Praise for Heather Cox Richardson's *Wounded Knee*

"In this provocative history Heather Cox Richardson traces the close linkages among late–nineteenth century politics, the West, and the horrendous Wounded Knee incident of 1890–91. No previous study has uncovered the full political account the author provides in this thorough, convincing volume."

—**RICHARD W. ETULAIN,**
author of *Beyond the Missouri: The Story of the American West*

"With a mastery that brings even her bit players to life, Heather Cox Richardson has given us a fresh and vivid account of the greed, partisan politics, prejudice, and butchery that led to the massacre at Wounded Knee. The result is a superb book, history at its very best."

—**LEONARD L. RICHARDS,**
author of *The California Gold Rush and the Coming of the Civil War*

"Heather Cox Richardson explodes the myth that the tragedy at Wounded Knee was simply an unfortunate accident or an outgrowth of cross-cultural misunderstandings on the frontier. Instead, she proves that the massacre emerged out of misguided federal Indian policies and, above all else, partisan politics. The story is chilling. You'll want to put it down, but because it's so well told here, you won't be able to."

—**ARI KELMAN,**
Associate Professor of History at the University of California, Davis, and author of *A River and Its City: The Nature of Landscape in New Orleans*

WOUNDED KNEE

WOUNDED KNEE

Party Politics and the Road to an American Massacre

HEATHER COX RICHARDSON

BASIC BOOKS
A Member of the Perseus Books Group
New York

Published by Basic Books,
A Member of the Perseus Books Group

Books published by Basic Books are available at special discounts for bulk purchases in the United States by corporations, institutions, and other organizations. For more information, please contact the Special Markets Department at the Perseus Books Group, 2300 Chestnut Street, Suite 200, Philadelphia, PA 19103, or call (800) 810-4145, ext. 5000, or e-mail special.markets@perseusbooks.com.

Designed by Brent Wilcox

Library of Congress Cataloging-in-Publication Data
Richardson, Heather Cox.
Wounded Knee : party politics and the road to an American massacre / Heather Cox Richardson.
p. cm.
Includes bibliographical references and index.
ISBN 978-0-465-00921-3 (alk. paper)
1. Wounded Knee Massacre, S.D., 1890. 2. United States—Politics and government—1889-1893. I. Title.
E83.89.R534 2010
973.8'6—dc22

[illegible]9592

10 9 8 7 6 5 4 3 2 1

For Lisa Adams and Lara Heimert

CONTENTS

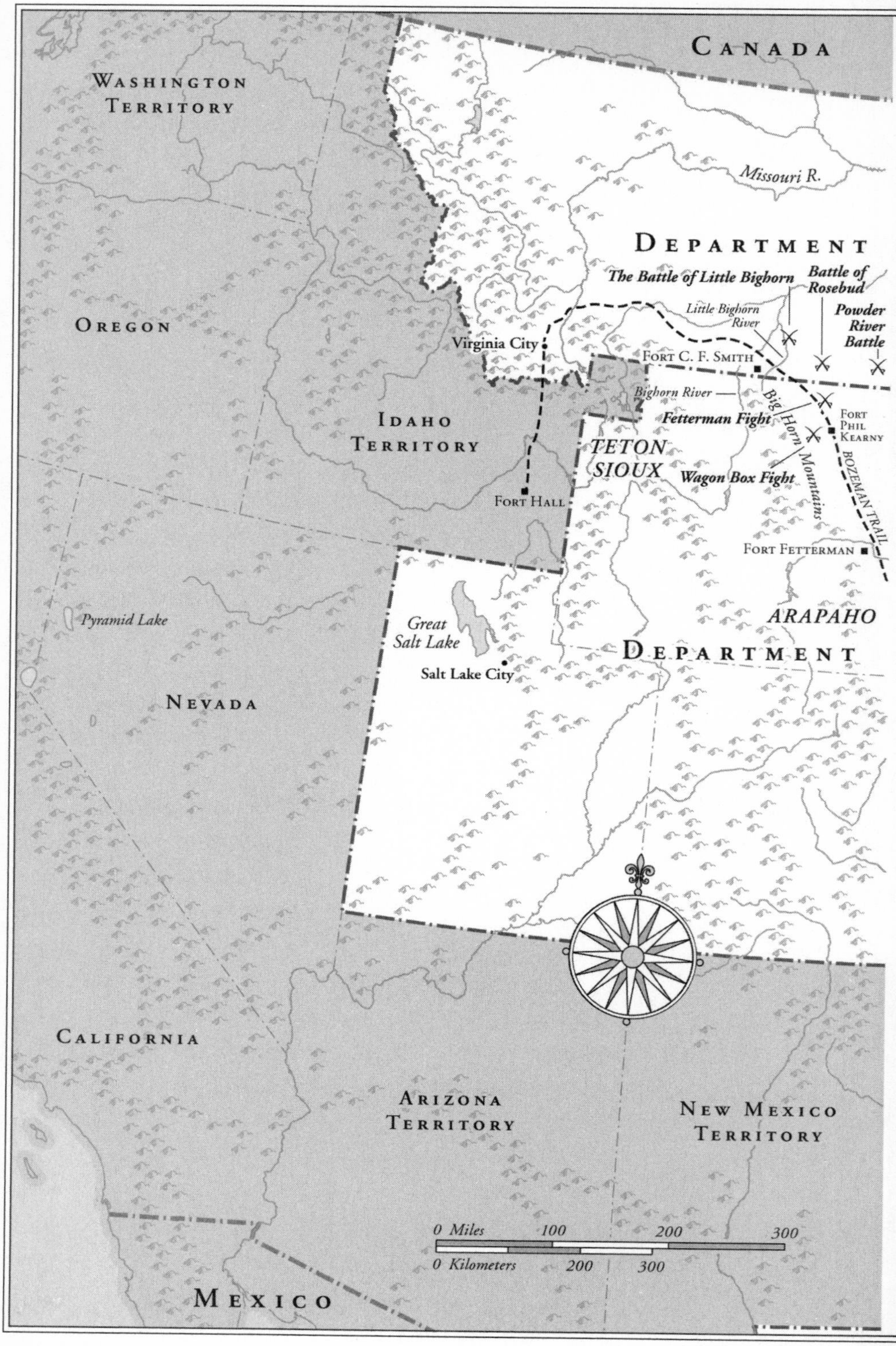

CANADA
WASHINGTON TERRITORY
Missouri R.
DEPARTMENT
The Battle of Little Bighorn
Battle of Rosebud
Little Bighorn River
Powder River Battle
OREGON
Virginia City
FORT C. F. SMITH
Bighorn River
Fetterman Fight
FORT PHIL KEARNY
IDAHO TERRITORY
TETON SIOUX
Big Horn Mountains
BOZEMAN TRAIL
Wagon Box Fight
FORT HALL
FORT FETTERMAN
ARAPAHO
Pyramid Lake
Great Salt Lake
DEPARTMENT
Salt Lake City
NEVADA
CALIFORNIA
ARIZONA TERRITORY
NEW MEXICO TERRITORY
0 Miles 100 200 300
0 Kilometers 200 300
MEXICO

· Map of U.S. West, 1866–1877 ·
Lake Superior
Yellowstone R.
Battle of Killdeer Mountain
of Dakota
Fort A. Lincoln
Crow
Grand R.
Wisconsin
Fort Snelling
(St. Paul)
Deadwood
Black Hills
Santee Sioux
Mississippi R.
Yankton Sioux
Missouri R.
Cheyenne
Fort Laramie
of the Platte
Illinois
Missouri R.
Sand Creek Massacre
Department of the Missouri
Mississippi R.
Department of Texas
Louisiana
©2010 Jeffrey L. Ward

INTRODUCTION

"The Sun Shone Forth Bright and Clear"

ON SUNDAY, DECEMBER 28, 1890, novice Nebraska newspaper reporter William Fitch Kelley wrote with a light heart from an army camp on the Pine Ridge Reservation in South Dakota. The Indian trouble of the last year was "practically ended," he explained to the readers of the *Nebraska State Journal*. The day had dawned beautifully, and "the sun shone forth bright and clear upon the camp of the Seventh Cavalry on Wounded Knee Creek."[1]

Relief pervaded the camp. Since mid-November, troops from as far away as Kansas and New Mexico had come to South Dakota to prevent an uprising of Sioux warriors. This had been the largest military mobilization of the U.S. Army since the Civil War, involving fully a third of the army. About nine thousand soldiers had moved to South Dakota; of those, about five thousand had been stationed at the Pine Ridge agency.[2]

Their arrival had panicked a number of the Sioux. When the soldiers had marched in, a band of thousands of Sioux warriors and their families had stampeded from their homes and holed up at a place called the Stronghold in the Badlands to the northwest. The soldiers had waited uneasily for weeks to see if the Badlands Sioux would fight or surrender. Indians and army scouts had made a number of forays from Pine Ridge to the Badlands to negotiate, and on this bright Sunday morning, reports had finally begun to indicate that the Badlands Sioux would come in to the Pine Ridge agency to surrender.

Only about a week before, another band had suddenly drawn the army's attention. Far to the north, on the Cheyenne River Reservation, a single group of about three hundred Minneconjou Sioux had been moving under army escort toward a fort where they would be held until things resolved in the Badlands. Unexpectedly, during the night of December 23, they slipped away from the officer in charge of delivering them to the fort and escaped south. These Minneconjous followed an old chief named Big Foot, well known as a cooperative negotiator, but also suspected of being hostile to the government. No one knew quite what the Minneconjous were up to in their flight, but officers had assumed the worst—that they were plotting to join the fighters in the Badlands and start a war.

In fact, the Minneconjous were not going to the Badlands. They were on their way to the Pine Ridge agency. The Indians at Pine Ridge had invited Big Foot to bring his negotiating skills there to help to calm the tensions between the Badlands Sioux, the reservation Indians, the army, and the government agents. The Minneconjous had decided to take up this invitation when rumor had reached them that they would be imprisoned if they stayed at Cheyenne River. They were worried about running from their army escort, but more worried that they were walking into a trap. Famous Oglala leader Red Cloud was at Pine Ridge, and they gambled that he could protect them from the army.

Army officers, anxious to make sure that Big Foot's people could not join the warriors in the Stronghold, sent a detachment from Pine Ridge to intercept them whenever they could be found. Following orders, the soldiers moved about eighteen miles from the agency to Wounded Knee Creek. They had arrived at the Wounded Knee settlement two days before and pitched their tents, hammering iron tent pegs in straight lines across the unbroken land. They set up camp near the trader's store and post office that were tucked into the sloping prairies under a few twisted cottonwoods.[3]

The settlement was typical of those scattered across sparsely inhabited South Dakota. It took its name from the nearby Wounded Knee Creek, which flowed into the White River on the southwestern edge of South Dakota near the Nebraska border. In this part of the new state, the dry ground was carved by dozens of long, shallow creeks that meandered through the region's gentle hills before draining into larger rivers. Those rivers in turn poured into the mighty Missouri, which commanded the center of the state as it wandered from its northern roots to the southern border and beyond. With its bright white tents and its straight lines, the army camp squatted awkwardly on the rolling land. There the soldiers settled in, reluctantly accepting that they might be facing a long winter campaign.

But the troops had been at Wounded Knee only a day or so when important news arrived from the Pine Ridge agency. On the morning of December 28, the officers at Wounded Knee had received reports that the Badlands Sioux were coming in to army headquarters. This would effectively end the threat of a shooting war that had loomed for the past six weeks.[4]

The troops who had been sent to Wounded Knee Creek rejoiced at the end of the standoff, but the morning was otherwise dull. They hung around and waited for scouts to locate the band of Minneconjou Sioux they had been sent to intercept. They performed the circle of their duties, then killed time as the chill prairie wind stirred the dust the army horses had churned up on the little-used road to the settlement. They likely speculated on where Big Foot's band might be and on when the Indian troubles would be settled, so they might be able to go back to their home army posts.

South Dakota was a strange place to most of these men. Many were soldiers from the Seventh Cavalry, General George A. Custer's old regiment, stationed since the 1880s in Kansas. Others were from even farther south and west. South Dakota might have sounded romantic in Custer's accounts of exploring it fifteen years before, but men used to warmer regions with their forests, milder climates, and bustling cities found the state cold and isolated and inhospitable.[5]

Most of the press corps covering the Sioux troubles had elected to stay back at the Pine Ridge agency waiting for the surrender of the Badlands Sioux, but Kelley and two others were tired of the boredom of an inactive army camp. They had made the trip to Wounded Knee Creek with the glamorous Seventh Cavalry to wait until someone found Big Foot's people.

Their initiative had paid off. According to Kelley's account of the next two days, while the Sioux coming in from the Badlands dawdled, scouts from the Wounded Knee camp found Big Foot's people. On Saturday and Sunday, Major Samuel M. Whitside, who commanded the Seventh's First Battalion, had sent out groups of Indian scouts to find the escapees.

Finally, they found their quarry or, rather, their quarry found them. As soon as the soldiers had established their camp on Wounded Knee, some Oglalas from Pine Ridge had ridden to Big Foot's camp to tell the chief that the army was trying to intercept his band. The Oglalas encouraged the chief to ride around the army camp and to go straight to the Pine Ridge agency, where the Badlands Indians would soon be arriving. The Badlands Sioux would need his intercession with the officers, and Big Foot's delay at Wounded Knee could be disastrous.

But the Wounded Knee camp was on Big Foot's route to the Pine Ridge agency, and the chief was in a hurry to get there. He had developed pneumonia in the cold winds during the trek across the state, and was terribly ill. He was too sick to add more miles to his band's journey and decided to head straight toward the army camp. Then the Indians and the troops could all go to the agency together.[6]

The army scouts were searching for the Indians, but the Minneconjous knew where the soldiers were. On December 28, Minneconjou men surprised four army scouts when they rode down a hill while the scouts were watering their horses on Porcupine Creek, about eight miles away from Wounded Knee. The Sioux captured two scouts by grabbing their horses' bridle reins. They took the men to Big Foot, who told them that he and his band were going to the army camp just as soon as they finished their midday meal. In the meantime, the other two army scouts had rushed back to Wounded Knee Creek to report that they had found the missing Indians.[7]

As soon as the men stationed at Wounded Knee heard the report, the officers ordered the bugle call for "boots and saddles," and four companies of men mounted and rode out of the encampment in double columns of four. The artillery men placed two Hotchkiss guns in front of the columns. With their operators under the command of Second Lieutenant Harry L. Hawthorne, an Annapolis graduate who had resigned his commission in the navy and become an expert in munitions tactics for the army, the guns were formidable. About a mile away from where the scouts told them the Indians had been eating, Whitside ordered the troops to dismount and string out in a half circle as they advanced. As soon as they spotted Indians in the advance of their band, the soldiers formed a line and set up their guns in a dry creek bed between the hills, a low ravine full of pines.[8]

The Indians finished their meal and began moving slowly toward the army camp, not a war party but a community band of about three hundred men, women, and children. The younger men were on ponies, smaller animals than army horses, but tough and well trained. The rest of the band—the women and children, along with the sick and the elderly—were in twenty-two rough wagons.[9]

The Minneconjou band had run from their reservation in fear of imprisonment, and had been in such a hurry they had taken little with them in the way of supplies. They had only old tepees and bedding, and a few cooking utensils. They were cold and ill-fed, bundled in ragged blankets wrapped over the overcoats and clothes that had been part of their annual distribution from their agency only weeks before. The trip across South Dakota in a bitter wind that had blown up days before had exhausted them, and some were ill.

The men and women of Big Foot's band were nervous as they headed toward Wounded Knee. They distrusted soldiers and knew they were in some trouble for running away from their army escort at Cheyenne River, but also knew they had done nothing wrong and hoped their unwillingness to join the Badlands Sioux would mitigate officials' anger. They were eager to get on to the Pine Ridge agency, where they expected to meet family members and take shelter with the Oglala leader Red Cloud.

They hadn't gone far from Porcupine Creek before they saw a cloud of dust behind the rise ahead of them. Crossing the rise, those at the head of the band saw the army marching down the hill in front of them. Wanting simply for their journey to end safely, the Minneconjous were shocked to see that army officers evidently considered them a dangerous war party.[10]

The Indians saw the line of soldiers and watched some of the men drop to the ground with their guns directed at the approaching Minneconjous. Major Whitside sent three scouts ahead of the soldiers to demand the Indians' surrender and to warn them that they were surrounded and must not fight. "This news, from appearances, produced great consternation in their midst from the howling and wailing heard," Kelley wrote. Lying in the back of a rough wagon, Big Foot counseled his people not to show fear but to proceed into the ranks of the soldiers calmly, without any warlike movements.[11]

The Indian men had no intention of fighting, and they followed Big Foot's advice. They quickly formed a line, each protected by his horse, at the front of the moving band, to shield the wagons with the women and children and the elderly and sick. The men advanced toward the line of troops. When they were about fifty yards away, three men left the band. They came forward, one on foot between two on horseback, carrying a white flag.[12]

Major Whitside refused to talk to the men. He demanded to talk to Big Foot. The men protested that the chief was sick. Whitside insisted.

Big Foot was indeed very ill. He was barely able to speak, and blood was dripping from his nose, but his nephew drove him up in a rough wagon to speak to Major Whitside. The officer asked if Big Foot and his band wanted peace or war. Weak and barely able to talk, Big Foot emphatically denied that he wanted to fight. He assured Whitside that his people were simply traveling to the Pine Ridge agency, where the Oglalas had asked him to come and help forge a peace out of the confusion of the last several weeks.[13]

Whitside demanded that Big Foot and his band accompany the soldiers to Wounded Knee Creek. Big Foot agreed, and the two men shook hands. Worried about Big Foot's terrible health, Whitside had soldiers lift him into an army ambulance wagon to make the trip to the encampment.[14]

Troops then rounded up the women and children, who were hanging about a quarter of a mile back from the men. The soldiers formed a column, with Big Foot's ambulance in the front, flanked on each side by a sergeant and a soldier on horseback. Behind him came the mounted Minneconjou men with columns of cavalry alongside. Next came the Indians with their tepees and horses and wagons filled with belongings. The rest of the soldiers brought up the rear.[15]

They started off for the army camp at Wounded Knee Creek. It was a "motley procession," one of the Indians later remembered; the soldiers' blue uniforms framing the variety of clothes and blankets the Minnconjous had jumbled together to stay warm. It must have been noisy, too, with hooves hitting the hard-packed earth, men calling to each other in both English and Lakota, wagons creaking, horses snorting, spurs rattling, people coughing.[16]

The group reached the camp in about four hours. Once there, the Indians set up their tepees just north of a ravine beyond the army tents. Soldiers provided the destitute Indians with three hundred soldier's rations.[17]

Whitside was determined that Big Foot and his people would not escape from him as they had done from the last officer charged with capturing them. He set two troops of cavalry around the Indians, forming a military cordon. He had the two loaded Hotchkiss guns set up on a slight knoll about fifty yards from the Indian camp and ordered all the artillerymen to stay on duty throughout the night. He ordered the troops not to undress for sleep, and he set a double guard on each tent to ensure that the soldiers couldn't be surprised by a sneak attack.[18]

Still nervous that the Indians might get away, Whitside sent to Pine Ridge for reinforcements. The Second Battalion of the Seventh Cavalry, commanded by Colonel James Forsyth, arrived at 8:00 in the evening, along with Light Battery E of the First Artillery. Forsyth outranked Whitside, and took over command. His orders were to move the Indians to Pine Ridge agency. From there they would be sent to Gordon, Nebraska, to a railhead where they could be put onto the cars and sent to Omaha until South Dakota calmed.[19]

As the Badlands Sioux headed to Pine Ridge and troops poured in to contain the Minneconjou, Kelley concluded that the Indian "uprising" had been brought to a successful close. The whole campaign had been "most remarkable . . . in many respects," he reflected. "I have heard a dozen officers of twenty to thirty years' experience in the army say that never had there been such a one before to their knowledge."[20]

Nonetheless, Kelley concluded that the soldiers had done themselves proud, especially those at Wounded Knee Creek. "Another laurel is added to the wreath of the famous old Seventh Regiment of cavalry; every man among them a veteran; scarce one that has not distinguished himself by some signal act of valor, some deed of daring in the Indian campaigns of the last twenty years, nearly, if not all of them, having been a participant. Custer's men they were once and like him will they ever be."[21]

Early on the morning of December 29, Kelley's cheerful dispatch went out by courier to the telegraph office thirty miles away in Nebraska, marking the happy conclusion of a tedious and cold campaign.

While the courier sped Kelley's report to Nebraska, the reporters and troops at Wounded Knee woke up at 6:00 to the smell of wood smoke from the campfires and the sounds of birds peeping in an unseasonably warm and windless South Dakota winter day. They ate a breakfast of hardtack, bacon, and coffee with sugar before being ordered to move at 8:00, when they joined the artillerymen surrounding the Indian camp.[22]

Whitside had not taken away the Indians' guns the previous day, but Forsyth had orders to disarm them before moving them to the agency. Through an interpreter, he asked the Indians to leave their tepees and come forward to a council, where they could be counted. Then he ordered twenty Indians to go and bring back all the arms from the encampment. They did so, but only produced a few guns—two, according to Kelley, although in reality they brought back about twenty-five, all of which were in poor shape. Confused and sullen, the younger Indian men had no intention of being disarmed in the face of such overwhelming military power.[23]

Angry at their recalcitrance, Forsyth commanded a detachment of about ten of his own men to search the tepees. The soldiers moved forward as ordered, but not cheerfully. Despite what Kelley had written the night before about the long experience of the soldiers of the Seventh in Indian wars, many at Wounded Knee Creek were new recruits. They had never been close to hostile Indians, but they had certainly read about them in blood-curdling dime novels and seen them portrayed in stage shows where brave cowboys protected innocent women from savages intent on taking blonde scalps.

These raw soldiers were frightened and vengeful. Many of the Indians lined up in front of the tepees had followed the great warrior Sitting Bull until agency police had killed him two weeks before as they tried to take him into custody. The soldiers probably suspected that these Indians had also been with him at the Battle of the Little Bighorn, where they had wiped out Custer's entire command and, stories said, torn out and eaten Custer's brother's heart. For months, the troops had been reading newspaper reports, written by men like Kelley, claiming that these same treacherous Indians were planning to exterminate nearby settlers. The soldiers were tense.

The detachment moved brusquely into the Indian camp. The troops rifled through the tepees, searching women, pushing children out of the way, and rummaging through sleeping robes. They were certain the Indians had hidden their guns in the camp, and they were determined to find them.

While the soldiers went about their work, Kelley and the two other reporters on the scene circulated comfortably among the Indians. C. H. Cressey, with the *Omaha Bee*, and Charles W. Allen, publisher of Nebraska's *Chadron Democrat*, looked over the encampment and its people for descriptions they could use in their daily newspaper reports. As they strolled around, Kelley recalled, an older Indian was dancing alone in a circle, singing a song from the new "Ghost Dance" religion. Occasionally he reached down to the ground and took dirt up in his fingers. He would raise his hand and throw the dust into the air, where it blew away. To the southeast of the line of troops and Indian men, eight or ten boys in gray reservation school uniforms played a noisy game of leapfrog and "bucking mare"—in which a scrum of boys tried to hold up as many of their friends as they could before they fell down. They ignored the tense line of men nearby.[24]

Eventually, the soldiers turned up about thirty-eight old guns. The search through the tepees had been slow, and Forsyth was frustrated and angry. He could not believe that the young men didn't have more—and newer—guns. It seemed clear to him that the Minneconjous were hiding their best weapons. Meanwhile, the Indian men were grumbling among themselves and milling about, and the soldiers were irritated.[25]

Determined to disarm the Indians once and for all, Colonel Forsyth ordered the warriors to submit to a personal search. The older men lifted their blankets to prove they were unarmed, but the younger men refused. Two soldiers were detailed to search the Sioux one at a time as they came forward. Kelley and the other reporters stood aside as the soldiers began to disarm the young men.

Three Indians had been searched without incident when a young warrior standing apart from the search held his new, valuable Winchester over his head and announced in Lakota that he had paid a good deal of money for the gun and would not give up such an expensive weapon without being paid for it. Three soldiers grabbed him from behind and they all began to struggle. Troops around them pointed their weapons at the Indian. As the men wrestled, an army scout shouted: "Look out! Look out! They are going to shoot!"[26]

As the soldiers and the warrior struggled, the gun fired into the eastern sky.[27]

An instant of silence marked the line between an anxious surrender and a full-blown military engagement. As the gunshot echoed, the soldiers, standing in ranks, fired a volley that felled half the Indian men immediately. The volley also brought down a number of soldiers, since Forsyth had given no thought to positioning the troops for battle when he arranged them. Bullets tore through the boys playing leapfrog; all of them died together.[28]

Those Sioux left standing counterattacked with knives, clubs, fists, and guns that they snatched from wounded soldiers. Kelley had been standing only yards from the Indians when the shooting started. An Indian warrior charged the shocked reporter with a raised tomahawk. Kelley grabbed a rifle from a dead soldier and shot the man. Then he laid aside the mantle of reporter and joined the battle. Deafening gunfire and dense smoke from the exploding gunpowder obscured the hand-to-hand fighting in the tight circle of combatants.

While the men fought in front of the tepees, the Indian women and children in the camp tried to flee. They whipped up the horses they had been hitching to wagons and ran to the northwest, or east on the road toward the shelter of the store and the post office. But most of the men and many of the women and children could not get to a wagon and the road. Instead, they ran to the south, where they could hide in a ravine that ran behind the camp.

The soldiers fired on the Indians as they tried to escape. They shot the running Sioux as the artillery turned the Hotchkiss guns on the fleeing wagons. Minneconjous fell on the plains, and fragments of bodies flew from wagons that exploded under artillery shells. Indians died in groups in the ravine when Hawthorne moved the guns so they could shoot directly down it. Forced out of the ravine by the firing, the Sioux crawled or crouched, running, to the hills. Cavalrymen followed them.

As soldiers moved off over the plains and the sound of gunshots grew more distant, Kelley put down his gun, quickly surveyed the battlefield, noted the dead, and wrote a new report. Brave soldiers had been murdered, he wrote in the first wire that told of the massacre at Wounded Knee. They were "victims of the treacherous Indians." Nothing but insanity could explain the Indians' suicidal attack, he pronounced, but fortunately the soldiers were shooting them down without quarter, even as he wrote. "Before night I doubt if either a buck or squaw . . . will be left to tell the tale of this day's treachery. The members of the Seventh Cavalry have once more shown themselves to be heroes. . . ."[29]

Over the next two hours, the soldiers hunted down and slaughtered all the Sioux they could find, riding them down and shooting them at point-blank range as they tried to escape. One woman was murdered after she had run three miles from the camp. Soldiers shot babies in their cradleboards. The only good Indian was a dead Indian, many of the troops had been taught, and they had just turned about two hundred and fifty Sioux into good Indians. The wounded Minneconjous lay moaning among the dead heaped on the prairie, ignored as soldiers hurried their comrades to shelter and then fought off sporadic forays by warriors who had rushed to Wounded Knee when they heard of the massacre. A day later, a plains blizzard roared down from the north and buried the carnage in pristine white.

The storm that buried the plains of South Dakota in snow quickly blew east. It traveled over the sluggish Mississippi River and the freezing Great Lakes, then swept south, bringing heavy fog and rain squalls to Washington, D.C. There, the social season was in full swing despite the miserable weather. Dignitaries and belles mingled at the many receptions of the new year. On January 1, as news of the events at Wounded Knee Creek were trickling east, President Benjamin Harrison and his wife held the traditional New Year's Day reception for government officials and visitors in the "blue parlor" of the White House. Braving the muddy roads that slowed their carriages, all the members of the cabinet and their wives, or eldest daughters, attended the reception in their finest clothes. Mrs. Harrison's pale blue dress glittered with peacock feathers and imitation jewels, but the diamonds she wore in her hair and carried with her bouquet were real.[30]

The splendid parties could not entirely cheer up the Republican officials who attended them. Only a year before, the Republicans had believed their party to be in a remarkable ascendancy. They had taken control of the House of Representatives, the Senate, and the White House for the first time since 1875. But somehow, in only a year, they had managed to lose all the ground they had gained against a surging Democratic majority. In the midterm elections held in November 1890, the Democrats had won the House and made alarming gains in the Senate.

President Harrison had been widely castigated for running an excessively partisan administration devoted to serving big business. He had been called a fool, ineffectual, a party hack, a tool of industrialists. Opponents pointed out that he had gained the Republican presidential nomination only when a corrupt deal cut out the far better qualified and far more able Ohio senator John Sherman. They also noted that Harrison had lost the popular vote and won the White House only through the offices of the Electoral College. They went so far as to call him the most hated president in history.

Such animosity only strengthened the president's resolve. The portly, bearded Harrison was a pious man who believed God had given him the presidency and that, in serving the businessmen who poured money into the Republican political war chest, he was doing what was best for America. Bewildered at the eclipse of his party, Harrison had spent the past year trying desperately to resurrect its fortunes before the election of 1892. If the political equation didn't change, it looked likely that the Democrats would take the White House and Congress.

Like other nineteenth-century Americans, President Harrison believed himself to be engaged in a titanic struggle over the soul of the country. Would the government that Abraham Lincoln had called "the last, best hope of earth" devote its considerable resources to promoting the growth of the economy, working hand in glove with rich industrialists? Or should the government work to keep the economic playing field level, guaranteeing that every hardworking man had an opportunity to rise? Republicans maintained that economic growth created jobs and fueled an ever higher standard of living, pointing to the fabulous houses of the nation's rich and the increasing wealth evident, for example, in Mrs. Harrison's jewels, as proof that their system worked. Their opponents, Democrats and members of various reform parties, countered by pointing to falling wages, child labor, and city tenements as evidence that the system was broken. While businessmen lobbied their friends in Congress and state legislatures for favorable legislation, workers took to the streets to protest poverty wages and dangerous working conditions. Each side was convinced that the other was destroying America.

Harrison's presidency had witnessed a desperate battle between Republicans and Democrats for control of the nation. Republicans had held the White House and controlled the Congress for most of the post–Civil War era, but by 1890 their grip was weakening. Pro-business Republicans still insisted that industrial growth was critical to the nation and they continued to pass legislation that benefited and sheltered business. "Individualism, Private Property, the Law of Accumulation of Wealth, and the Law of Competition" were the very height of human achievement, multimillionaire steel baron Andrew Carnegie cheerfully pronounced. Like other powerful industrialists of the age, Carnegie had promoted the widespread organization of trusts, which brought competing corporations together into large monopolies that carved up markets and fixed prices. In the 1880s, these trusts began to dominate most industries, crush small businesses, and control the meat, fruit, sugar, cloth, electricity, and transportation the average American needed to survive.

By 1890, a formidable challenge to the Republicans' policies had emerged. Leaders of the Democratic and western farmers' parties were holding rallies in eastern cities and were barnstorming the West. They lectured to wage laborers, poor farmers, and young entrepreneurs about laws that put the fruits of their labor into the pockets of the rich. "Wall Street owns the country," western organizer Mary Elizabeth Lease thundered in the summer of 1890. "It is no longer a government of the people, by the people, and for the people, but a government of Wall Street, by Wall Street, and for Wall Street." Seasonal factory closings and lockouts meant that hunger and homelessness haunted urban workers; soaring shipping costs meant that farmers spent the price of two bushels of corn to get one to market. On shop floors and in western fields people shoveled coal or broke sod for fourteen to sixteen hours a day; if their health broke down or they lost a limb, they were out of both work and luck. The little money that went into their pockets didn't go far—the restrictive tariffs that protected businesses against foreign competition drove up consumer prices. "The great common people of this country are slaves, and monopoly is the master," Lease snarled.[31]

As the midterm election of 1890 approached, Democrats had battered at the Harrison administration's support for big business and toleration of the trusts. For the Republicans, much was at stake. If they lost control of the government, there was little doubt that their opponents would sever the close ties between government and business, and bolster the position of workers and farmers. This was heresy, and party members were determined not to let it happen.

In an attempt to secure the outcome of the midterm elections, the Republican Congress tried to shore up the numbers of Republican voters. They tried to cut back the numbers of Democrats who could vote by passing a federal elections bill that placed the military at polls in the South and in New York City. If enacted, this law would help to protect black Republicans in the South, who had lately been kept from the polls by Democratic opponents, and would also intimidate immigrants in New York City, who tended to vote Democratic, keeping them from voting in the swing state of New York. While Republicans argued they were trying to prevent voter fraud, Democrats and Populists chided them for simply trying to stack the vote for the Republicans.

Both parties knew that control of the government in 1890, and then in 1892, would turn, in part, on western voters. Harrison's men believed that westerners tended to be Republican, so they worked to bring western states into the Union as quickly as possible. Dakota Territory might make two new states if it could be divided, but most of the land in the southern part of the Territory consisted of the Great Sioux Reservation. It belonged to the Teton Sioux. Torn between traditional cultures and modern America, unable to vote, and uninvolved in the political war, the Sioux nonetheless became crucial figures in the 1890 election.

To court settlers in Dakota Territory, in 1889 Harrison's men subdivided the Great Sioux Reservation into small blocks, opening up more land for private development. An influx of settlers would give the Territory enough people to make a case for two new states.

The destruction of their huge reservation proved disastrous for the Sioux. The bison herds that had once roamed the Plains had largely been destroyed, and the smaller reservations had too little game to support the native populations living on them. When a drought killed the few crops the Indians could raise on the dry prairies, they got little relief from the government, for new census numbers gathered in 1890 suggested that the agencies had been providing more food than treaties required, and officials cut back rations.

Destitute and in real danger of starvation, the Sioux turned to a new religious movement. The Ghost Dance promised to bring back the world of game and plenty that had been theirs before the coming of whites. If they danced on certain nights, stopped fighting amongst themselves, and dealt honestly with all men, they believed, their ancestors would come back from the afterworld, herding before them the vanished game that would sustain the tribes. Settlers on their lands would be buried in a landslide or drowned in a flood as the ancient world returned. The religious excitement burned across the dry prairies.

The new religion and the political maneuverings of the Harrison administration dovetailed to create a crisis. The Ghost Dancers never hurt their non-Indian neighbors and few settlers paid them much attention, but Republican political appointees did. Incompetent and frightened by the Indians, they interpreted the religious enthusiasm as tremors of an approaching war.

Indian agents were a particularly problematic aspect of the Harrison administration's push to court the West. The new reservations covered huge expanses of land with wide-flung camps of different Indian bands. Each was overseen by a single politically appointed government agent who was responsible for seeing that the Indians received all the goods and payments guaranteed to them by treaty. Those agents disbursed the money that Congress appropriated for the Indians every year, and they held complete authority over how the funds were spent. The agents were supposed to contract for food, farming supplies, the construction of schools and hospitals, and so on, but everyone knew that the positions were a rich reward for political service. Agents made a practice of awarding inflated contracts to their friends, who fulfilled them with rotten food, shoddy clothing, and poor construction . . . if they bothered to fulfill them at all. The agency system had been corrupt long before Harrison took office, but a bad system was made worse on Harrison's watch, and the Sioux in South Dakota suffered more than other tribes in other states.

The problem intensified in 1890. In the summer of that year, South Dakota's voters started to sway toward the Democratic Party because they resented the obvious bias of the Harrison administration in favor of big business. Harrison's men replaced seasoned agents with hacks in the fall, distributing the lucrative agency jobs to loyal party men. This turnover at the agencies would be catastrophic for the Sioux.

On the Pine Ridge Reservation, the new Republican agent was good at drumming up Republican votes, but he feared and hated Indians. Insisting that the Ghost Dancers on his reservation were plotting a war, he demanded army protection. He peppered his superiors with daily telegrams insisting that renegade Sioux were about to launch a massacre against settlers in South Dakota and Nebraska.

Experienced Indian agents and army officers dismissed the scaremongering of the frenzied agent. They assured the administration that the Indians were not a military threat and begged Washington to fulfill the neglected treaties, sending rations for the reservation Indians before they starved.

Army officers' complaints about the ineptitude of Republican agents fed right into the hands of Harrison's political opponents. Back East, Democrats took the panicked agents at their word when they foretold a war. Democrats argued that the corruption that characterized the Republican Party under Harrison had sent pacified Indians back to the warpath, where they threatened the lives of settlers. Too late, the president's agents recognized their error. They countered with protestations that they were only trying to do what was best for the Indians, but that the Sioux were bloodthirsty savages who refused to be civilized.

Harrison had little interest in the whole South Dakota problem except as it affected potential votes. He insisted that his administration had treated Indians well and that they had no excuse for a war. He recognized, though, that westerners were defecting to the Democrats' economic vision and that the stories of Republican corruption were helping to push them away. Western voters must be retrieved or the Republicans would lose the presidential election of 1892.

The election of 1890, held early in November, made Harrison's political fears a reality. The Republicans lost control of the House of Representatives by a margin of two to one. Although prepared for Democratic gains, this was far beyond what Republican strategists had convinced themselves they would face.

Worse, though, was that Republican control of the Senate remained in doubt even after the elections were over. The administration had counted on controlling the Senate, and initial election returns suggested that the Republicans had held on to a majority by four seats. But this was not the relief it should have been, for those four senators were not firmly pro-administration Republicans. Three were from western states that had gone Democratic in the election, and had themselves recently voted against Republican pro-business economic policies. That left one Republican seat to assure the Republicans a majority in the Senate. Only with that majority could they block a repeal of the laws the administration had pushed through the previous Congress.

That seat was from South Dakota. It had been held by a staunchly Republican senator who claimed at first, loudly and proudly, to have won reelection. Within days, though, evidence emerged that ballot boxes had been broken open and tampered with. Immediately, opponents charged the Republicans with fraud and claimed that they, rather than the Republicans, had won the seat.

The outcome would remain in question until the state legislature met in January 1891. The results of the election depended on more than settling the issue of the ruined ballot boxes. In the nineteenth century, senators were still chosen by state legislatures rather than directly by voters. Legislators could be—and usually were—lobbied, between the time of their election and the time the senators were named, to vote for one candidate or another. And in late 1890, South Dakotans were especially susceptible to encouragement from the administration to back a Republican. The new state was mired in a recession and desperate for money and contracts to boost the local economy. Such a situation demanded attention from the Harrison administration.

Westerners had a long, and what one historian has called a "diabolical," history of support for government involvement with Indians. They liked the government either to send contracts to Indian reservations or to send in the army to fight them, for either policy brought money into the local economy. As early as 1866, William Tecumseh Sherman privately acknowledged that the western cry for military action against Indians was a veiled attempt to create a nearby market for agricultural products.[32]

Once Indians were on reservations, Indian agents bought beef and grain, as well as shirts, shoes, blankets, and so on, to feed and clothe their charges. Army mobilizations were even more profitable. Soldiers needed rations, of course, and so did their horses and pack animals. Officers wanted rooms to rent, as well as board and liquor. With their pay, soldiers and officers bought meals and dry goods, hired laundresses, and had their mustaches curled. Sometimes they brought their wives and families on assignments, and the ladies bought cloth and hair combs, candy and children's toys. Western towns liked having the army around, and this fondness was undoubtedly in the minds of Republican politicians as they wondered how to placate the legislators who would soon be electing a senator in economically distressed South Dakota.

Meanwhile, the Pine Ridge Indian agent continued to insist that the Ghost Dancing Sioux were about to take up arms. There had been no lives lost and no property threatened around Pine Ridge or any of the other reservations, and experienced army officers continued to discount the agent's fears. But in mid-November 1890, as the South Dakota legislators were getting ready for the new session and gathering last instructions from their constituents about electing a new senator from the state, Harrison ordered the army to South Dakota to protect settlers against the Indian "uprising."

Six weeks later, snow fell on Washington and the dignitaries shivered coming in from the cold to the warmth of the White House. President Harrison and the wealthy men squiring their glittering wives to the capital to shake his hand seemed a world away from the bodies frozen beside Wounded Knee Creek. But the road to the massacre had begun in Washington. It had hammered its way across the Midwest, then pushed its way into South Dakota. Finally, it faded into a bloody track beside a South Dakota stream. The fate of the Minneconjous at Wounded Knee was sealed by politicians a thousand or more miles from the rolling hills and cathedral clouds of the Great Plains. The soldiers who pulled the triggers in South Dakota simply delivered the sentence.

CHAPTER I

A New Nation, a New Economy

IN THE WET CHILL of late December 1890 in Washington, Senator John Sherman was spending his days bickering with opposition senators while they waited for their colleagues to return from the holidays. As was his wont, the sixty-seven-year-old Sherman, Congress's leader on financial affairs and the chief architect of Republican economic policies, was irascible during the congressional days, but had much to enjoy in the evenings during the Washington holiday social whirl. His older brother, General William Tecumseh Sherman, was in town, and the two aging men cherished their hours together. Each had, in his own way, been a chief actor in the American drama that had created the modern nation, and they had compared notes and helped each other's careers for half a century.[1]

Closeted in the library of Senator Sherman's elegant K Street residence, the two men—each tall and lean almost to gauntness, John with a closely cropped white beard and William Tecumseh clean shaven so that his prominent cheekbones dominated all but his piercing eyes—undoubtedly reminisced about their childhood years and the Civil War. They also surely discussed their worries about the direction of the country and chatted about their families, particularly because their niece, Mary Miles, was also in town on the winter social circuit. For more than two decades, her husband, General Nelson Miles, had availed himself freely of the Sherman brothers' influence to advance a career that, although enviable by any standard, was never as good as he thought it should be.

Mary's husband was the Commander of the Division of the Missouri. He was not in Washington with his wife, for he was overseeing the Sioux "outbreak" in South Dakota.[2]

The fortunes of the Sherman family had been inextricably entwined with those of the nation since the 1850s. Born in the heady days of the nation's westward expansion, the Sherman siblings represented a new kind of American, one who believed in the aggressive economic development of the country. The Shermans had helped to create a worldview based on that development, they had fought for it against Southern slaveholders, and they had pushed it into western lands. There it clashed, inevitably—for the two were incompatible—with the traditional culture of the Plains Indians. As John and William Tecumseh chatted in John's comfortable mansion, a final collision between the world they had constructed and the world of the Sioux turned tragic.

The Sherman brothers' childhood was much like that of their contemporaries. In the early years of the republic, their parents had taken part in the popular push west. After the American Revolution opened the lands west of the Appalachians to settlement, their father, Charles Sherman, had joined the rush to the newly opened land of Ohio. Traveling by horseback and carrying their oldest son, Charles Junior, on a pillow, Charles and his wife had settled in Lancaster, Ohio, in 1811. Charles Senior soldiered for his country in the War of 1812, helping to cement the West to the new nation.

The Sherman clan grew quickly, and the brothers were close. William Tecumseh (named for the Shawnee leader his father had admired during the War of 1812) and John, along with their eight other siblings, arrived one after the other in the first few decades of the nineteenth century. The eleven Sherman siblings lost their father in 1829 when Charles, the oldest, was just eighteen. It was William, nicknamed "Cump" within the family, who taught John how to aim a gun; when the boys hunted for pigeons and squirrels he made John carry their game. Cump became the family scholar, quiet, mannerly, and emotional; John learned Latin and mathematics but gained a reputation as a wild boy, always ready for a fight or a drink.[3]

Like most of their neighbors, the Sherman boys were ambitious. Losing their prominent father had dimmed their prospects, but they managed to cobble together first an education and then jobs with the help of family friends well connected in Ohio's young legal and political community. Men on the make, Charles became a lawyer, James became a merchant in Iowa, the quiet and studious William Tecumseh garnered a prestigious appointment to West Point in 1836. John cleaned himself up, studied law, and went to work with his older brother Charles. Eager to see their fortunes grow along with their region, the brothers invested in manufacturing and railroads and supported the Whig politicians who called for government protection of domestic industries.[4]

An observer watching the brothers in young adulthood would have predicted that the Shermans were a vanguard of upwardly mobile businessmen and professionals embarking on long, prosperous, and relatively uneventful lives. Cump graduated from West Point and was stationed first in Florida to fight Seminoles and then at Fort Moultrie in Charleston, South Carolina; John and Charles became partners in business law. The young men watched their home state grow as railroads and telegraph wires cut its hills and bound its people to distant markets. Investing in a lumber concern, John managed to turn his law earnings into a nest egg of more than ten thousand dollars.[5]

But, as it happened, the Shermans and their contemporaries were headed not for unruffled success but for a cataclysm. The calm prosperity the 1840s promised depended on an enduring compromise between the nation's free states and slave states. By the time Cump and John Sherman were born in 1820 and 1823, respectively, just such a balance seemed to have been achieved. After a battle for control over the huge Louisiana territory the United States acquired from France in 1803, the North and the South had found a way to coexist in the region. New states were admitted to the Union in pairs—one free and one slave—to keep the two sections balanced in the Senate, and the Missouri Compromise of 1820 guaranteed that slavery would not spread north of a line that ran east to west below the southern boundary of Missouri. The sections neatly divided the Louisiana territory between them.

For nearly thirty years, this compromise bought a truce, and people went about their everyday lives. But this complacency ended abruptly in 1846, when the United States went to war with Mexico. Southerners, backed by Democratic president James K. Polk, were eager to take

Mexican lands. Northern Whigs like the Shermans, though, were convinced that the war was a Southern plot to annex much of Latin America, bringing in new Southern states and swinging the balance of power in the nation decisively toward the slave states.

The war unsettled the Shermans in much the same way as it unsettled other Americans. On the one hand, they were eager to try out the power of their young nation and of their own maturity. U.S. soldiers quickly fought south into Mexico and pushed west into Mexico's California territory; newspapers trumpeted military victories over Mexican troops and the quick and easy conquest of California, where American soldiers rode in unchallenged. John Sherman believed that the war was unjust, but the excitement of battle was almost enough to get him to enlist anyway. Cump, then a captain in the regular army and on recruiting detail in Ohio, was eager to fight. He chafed at the orders that took forever to arrive, and then had him sailing on a two-hundred day journey around Cape Horn to occupy California. The bloodless conquest of California meant that Cump would not see battle in the war, and he bemoaned the loss. "I felt deeply the fact that our country had passed through a foreign war, that my comrades had fought great battles, and yet I had not heard a hostile shot. Of course, I thought it the last and only chance in my day, and that my career as a soldier was at an end," he later mused.[6]

On the other hand, though, the war threatened to hand national power to slave owners, perhaps forever. As U.S. troops pushed far into Mexico, horrified Northerners realized that if the nation kept the land it was rapidly conquering, the South could create enough new slaveholding states to overwhelm the northern states. With troops still in the field, Whigs in particular, and Northerners in general, demanded a law that would prohibit slavery in the new lands. The Northern-dominated House of Representatives passed such a bill, but the Southern-dominated Senate repeatedly rejected it. In the 1848 Treaty of Guadalupe Hidalgo that settled the conflict, Mexico gave America an enormous tract of land, including the territory that would later make up most of the states of Texas, New Mexico, Arizona, Utah, Nevada, and California. This was less land than Northerners had feared as the troops pushed farther and farther south, but it was enough to endanger the uneasy truce between the sections.

Tension built further when workers discovered gold at Sutter's Mill in California only months after the region fell into American hands. The rush of young men into the territory, working and roving, drinking and fighting, made it imperative to establish a government that could enforce order, but debate over whether the state would be free or slave increased the strain back East between Northerners and Southerners. Traveling through the territory, Cump professed to be shocked by the breakdown of normal lines of authority. Soldiers and sailors were deserting their posts. Worse, so were their commanders. These renegades could not be punished, because once they reached the mines, other miners shielded them. Making money was the order of the day. Preachers and professors were abandoning their principles and opening gambling houses. Sherman himself caught the infection. Although a professional soldier, he invested in a store and in city lots in Sacramento "in order to share somewhat in the riches of the land."[7]

The chaos in California demanded the establishment of governmental law and order, but under what principles could this western state be organized? The stunning speed with which the area had gone from backwater to teeming settlement meant that there was no partner state to offer to whichever section didn't get California, and, in any case, the new territory was far beyond the Louisiana territory that had been divided by the Missouri Compromise. Tempers ran high over the question of organizing California. That question, in turn, raised the issue of how to organize the other new territories acquired from Mexico. Southerners were determined to spread their economic system of plantations worked by slaves into the new lands; Northerners were just as adamant that Southerners would not dominate the new regions. Arriving in New York City in January 1850 to deliver dispatches, Cump was startled to hear from Commander of the Army Winfield Scott that "our country was on the eve of a terrible civil war."[8]

To calm the crisis, congressmen hammered out a compromise that made California a free state but offered Southerners the two huge Territories of New Mexico and Utah, Territories that eventually became the five states of Nevada, Utah, Colorado, Arizona, and New Mexico. In these large hunks of land, slavery could be established if the settlers decided they wanted it. The Compromise of 1850 was a panacea for those eager to believe that economic development could override sectional tensions. Although John Sherman was far from the military world in which Cump had heard rumors of civil war, the young Ohio lawyer had begun to pay careful attention to politics, and he "heartily supported" the compromise as "the best solution of dangerous sectional divisions."[9]

Those busy developing the American economy clung to the idea that the Compromise had calmed the sectional storm. Cump happened to be in Washington, D.C., in early 1850 while congressmen argued over the measure. He was there for his wedding to the daughter of the Secretary of the Interior, with whose family he had lived after the death of his own father. Cump didn't bother himself much with the congressional debates, which he found dull. He was much more interested in his own upcoming appointment as a Commissary Department captain, to be stationed in St. Louis. This appointment was undoubtedly garnered for him by his new father-in-law to enable the two men to look after family financial interests together in the western town. His experience with the private sector in St. Louis convinced Cump to build his fortunes in business rather than in the military; in 1853, when he was offered a good salary and the potential to accumulate a decent fortune, he resigned from the army to direct a bank in San Francisco.[10]

The Compromise did not, in fact, end tensions between the sections. Trouble erupted again in 1854, arising, as before, over the settlement of western lands. In a drive to promote a railroad to California, Illinois senator Stephen A. Douglas introduced a bill in Congress to organize a huge Territory of Nebraska—the land that now includes parts of North Dakota, South Dakota, Nebraska, Wyoming, and Montana—as a free state. Southerners announced that they would never agree unless he arranged for a corresponding slave state at the same time. He obliged, adding to his measure the much smaller Territory of Kansas—including part of what is now Colorado as well as today's Kansas—where slavery would be allowed if the settlers wanted it.

The hitch in this plan was that the proposed Kansas Territory lay to the north of the Missouri Compromise line that had divided slavery from freedom since 1820. After the passage of that law, Northerners had watched Southerners settle all the land that fell to them under the deal and then, when it ran out, involve the nation in a war to take more land from Mexico. Now, when Northerners proposed to move into the land that was theirs under the Missouri Compromise, Southerners abruptly changed the rules. When Congress passed the bill after great Southern pressure, Northerners howled. Across the free states, men turned their attention from their plows and their stores and their law books to politics. John Sherman was one of them.

It was not so much that Northerners like Sherman wanted to end slavery. Most of them didn't care about the welfare of slaves one way or the other. Rather, they worried that free workers would never be able to compete with slave labor. Slaves were cheaper than free workers, they thought, because slaves could be forced to work with less food and worse housing than a free worker, in conditions a free worker would never tolerate. Southern planters, though, were determined to spread the slave system because it would let them dominate the western economy the same way they dominated the South. If slavery were permitted to spread, Northerners argued, it would eventually force free workers into a sort of slavery of their own, living on a pittance and dependent on the goodwill of their employers for their very survival.

For the Shermans and Northerners like them, who were rising from their own impoverished backgrounds, the promise of free labor seemed to be the very heart of American society. They contrasted their own society of men who farmed their own land, fished from their own boats, or worked for wages until they could afford a farm or a boat or a business, with the slaveholding South, where the 4 million black people who bore the brunt of the region's hard labor could never hope even for a decent standard of living.

Northern free labor advocates believed that the fundamental element of American society was that every man had the right to the profits of his own labor. A society based on this principle honored God's plans for America (and perhaps for the world), while promising its citizens an ever increasing standard of living. A benevolent God had created a bountiful world of nature, guaranteeing that any man who worked hard could produce more than was necessary to support himself and his family. He could sell the surplus he created (which is why they called capital "pre-exerted labor"). He could then invest his money either in hiring workers to increase productivity or in ventures like trade or manufacturing.

This theory played out concretely in ways Northern men recognized from their own pasts. Young men fresh from their father's house would work for older, established men, accumulate their own capital, buy their own farms or businesses, and begin the cycle again in a never-ending upward spiral, just as the Sherman brothers and thousands of their contemporaries had done. Slavery was incompatible with free labor, they insisted; it destroyed free workers by providing cheap competition that put free men out of work.[11]

Democratic Southern slave owners were trying to take control of the national government to guarantee the spread of slavery, Northerners thought. Northerners saw a concerted effort to swing the power of the government to the South. There had been the Mexican War, then the fight over California, then the Kansas-Nebraska Act. Slave owners, it seemed, were organized as a "Slave Power" to destroy American free society.

John Sherman was only one of the many men determined to stop them. He later recalled that he had vowed to oppose anyone who had supported the Kansas-Nebraska Act and to make sure that slave owners never derived any advantage from overturning the Missouri Compromise. Sherman abandoned his former Whig associations and decided instead to act in concert with anyone who was part of the growing movement to preserve the West for free labor.[12]

Initially, it was not clear exactly what political shape this movement would take. Men of all political persuasions in the North dedicated themselves to a world based on free labor, but it took time to organize into a single form of opposition. John Sherman ran for Congress against the Democrats who had bent to the demands of Southern slave owners and permitted the westward spread of slavery. He was elected in 1854 without a firm party affiliation, having "never presided over any assembly except an Odd Fellows' lodge," he later remembered.[13]

By 1856, Northerners who opposed the spread of slavery had formed the Republican Party, and John rose with the party. He had found a new field for his fighting spirit, and he took to the political stump to oppose the Slave Power and get Republicans who had pledged to stop the spread of slavery elected to office. In the run-up to the election of 1860, Congressman Sherman spoke in Ohio, Pennsylvania, Indiana, New Jersey, and Delaware, all closely contested states, where he rallied men to vote for Abraham Lincoln, the backwoods lawyer from Illinois.[14]

"Well, Lincoln is elected," John wrote to Cump after the 1860 election. Unwilling to abide by the election results, eleven Southern states greeted the new president with articles of secession. The administration turned to its friends to preserve the integrity of the Union. Among those tapped for positions in Washington was Ohio senator Salmon P. Chase, chosen to become Secretary of the Treasury. John Sherman took over Chase's Senate seat in March 1861. Less than a month later, Confederate forces opened fire on Fort Sumter, the Union's outpost in the harbor of Charleston, South Carolina. Four bloody years of war had begun.[15]

The outbreak of war brought Cump to Washington. The military Sherman brother had never shared John's zeal for politics. He had ignored the political tensions that drove John into Congress and had spent the tense antebellum years concentrating on building a successful career, one way or another. After his San Francisco bank failed, in 1858, he had briefly joined his brother-in-law's law firm in Kansas despite his lack of legal training. Then, chafing under his poor salary in a profession not his own, he turned back to the military. Applying to the War Department for a political appointment as a paymaster, Sherman instead was appointed the superintendent of a new military college in Baton Rouge, Louisiana—an institution that became Louisiana State University—taking up his new duties in late 1859. "I gave no heed to the political excitement of the day," he recalled, but he was sometimes treated with suspicion by Southerners who loathed his famous brother John, who they believed was plotting to end slavery across the South.[16]

Cump loved his post in Louisiana, but loved the Union more. When the South seceded, he resigned from the military college and moved back to Ohio. But he resented the atmosphere that had stolen from him a job he loved, the first job that seemed likely to give him the respect and salary he needed to live up to the expectations of his well-connected wife. He and John were in frequent contact as the crisis mounted, and Cump was furious with "the politicians" on both sides, whom he blamed for the troubles that had forced him to leave his congenial and lucrative position in Louisiana, and who could, as far as he was concerned, "fight it out" amongst themselves. Visiting Washington at John's urging in early 1861, he recalled, "I broke out on John, d—ning the politicians generally, saying, 'You have got things in a hell of a fix, and you may get them out as you best can.'" In April 1861, Cump stormed back to St. Louis to run a local railroad line.[17]

By May, he had cooled off and decided not to miss his chance at rising to a position of eminence in a real shooting war. John had received permission to raise an Ohio regiment and, clearly hoping to get a command for his brother, solicited the president for two West Point graduates to drill the volunteers. Cump did not get that assignment—it went to another Ohio man, Second Lieutenant James William Forsyth—but he received a different appointment as a colonel in May 1861.[18]

Cump's war service meant that he would eventually eclipse John in Americans' memories of the nation's nineteenth-century history. General Sherman was a ferociously successful military leader, the right-hand man of General Ulysses S. Grant. He was author and executor of the March to the Sea that demoralized the Confederacy by devastating a swath of countryside three hundred miles long and sixty miles wide from Nashville to Savannah. He was a crucial figure in the North's successful prosecution of the war. Cump fought because he was good at it, and because by doing so he could guarantee the survival of a world where a man could succeed through hard work. By spring of 1865, "Uncle Billy," as his soldiers knew him, had become one of the most loathed and loved generals in America.

Cump became the better remembered brother, but in his role as a legislator, John Sherman was just as vital to the North's success. He was one of the chief architects of the government policies that financed the enormously expensive war, and in the process of funding the treasury he helped to transform the American economy. By the end of the century, the American nation itself reflected the shape that Sherman and his fellow Republican congressmen had cast for it. Reflecting their belief in free labor, John and his colleagues committed the postwar nation to a policy of economic development that made it the economic juggernaut that it had become by the 1890s. While that economic dynamism came at a high price, men like Sherman had no idea of that cost when they set out to fund the war.

When the Confederates fired on Fort Sumter, Congress realized that it had to find money for the monumentally expensive task of equipping, feeding, caring for, and moving an army that would eventually include more than a million men. As chairman of the powerful House Committee on Ways and Means charged with preparing all financial bills, and then, beginning in July 1861, as a member of the Senate Finance Committee, the younger Sherman was one of a handful of Republicans who developed an economic policy for the fledgling party. Their dramatic success determined the path of American history for the rest of the century.

In December 1860, the treasury was empty. Sherman was confident that the government could get volunteers to fight, but he was not convinced that it could find money to pay them. There was not even enough money, he recalled with chagrin, to pay the salaries of members of Congress. Secretary of the Treasury Chase greeted an emergency session of Congress with the news that the nation would need about $319 million for the upcoming year (a woefully low estimate, as it turned out). Sherman was a close friend of the treasury secretary and had chaired the House Committee of Ways and Means, making him well acquainted with financial matters. He quickly became the Senate go-to man for financial legislation. Recognizing that Lincoln's military power was extraordinary, and that the administration had "almost unlimited power of taxation," Sherman and the Republicans set out to find ways to fund the war.[19]

They started with taxes. New luxury taxes covered tobacco and liquor; new manufacturing taxes fell on every industry; new graduated income taxes swept in all those above poverty. Senators joked that when one complained that everything was taxed except coffins, another senator warned: "Don't say that to Sherman or he will have them on the tax list before night!"[20]

At the same time, though, men like Sherman understood they needed to enable Americans to pay the new taxes that they had placed on practically everything. The Republican congressmen set out to clear the way for individuals to move up the economic ladder more quickly, developing the economy as they prospered. Congress provided free western land for those willing to farm it, then funded the construction of a transcontinental railroad line to enable young families to reach the western farming regions. Eager to increase production by bringing workers into the country, they also made it cheaper and safer for immigrants to travel to America.[21]

Sherman and his colleagues also encouraged trade and industry. Before the war, the nation's buying and selling had been accomplished with state banknotes, but Congress replaced this notoriously volatile currency with the country's first national money, printed on the back with green ink. When too many greenbacks inflated the currency, Congress established a more stable currency backed ultimately by gold, to be distributed by new national banks.

Most dramatically, the wartime Republican Congress changed the nation's system of tariffs. These fees, which were essentially taxes on imported goods, raised funds for the treasury at the same time that they gave domestic industry an advantage in home markets. Tariffs added surcharges to cheap foreign products to make sure that American-made products could compete with them even if the domestic product was more expensive to produce. Before the Civil War, manufacturers had begged for tariffs that would protect their fledgling industries from foreign competition, but American consumers demanded the low tariffs that would keep inexpensive foreign products flowing into the United States. In the prewar years, the government bowed to consumers and imposed tariffs solely with an eye to raising the low revenues the inactive government needed.

During the war, though, the desperate need to raise money to fight the war inspired Republicans like John Sherman to develop a new kind of American tariff that would protect industry. Rather than using tariffs simply to raise revenue that would flow directly to the treasury, the Republicans put tariff walls around virtually all of the nation's production, agricultural as well as industrial, believing that by supporting the entire economy the government would improve everyone's standard of living and enable Americans to pay the new taxes Congress had imposed.[22]

The wartime tariffs worked, increasing revenues both for the treasury and for businessmen. Congress increased them as necessary to bring in money until, by the end of the war, tariffs of 47 percent of an item's value protected American industry. Under this protective system, American manufacturing thrived just as Sherman had always thought it would, but the arrangement did little for farmers, who were exporting their produce rather than competing with imported crops. Still, farmers didn't care much; their products were in demand and prices were high.[23]

The measures set in place during the war to develop the national economy created great prosperity and fundamentally reshaped the economy. To feed, clothe, equip, and move the army, government officials dealt contracts to expanding factories and the railroad industry. Henry Burden & Company in Troy, New York, made the horseshoes on which the army spent almost $5 million during the war; the Union India Rubber Company of New York and Connecticut turned out more than $5.7 million worth of waterproof blankets and ponchos for the soldiers; the Springfield Armory in Massachusetts employed about 2,500 workers by 1862 and shipped about 20,000 rifles a month to the army. The new greenbacks and the new national banknotes made it feasible for the first time for businesses to operate across state lines, and new, national companies developed. The tariffs guaranteed that American business could sell products domestically at a profit, providing more cash to pour into development. The iron industry, especially, boomed under the influence of the protective tariff, driving the rapid growth of the railroad industry, and workers laid 5,000 miles of new railroad tracks across the North during the war. The railroads symbolized and bolstered the nation's great industrial growth. Americans dreamed of pushing the railroads all the way across the continent.[24]

Indeed, the West was still at the heart of the Republican vision of the world, just as it had been when Northerners took a stand against the Slave Power. The government encouraged settlers to move west during the war, claiming the region for the Union. In July 1862, Congress passed the Homestead Act granting free western farmland, and in the same month chartered the Union Pacific Railroad to tie the West into the national economy. Farmers sweated to bring new acres under cultivation, feeding not only the Union troops but also Europeans suffering under repeated crop failures. Miners swung their picks into newly discovered lodes in the western mountains; the treasury coveted the gold they dug to pay mounting war bills.

Congress organized western lands as quickly as it could. In 1861, it admitted Kansas as a state and organized Colorado, Nevada, and Dakota as Territories. Two years later, in 1863, it organized the new Territories of Arizona and Idaho, carving Arizona out of the older Territory of New Mexico. Montana Territory was organized in 1864 after prospectors discovered gold there, and John Bozeman cut up to Virginia City, Montana, from the old Overland Trail, blazing the Bozeman Trail through the Powder River country in what is now Wyoming to reach the Montana mines. Before the war, the plains were unorganized land, but by the end of the Civil War, Congress had carved the West into Territorial blocks, a configuration that looked almost like it does today.[25]

But the lines on the map belied the reality of the West. In the hills and river bottoms of that vast region, on the sweeping plains and in the remote mountains, lived people whose livelihoods depended on holding the land as it was. The two worldviews could not coexist. Very soon, they would come into conflict.

The powerful Plains Indians held the ground that American miners and settlers hoped to turn to their profit. Before horses had come to North America with the Spanish explorers, Plains Indians were poor and relatively weak, but the arrival of horses had dramatically changed Indian cultures. While those changes were a mixed blessing for most, they made the Sioux wealthy and militarily strong. They would be the most powerful foreign fighting force the U.S. Army would meet until World War I.[26]

Plains Indians were master equestrians and formidable fighters. The Comanche warriors of the Southwest were perhaps the most famous horsemen on the plains, but it is fair to say that all of the horse tribe's warriors could outride all but the very best U.S. cavalry. A Plains Indian warrior could ride full speed into battle with one leg slung over the neck of his horse and his own body hung over the side of the horse's neck, keeping the body of the horse between him and his enemy. From beneath the horse's neck he could shoot arrows that were as sharp as scalpels with enough force to go through a buffalo. And while U.S. troops were still tied to muskets or rifles that took a skilled soldier about thirty seconds to load and fire, a mounted Indian could shoot his arrows fast enough to keep one in the air at all times. The coming of the modern gun in the late nineteenth century gave even greater military power to those Indians wealthy enough or lucky enough to own one, although they continued to prefer to use their ammunition on animals and to grapple with men at close range. Killing an enemy by shooting him from a distance was "just shooting," and carried no particular honor.[27]

Fiercely protective of their land, the Plains Indians prized it in its uncultivated state. They depended for survival on game, especially the bison, called "buffalo" but a very different animal from the Asian water buffalo and the African Cape buffalo that give that species its name. Bison, standing over six feet tall at the shoulder and weighing up to 2,000 pounds, ranged over the plains in numbers estimated as high as 40 million; before the arrival of settlers, observers wrote of herds that covered fifty square miles. These huge numbers of animals were possible because, over time, Indian societies had altered the landscape of the plains to nurture the bison herds. It was imperative to their economy that the land be preserved as it was.[28]

Plains Indians constructed their world around the bison. They followed the animals, eating the meat of the buffaloes they killed, of course, as well as the internal organs that were rich in vitamins and minerals. The tough buffalo skins were their fabric; they made leggings and shirts and dresses from them, slept under the warmth of the rough buffalo pelts, and used buffalo skins to cover their tepees. Horns of the animals became cups and spoons as well as powder horns. Bones were filed into arrowheads, knives, and dice. Indians twisted bison hair into rope and used it for saddle padding or the stuffing for dolls made of buffalo skin. They kindled their fires with buffalo chips. Their very identities derived from the bison: great Sioux leader Sitting Bull took his name from the buffalo. A notable artist, Sitting Bull painted the story of his life on buffalo skin. The bison filled every need of the Plains Indian and created the culture of tribes like the Sioux. Using the buffalo for food, shelter, tools, and blankets, bartering buffalo skins for anything else they desired, the Plains tribes were powerful and wealthy.[29]

Indians needed to preserve the land as it was to conserve the animals at the heart of their economy. Before the coming of Americans, they hunted in their own territory and patrolled their lands for intruders from other tribes, fighting skirmishes to keep their lands and honoring the warriors who defended their dominions.

When American migrants pushed onto the Plains in the late 1850s, Plains Indians defended their lands against them, too. When U.S. soldiers came to back up the interlopers, they fared no better. In 1861 in the Southwest, an officer wrongly imprisoned Apache leader Cochise and his family for the theft of a white boy by another band of Indians.

Cochise escaped by cutting his way out of the back of a tent, and the two sides commenced a guerrilla war. By 1863, just north of the Apache lands that spanned the border of Mexico and Texas, Comanches raided the camps of the men building the Kansas Pacific branch of the new transcontinental railroad, terrifying the workers and slowing progress.

Farther north, vicious fighting had begun even earlier. The Northwest was the land of the Sioux and their allies, and they held their land so effectively that famous Sioux leaders like Sitting Bull became for Americans the hated symbols of Indian resistance to government authority. "Sioux" was a name that meant "enemy" and had been fixed upon the Lakota by their own enemies. The Sioux were divided by different dialects into three groups: an eastern, a middle, and a western group, named, respectively, the Santees, the Yanktons, and the Tetons. Each of these larger language groups was made up of a number of distinctive bands. These bands ranged along the rivers, which ran generally northwest to southeast, in the region from Minnesota to what is now Montana.[30]

The Santees, the Sioux farthest east, were the first to clash with the Americans. By 1858, settlers moving into Minnesota had forced the Santee Sioux from their 24 million-acre territory onto a single strip of land twenty miles wide and 150 miles long, along the upper Minnesota River. No longer able to feed themselves, the Santees depended on the rations the government had promised them in exchange for their land, but the unprecedented expenses of the Civil War delayed funding for Indian appropriations.

By 1862, Santees in Minnesota were starving. After the agent charged with their care refused to provide emergency rations (one of his supporters told the Indians to "eat grass or their own dung"), the young men of the tribe fought to push whites back east across the Mississippi. They killed between four hundred and eight hundred settlers before the Minnesota militia and the U.S. Army crushed the rebellion. Angry Americans condemned the "Santee Uprising" and demanded retaliation. Military authorities sentenced 303 Indians to death by hanging. President Lincoln ultimately spared the lives of all but thirty-eight of the Indians, who were hanged on December 26, 1862, in what remains the largest mass execution in American history.[31]

The Santee crisis sparked a drawn-out war between the Sioux and the United States government. After the uprising, soldiers and civilians working for the army as scouts retaliated against western Indians generally, while Santee refugees chased by the army fled west in disarray to enlist the Yankton and the Teton Sioux in their struggle. One young, mixed-race boy, later known as Ohiyesa, the Winner, recalled a helter-skelter scramble with his extended family from Minnesota across the plains and eventually across the Missouri River to Canada after hearing that his father, Many Lightnings, had been hanged for his part in the uprising. Ohiyesa was adopted by his uncle and trained as a warrior to avenge his father.[32]

Eastern expansion had pushed the Yankton Sioux west from their lands along the James River onto the Yankton Reservation on the eastern bank of the Missouri River in 1858. There, the Yanktons had learned to fear the soldiers stationed nearby and weren't much interested in going to war alongside the Santees, especially after a company of soldiers was stationed at their agency, and a new block-house—a log stockade—protected area settlers while scouts deliberately murdered roving Santees.[33]

Farther west, the Teton Sioux were not as wary of war as the Yanktons and were willing to entertain the idea of fighting the army. They had twice as many people as the other two Sioux divisions combined and did not fear soldiers, since they had not had any contact to speak of with them. They lived west of the Missouri River, in the area around the Powder River and in the Black Hills and Big Horn Mountains, in the lands that became Dakota, Montana, and Wyoming Territories. This was an area still out of reach of eastern interlopers. The Teton Sioux included seven main groups—the Oglala, Minneconjou, Hunkpapa, Brulé, Sans Arc, Two-Kettle, and Black Foot Sioux—themselves broken down into bands. Members of these different groups interacted freely, but followed their own chiefs and camped as a unit whenever the groups came together.[34]

As the Santees moved west to get the Tetons to join the war against the soldiers, the soldiers followed behind them. In 1863, army troops marched west to dominate the Teton Sioux, skirmishing with Tetons on the eastern side of the Missouri River in the Dakotas. One of the warriors they fought there was Hunkpapa leader Sitting Bull. The chief was a grown man by the 1860s, famous for his utter recklessness in battle, his magnetic personality, his wisdom, and his kindness. He was especially fond of children; his people marveled at his patience with them. Both sides suffered in the drought conditions in the Dakotas during the summer of 1863, and the skirmishes were inconclusive. In the fall, the Tetons crossed back across the Missouri, while the soldiers went into winter quarters.[35]

The following summer, troops crossed the Missouri River and engaged an encampment of Santees and Yanktonais—relatives of the Yanktons who had not settled onto a reservation—as well as hunting Sioux, at Killdeer Mountain in what is now North Dakota. The soldiers eventually pushed the Indians back, but soon found themselves desperately short of supplies. Their journey west toward the Yellowstone River to supply ships for water and food turned into a flight in which they were pursued by angry Sioux. Sitting Bull looked with some disdain at the army's assault as he and his people pushed the soldiers toward the river. "Why is it the whites come to fight with us?" Sitting Bull wanted to know.[36]

It didn't really matter, for within months, Sitting Bull's people would stop their halfhearted skirmishing with soldiers and commit themselves to a full-blown war against eastern incursions. A vicious attack on their allies to the south, the Cheyenne, prompted the Hunkpapa to abandon their sporadic warfare and undertake to throw the interlopers out of their territory altogether. The Cheyenne had been clashing with eastern emigrants since 1858. Those clashes escalated until, in 1864, they came to a conclusion so horrific it convinced many of the Teton Sioux bands that they must stand together against the Americans.

The Cheyennes' problems with easterners began with the discovery of gold on the eastern edge of the Rockies in 1858, which sparked a rush of more than 100,000 Americans into land that the U.S. government had guaranteed to the Southern Cheyenne and Arapaho. As miners continued to pour into the area, the government organized the region as Colorado Territory and tried to force the Cheyenne and Arapaho onto a reservation at Sand Creek on the Arkansas River in southeastern Colorado. This arid piece of land could not support the Indians, many of whom ignored orders to move to Sand Creek and continued to hunt on lands now claimed by miners and settlers.[37]

By 1864, settlers' anger had reached a boiling point as Cheyennes and Arapahos who had never agreed to the land cession were raiding farms and wagon trains for food. In an atmosphere of Indian-hating that had been exacerbated by the "Santee Uprising," the militia retaliated. Raids became battles, until in the summer of 1864 the governor of the Territory called for every Colorado citizen to "kill and destroy . . . all . . . hostile Indians." A group of volunteer soldiers took him at his word. On November 29, they opened fire on a friendly band of Cheyenne and Arapaho people, mostly women, children, and old men, camped for the winter under a flag of peace at the Sand Creek Reservation. The soldiers killed about 125 Cheyennes and Arapahos. Then they butchered the bodies, taking as trophies the scalps and genitalia of their victims.[38]

The murder and mutilation of surrendering innocents sent a number of Cheyennes north to the Sioux. In the spring of 1865, they arrived at Sitting Bull's camp and appealed for help. "We were told that white men would not kill women and children, but now we have lost all faith in white men," they explained. "We took pity on them in the past, but we shall never do so again. We plan to strike the whites all along the Platte, and after that the settlements to the west. Are you with us?" they asked Sitting Bull. He was. From this time on, Sitting Bull would stand firm against eastern incursions into Indian lands.[39]

More important, in the short term, was that other Teton Sioux bands had also wholeheartedly determined to fight intruders. While Sitting Bull's people drifted northwest after game during 1865, drastically limiting their contact with easterners, Teton Sioux farther southeast were angry over emigrant intruders into their territory and were ready to organize against them once and for all. By mid-1865, they began to push back against the troops marching into the Plains.

What was at stake was some of the best hunting land on the continent, land critical to the Sioux way of life. In 1864, John Bozeman had blazed the Bozeman Trail directly through the Indians' prized Powder River hunting lands. Here, the plains, with their crowding buffalo, were broken by wide sheets of water teeming with waterfowl from the majestic Trumpeter swan to brant, mallard, and tiny little teal. As prospectors headed to the Montana mines, the army was determined to protect the Bozeman Trail.[40]

The Indians were just as determined to keep the settlers out of the Powder River region. By the end of the Civil War, the Oglalas held the northern plains, led by famous chief Red Cloud, a merciless warrior whose great height—six and a half feet, according to an awed reporter, although this was generous—gave him a commanding presence. Some of the Brulés, as well as Cheyennes and Arapahos, joined his forces, pushing settlers back from the tribes' prime hunting grounds in the Dakotas and the Powder River Valley.[41]

By 1865, the U.S. government was eager to stop the Sioux's successful campaign against interlopers. As Americans saw it, millions of Northern men had charged the heights at Fredericksburg and held their dying friends at Shiloh, protected Little Round Top at Gettysburg and foraged through Georgia, to guarantee that the West would be a free field for American settlers and businessmen. Now, miners were poised to rush to the new lodes of Montana, but Indians promised to kill them if they tried. Railroad men were eager to pound their rails across the Plains, but Indians insisted on keeping the land as it was. The fledgling cattle industry was taking off, and wildly picturesque cowboys herded long-horned beeves from Texas either to western army forts or to railheads for shipment back to eastern cities, but they risked their lives when they traveled through the lands controlled by Indians. Farmers and storekeepers, blacksmiths and carpenters were ready to build new, thriving communities on the Plains, but Indians clung to their ancient ways. Americans had fought and died for economic progress, and they were not going to be stopped by savages. Not if men like the Shermans had any say in it.

And who better to put in charge of breaking the Indians than the man credited with breaking the Confederates? When the postwar nation was divided into five military divisions, General Grant placed William Tecumseh Sherman at the head of the Department of the Mississippi, charged with overseeing the volatile West. Sherman's time in California and St. Louis had convinced him of the enormous value of western land for development, and he was determined to bring the West into the free labor economy he had just fought so hard to defend. From his headquarters in St. Louis, Sherman plotted to absorb the West into the rest of the nation.[42]

His first job was to defend American emigrants in the West from Indian attacks. In the Southwest, the army needed to protect the workers on the Union Pacific, where Comanches and Apaches attacked with deadly success. Sherman's guidance was not imperative there, for in the Southwest the Indians and Americans had rubbed elbows for decades and there were already established officials with contacts in the tribes. Officials negotiated treaties with different tribes, and although the treaties did not establish a lasting peace, they kept violence sporadic.[43]

Sherman turned his attention to the Northwest. There, American incursions were so recent that there was no existing policy for Indian relations—and a policy was imperative, for Sioux fighters threatened the Bozeman Trail. Throughout the spring of 1866, army officials at Fort Laramie, in what is now Wyoming, worked to get the warriors to come to the fort and make peace. They had little luck at first, but they were encouraged in March 1866, when Spotted Tail of the Brulés came in with the body of his daughter, who had begged on her deathbed to be buried on the grounds of the fort where she had lived earlier when her father was on better terms with the officers. A legendary leader by this time, Spotted Tail was a stocky man known for a subtle and hilarious sense of humor, a very keen appreciation for female companionship (his nickname was Speak-with-the-Woman, and in Lakota to "speak with" a woman meant to make love), and his emotional intensity. The death of his daughter was a blow indeed, driving Spotted Tail to the great length of appealing to an enemy to fulfill her final wish. Acceding to the request, the fort commander organized a fine funeral, and the brokenhearted father, who had been fighting the army for four years, agreed in exchange to listen to government proposals for a treaty.[44]

Spotted Tail was the first Sioux leader to consider peace, but others followed close behind. Friendly feelers and presents of gunpowder and food to the other fighting Indians brought a number of Sioux leaders to the fort on June 13 for a council. Sitting Bull and the northern Teton Hunkpapas, who still lived a traditional life far from white settlement, did not attend, but important Oglalas closer to army forts did. Forty-three-year-old Oglala chief Red Cloud was there, along with Man-Afraid-of-His-Horse, whose ferocity in battle made enemies fear even the sight of his pony.[45]

The talks broke down almost as soon as they began. With remarkably bad timing, army troops charged with reinforcing the Bozeman Trail marched into camp right after the council started. Red Cloud angrily accused the officers of bad faith, claiming to negotiate when they had already decided to take the land. He and Man-Afraid-of-His-Horse, along with their people, rode their ponies out of the fort vowing to defend their lands. Not everyone joined them. Spotted Tail, whose people preferred to live on the Platte rather than in the Powder River country anyway, and who still felt kindly toward the officer who had honorably buried the chief's favorite daughter, joined less important men in signing a peace treaty allowing whites to use the Bozeman Trail. The army could claim to have achieved a signed treaty but, in fact, the warriors who posed the most danger to settlers had left the fort angrier than ever.[46]

Despite Red Cloud's hostility, General Sherman was willing to bank on the treaty. He was not overly concerned with ongoing Indian troubles. He believed they were largely the work of a few hostiles and that white settlement would soon overrun the tribes. His confidence underestimated the powerful Red Cloud, who was marshaling his warriors into a resistance that would be so effective it would become known as Red Cloud's War.

Believing that the West was now under American control, General Sherman asked his brother John to come tour the land that Cump oversaw. In August of 1866, the War Department reorganized military districts and put Sherman in charge of the Division of the Missouri, overseeing four departments that covered the Plains from the southern border of New Mexico to the Canadian line. The new organization of the military in the West did not change Cump's duties much, but it did recognize that the center of military activity was now in the western, rather than the eastern, theater.[47]

Cump invited John on a tour through the two northernmost departments of his western command. They traveled through the Department of Dakota, which oversaw the northernmost part of the Plains, including Minnesota, Montana Territory, the Dakotas, and the Yellowstone part of what would become Wyoming; they continued on through the Department of the Platte, which covered the region south of the Department of Dakota, overseeing Iowa, Nebraska, Colorado, Utah, and Wyoming except for the Yellowstone region.

Although the Shermans took the precaution of traveling with a guard, they had no trouble with Indians on their journey. On the contrary, it seemed to the brothers that the region was peaceful and ready for intensive settlement. John Sherman was impressed with the beautiful landscapes, especially the mountains, which he predicted would be very valuable. He also approved of the boosterism he found among the farmers and miners he met, although he worried about the "Indian depredations" that cut into settlers' efforts. For his part, Cump told John that he shouldn't believe the stories he heard about Indian troubles. Those reports were just another sign of the same boosterism John approved. Settlers complained about Indians, Cump thought, so they could convince the government to send in troops and then profit by supplying the soldiers with meat and goods.[48]

General Sherman believed that the Indians would eventually give way to settlement, but it wasn't happening as fast as he would like. In November 1866, he came up with a plan to speed things along. He proposed to push the Indians out of the way of railroad construction onto reservations to the north and south, leaving a corridor through the middle of the country "for our people exclusively. . . ." He also wanted the commander of the Department of Dakota, General Alfred H. Terry, to protect navigation on the Missouri River and travel across the plains.[49]

Army officials insisted that the treaty with Spotted Tail and his kin permitting settlers to use the Bozeman Trail had established peace but, in fact, war was brewing. Red Cloud and his men had no intention of allowing eastern incursions into the Powder River region. Even some of the warriors who had signed the treaty warned officers that any whites venturing into the Powder River country should "go prepared and look out for their hair." Indeed, warriors with Red Cloud and Man-Afraid-of-His-Horse preyed on those journeying in the Powder River region, running off stock and picking off men who were traveling alone.[50]

Soldiers doggedly marched up the Bozeman Trail and established forts to protect American migrants. They built Fort Phil Kearny, then marched another ninety miles to the Bighorn River and established Fort C. F. Smith. These forts, together with Fort Reno—which had been built in 1865—were supposed to defend the Bozeman Trail. The troops stationed at the forts, though, were understaffed, underequipped, and undertrained, and their commanding officer did not venture out to engage the Sioux, who continued to mount limited offensives against settlers and army details in the area.[51]

In December 1866, the simmering trouble erupted dramatically, shattering the complacency of those officers who believed the Indian threat had been contained. An arrogant and inexperienced officer at Fort Phil Kearny, Lieutenant Colonel W. J. Fetterman, believed he could whip the Sioux once and for all. Ignoring orders to stay close to the wood train he was supposed to protect, Fetterman led eighty men into an ambush set up by Red Cloud and the wily American Horse. The Sioux killed Fetterman and all of his men.[52]

This event, immediately dubbed the "Fetterman Massacre," turned Sherman's eagerness to push the Indians aside into an eagerness to kill them off. "This massacre should be treated as an act of war and should be punished with vindictive earnestness," General Sherman wrote, "until at least ten Indians are killed for each white life lost. . . ." He told his men not to worry about finding the men who had actually killed Fetterman and his command but rather to kill any Indian they could find, to "destroy all of the same breed." This suggestion perhaps reflected just how hard it was to track down warriors and how much easier it was for soldiers to take revenge on friendlier Indians, the same calculation that had fed the Sand Creek Massacre. Sherman told the commander of the Department of the Platte to consider all Sioux in the Powder River region hostile, and to "punish them to the extent of utter extermination if possible." He wrote to John that the Sioux and the Cheyenne "must be exterminated, for they cannot and will not settle down, and our people will force us to it."[53]

The Fetterman affair also galvanized government officials back East into finding a solution to the conflict with the hostile Sioux. Congressmen were eager to stop Indian attacks on settlers and on the train crews that were hammering west, but were not willing to follow General Sherman's advice that the Indians be exterminated. Sherman, Grant, and indeed, army officers in general, demanded that the War Department be given control of Indian Affairs, but politicians refused. Many easterners leaned instead toward the advice of reformers who insisted that soldiers were drunken butchers whose proximity to the Indians would, at best, introduce them to liquor and sin, and at worst, eliminate them. Reformers wanted to devote resources to "civilizing" the Indians. For their part, army officers dismissed the reformers as starry-eyed idealists who created problems with the Indians that the army then bore the brunt of cleaning up.[54]

Congressmen had their own interests to serve as they managed Indian policy. Government officials clung to their control of the vast political machinery of Indian management, and hated the idea of handing that appointment power over to the military. The Interior Department managed Indian affairs, meaning that its officers—themselves appointed by the administration in power—dispensed the valuable government jobs and lucrative contracts for Indian supplies to political supporters. By siding with reformers on the issue of managing the Indians, politicians kept this significant patronage power in their own hands.[55]

In July, Congress established an Indian Peace Commission charged with ending the hostilities. It designed the commission to balance the rivalry between army officers and politically appointed government officials. The commission had three current military leaders and four men who had been interested in some fashion in Indian affairs, either as politicians or reformers. At the head of the group was the Interior Department's Commissioner of Indian Affairs, but General Sherman was also on the mission, along with Major General William S. Harney and Major General Alfred H. Terry. Congress also tried to balance the wishes of the army and reformers when it instructed the commission. It charged the commissioners with pushing the Indians onto reservations in the northern and southern Plains to open up a corridor through the country, as Sherman wished. At the same time it asked them to find a way to "civilize" the Indians by turning them into farmers, a sop to reformers.[56]

While all the members of the commission fervently wanted to move the Indians out of the way of American economic development, they had different ideas about how to accomplish the task. The reformers on the commission wanted to "civilize" the Indians by providing them with agricultural instruction and tools, churches, schools, and the provisions to help them make the transition to self-sufficiency. The military men wanted a military solution to "the Indian problem."[57]

The commission had its work cut out for it, for by the summer of 1867, the traditionalist Sioux controlled the Bozeman Trail and the Powder River country, keeping the resident troops holed up in their raw forts. In August, the Sioux attacked men haying near Fort C. F. Smith. The Indians were driven off, but the next day they descended on a corral made of wagon boxes near Fort Phil Kearny, killing an officer and five soldiers. Within days of the "Wagon Box Fight," Sioux fighters attacked a Union Pacific freight train in Nebraska, causing the president of the Union Pacific to warn the Secretary of War that work on the road would have to stop until the government could protect railroad workers.[58]

General Sherman insisted to Senator Sherman that the government must take responsibility for pushing the Indians out of the way of economic development. Existing treaties meant that Indians had the right to hunt across the lands the railroads wanted, and they kept doing so, he complained. It was ridiculous to suggest that the railroad companies should defend themselves. Defining government duties toward private enterprise expansively, the general reasoned that Congress had a duty to protect the railroads. It had provided legal charters and granted lands to the transcontinental railroad companies to build across the country. The act of granting the charters and giving away land that the Indians claimed was "an implied promise" that the government would provide military protection for the construction of the roads. Certainly, he wrote, everyone knew that Congress could not simply "surrender the country to a few bands of roving Indians."[59]

The commission decided to negotiate two treaties with the Indians, one with the tribes in the Southwest and the other with the Sioux and their allies in the Northwest. They began by taking the Union Pacific up to the North Platte River, where in September they met with cooperative Teton Sioux. Spotted Tail led the Indian side of the discussion, and his weakening friendliness toward the soldiers indicated that the commission was going to have trouble with the rest of the Sioux. Spotted Tail complained about settlement along the Bozeman Trail and asked for ammunition and guns for his people to continue to live as hunters. Sherman answered him with a warning that the railroads and whites were coming, and they must either cooperate or be killed. It was clear that there was little point in expecting finality from anything agreed on with the Sioux at the conference, with warriors still in the field. The commissioners could not do much until they found out whether or not Red Cloud and the other warriors would negotiate. They dispatched a Sioux trader to try to summon Red Cloud to a council.[60]

Giving hostile Sioux time to come to Fort Laramie for talks, the commissioners traveled south to Medicine Lodge Creek in Kansas. They went without Sherman. He had gone to Washington at the command of President Andrew Johnson, who was trying without success to use the general as a pawn in his ongoing fight with Congress. General C. C. Augur, commander of the Department of the Platte, took Sherman's place. In October the commissioners persuaded many southwestern Indians to sign a series of treaties, known collectively as the Treaty of Medicine Lodge. Under its terms, the Apache, Comanche, Kiowa, Cheyenne, and Arapahoe exchanged their claims to about 90 million acres of their lands for firm titles to about 3 million acres of land in Indian Territory, in what is now Oklahoma. They promised to stop attacking railroad crews and settlers. In return, the government promised annual distributions of clothing and food; the provision of a doctor, a blacksmith, a miller, an engineer, a carpenter, a farmer—to show Indians how to grow crops—and teachers; and the construction of schools.[61]

The commissioners then turned north again. Augur was still sitting in for Sherman, and it turned out that Cump was not missing anything. When the commissioners got back to Fort Laramie in November, they found only friendly Indians waiting for them. Red Cloud and his people refused to have anything to do with the negotiations. The chief sent word that he had every intention of protecting the Powder River valley, and that he would talk only when troops were removed from Forts Phil Kearny and C. F. Smith.[62]

Red Cloud's warfare and determination finally won his main point. Tired of the expense of the war and convinced they could not protect both the Union Pacific and the Bozeman Trail, government officials reluctantly agreed to abandon the troublesome forts—Reno, Phil Kearny, and C. F. Smith—and to permit those Indians unwilling to live on a reservation to continue to live untrammeled, following the buffalo so long as they should last. Sherman was reluctant to admit defeat, and urged his officers to remove their troops as slowly as possible to make sure the Indians understood that the army was not weak, just more interested in targets other than Red Cloud.[63]

The commissioners invited Red Cloud, Man-Afraid-of-His-Horse, and their people to meet them at Fort Laramie in mid-April 1868. The

Sioux fighters ignored the invitation. Red Cloud was angry at the dawdling soldiers and held firm that the forts must be abandoned before he would negotiate. "We are on the mountains looking down on the soldiers and the forts," he said, according to newspapers. "When we see the soldiers moving away and the forts abandoned, then I will come down and talk." The commissioners were left to negotiate with Spotted Tail and the Brulés, who were already friendly, and who signed a peace treaty along with friendly Crows, Northern Cheyennes, and Arapahos. As troops slowly drained out of the forts, the commission went back East, leaving behind a copy of the treaty for Red Cloud and Man-Afraid-of-His-Horse to sign.[64]

By August the troops had finally left the forts along the Bozeman Trail and Red Cloud's people had burned Forts C. F. Smith and Phil Kearny. Still, Red Cloud took his time about coming to Fort Laramie to negotiate. It wasn't until November that he and Man-Afraid-of-His-Horse arrived there. They rode in with an impressive crowd of followers, including about 125 chiefs of the Hunkpapa, Brulé, Black Foot, and Sans Arc Sioux.[65]

Red Cloud had won. He had proved that he had the upper hand over the U.S. Army, and his power was at its zenith. He signed the treaty with only a vague understanding of what was in it, ignoring the provisions about farming and reservations because his people flatly refused to have any part of that sort of lifestyle. Red Cloud signed the treaty primarily because he wanted trading rights at Fort Laramie. He had also heard that the soldiers had provided powder and lead to his enemies the Crow, and he thought it only fair that he got the same deal. He announced that, while he would stop killing settlers, he had no intention of changing his way of life.[66]

It seemed that Red Cloud had successfully defended his way of life against the new ideas coming in from the East, but in fact his world was doomed. The 1868 Treaty of Fort Laramie ended "Red Cloud's War" with Red Cloud in charge, but it also established what became known as the Great Sioux Reservation, where horse warriors would be forced into farming. The reservation was a 22-million-acre tract of land that was essentially the western half of what later became the state of South Dakota, divided along the Missouri River, along with a piece of Nebraska. The commissioners anticipated turning the Sioux into farmers but, recognizing the general unpopularity of that idea, it guaranteed them the right to hunt in the lands to the west of the reservation in what is now western Nebraska and eastern Wyoming, an area encompassing the Black Hills, so long as the bison lasted. The Indians had never known a life without bison and, while they knew the herds were getting smaller, did not understand the extraordinary rate of their extinction. They believed them to be a permanent fixture of the landscape. Confident that bison would be around forever, Red Cloud and his people undoubtedly believed that the hunting rights guaranteed in the treaty would last forever.[67]

General Sherman knew better. He was pleased to have moved the Indians away from the railroads, and could live with the commission's concession about buffalo hunting outside the reservation proper. "It will not be long before all the buffaloes are extinct near and between the railroads, after which the Indians will have no reason to approach either railroad," he wrote. Three months later, with railroad men complaining about the roving hunting parties that made them fear for their lives, his views had hardened. "All who cling to their old hunting grounds are hostile and will remain so till killed off."[68]

Sherman and the other commissioners had every intention of ending the traditional world of hunting. They planned to turn the Sioux into farmers in the American model. In exchange for the Sioux's acceptance of limits on their land, the government promised to underwrite each Indian family willing to take its chances on a reservation to be established somewhere along the Missouri River. It would provide every family with farm tools, seeds, farm animals, clothing, and a yearly annuity, enabling them to join the American free labor system. Government officials would count the Sioux every year to adjust the articles properly according to the population. The government would build a storehouse for the Indians, an agent's house, a doctor's residence, a sawmill, a gristmill, a school, and housing for a carpenter, engineer, miller, and blacksmith, and would provide a farmer to instruct the Indians how to farm and a teacher for every thirty students. It also promised to anyone who began farming a pound of flour and a pound of meat a day for their first four years on the reservation, as well as a cow and a well-broken team of oxen. All together, this sounded like a pretty good formula for creating prosperous farmers out of any young men willing to work at it.[69]

In the end, it turned out to be an utterly unworkable formula, but that was ultimately of less concern for late nineteenth-century Americans than a small, final clause in the treaty that seemed a good way to protect the tribes from speculators who might try to take advantage of them. The Treaty of Fort Laramie guaranteed that the treaty could not be changed without the signatures of three-quarters of the men of the Sioux tribe.

The same Republican free labor vision that had condemned the economy of the free Sioux had brought the Shermans and their kin to wealth and national prominence. Nothing made this clearer than the contrast in the summer of 1868 between Red Cloud's fight to hold his land in the West and a lavish Sherman wedding in Ohio.

In June 1868, the Sherman brothers' niece Mary—daughter of their brother Judge Charles Sherman—married an up-and-coming young army officer, Nelson Appleton Miles. They had met at Senator Sherman's Washington, D.C., home, and the senator helped to fund their fancy wedding in part with a $1,000 check. The guest list for the wedding included a number of prominent army men, including General Sherman, General Grant, and General Philip Sheridan, as well as a Supreme Court justice and a senator. Miles asked General Alfred Terry to be best man. Terry had accepted, but then had to back out when his work on the Indian Peace Commission necessitated his presence at Fort Laramie.[70]

While Terry negotiated with the Indians in frontier Wyoming, which would be organized as a Territory in the following month, the Sherman family gathered at Trinity Church in Cleveland, Ohio, on June 30, 1868, without him to celebrate the marriage. Miles was an irascible and ferociously ambitious man who relished the growing political and social connections that would advance his career. And the Shermans were happy to have him on board. Through Miles, with his military prowess and political ambitions, the Shermans would extend their reach into the late nineteenth century.[71]

The Treaty of Fort Laramie bought a few years' peace in the westward march of the new American economy but, far from resolving the incompatibility of the two economies, it simply set the stage for a showdown. Red Cloud interpreted the treaty to guarantee the perpetuity of his people's way of life on their traditional lands. Eastern settlers interpreted the treaty as an unfair infringement on what they believed was their right to move west and settle. They continued to push onto the Sioux lands.[72]

Government officials sided with the settlers over the Sioux. They tried to force Red Cloud's people to get their supplies and annuities from an agency next to Fort Bennett on the Missouri River, but the Oglalas were high hill Sioux and wanted no part of moving east to a reservation on the low-lying Missouri River. Red Cloud also expected to trade at Fort Laramie, while Sherman wanted to make sure he would not. The Oglalas were determined to continue hunting in the western hills; Sherman was just as determined that they would move to a reservation on the Missouri River.[73]

Red Cloud repeatedly insisted on his rights, but to no avail. Finally, in the summer of 1870, he took the drastic step of leaving the Plains and taking his complaints directly to the president. He led a delegation of Sioux to Washington to complain that the government was disregarding the treaty and white men were pushing onto Sioux lands. In the city, he met up with Spotted Tail of the Brulés, who had been summoned to the capital by government officials to try to undercut Red Cloud. The two leaders buried their differences over the treaty and the past years of war in their mutual desire to protect their people.[74]

The Sioux visitors to Washington created much excitement. Everyone wanted a chance to meet them, or at least to see them. Even the president hosted a levee for their entertainment. After days of fetes and excursions to see the local sights, Red Cloud was finally able to get down to business. He and his men met with officials from the Interior Department that oversaw Indian affairs and listed their complaints. "Our nation is melting away like the snow on the side of the hills when the sun is warm," Red Cloud told officials, "while your people are like the blades of grass in Spring when Summer is coming." He refused to accept reservation life on the Missouri River, a place that killed children and old men "like sheep." He demanded that the government remove Fort Fetterman, which the army had been constructing on the Bozeman Trail in what is now Wyoming since 1867 and had finally finished in 1870. He also insisted that the army remove settlers' land claims from the Sioux hunting lands in the Black Hills and Big Horn Mountains.[75]

It soon became clear, though, that the two groups of men had incompatible ideas about the future of the Indians. While Red Cloud wanted to continue living the life of a traditional Sioux, Interior Department officials wanted him to farm. The Secretary of the Interior told the delegates they should teach their young men to plant and tend their fields, a comment that reflected just how poorly he understood the reality of western life. The men laughed scornfully. One of the delegates, Fast Bear, showed the secretary the scar in his side from a bullet wound, courtesy of an army officer who had shot him when he returned from a hunt to check on his corn crop.[76]

The secretary then tried to impress upon Red Cloud that he had given up his land in the treaty of 1868. Red Cloud retorted that he had never heard any such terms. In any case, it didn't really matter, for the whites had no intention of coexisting with Indians. "All the promises made in treaties had never been fulfilled," Red Cloud said. "The object of the whites was to crush the Indians down to nothing. The Great Spirit would judge these things hereafter." Red Cloud and his men left Washington in bitterness.[77]

Red Cloud's complaints to the president did not stop the press of easterners into Indian lands. In 1871, workers for the Northern Pacific Railroad began to survey land for tracks along the southern bank of the Yellowstone River where more than half of the Sioux still hunted for game. With the railroads came emigrants and buffalo hunters, who slaughtered the bison indiscriminately, sometimes to ship their hides back East to become belts for the new machines in the nation's multiplying factories, sometimes just for sport. The newcomers were destroying the very lifeblood of the Sioux.[78]

As the soldiers and settlers hemmed in the Indians, Red Cloud's influence with other Sioux began to fade. Red Cloud had embarked on the delicate work of trying to balance his people's needs and expectations with government demands, and it was thankless work. For Red Cloud, like other Sioux leaders, it meant posturing, delaying, talking, cajoling, and sometimes appearing to misunderstand members of both sides, generally irritating everyone while he provided an important buffer of distance and time to bring about compromises that protected his people. Red Cloud's trip to Washington bore fruit, for example, when the government finally compromised and established agencies for his Oglalas and Spotted Tail's Brulés in northwestern Nebraska, locating Fort Robinson nearby. But by the time that happened, Red Cloud's support in the tribe had slipped as his followers had come to perceive him as weak.[79]

Red Cloud lost control primarily over those warriors who resented the loss of their traditional life. Some of the more traditionalist Sioux had opposed signing the Treaty of Fort Laramie back in 1868, and moved northwest to join Sitting Bull's Hunkpapas, who lived in the Powder River country and had little contact with whites apart from an occasional trader.

One of the most famous Oglalas to abandon Red Cloud's course was the fighting visionary Crazy Horse. Disgusted by Red Cloud's willingness, however grudging, to talk to government officials, he brought his warriors north to work with the traditionalist Sioux who still held their own against the army. This slight, light-skinned man, who painted his face white and wore his hair loose for battle, was known as an inspired warrior.[80]

As Red Cloud prepared to sign the 1868 treaty, Sitting Bull emerged as the leader of the traditionalist Sioux. Probably in the summer of 1869, on the banks of Rosebud Creek, a large band of Indians gathered. The warrior societies of the Hunkpapa Sioux had proposed to bands of Cheyennes and Arapahos, northern Sioux Minneconjous, Sans Arcs, and Crazy Horse's Oglalas, and a few Yanktonais and Two Kettles, that they elect a single leader to marshal them against the whites. The group fell in behind Sitting Bull, now a warrior in his early thirties who had gained a reputation as a deadly fighter and a holy man.[81]

Present at this historic moment were a number of leading Sioux, including Gall, a famous Hunkpapa warrior about ten years younger than Sitting Bull, a big man who ran to fat and who was unusually communicative about his feelings and actions. Crazy Horse, who would soon become Sitting Bull's close friend and second in command, was also there. Slowly circling the encampment on a white horse given him upon his election, with all the mounted chiefs who had just pledged their confidence in him following behind, Sitting Bull sang:

Ye tribes, behold me.
The chiefs of old are gone.
Myself, I shall take courage.[82]

He would need it, for he had taken up the mantle of Red Cloud. From now on, he would be the leader of the traditionalist Sioux who would continue to stand against the spread of eastern settlement.

With the eclipse of compromise, traditionalist Sioux and eastern interlopers squared off. In the summer of 1872, Gall and his men repeatedly skirmished with the army escort protecting the Northern Pacific survey. Sitting Bull had been fighting the Crows that summer, but in August, he turned his attention to the railroad men. He led a war party against the railroad's army escort, warning them to get off his land. Younger warriors wanted to show their mettle in the fight, and grumbled that Sitting Bull was too bossy about the way they handled the skirmish. Sitting Bull was determined to prove to the younger men in his band that they should never challenge his authority. As the battle raged around him, he strolled into the area between the two armies. He lit a pipe and sat calmly smoking it, then invited the younger warriors to join him. They did, but smoked as fast as they possibly could, then darted back to cover. Sitting Bull's sheer nerve cemented his leadership in the war with the interlopers.[83]

Military retribution was swift. In September 1872, Congress sent a thousand guns to settlers in eastern Montana to protect themselves, and two months later, the army established Fort Abraham Lincoln on the west side of the Missouri River near what is now Bismarck, North Dakota. Military officials stationed the dashing General George Custer and his Seventh Cavalry at Fort Lincoln to protect the Northern Pacific Survey. Custer was a popular Civil War veteran who was fast friends with Nelson Miles. Custer and his adoring wife, Libby, quickly gathered a fashionable society around themselves at the fort, making the doings of the Seventh Cavalry newsworthy. The pressure of the military on the Indians grew.[84]

There was another way that Indians could try to negotiate the tension between their traditional culture and the new economy pushing in on them from the East. Some Sioux, who recognized that the pressure of Republican economic policy on Indian life was inexorable, were willing to try to live like white men.

Ohiyesa's father, Many Lightnings, had not, in fact, been hanged with the other Santees in 1862. He had been sent to prison in Davenport, Iowa, where he converted to Christianity and added the name Jacob to his wife's surname—Eastman—to rechristen himself Jacob Eastman. Rather than settle on the reservation at Santee, Nebraska, where the government had placed other Santees, Eastman and some of his neighbors homesteaded in what became Flandreau, about forty miles from Sioux Falls, South Dakota, on the Big Sioux River. Once settled, Jacob sought out his son, brought him to Flandreau, and encouraged him to adopt white ways. Ohiyesa became Charles Alexander Eastman and began working his way through white schools, a task that required his people's "undaunted bravery and stoic resignation," he later recalled with a glint of humor.[85]

Men like the Shermans believed that their new free labor economy was the best in the world and that it would attract any man who was not utterly blind to its obvious benefits. As evidence, they could offer the 4 million African American freedpeople who had fought to be included in the new economy, the hundreds of thousands of immigrants who arrived each year to participate in it, and even some Sioux, who recognized that the pressure of Republican economic policy on Indian life could not be ignored and who were willing to try to live like white men.

CHAPTER 2

A Divided Nation

BY THE 1870s, as even former warriors settled down to their books in white classrooms, the way seemed clear for the triumph of the Republican economic vision. American ideas about free labor had been developed in the early years of the nineteenth century, forged into law during the 1860s, and had reigned triumphant during the Civil War. Under this system, Republicans promised a future of unlimited prosperity and power. It seemed that America was on its way to becoming the greatest nation on earth, just as wartime Republican congressmen had predicted.

Senator Sherman certainly believed that the nation was entering a new era of remarkable prosperity. As soon as the Civil War had ended, he had left his new mansion on K Street in Washington to hobnob with capitalists in New York City and tour coal mines in Pennsylvania, where he marveled at how valuable coal had become. It seemed he would be a key player in bringing the new economic expansion to fruition. After entertaining a group of British capitalists that John had sent to meet him at his headquarters in St. Louis, Cump mused to John that Europeans seemed to have come to the conclusion that "Grant and I accomplished the military problem, and now they look to you to bring order, system, and prosperity out of the wreck."[1]

It was precisely the right assignment for John Sherman. He knew more about the brand-new economic system of the Union than almost anyone else, and he was an expert on the government's fledgling monetary system. He was the natural leader of the nation's postwar economic policy makers. His exalted position, though, did not mean he had a nuanced understanding of economics, which was a subject only in its infancy in the mid-nineteenth century. Like other Americans, Sherman filtered his understanding of economic affairs through his own morals, prejudices, and impressions of the changing world around him.

In the decades after the war, Sherman readily believed that God was blessing the economic system he had helped devise. The new plan seemed to be delivering an ever increasing standard of living at an astonishing rate. New national markets and the national financial system made business boom. Factories grew. This meant more jobs in urban areas, and cities expanded. The populations of New York City and Philadelphia quickly rose toward a million people each. Chicago, which before the Civil War had been a backwater where pigs rooted in the streets, followed suit, with close to a million inhabitants in 1890. This growth extended to industrial towns in the South, too, where railroads and cotton mills created cities like Atlanta, which had a population of more than 65,000 people by 1890, and Nashville, home to more than 80,000 people by 1900. Founded as a steel town in 1871, Birmingham claimed 26,000 inhabitants by 1890.

These bustling cities offered new entertainments, streetcars, restaurants, museums, bookshops, and a vast range of consumer goods in new department stores. Those who remembered the antebellum world of small towns with local economies and quiet lifestyles marveled at the prosperity, novelty, and excitement of the modern urban world.

The East Coast, in particular, benefited from the postwar economy. The development of wheat farming in California meant surpluses of wheat with a kernel hard enough to withstand months at sea, and this new crop, combined with increasing trade of eastern manufactured goods, brought real wealth to the East. Up and down the New England coast, shipyards turned out the trim and ship-shape "Down-Easters" that carried American goods to harbors all over the world. Shipbuilding boomed along the coast and coastal rivers, while eastern harbors bustled with teamsters moving goods, wholesalers selling new shipments of products, and financiers underwriting ocean voyages.[2]

When the Shermans visited New York City they saw a lively harbor bristling with masts and a business district crowded with managers, clerks, salesmen, and secretaries who worked in the growing industries. The thriving economy brought these newly minted white-collar employees a standard of living unimaginable only a decade earlier, when their fathers and brothers had sweated and bled at the Battle of the Wilderness, or shivered under their mildewed tents during a Potomac winter, or huddled in trees during General Sherman's rain-soaked March to the Sea.

The nation's new businessmen had a steady income that permitted them to enjoy the novel products pouring out of the factories. Thanks to the development of refrigerated railroad cars that enabled butchered meat to be moved from the western plains to the eastern cities without spoiling, their families had fresh meat on the table, and vegetables trucked in from local farms. Refrigeration also made ice cream an affordable luxury in hot summers. Their wives' fashionable dresses were fastened with celluloid buttons that had been pressed into fancy shapes; they wore coats made from the fur of seals culled from the islands off Alaska and sported hats decorated with the feathers—and sometimes the bodies—of rare birds. Their families lived in comfortable homes, with servants to cook their meals and clean.

By 1890, a manager's family would have luxuries unimaginable just a generation before. Their house would have a newfangled bathroom with fancy porcelain bowls, possibly painted in France, and pipes that brought water into and waste out of the house, a far cry from the traditional outhouses and wells that were part of the rural American landscape until the end of the twentieth century. For children, this new prosperity translated to an expectation that they would get an education at least through high school, and they would wear finer clothing to school than their parents had. When they were out of the classroom, they diverted themselves with manufactured toys—metal fire engines with moving wheels, cranes that lifted up and down with the turn of a crank, and carved puppets—and candy to eat while they played.

Servants, manufactured products, and household conveniences gave prosperous men and women not only more material goods but also more leisure time. Gentlemen and ladies of this era adopted "lawn tennis"; some daring men tried the newly imported Scandinavian sport of skiing. Men and women both experimented with the new bicycles that became a fad in the 1890s and that dramatically increased the range a man could travel, requiring civic-minded governments to pave city streets with asphalt because cobblestones were so dangerous to the narrow-wheeled machines.[3]

Leisure and money also translated into more elaborate holidays. Weddings became relatively lavish affairs compared to those of the previous generation. Women wore special white dresses of satin with tulle and trimmings, flowers decorated the church, and a party after the wedding for the couple's friends sometimes featured musicians and a tiered white cake that matched the bride's dress. The Thanksgiving table was marked less by the prayers around the table than by the wide variety of foods on it; Christmas now meant a tree decorated with ribbons and small ornaments, with presents tied to the branches; a child's birthday was now celebrated with a cake and a party, sometimes with small favors for the attendees.[4]

For those thriving in the industrial world, the new economy created by the Republicans seemed to have brought to life all that their wartime free labor dream had promised. Eastern Americans had money, novel ways to spend it, and leisure time to enjoy their new purchases. America's postwar economic system seemed to be the pinnacle of human organization. It was impossible to believe that everyone would not want to share in it. To those who enjoyed this new world, it only made sense to spread an industrial economy across the nation, all the way to the West Coast. As it spread, it would sweep across the Plains and absorb all the Indians there who still followed an ancient and far less materially prosperous way of life. How could the Indians see this as anything but a great gift?

The extension of the new industrial economy to the West had begun during the Civil War, when Congress had pushed farmers to produce more and more wheat and corn for the troops and for export. It had passed homestead legislation to get farmers onto land, relaxed immigration laws to draw more workers into the country, and chartered railroads to make it easier to go west. The drive to increase agricultural production would show dramatic results in the ten years after 1865, when American farmers turned more than 100 million new acres into crops of corn, wheat, oats, hay, and cotton.[5]

After 1874, two developments made even more farmers decide to try their luck on the Plains. First, barbed wire became widely available. Until then, farmers had found it next to impossible to fence their fields on the treeless plains. They had tried all sorts of methods to create boundaries, even attempting to cultivate thorn bushes to keep animals from their crops, to little avail. With the advent of barbed wire, though, fencing became cheap and easy. Barbed wire went west by the trainload as farmers snapped it up.

The second development was the start of a wet weather cycle that brought unusual amounts of rain to the dry prairies. Farmers who had previously believed the region was "the Great American Desert" ventured onto the Plains in hopes that the weather had changed for good, and that the rich soil there would now be complemented by sufficient rainfall to deliver bountiful crops. In the late 1870s and early 1880s, unusually heavy spring rains made their dreams seem justified.[6]

With the spurs of barbed wire and rain, farmers moved onto the Plains in large numbers, cutting prairies into cultivated fields. They were so successful in changing the landscape that furious cattlemen, who needed open ranges to move their beeves to market, blamed barbed wire for destroying their industry.

Railroad companies encouraged Americans' vision of the West as an agricultural paradise. In order to fund the building of the transcontinental railroad, Congress had given western land to the railroad companies, which they then sold to settlers to pay the expenses of the railroad's construction. While this bargain kept the government from having to assume the financial burden of building a road across the unprofitable plains in a push to reach the West Coast, it also gave the companies every incentive to exaggerate the charms of life on the prairies. Railroads enticed settlers west with promises of easy farming and mild climates, promises that seemed realistic in the atypical wet decade that began in the mid-1870s.

Railroad promoters' claims about the charms of western farming were especially exaggerated in regard to the Dakotas. In the railroad boom of the late 1870s, as new western railroads cut into the Dakota Territory formed from Sioux land, Dakota railroads had to work to entice settlers away from other rail lines. Railroads offered financial aid for settlers' travel west, built "reception houses" in big towns to shelter arriving emigrants, sold land at two to ten dollars an acre, and gave rebates to those breaking land. Railroad literature and advertisements offered the "Best Wheat Lands, Best Farming Lands, Best Grazing Lands in the world . . . FREE TO ALL." Trying to portray even the nearby Indians as an advantage, promotional materials pointed out that the government bought supplies for the army posts and the Indian agencies, creating a ready market for crops and provisions. Farmers promoted their towns, promising that each would be the next Chicago.[7]

Eastern migrants, black as well as white, bought into the vision of a free labor West, a place where anyone who worked hard could rise. Settlers poured into the plains, envisioning their futures as solid citizens of prosperous towns. Their approach to the Dakotas was no exception. A migrant himself, newspaperman and future author of *The Wizard of Oz* L. Frank Baum boosted his small South Dakota town even as he poked fun at it, insisting that Dakota was a land destined to prosper. "Oh, the wet, the elegant wet!" he rhapsodized:

Continue to arrive, my pet.
All of our troubles we'll now forget,
Over the crop we'll cease to fret.
Who cares now if we are in debt?
We'll get out again in the fall, you bet![8]

African Americans in the West were at least as enthusiastic about the region as white settlers. By 1889, there were 540 black citizens in South Dakota. Living in Yankton, the center for black life in South Dakota, poet Kate Chapman contrasted the racial uplift and harmonious race relations she experienced in the West with "the crowded tenement houses, loathsome streets, foul air, bitter prejudice" of the South. She detailed how her black neighbors had been able to work their way to prosperity and advised freedpeople: "For the sake of health, wealth and freedom, come west."[9]

Western boosters saw themselves as agents of progress united against a common enemy: the western Indians who insisted on keeping their lands undeveloped to protect the game on which their economy depended. The mission to contain and domesticate the Indians overrode eastern racial distinctions. At the end of her life, when she told the story of South Dakota's struggle against the Sioux, one dark-skinned former slave described herself as the first white woman in the Black Hills. The "whites" who were moving west were eastern Americans of all ancestries, united in a cause against the Indians whose way of life stood in the way of economic "progress."[10]

The push of settlers west did not spare the Great Sioux Reservation. Even before large numbers of farmers started to carve out their homesteads from the Dakotas, prospectors who expected to find gold in the Black Hills started their own stream in the relentless flow of Americans westward. They trudged toward the Black Hills, pushing through the pale green tufts of buffalo grass in the territory guaranteed to the Sioux by the Treaty of Fort Laramie. The army was charged with keeping the settlers out of Sioux lands, but they found their work harder every day.

The Sioux insisted that the intrusions into their territory must be stopped. They were furious at the incursions of prospectors and the Northern Pacific Railroad survey onto their land. Sitting Bull, Crazy Horse, Gall, and their men harassed the surveyors and prospectors, while demanding that the army keep intruders out of Sioux land.

In 1874, Philip Sheridan, who in 1869 had succeeded Sherman as the Commander of the Division of the Missouri, concluded that the way to calm the Sioux complaining about eastern interlopers was to establish a major new fort in the Black Hills. He ordered General Alfred Terry, who oversaw the Department of Dakota in which the hills lay, to investigate the region. Terry sent the colorful "Boy General," George A. Custer, and more than a thousand soldiers, teamsters, Indian scouts, scientists, and reporters—who required a thousand horses, 110 wagons, and a herd of three hundred beeves to supply them—on an expedition to investigate the region around the Black Hills.[11]

While Sheridan wanted a military report, Custer and his men were much more interested in the economic value of the area. Custer's report noted the potential of the region for timbering, farming, and mining. His dispatches back East confirmed that there was, indeed, gold in the Black Hills. It was easy to find, he claimed, and there was enough of it to make mining a paying proposition.[12]

Custer's report created a stampede into the Great Sioux Reservation. By 1875, men were pouring into the Black Hills to find their fortunes, and prostitutes and gamblers followed them to find theirs. Custer City sprang up at the site where Custer's expedition had found gold, and by the end of August 1875, prospectors had made it north to Deadwood Gulch, where they found far richer deposits than those farther south. Deadwood, South Dakota, became a boomtown, bringing in men like Wild Bill Hickok, whose death at a gambling table holding two eights and two aces gave us the term "deadman's hand." By late 1876, there were as many as twenty thousand people in the area around Deadwood, establishing settlements around the newest promising mines.[13]

Emigrants to the Sioux land could not understand why the Indians were so determined to hold on to the Black Hills, which it seemed they only used occasionally for hunting and the cutting of lodge poles. Settlers thought it was only a question of finding the right price—a low one—to get them to give up their claim. The government appointed a commission—once again drafting Alfred H. Terry as a commissioner—to convince the Sioux to sell or lease the Black Hills.[14]

The commission had no luck. Red Cloud and Spotted Tail, along with their men, were willing to confer, but not to sell the land. They wanted the army to do its job, keeping miners out of the Black Hills. When asked to sell the land, they put such a high price on it they made it clear that selling was not on their agenda. Red Cloud enumerated for the commissioners a long list of everything the Indians needed to live as comfortably as whites did, and made it clear he expected all of that and more in exchange for his land. The Black Hills were priceless, he concluded, and to get them the whites would have to make an equivalent offer. "God Almighty placed these hills here for my wealth, but now you want to take them from me and make me poor, so I ask so much that I won't be poor."[15]

The commission reported back to Washington that the Indians were asking for more than the government would ever be willing to pay. It concluded that it was useless to try to negotiate with the Indians in council.[16]

Sitting Bull, Crazy Horse, and their warriors were not even willing to talk. They answered unequivocally the commissioners' request that they sell the Black Hills. "We want no white men here," Sitting Bull said. "The Black Hills belong to me. If the whites try to take them, I will fight." To traditionalist Sioux, the Black Hills were sacred. Their red rock was the blood of Sioux forefathers; their heights, the place from which humans had come to earth. The Black Hills could never be sold.

Like Red Cloud, the traditionalists demanded that whites respect the Treaty of Fort Laramie.[17]

Government officials chose to interpret Sioux refusal to sell their land as hostility to Americans. After months of ongoing clashes between Indians and intruders in the Black Hills, officials simply stopped trying to honor the 1868 treaty. They removed the soldiers who had been charged with keeping miners out of the reservation, and advised those going in to arm themselves against "hostile" Indians. Then, in December 1875, government authorities told the Indian agents to inform Sitting Bull and other "hostiles" to report back to their agencies by the end of January or to expect war.[18]

For their part, the fighting Indians kept to their normal winter routine, hunkering down to survive the brutal Dakota cold. Sitting Bull and Crazy Horse had never had any use for the agencies and had never accepted them, telling the Hunkpapas who frequented the Standing Rock agency set up for them: "You are fools to make yourselves slaves to a piece of fat bacon, some hard-tack, and a little sugar and coffee." Sitting Bull and Crazy Horse were 250 miles away from their agency and probably never heard the order to come in; in any case, neither of them braved the treacherous journey in the dead of winter to do so.[19]

The Indians' noncompliance with the order to report to their agencies confirmed for government officials that they must be brought to heel. On February 1, 1876, the War Department ordered the military to subdue the Sioux. The task fell to General George Crook, who, in 1875, after corralling the Apaches onto reservations, had recently been appointed head of the Department of the Platte into which Wyoming Territory fell.[20]

On March 1, General Crook led eight hundred men to war against Sitting Bull and the hunting Sioux bands. He planned to march up the old Bozeman Trail while the Sioux ponies were still weak from the winter and to engage the Sioux when he found them.[21]

Crook and his men started out in weather that sometimes fell to twenty or more degrees below zero; it was so brutally cold that he could not let the men sleep through the night for fear they would freeze. In mid-March, Crook split off a column of about four hundred men under Colonel Joseph J. Reynolds to follow a couple of Indian scouts they had spotted. On the morning of March 17, the soldiers stumbled onto a large camp of Cheyenne and Oglala Sioux on the Powder River and, believing the people there to be Crazy Horse's band, attacked the village. They drove off the Indians, who scrambled out of their sleeping robes and cut their way out of the tepees that had been fastened tightly against the cold. Soldiers killed two Indians and wounded several others, then burned the camp. Warriors shot at the troops from gullies, killing four of the soldiers and wounding six others.[22]

While the soldiers had taken the camp, the raid was a strategic loss. Crook had planned to capture the supplies in the camp and, when they were burned, he couldn't continue his campaign. He was furious at Reynolds, who was court-martialed for his poor handling of what the army called the Battle of Powder River.

The attack also hurt the army by cementing Sioux determination to fight. Cold and hungry Cheyenne refugees from the attack fled down the river to Sitting Bull's camp. They had lost their homes and their possessions in bitterly cold weather and they desperately needed shelter. Sitting Bull took them in. He was furious. "We are an island of Indians in a lake of whites. We must stand together, or they will rub us out separately. These soldiers have come shooting; they want war. All right, we'll give it to them!"[23]

Sitting Bull began to prepare for a full-blown war. He sent runners to the agencies and the traditionalist Indian bands, calling people to his camp at the Big Bend of the Rosebud River to make a stand against the soldiers. Not everyone was as keen as Sitting Bull to take on the U.S. Army, though. Red Cloud had seen the power of the American military during his days in Washington and advised his people not to go. But his own son, Jack Red Cloud, rode away with the younger men. Others joined Sitting Bull in fear that, when the clash came, the weight of the army's wrath would fall on reservation Indians as well as the fighters, and they would be safer with their own warriors.

Thousands of men rallied to Sitting Bull. In the spring of 1876, Indians from almost every Sioux band, including the Santees and the Yanktonais, gathered with Sitting Bull in the Rosebud River valley and named him the leader of their campaign. It was the largest camp of Indians the Sioux had ever known; participants estimated that there were 1,400 lodges, plus individual men sleeping on their own or as guests in the tepees. The camp was a lively place, with feasts, families gathering, couples courting, and warriors dancing every night.[24]

In mid-June, as a final preparation for war, Sitting Bull performed a Sun Dance to pray to the Great Spirit for revelation and blessing. He asked Wakan Tanka to provide food for his people for winter, and to "let good men on earth have more power." In this traditional dance, a warrior mortified his flesh, either by cutting himself, hanging from thongs laced through his back muscles, or staring into the sun. A friend cut a hundred pieces of flesh from Sitting Bull's arms, and the chief danced, staring at the sun, for a day and a night and into the next day. Finally, he fell. Then, in a vision, he saw soldiers dropping upside down from a clear sky into the Indian camp. A voice from above spoke to him: "I give you these because they have no ears." Sitting Bull's vision galvanized his warriors. They had seen the chief's prophecies come true before, and were sure that the soldiers, who refused to listen to wisdom and made war for no reason, were coming. The vision showed them upside down, so the warriors knew the soldiers would die.[25]

Sitting Bull's vision was right. Army leaders believed that there were only about three thousand "hostile" Indians, of whom only about five hundred to eight hundred were warriors. They expected this small fighting band to fall quickly under a display of force. In fact, Sitting Bull's camp boasted almost a thousand warriors at the time of his Sun Dance, and the number was growing every day.[26]

In the spring of 1876, the job of subduing the Indians fell to General Crook. He was in charge of a plan for a three-pronged attack on the Sioux in the Powder River country. Crook's column would move north from Fort Fetterman; Colonel John Gibbon's column would move east down the Yellowstone River from Fort Shaw in western Montana. Nelson Miles's old friend General Alfred H. Terry would lead a column, which included the Seventh Cavalry under George Armstrong Custer, west from Fort Lincoln. They would meet up near the confluence of the Yellowstone and the Little Bighorn rivers, where the traditionalist Indians were hunting.[27]

By mid-June, Crook's command of more than a thousand soldiers and more than two hundred Crow and Shoshone scouts was marching toward the Rosebud River. The Sioux had previously been camped there, but had moved from the Rosebud toward the river they called the Greasy Grass in search of more food for the horses. Sitting Bull's scouts still scoured the valley, though, and spied the troops. They brought word back to camp on June 16 that "the valley of the Rosebud was black with soldiers."[28]

Sitting Bull, Crazy Horse, and about a thousand warriors from all the Teton Sioux bands and their allies rode out to meet Crook's troops on June 17. They were hungry for battle, pleased at the chance to exact revenge on the men who had launched the attack on the Cheyenne at Powder River in March. Still weak from the Sun Dance, Sitting Bull left the leadership of the battle to Crazy Horse, contenting himself with riding behind the lines and cheering his warriors on.[29]

The Sioux and Cheyenne barreled into the valley on their ponies, whooping and yelling. With the strength of Sitting Bull's prophecy behind them, they fully expected to destroy their enemies. They pushed into the hastily organized troops, who had not been expecting an attack, but who managed to pull themselves together and repulse the Indians with heavy fire. The battle raged all day. First the Sioux advanced and were pushed back; then the soldiers did the same. The smoke from the powder and the dust from the pounding horses obscured the battlefield, but it was "a great fight," according to one of the Sioux participants.[30]

At sundown, the Indian attackers turned for their home camp, hungry and worn out from the fight. They left behind dead and wounded enemies: nine dead soldiers and one dead Indian army scout, and twenty-three wounded soldiers and seven wounded Indian scouts. One of the most badly wounded was black soldier Colonel Guy V. Henry, who had taken a bullet through the face and was not expected to live. For their part, the Sioux had lost twenty men and had a number wounded, and the Cheyenne had one dead man and several others wounded.[31]

Crook reported to his superiors that the Indians had retreated in great confusion and tried to claim that he had prevailed. In fact, the victory had gone to the Sioux and the Cheyenne. Crook's advance stopped dead after the Battle of Rosebud as he fell back to the south to his base camp and waited for reinforcements. Effectively, his men were out of the campaign for the next six weeks, six weeks that would prove crucial. Sitting Bull's warriors pronounced themselves "quite content" with the outcome of the Battle of the Rosebud.[32]

The Sioux feasted and celebrated. For six days they rejoiced that they had turned back the soldiers. As they basked in the warmth of the victory, more and more people poured into camp. Families who had spent the winter at the agencies joined the gathering fighters, partly because they always left the agencies in summer to hunt, partly because they had heard of the great victory and wanted to join the celebration. The size of the Sioux camp more than doubled. It went up to about 7,000 people, 1,800 of whom were warriors.[33]

After the celebrations, Sitting Bull moved his people to the Greasy Grass in search of better hunting, despite the terrible flies on the river that summer. The crowd of Indians was much too big to stay in one spot for more than a day or two, as they constantly had to find forage for the horses and food for the cooking pots. By June 24, they had settled down in a camp that stretched three or four miles on the west bank of the Greasy Grass. They still anticipated the attack that Sitting Bull had foreseen. They knew that the soldiers would be coming, but they also knew that Crook had moved back to his camp. They watched him to see what he was doing, but so long as he remained hunkered down, they didn't anticipate a pitched battle.[34]

On June 21, unaware that Crook had been stopped by the Battle of the Rosebud, the other two commanders, Gibbon and Terry, met up on a steamer at the confluence of the Yellowstone and Rosebud rivers. They agreed to trap the Indians between the two commands by moving the main body of their forces up the Yellowstone, then up what they called the Bighorn River, and then up the Little Bighorn River—the Indians' Greasy Grass. This big command under Gibbon and Terry would bivouac at the mouth of the Little Bighorn. There they could stop the Indians' escape from an attack launched by an offshoot of Terry's command under General George A. Custer. The plan was for Custer to break off from Terry's command with about 750 soldiers from the Seventh Cavalry. The Seventh would travel up the Rosebud to attack the Indian camp.[35]

Custer set off up the Rosebud on June 22. For three days his men rode upstream, following the trail the Indians had left as they had abandoned camps, one after another, early in the summer in search of better grazing. On June 24, Custer marched his men until a little after 2:00 A.M. to position them near the place where he believed the Indian camp to be. He planned to let them rest through the next day, and then to attack on June 26. Soon after his men arrived in camp on the twenty-fifth, though, Custer's Crow scouts spied the Indian village. Worried that the Indian camp would break up and the Sioux would flee when their own scouts discovered the soldiers, Custer changed his plans.[36]

On the hot, windless afternoon of June 25, Custer attacked the Sioux. About fifteen miles from the camp, he divided his tired command into three battalions, taking charge of the largest force, about 210 men (and a newspaper reporter) himself, and giving to Major Marcus Reno and Captain Frederick Benteen command of the other two. He dispatched Benteen and his men up the valley to hunt for roving Indians, putting them out of communication. Then he ordered Reno and his 175 soldiers and Indian scouts to cross the Little Bighorn River to attack the Indians and force them to fight.[37]

The Indians had been watching Crook, and had been lulled into a sense of security by his retreat. They were not expecting soldiers that afternoon. Some of the youngsters were fishing, women were tending their babies or digging wild turnips, and the men were watering their horses or drowsing in the heat. The attack threw them into confusion. The women and children ran to the north while the warriors covered their escape or pulled their relatives onto ponies to carry them out of the hail of bullets. Once their people were safely in the hills, the men circled back to the battle.[38]

Reno had forded the river and directed his battalion onto the Hunkpapa end of the camp. Rather than charge into the tepees, though, he ordered his men to dismount and fight in a skirmish line. Sitting Bull's warriors had armed and horsed themselves instantly. Once the women and children were safe, they pushed Reno's men off the plains in about fifteen minutes, forcing them into the timber that lay to their east, along the riverbank. Under the poised Crazy Horse, who restrained the eager men until Reno's men had fired their guns so many times they were too hot to fire effectively, the Hunkpapas forced the soldiers out of the woods back across the river. As they floundered with their horses through the water far from the ford where they had crossed over, the Sioux cut them down. By the time Reno's men made it to the bluffs on the other side of the river, forty had been killed, thirteen were wounded, and sixteen were missing in the timber.[39]

Meanwhile, Custer had cut around to the north and attacked the Indians from that side, but by that time the warriors from the whole camp were mounted and threw themselves into the fight with a will.

Hunkpapa warrior Gall had lost his two wives and three children in the early fighting, and he fought to avenge their deaths. He led hundreds of warriors from all the different bands at the camp in a counterattack on Custer's two hundred soldiers. The ensuing battle lasted only about thirty minutes. The troops dismounted and made a stand on a long, low hill. Quickly, though, their organization fell apart. The Indians stampeded the army horses, so there was no escape. Soldiers fought or ran, singly or in bunches, in the heat and smoke and whoops and screams, until the Indians had killed them all.[40]

While white legends later claimed that the Indians fought to destroy the man they knew as "Long Hair," both Gall and Sitting Bull later told reporters they did not have any idea they were fighting Custer. They were simply repelling an attack, fighting in the normal noise and confusion of every major battle.[41]

Shocked that the army officers would have put themselves into such an untenable military situation, Sitting Bull believed that the attacks had been a feint intended to distract the Indians from a major offensive to come. He stayed out of the fighting to survey the battle and marshal his forces against a final major attack. It never came.[42]

Instead, the Indians continued to cut the soldiers apart. After finishing off Custer and his cavalrymen, Gall and the other warriors turned back to Reno. While the Indians had been occupied with Custer's men, Benteen had reinforced Reno and their commands now numbered about 350 soldiers. They were in dire straits, though, pinned in the blazing heat at the top of a bluff without water. The Indians surrounded them and fired on them all night. The soldiers were rescued from their predicament only by the timely arrival of General Terry's command the next day. Aware that Terry was on his way, Sitting Bull urged his warriors to stop the attack. "Let them live," he said. "They came against us, and we have killed a few. If we kill them all, they will send a bigger army against us."[43]

The Indians moved into the foothills of the Big Horn Mountains and celebrated their victory. They had killed 263 soldiers and wounded 60 others. Their own losses were relatively slight, probably no more than 40 killed and 60 or so wounded. While they mourned their losses, there was no doubt they had won a great victory.[44]

Army officers knew that the Custer fiasco had been an unmitigated disaster. On June 27, 1876, from his camp on the Little Bighorn River,

General Terry telegraphed the terrible news back East. "It is my painful duty to report that day before yesterday, the 25th, a great disaster overtook General Custer and the troops under his command," he told his superiors.[45]

The only survivors of Custer's escapade were a few Indian scouts, who had run from the general's suicidal plan, and a badly wounded horse, "Comanche." The Seventh Cavalry kept Comanche unridden and unworked thereafter, but at all ceremonial occasions they saddled and bridled him and draped him in mourning. He was led by a mounted trooper and paraded with the regiment. The profound symbolism of the lone horse draped in black indicated the fury of members of the Seventh Cavalry at what they saw as a heroic stand against murderous Indians, a willful view of a battle that, after all, Custer had launched against an encampment of Sioux in their own territory.[46]

Sitting Bull saw the engagement more clearly. "I feel sorry that too many were killed on each side," he later reflected, "but when Indians must fight, they must."[47]

Eastern Americans sympathized with Custer, not Sitting Bull, and they would come to regard the fight at Little Bighorn as the height of Indian treachery. Their demand for vengeance would echo for decades.

Stationed in Kansas, where he and Custer had become good friends, Nelson Miles read of the debacle in the July 5th newspaper with horror. Immediately, he received orders to reinforce Crook and set out for Dakota Territory, stopping on the way to pay his respects to Custer's devastated widow. Custer's demise opened the way for Nelson Miles's career to take off.[48]

Once in Dakota, Miles found that the Sioux had retreated into the Big Horn Mountains while Terry and Crook halfheartedly were marching their soldiers through the Powder River region in search of them. Miles chafed at their ineffectuality and jumped at the chance to guard the fords of the Yellowstone. As winter approached, Miles's men threw up a rough fort and scrounged for warm clothes. Determined to locate the Sioux in their winter camp, Miles hired scouts, including the famous Buffalo Bill Cody, to find the Indians. Whether he would fight them or capture them depended on the circumstances of their meeting.[49]

For his part, Sitting Bull preferred to talk rather than fight. His coalition had been steadily crumbling as groups broke off to find fresher hunting ground, and those who remained were tired of war and eager to settle in for the winter. In October, with bitterly cold weather already dropping down and with Miles's men on his trail, Sitting Bull requested a conference with Miles. Sitting Bull asked the general to take the soldiers out of his country. He wanted to live as a free Indian. Miles countered with a demand that the Indians submit to the government. The meeting broke up with gunfire, and Miles's 398 soldiers advanced on the warriors. Over the next several days, the troops overran the Indian camps, then chased the Sioux forty-two miles to the south side of the Yellowstone. Both the soldiers and the Sioux had lost their conviction that the Indians were invincible.[50]

Over the next six months, Miles wore down Sioux resistance. Rather than letting his men hole up in winter quarters, he outfitted them in buffalo skin coats, had a bearskin coat made for himself, and then chased the Sioux through snow and frigid temperatures that sometimes reached 35 degrees below zero. The constant moving in the dead of winter ruined supplies and wore out the Indians as much as the few skirmishes and the one battle they fought. As the Sioux wearied, Miles and Crook kept the pressure on them in negotiations as well as on the field, promising them that they could keep their ponies and arms if they surrendered. By the spring, groups of former fighters were turning themselves in to Miles and to Crook and at the Cheyenne River agency. About 300 surrendered to Miles, 2,200 to Crook, and several hundred at the agency.[51]

It seemed the back of Sioux resistance had been broken. On May 6, even Crazy Horse gave up. He brought almost nine hundred followers to Camp Robinson to surrender. The Indians had counted on lenient terms, but what happened at Fort Robinson suggested that their hopes were unfounded. When Crazy Horse rode into the fort he expected to be able to speak with the officer in charge. Instead, he found himself escorted to the guardhouse. When he realized he was on his way to jail, he threw himself backward, screaming: "Let me go!" Struggling, he twisted a knife into the arm of the reservation Indian holding him. A sentinel swung his bayonet just as Crazy Horse turned. The bayonet stabbed the great warrior through both kidneys. He sank to the ground and died in minutes.[52]

Sitting Bull and about four thousand of his people wanted no part of such leniency. They fled to Canada, insisting they would not be controlled by federal authorities.[53]

For Miles, the campaign was an enormous success. He had both subdued the fighting Sioux and bolstered his own career. "I . . . have fought and defeated larger and better armed bodies of hostile Indians than any other officer since the history of Indian warfare commenced, and at the same time have gained a more extended knowledge of our frontier country than any living man," he boasted to his wife's uncle, General Sherman. From a relatively forgotten army officer at a minor post, Miles had become one of the nation's most famous Indian fighters.[54]

Miles's victory further eroded the Sioux's traditional way of life. In the aftermath of the fighting, angry government officials forced the Indians to give up the Black Hills, along with about a third of their reservation. Estimated at about 20,000 people, the Teton Sioux were forced onto a tract stretching across about 35,000 acres in the middle of what is now South Dakota. Government agents took thousands of horses from the Sioux at Standing Rock and Cheyenne River, severely curtailing their ability to hunt. The punishment of the agency Indians who had stayed on the side of the government as well as those who had gone to war shook the confidence of agency Indians that they would be safe with the government. They were convinced that they could expect in the future to share in whatever punishments fighting Indians endured.[55]

The agency Indians might have been less secure in their new way of life, but they no longer had any other options. Pushing the Sioux out of the hills, government officials intended them to dry farm on the plains of Dakota Territory. Those Sioux who continued to try to follow the buffalo were quickly disillusioned, for the settlers pouring into the eastern part of the Territory killed off the game. By 1878, the huge buffalo herds had been decimated and the Sioux tribes were assigned to agencies for rations.

Because Red Cloud's and Spotted Tail's agencies, located in Nebraska, were now outside the reservation, the government established new ones. Red Cloud's Oglalas were moved to Pine Ridge and Spotted Tail's Brulé to Rosebud, agencies near each other in southern Dakota Territory. At Standing Rock in the middle of the Territory were the Upper Yanktonais, the Hunkpapa, and some of the Black Foot Sioux. South of Standing Rock, Cheyenne River became the agency for the Two Kettle Sioux, the rest of the Black Foot Sioux, the Minneconjou, and the Sans Arc. In between the northern and southern agencies were the Lower Brulé and Crow Creek agencies, where relatives of Spotted Tail's Brulé and the Lower Yanktonais Sioux lived, respectively.[56]

On the reservation, the agents tried to induce the Sioux to accept the American economy and adopt white ways. Each left to act as he thought best, the agents achieved varied results and left varied legacies. At Rosebud, political appointee Cicero Newell had grandiose visions of making his Brulé Sioux model citizens, and he launched into the project of turning these hunting people into dry farmers with an unbridled enthusiasm that bemused even his government supporters. Made in the same western booster model as L. Frank Baum, he imported settlers from his hometown of Ypsilanti, Michigan, to fill agency posts and flitted from one new project to another—prosperous farms, a steam bakery, a sawmill powered by a dam—while fields dried up, the bakery failed, and pieces of the sawmill went missing only to reappear as a privately owned mill in the Black Hills.[57]

Newell did not force his charges into the new ways. In his eagerness to turn Rosebud Indians into members of model farming communities, Newell left Spotted Tail—whom he liked and respected—in control of his own people, actually sitting in the agent's own office, managing Indian affairs at the agency. Spotted Tail left no record of his impression of Newell, but one can easily imagine him making wry observations to his friends as Newell whipped up his team and set off to promote one or another of his extravagant ventures.[58]

Spotted Tail learned the hard way, though, that not all white reformers were so easy to manipulate. In 1879, Indian reformer Captain Richard H. Pratt opened the Carlisle Indian Industrial School in Pennsylvania, taking as a principle to "kill the Indian and save the man." Removing children from their communities, he believed, would eradicate their heritage and enable them to assimilate into American life. Sioux parents wanted no part of what seemed to be abandoning their children, but Spotted Tail finally agreed to send four of his sons and a few grandchildren to the school after Pratt agreed to hire Spotted Tail's white son-in-law to look after them.[59]

A year later, when Pratt proudly showed off the Brulé children to Spotted Tail and a number of other Brulé leaders whom he had brought east, the adult Brulés were horrified. Their children had been forced into menial labor, had had their hair cut, and had been baptized as Christians without their parents' consent. Spotted Tail was enraged and announced that he was taking all thirty-four of the Rosebud Brulé youngsters home. The government authorities tried to stop him, fearing that the withdrawal of the children would undermine the school's reputation. But Spotted Tail utterly refused to leave his own relatives at the Carlisle School and took them back to Rosebud. The episode taught the Sioux to loathe Pratt and to distrust reformers' promises to "teach" their children.[60]

On Pine Ridge, Agent Valentine T. McGillycuddy, a dictatorial former army surgeon, thought much like Pratt. He and Red Cloud clashed from the start. The agent was determined to break the Oglalas free from what was left of their traditional culture and make them adopt white ways. According to both tradition and treaty, agents delivered rations to the chiefs, who divided and distributed them. McGillycuddy tried to end this practice—in violation of treaties—in order to undermine the authority of the traditional leaders. Chiefs consolidated power through gifts, and without the power to dispense rations they would lose the basis of their influence. In their place, the agent cultivated different men in the tribe, making them police officers or giving them agency jobs. The agents hoped these men, raised to prominence by the agents rather than through tribal customs, would work with the government to bring the Indians to accept reservation life.[61]

Determined to get rid of all elements of tribal culture, McGillycuddy also forbade the practice of the Sun Dance, which played a vital role in Indian religion. One man later recalled the reason for McGillycuddy's hostility to the Sun Dance: "The dance took the people from their homes & caused them to neglect their gardens, their poultry and pigs and other affairs, and for this reason must be abandoned." Dancing stopped first at Pine Ridge, and then other agencies followed suit.[62]

Because of his loathing for McGillycuddy, Red Cloud dismissed anyone who cooperated with him as a man of no account. They collaborated with the agent, he thought, only because they were incapable of earning influence in real Sioux ways, such as wisdom or battlefield honor. Red Cloud was, of course, somewhat cynical in his characterization: while it was undoubtedly true that McGillycuddy and the other agents hoped to break the chiefs by replacing them with a different set of Indian leaders, it was not always young men unable to succeed who allied with the agents. At Pine Ridge, for instance, McGillycuddy managed to recruit in 1879 a police force of forty-five men, led by Man Who Carries the Sword (who took the name George Sword), who had fought bravely against the soldiers at the Wagon Box Fight. The men in the force had an average age of thirty-three—five years older than McGillycuddy—most had large families, and many had previously served their tribe as *akicitas*, or traditional law enforcers.[63]

Indians joined the police force for a number of reasons. As police officers, they were able to protect their people from gangs of non-Indian horse thieves, against whom *akicitas* had no authority. In keeping order themselves, many surely believed, they were able to forestall the need for further military occupation troops to enforce order in the reservation. Far better to police themselves than to have soldiers policing them. Many also joined for the pay and goods McGillycuddy sent the way of the Indian policemen.[64]

Sword himself suggested a further reason for joining. The nephew of Red Cloud and an honored warrior and holy man, Sword greatly respected tribal tradition but also understood that American expansion could not be stopped. "I went to Washington and to other large cities, and that showed me that the white people dug in the ground and built houses that could not be moved. Then I knew that when they came they could not be driven away." Sword hoped to save what was left of his people by leading them into the white man's world.[65]

The Indians on the reservation faced a stark choice: They could try to adopt white ways or they could accept government rations while trying to protect their cultural heritage. Those who chose to adapt were referred to as "progressives" by white observers; those who did not were dismissed as "blanket Indians," or "hostiles." Within the tribes, those trying to adapt to new ways often clashed bitterly with traditionalists.

There was tension between these groups at all the agencies, but it was especially intense at Standing Rock and Cheyenne River once members of Sitting Bull's band arrived on the reservation. Sitting Bull and his people had starved in Canada, and had finally surrendered to the U.S. Army in July 1881. Gaunt and exhausted, Sitting Bull had handed his gun to his young son Crow Foot to give to the soldiers. "My boy," he said, "if you live, you will never be a man in this world, because you can never have a gun or pony."[66]

The army split Sitting Bull's band between Standing Rock and Cheyenne River. Settling there, they stirred up the agency Indians with their stories of their free years in Canada, making it plain that they were at the agencies now only as a last resort. "Let it be recorded that I am the last man of my people to lay down my gun," Sitting Bull told reporters. The traditionalists were four years behind their kin in adapting to agency ways. Many of them continued to hold themselves apart, making their disdain for their more compliant relatives clear.[67]

Officers negotiating Sitting Bull's surrender promised the chief that he would be settled at Standing Rock agency, but the government did not honor this agreement. The army held Sitting Bull at Fort Yates, then transferred him down the Missouri to Fort Randall—ironically, aboard the steamer *General Sherman*. The government held him a prisoner of war for two years.[68]

Officials moved Sitting Bull to Standing Rock in 1883. There, the tensions between his followers and the agency Indians escalated. Sitting Bull fully expected to regain the leadership of his people; Standing Rock agent James McLaughlin, in turn, expected to turn Sitting Bull into just one more Indian farmer. They clashed at every turn. Sitting Bull and his people were on the Great Sioux Reservation, but they were not converts to the American way of life. The agents watched them with trepidation.

As soon as the fighting Sioux had been pushed onto the reservation or into Canadian exile, the way was clear for settlers and miners to pour into their land. The year 1878 saw the beginning of what was called the Great Dakota Boom, when settlement took off in Dakota Territory. In 1870, the Territory was populated by a mere 11,766 non-Indians, living on 1,700 farms clustered around six towns. But the terrible "Hard Winter" of 1880 to 1881, during which frequent blizzards from October to the end of April covered the prairies eleven feet deep in snow and froze entire herds of cattle, also saturated the topsoil. That water, together with unusually heavy spring rains, made crops flourish for the next few years. Newfangled barbed wire enabled farmers to fence off their fields from roving cattle and the few remaining bison; new methods of milling hard red spring wheat made wheat farming profitable. Railroads laid more than two thousand miles of track across South Dakota between 1878 and 1887, carrying in settlers and the food, fencing, and goods they needed to survive. The growth was explosive: By 1890, the non-Indian population of the Territory had jumped to 328,808. The six towns of 1870 had become 310; 1,700 farms had become 50,158.[69]

Nothing could have pleased the Shermans more. When he retired in 1883, General Sherman reflected that, since the Civil War, he had done everything in his power to promote the growth and development of the West. In twenty years, the land had passed from the hands of dangerous "savages" to those of industrious families. Comfortable railroad cars now traversed more than ten thousand miles of land that had previously been empty plains. Sherman congratulated himself for his role in this dramatic transformation. "I honestly believe," he told his wife, that "in this way I have done more good for our country and for the human race than I did in the Civil War."[70]

It seemed that nothing now stood in the way of the triumph of the Republican economic system. The Plains Indians, with their traditional economy, had been corralled onto a reservation and were being taught how to become good American farmers. It was only a question of time until everyone was rising together in the new industrial economy. Everything seemed to point to the harmonious achievement of universal prosperity throughout the nation. Cump and John Sherman certainly believed that the Republican economic system was the best one on earth. For proof, they had to look no further than the westward expansion of the country and the rising standard of living among the new professionals.

But those who championed the industrial economy ignored that its benefits did not spread to everyone. The new economy bought prosperity for some at the price of suffering for others. Even as the army was forcing the Sioux to accept the free labor system, the new economic organization was under attack by Americans who were beginning to see its shortcomings. The idea that a man could rise if only he worked hard enough might have been true in the rural economy of prewar Ohio, but it was not so in the industrial factories or on the arid Plains. Workers and farmers left behind by the postwar prosperity began to take a stand against Republican economic policies that promoted business growth at their expense.

The new world of industry was harsh for many wage laborers. Unskilled workers were easily replaced by others, and they had no bargaining power to protect their wages or to guarantee decent working conditions. In Pittsburgh's steel mills, men shoveled coal into the white-hot furnaces twelve hours a day, seven days a week, for less than two dollars a day (the equivalent of about $34 today). In New York City's garment factories, working girls sewed at industrial machines that could puncture their fingers and that produced highly flammable cotton lint. In the Southern cloth mills, young children climbed between the looms and poked their small fingers into the machinery to retie broken threads for pennies.

Wage laborers found themselves increasingly isolated from rising Americans. Growing factories pulled workers from Europe, and these new immigrants were different than the ones who had come to America from England, Ireland, and Germany before the Civil War. The newcomers were southern and eastern Europeans: Italians, Poles, Russians, Slavs. Native-born Americans shied away from the new arrivals, who seemed to them alien and uncouth. They spoke languages most Americans had never heard; they were often Catholic or Jewish, religions largely unfamiliar to America's Protestant majority. These new immigrants wore the distinctive clothing of their homeland—black babushkas, loose cotton blouses, yarmulkes; sometimes they fought—not with fists or guns, like Americans, but with knives. The new immigrants, in turn, generally preferred to live with their countrymen. The distrust with which they were viewed by native-born Americans meant they were often forced into dirty ghettos of crowded tenements, where strep infections, smallpox, tuberculosis, and typhoid ran rampant, creating fear among outsiders that the newcomers might be carrying deadly germs.[71]

Immigrants had little power to improve their conditions. Eager for work of any sort to keep their families from starvation, they had to accept low-wage jobs shoveling coal into the furnaces of steel mills, stirring the vats on the floors of meat-packing plants, or unloading cargo from the ships on the wharves. If they complained, they were fired. Wage laborers were also at the mercy of seasonal markets. It was a rare industry that needed workers year-round, and a closed factory gate meant that a man's family had to survive on whatever his children could scrounge, his wife could earn, and he had managed to save. Unlike the upwardly mobile native-born population that the Sherman brothers celebrated, many of these people had little hope of rising far.

Western farmers also suffered in the new economy. While boosters had promised prosperity and easy farming on the plains, the reality of life there was often far more difficult. The High Plains, which stretch from Canada to Mexico in a band that reaches from approximately the southernmost tip of Texas to the Rocky Mountains, have a topography and a climate quite unlike that of the rest of the country. The region is flat, and its rivers tend to be shallow and difficult, if not impossible, to navigate. At the end of the nineteenth century, even the great Missouri River, which dominates the northern Plains, could accommodate riverboat traffic only from the end of March through the beginning of November. The climate is harsh: the Plains region has significantly less rainfall than the lands to the east of it. The lack of trees and the tearing winds, unbroken by mountains for hundreds of miles, mean the region has high evaporation rates. The evaporation creates the dramatic cathedral clouds that fill with light and dominate the landscape; in the absence of modern wells, it also makes agriculture a losing proposition. Those same winds, whipping down from the arctic or up from Mexico at an average speed of more than ten miles per hour, make summers scorching and winters frigid. The plains are a natural corridor for tornadoes and for the blizzards that drop the temperatures by as much as fifty degrees and churn snow into whiteout conditions in minutes.[72]

Many easterners who had gone west banking on the bumper crops and mild climates promised in railroad advertisements found themselves instead on a monotonous, dirty trek behind oxen that either refused to move or refused to stop, in wagons whose wheels broke far from the towns that held wheelwrights, quelling arguments between bored children, and camping wherever nightfall found them. When, finally, they reached their destination, they found not the thriving towns the railroad literature described, but a boundless prairie that offered no obvious building material. Compelled either to dig out a hollow in the side of a bluff for shelter or to build a house of sod bricks, settlers found themselves living in dirt and marooned in a sea of grass, their closest neighbors miles away. They fought constantly to hold their fields against the buffalo and cattle that roamed the plains.[73]

Few people who had extra cash tried to homestead. Congressmen designed the Homestead Act to put poor families on western land, and while the plan worked, it also meant that homesteaders had no money to buy the supplies they needed to establish a successful farm. Most had to borrow money from back East at interest rates of 10 to 15 percent in order to buy lumber for a claim shanty, fencing, seeds, tools, clothing, lamp oil, and food. In the 1880s, people in the farming state of Kansas carried personal debt four times the national average. Transportation of crops, too, was expensive. Sometimes it cost two bushels of corn to get one to market.[74]

Such debt might have been tolerable had crop prices been high, but they fell precipitously after the Civil War. Production of grain increased even after Europe's fields recovered from the droughts of the mid-1860s, so Americans dumped their huge crops into a saturated international market. Southern cotton farmers, who had dominated the world cotton market before 1860, found after the war that farmers from India and Egypt had taken their place. This meant that American cotton growers also had to contend with a glut. Overproduction kept prices dropping in the later decades of the nineteenth century, but the tariffs designed to protect agriculture could not help American farmers because they were exporting rather than importing crops. Farmers were pinched at the other end, too, as tariffs inflated the prices of farm machinery, cloth, sugar, kerosene, and, indeed, virtually everything they needed to live.

Workers and farmers began to bridle under the Republican push for economic development even as Republican administrations pressed that development west. While Republicans regarded the triumph of the army in the Dakotas as the stroke that would enable their economic vision to become truly national, opponents were starting to challenge the very premises of that vision.

Urban workers unable to work their way off the gritty factory floors and farmers ground into poverty turned to politics to bring back a world in which hard work led to success. They believed that they were falling behind because Congress had tilted the economy in favor of industrialists, and strongly resented what they saw as an unfair alliance between the government and big business. They began to call for legislation to level the playing field between them and the businessmen and bankers who seemed to control their lives. Workers agitated for the regulation of wages, hours, and working conditions; farmers called for laws that regulated the storage, sale, and transportation of crops. Only the restoration of economic fairness, they thought, could make their work as valuable as it ought to be.

Their call for legislation was based in the widespread idea that hardworking Americans should be able to rise, but horrified Republican politicians and businessmen didn't see it that way. Farmers and workers were trying to destroy the very fundamentals of American life, they insisted. Every man had a right to make his own decisions about where to work and under what conditions, Republicans argued, and every businessman had a right to arrange his affairs as he saw fit. Those who could not rise were responsible for their own failure; they should get an education and work more efficiently.[75]

Protesters would ruin the country, Republicans claimed. If the government helped any specific group, that interference would destroy America's unique political economy that allowed everyone to rise together. In its place would arise a society with different interests pitted against each other, snarling over the remnants of a decreasing prosperity. The principle of American government was laissez-faire, they argued; it should not help any particular sector of society.

The Republican celebration of a laissez-faire government was deceptive. Laissez-faire was an elegant term, but the reality was that the postwar Republican government was closely allied to business interests, just as farmers and laborers claimed. During the war, when government and industry both shared an interest in developing the country, businessmen and lawmakers worked hand in hand. Congressmen explained their need to keep constituents happy; businessmen told government officials what they needed to keep their companies thriving and, thus, their workers employed. Even during the war, this cozy relationship often gave businessmen too much influence on policy. Banker Jay Cooke made a fortune from his monopoly on the marketing of government bonds; he used some of that money to pick up the tab for the shopping bills run up by the daughter of the Secretary of the Treasury, who awarded Cooke his contracts.

After the war, this kind of corruption became institutionalized. Businessmen offered all sorts of benefits to legislators. Congressmen traveled across the country free on railroad "passes," railroad men offered valuable stock to their government friends at fire-sale prices, and government officials at all levels accepted expensive presents—including cash—from business owners. Politicians justified their actions on ideological grounds. Republicans had adopted into their political worldview the idea that the government's role was to promote business, and they legislated to do just that. Economic development, they argued, would promote the good of all Americans.

The Republicans' use of the government to push postwar economic development centered at first on monetary policy. First from his post on the Senate Finance Committee and then as Secretary of the Treasury from 1877 to 1881, John Sherman was a leader in the effort to manipulate the money supply to clear the way for business development.

Eastern businessmen demanded an early return to hard money after the war, but congressmen dragged their feet at retiring the greenbacks, which were enormously popular with cash-starved, indebted westerners. Hard money, backed ultimately by gold, prevented inflation and kept debt stable. The greenbacks had been created as a temporary measure during the war and were not backed by anything but the government's declaration that they were legal tender. Their value fluctuated, although they almost always were worth considerably less than hard money. Greenbacks' lower value created inflation that helped farmers by permitting them to repay loans with money worth less than when they borrowed it. Capitalists hated the greenbacks for the same reason.

Although debtors liked the greenbacks, Sherman pushed hard for the resumption of the gold standard. When the national economy fell into a recession in the mid-1870s, he blamed the crisis on the unstable currency and forced through the resumption of specie payments. While this pleased eastern creditors, whose loans would be paid back in money more valuable than it was when they lent it, westerners and workers loathed both the deed and the man behind it. Sherman also began to pay off the national debt, which further tightened the money supply by taking cash out of circulation. According to an angry supporter of paper money, Sherman was one of the two most dangerous men in the nation, and should be hanged or shot as a traitor. His deflationary financial policy was taking the wealth produced by laborers and redistributing it to those already well off.[76]

Opponents resented government's concessions to business in part because businessmen spent their wealth in spectacular displays that left poorer Americans agog. In 1883, Alva Vanderbilt, who was married to the wealthiest man in the nation but still excluded from the elite "Four Hundred" by social leader Caroline Astor, threw a spectacular party to break into that exclusive club. Vanderbilt and her husband began by building a stunning new home on Fifth Avenue and Fifty-first Street at a cost of more than $2 million—upwards of $44 million in today's dollars—including stables finished in black walnut, cherry, and ash, with sterling silver metalwork.[77]

To christen the house, Mrs. Vanderbilt planned a costume ball. For weeks, fancy dressmakers, costumers, and milliners all along the East Coast were commissioned to produce costumes that imitated famous queens and kings, or characters from literature. The nation was atwitter with gossip about the upcoming event. Terrified that her unmarried daughter Carrie would be excluded from the most important social event of her generation, Mrs. Astor swallowed her pride and admitted the Vanderbilts to her social circle. On March 26, Carrie joined the throng of about twelve hundred guests at the Vanderbilt mansion, where one guest dressed as a peacock, another as a hornet, others as Joan of Arc, Marie Antoinette, Spanish knights, and French kings, all glittering with jeweled headdresses and rustling with satin and lace and tulle. Guests used golden spoons at their $25,000 meal, sitting at tables decorated with hothouse crocuses, tulips, and ascension lilies. The party proved a smashing success, and it launched a social competition that the popular press followed slavishly.[78]

The Astors and Vanderbilts were hardly alone in their extravagance. In cities across the nation, the wealthy dressed their horses and coachmen in expensive livery that competed with the costumes previously seen at Barnum's circus, gave $1,000 dinners for twenty people and, according to a scandalized observer, had "gotten into the habit . . . of spangling and emblazoning their own persons [with] diamonds, rubies, and emeralds." Newly rich couples bought their way into society by throwing magnificent parties. A newspaper society column noted that when Miss Tessie Fair, the daughter of a former senator from California, married Hermann Oelrichs, she wore a $10,000 dress, her mother gave her a diamond tiara, and others sent "necklaces of diamonds, bracelets of diamonds, sapphires, and rubies. [Newspaper editor] Mr. James Gordon Bennett sent a yachting bracelet, a curiously woven chain of rich yellow gold set with diamonds, rubies and sapphires." Her dowry was between one million and five million dollars.[79]

To a factory worker, eking by on pennies, or a farmer unable to pay his mortgage, such displays of wealth seemed outrageous. The parties and pricey jewels were not merely offensive, they also seemed to indicate that something was terribly wrong with America. With workers and western farmers sliding into destitution while the Four Hundred dressed their coachmen in suits with $300 buttons, many Americans began to worry that the nation had gone badly astray. Surely, the idea behind a republican government was that it would treat everyone in society evenly. The burgeoning wealth among the upper classes suggested that the cozy friendship between business and government had tilted the scale in favor of businessmen. If the government was going to act as it should, treating all interests equally, that close relationship had to end.[80]

The Senate, especially, seemed the private domain of big businessmen. "Behind every one of half of the portly and well-dressed members of the Senate can be seen the outlines of some corporation interested in getting or preventing legislation, or of some syndicate that has invaluable contracts or patents to defend or push," the *Chicago Tribune* lamented in 1884. Even the business-minded *New York Times* accused senators of doing the bidding of the corporations that had bought their election.[81]

Senators worked for business most dramatically by strengthening the tariff system the Republicans had established during the Civil War. Protective tariffs had been wartime measures to raise revenue and protect fledgling industries, but after the war they became vital supports for big business. By placing high walls around domestic industry, tariffs protected national businesses from the competition of cheaper foreign products. This protection was vital to the business trusts that increasingly controlled the economy by the 1880s. So important were they that it was not a stretch to conclude that trusts could not survive without tariffs.

Tariffs were a disaster for workers and farmers because they kept prices for consumer goods artificially high. They enabled domestic manufacturers to collude in raising the prices of their products, which they did with astonishing speed. After the war ended, businessmen had ridden the volatile waves of economic booms and busts by consolidating their industries. They first developed informal organizations called pools, in which participating members carved up markets and set prices across the industry. By the mid-1880s, though, business leaders pulled industries together into larger trusts that eliminated competition and fixed consumer prices at artificially high levels. By the late 1880s, trusts controlled most of the nation's industries, keeping buyers at their mercy for sugar, meat, salt, gas, copper, transportation, and the steel that fed railroads and urban construction. In 1889, New Jersey passed a general incorporation law that permitted one company to hold stock in others. These new "holding companies" consolidated business to an even greater degree than the previous trusts. In the late 1880s, one observer writing for a magazine fumed that corporations "dominate all channels of activity; they control governors, judges and legislatures; they make hewers of wood and drawers of water of all who are outside of their charmed circles."[82]

Americans who did not directly benefit from the trusts resented the prices they demanded for their products. Consumers would gladly have seen the trusts eradicated, but it was not immediately clear that Congress had the Constitutional power to do so. What Congress did have power to do, though, was to regulate the tariff.

Tariff revision seemed an obvious way to restore fairness to the American economy. To Americans watching the excesses of the Four Hundred, and the scores of nouveaux riches who sought to emulate them, the idea that American businesses continued to need protection seemed ludicrous. Tariffs had eventually come to represent almost half of a product's value, and by 1888, so much money was pouring into the U.S. Treasury from tariff duties that the government ran an annual surplus of almost $120 million.

Republicans nonetheless staunchly supported the protective system, arguing that it was key to the nation's industrial growth. Money spent domestically stayed in the country for reinvestment, they contended, while money spent on imports was lost forever. Money invested at home would develop more and more domestic industry which, theoretically, should eventually create more jobs and higher wages for American workers. This was, after all, the vision behind the Republicans' wartime economic policy, and advancing that vision had brought a way of life that Republican politicians enjoyed. Their arguments did not convince workers and farmers, though, who paid higher prices but never seemed to see money come back to them in higher wages or grain prices.

By the early 1880s, the fight over the tariff had become a defining issue for Republicans and Democrats. Since before the Civil War, Democrats had tended to support wage laborers and dislike a strong federal government. They had watched the Republicans' wartime economic legislation with distrust, carping that it benefited the wealthy at the expense of the average American. As soon as the war ended, taking away party members' common ground of the Union cause, Democrats found themselves at odds with the Republicans over monetary policy, with Democrats taking the side of the pro-inflation farmers and laborers.

They continued to oppose measures that seemed to favor the wealthy, and nothing irritated them more than the protective tariff. They found it unconscionable that tariffs took taxpayers' money and put it in the hands of wealthy businessmen. They had been opposed to a protective tariff since the early nineteenth century, and had always insisted tariffs should be used only to raise revenue. As tariffs and the money they raised steadily climbed, Democrats waxed angrier and angrier at the men who advocated them. That tariffs enabled trusts simply illustrated that Republican-controlled government was in thrall to business, the Democrats thought. They insisted that the government must work for all Americans, and worried that it had become the servant of the rich at the expense of the poor.

By 1884, Democratic opposition to the tariffs had begun to attract a wide audience. Even many Republicans had come around to the view that party operators had tied themselves too closely to the big businessmen who funded their political war chest. Moderates worried that the party needed to reform and to realign with its earlier principles of individual success through hard work. When the 1884 national convention nominated James G. Blaine, famous for taking large bribes from railroad companies, for the presidency, along with a notoriously corrupt vice-presidential candidate, some broke away from the party and voted Democratic.

Others stayed within the party but also worked for change. Even staunch Republican John Sherman balked at electing the tainted Blaine to the White House. While he didn't endorse the Democratic candidate, New York's reform-minded governor Grover Cleveland, Sherman was a lukewarm advocate for the Republicans. Each voter should figure out for himself which party would most likely be better for the country, he said. While the Blaine wing of the party insisted on the sanctity of tariffs and trusts, Sherman had come to believe that large entities like the Sugar Trust were dangerous and wrong, because they stifled competition and artificially raised prices. The tariff laws had created the trusts, Sherman said, and the laws could certainly be revised to curb them.[83]

In 1884, for the first time since the Civil War, Americans put a Democrat in the White House. Democratic candidate Grover Cleveland was famous for fighting corruption in New York and stood firmly against the control of government by business. The Blaine campaign tried to sidestep the issue of corruption by tying Cleveland to the "bloody shirt" of the Civil War, but many voters thought that less important than the takeover of the government by business. During the campaign, Democrats made much of Blaine's tainted relationships with the railroads. Their hits scored. In the election, Republicans disgruntled by their party's close relationship with commercial interests voted for the Democratic reformer rather than their corrupt standard-bearer. These "Mugwumps," as they were called, swung the very close election and sent a Democrat to the White House.

Emphasizing the duty of the government to represent the interests of all the people rather than "private interests," Cleveland's inaugural address took a stand against tariffs. And he continued to try to strike a new balance, making no secret of his desire to divorce the government from the businessmen who insisted they should be part of his administration. But he could not force Congress to pass new legislation. It was not until 1888 that the Democrats managed to bring forward their own tariff bill. The Mills Bill of that year, sponsored by Roger Q. Mills from the agricultural state of Texas, sought to lower tariffs dramatically and to use them primarily for revenue. Defending it, Mills echoed the Civil War Republicans when he called for "free men, free labor and free trade."[84]

Although Democrats had won the White House and represented the growing sense of the nation that tariffs must come down, they did not control Congress. Republicans still held the Senate, and businessmen had bought and paid for the senators. They refused to entertain the idea of any system but that of industrial protection. Attempts to reform the tariff came to nothing.

Meanwhile, business-oriented Republicans were determined to retake control of the government and to protect the tariff. They aggressively organized local clubs to distribute pro-tariff literature. For a presidential nominee in 1888, they bypassed frontrunner John Sherman in favor of the weak, little-known war hero Benjamin Harrison, grandson of President William Henry Harrison. Unlike Sherman, who was willing to negotiate over lower tariffs to break certain trusts and who had wavered during the election of 1884, Harrison showed every sign of being willing to do what he was told. Harrison's nomination was a shock to most Republicans, Sherman himself not least. He had expected the nomination and had even begun campaigning for the presidency along with friends and relatives like General Miles. Sherman and his many supporters believed that the Republican convention had abandoned him only because a railroad mogul had convinced the New York delegation to throw its weight to the far less qualified—but more reliably pro-tariff—Harrison.[85]

Certainly businessmen staunchly supported Harrison. John Wanamaker, the Philadelphia entrepreneur who pioneered the department store, designed an innovative fundraising system for the campaign. He created a network of committees that solicited donations from the nation's business leaders, touting Harrison as the pro-business candidate. Across the country, businessmen generously poured campaign money into the well-oiled Republican machine.

Harrison's men ran an extraordinarily corrupt campaign. Their platform defended the protective tariff, but on the stump Republicans allowed that some "reform" might be appropriate. They charged the Democrats with disloyalty and with stealing the previous election; they reminded voters of the great Republican heroes of the Civil War. Most important, perhaps, they spent their enormous war chest where it would do the most good. Harrison lost the popular vote by about 100,000 votes but won the Electoral College. After the election, the president-elect piously told one of his campaign managers that "Providence has given us this victory." The surprised operator later grumbled that "Providence hadn't a damn thing to do with it. [A] number of men were compelled to approach the penitentiary to make him President."[86]

In his 1888 annual message to Congress, delivered a month after Harrison's election, outgoing President Cleveland warned his countrymen of the danger they faced. He despaired of the country if the government did not divorce itself from big business. The gulf between employers and employed was growing every day, he noted. America had formerly been a land where all could rise, but now classes were forming. On the one hand were the rich and powerful; on the other, the toiling poor. Corporations had been created by the government to serve the interests of the people, but they had gained the upper hand. Soon they would be the masters of the people, rather than the other way around. The government had been lost to business, Cleveland lamented. The people must take it back, he insisted, or America as the hope of mankind would be lost.[87]

Harrison's supporters, in contrast, were elated that the future of America had just been secured. Convinced as they were that protectionism was the heart of the nation's success, they believed they had just managed to save the country from imminent peril. They interpreted their eked-out victory as a mandate for protectionism, but this was wishful. While the Democrats had lost the White House and the Congress, they had not lost on the tariff issue. By 1889, even many Republicans had turned against tariffs because of their role in supporting trusts. Most voters backed lower tariffs, and they expected the Harrison administration to "reform" the tariff, as Republicans had promised during the campaign.[88]

The ongoing unpopularity of big business was clearly apparent in the wake of a decision handed down by the New York Supreme Court in January 1889, in the last few months of President Cleveland's administration, before President Harrison took the oath of office in March. The court revoked the charter of the North River Sugar Refining Company because it had joined the "the great Sugar Trust." The decision was predicated on the idea that a trust had a public duty, and if a judge believed a trust to be neglecting that duty, he could take away the legal basis for its existence. Businessmen panicked, recognizing that this sweeping decision threatened the existence of all trusts. But outside of business circles, the judgment was widely popular. Even the staunchly Republican magazine *Frank Leslie's Illustrated Newspaper* cheerfully reported that it amounted to a new charter of liberty for the people. *Harper's Weekly* agreed. It suggested that any business combination that limited production or raised prices was illegal, a conspiracy against the public welfare, and should be condemned.[89]

Protectionist Republicans, however, continued to defend a high tariff, claiming it was the economic wall that kept the American economy healthy and growing. Free trade, they insisted, would destroy business, undermining the very workers tariff reformers claimed to be defending. Cheap foreign imports would destroy the market for American goods, ruin businesses, put American laborers out of work, and send capital fleeing across the Atlantic. As Democrats and reformers called for lower tariffs, pro-tariff Republicans more and more stridently insisted that the tariff must be preserved. It was their duty, they claimed, to cement a permanent Republican majority that would keep the nation from disintegrating under the demands of those suffering in the new industrial system.

The tariff issue divided the parties, and divided America. Many considered it the key to the success or the destruction of the nation. And the nation was, as Abraham Lincoln had said, the "last best hope of earth" to prove that a republican government could survive. On the tariff, it seemed, hung the fate of the world. As a leading Republican put it: "The difference between the parties is as the difference between the light and darkness, day and night. Either the Republican party must be right and the Democratic party wrong, or the conditions must be reversed. One is certainly right, and if so, obviously the other is wrong." He, for one, was sanguine about the outcome of this contest. He continued: "The Republican party is in power. For the first time in fifteen years it is in control of the Federal Administration. . . ."[90]

Harrison's men were convinced they must protect the tariff, and they knew they had a very tenuous grip on power. They had won the election, but even with the help of a huge war chest, they had lost the popular vote. If they were to hold on to their control of the government, first in the midterm elections of 1890 and then in the presidential election of 1892, they would have to use every tool at their disposal to skew votes toward the Republican ticket. Harrison's men did not hide this plan; indeed, they trumpeted it as proof that they had the best interests of the country at heart. To defend America, they were willing to try to make sure that correct policies could not be overturned by the votes of ignorant people who did not understand what was good for the country.

Once in office, Harrison's people did everything they could to strengthen their position and weaken that of the Democrats and reformers who wanted to lower the tariffs. They turned first to the patronage machine that would funnel government jobs and government contracts to friends of the administration. As soon as the new administration took over, the first thing it did was to clear out of office the supporters of the previous administration and replace them with their own men. This practice was called the "spoils system"—for to the victor go the spoils—and it had been a staple of American government since the 1830s. Party politicians gave jobs to the men who could deliver votes to the party ticket; the more they could deliver, either through money or influence, the higher the office they received. This system trickled down to individual voters, who could count on a job from a ward boss as long as they voted the correct way.

The spoils system thrived in nineteenth-century America, and never so well as in the years after the Civil War. With the enormous expansion of the government during the war, the number of positions available for politicians to offer to political friends swelled. So, of course, did the opportunities for corruption, as politicians offered government contracts to supporters. So bad had the system become by the 1880s, that in 1881 an office seeker assassinated President James A. Garfield in the hopes that Garfield's vice president would give him a job when he took over from the dead president. Horrified, the public demanded that the spoils system be cleaned up. In 1883, Congress passed a law to establish a new "civil service" system by which government jobs would be awarded according to a candidate's fitness for the position rather than his party loyalty. Nominees for office had to take an exam and, once in a job, could not be removed simply to make way for someone else under a new administration. The rules covered only a few jobs in the beginning, but since presidents could expand it to protect their own appointees when they left office, the system steadily grew.

The first president to inherit the new civil service rules was Democrat Grover Cleveland. A reformer himself, Cleveland tried to abide by the spirit as well as the law of the new system. Republican Benjamin Harrison had no such scruples. Elected by railroad men and trust officers, he knew the value of well-placed jobs and contracts in shoring up political support. Within a week of his inauguration, observers estimated the number of job seekers in Washington to be at least seven thousand.[91]

John Wanamaker symbolized Harrison's idea of a good public servant. Wanamaker was a fervent Christian who was a trustee of the national Christian Endeavor movement to evangelize the nation and the world, he taught Sunday school, and sometimes even preached to "drunkards and abandoned women" in Philadelphia missions. The campaign financier's zeal for spreading Republicanism paralleled his zeal for spreading the word of God. To Wanamaker went the office of Postmaster General, the key patronage position of the government, for almost every town in American had a government postmaster. Having a businessman in charge of such an important government position so pleased the members of the Manufacturers' Club of Philadelphia that they gave Wanamaker a "brilliant reception" that coincided with the opening of their "magnificent" new $250,000 quarters, with each room furnished in a different kind of wood, on Walnut Street. As businessmen expected, Wanamaker used his position to advance their interests. Within months of Wanamaker's appointment, supporters were forced to defend his endorsement of clients for government jobs, his use of his position to retaliate against Democrats, and his attempts to contract out government services to friendly industrialists.[92]

Wanamaker was just the most prominent example of widespread patronage corruption in the Harrison administration. Harrison's men intended their appointments to shore up the Republicans, but putting unqualified and corrupt men into bureaucratic positions badly damaged the functioning of government. Their appointees failed to do their jobs adequately. That incompetence would reverberate all over the country, from the Cabinet all the way to the Indian agencies.

The patronage feast was so grotesque that the Civil Service Reform Association publicly reproved Harrison only two months after he took office, and even moderate Republican papers began to protest. As men swarmed into Washington to beg for appointments, the Republican owner of the popular *Frank Leslie's Illustrated Newspaper* asserted that respectable members of both parties could agree on one thing: "The greed displayed by the office-seekers has never been surpassed in our political history." Harrison's men had proved that it was high time to clean up the civil service.[93]

Harrison's people retaliated aggressively against their critics. Irritated when the owner of *Frank Leslie's* bristled about Harrison's sell-out of the government to businessmen, W. J. Arkell, the wealthy and well-connected son of New York Republican ex-senator James Arkell, bought the paper and installed the president's ne'er-do-well son, Russell B. Harrison, as its co-editor. From the paper's new headquarters at the Judge Building at 110 Fifth Avenue in New York City, they produced the first issue of the administration's mouthpiece on May 11, 1889. At thirty-two pages, it was double the paper's old length and claimed to be the largest illustrated paper ever printed in the United States.[94]

The first issue of the new *Frank Leslie's* contained a thorough attack on civil service reform, written by Republican machine kingpin Thomas C. Platt. Platt dismissed the idea that the government was supposed to represent all the people. Rather, he wrote, it was supposed to represent Republicans. That was the whole point of an election. "When the people elect a President and Congress, they presume that they also elect policies and men of their political faith to carry them out. They expect that all the subordinates of the Federal service will be put in full accord with the new Administration."[95]

The new *Frank Leslie's* unabashedly celebrated President Harrison's connections to the business world. Harrison's people made much of the fact that his inauguration marked the centennial of George Washington's, and New Yorkers used this coincidence to boost both their new president and their businesses. The first issue of the new *Frank Leslie's* highlighted Harrison's visit to New York City for its celebration of the centennial. It showed him visiting the "Lawyers' Club" and Wall Street, and offered a full-page illustration of schoolgirls strewing flowers in front of the new president as he entered New York City Hall. A supplement to the paper had a sketch of Washington on one side and Harrison on the other, below eight illustrations of New York businesses decked out for the celebration.[96]

Frank Leslie's became increasingly brash in its celebration of the business community. The second issue of the new paper praised an amateur circus put on by "the leaders of the '400'" at a cost of $30,000. By August, it was running puff pieces on "representative society ladies," the wives and daughters of New York's wealthy men.[97]

Frank Leslie's echoed pro-tariff men like Andrew Carnegie, who in an 1889 article in *North American Review* argued that the huge fortunes of the new industrialists were good for society. The wealthy were essentially stewards of the nation's money, gathering vast amounts of it together so it could be used for the common good, wrote the great steel baron. With their great resources, responsible capitalists built libraries and schools, museums and symphony halls. Indeed, Carnegie argued, American industrialism was the highest form of human civilization.[98]

Carnegie urged capitalists to use their wealth for the good of their fellow man, but Arkell and Harrison of *Frank Leslie's* went further and claimed the rich had already done so. Many of New York's wealthiest men were quite charitable and benevolent, they insisted, but they couldn't let anyone know because they would be overwhelmed by appeals from people who were unworthy of charity. According to *Frank Leslie's*, virtually every millionaire in the city did great good with his money.[99]

"This is to be a business-man's Administration," *Frank Leslie's* announced as soon as the first Congress of the Harrison administration assembled in December 1889. The paper's editors expected expansive legislation, wise financial policies, and a resulting "business boom." This is "A BUSINESS MAN'S ADMINISTRATION," the editors boasted again, and predicted "that before the close of the present Administration business men will be thoroughly well content with it. . . ."[100]

CHAPTER 3

The Westward March of Civilization

FOURTEEN HUNDRED miles away, in his cabin at Grand River on the Standing Rock Reservation in the new state of South Dakota, Hunkpapa Sioux leader Sitting Bull couldn't read the new *Frank Leslie's Illustrated Newspaper*, but he didn't need to. He had no doubt that Harrison's administration served businessmen. He had spent the past twenty years trying to defend his land and way of life from American development, and had suffered his most thorough defeat only months before at the hands of Harrison's people. What he couldn't know was that, with the election of President Harrison, the general American impulse to take Indian land had become a stated government policy with a clear political goal. Opening the Great Sioux Reservation for settlement had become a matter of political survival for the Harrison administration.

In 1881, starvation had forced Sitting Bull to bring his band back to the United States from Canada. After spending almost two years in prison at Fort Randall, he had been settled at Standing Rock in 1883. He had accepted it all, bitterly, but he couldn't resign himself to the latest attack on his people.

Sitting Bull was close to sixty in 1889 and living in a log cabin on the reservation, but he had spent most of his years leading a traditional Sioux life of hunting and horses, fighting and family. His very name derived from the bison, an animal that was stubborn, determined, unafraid, and unwilling ever to turn back, even if marching forward meant death. By 1889, with President Harrison in office, it seemed he would be forced to imitate his namesake.[1]

The troubles that would explode during Harrison's administration had begun only a year or so after Sitting Bull surrendered to the army. Settlers who had come to Dakota Territory in the Great Dakota Boom wanted more land, and couldn't bear seeing rich fields lying unplowed on the Great Sioux Reservation. In 1882, Dakota Territorial Delegate Richard Pettigrew, who was working to build a political following, sought to cut the Great Sioux Reservation in half. His plan would give settlers 11 million acres of land in a broad band across the middle of the reservation from the Missouri River to the Black Hills.[2]

Pettigrew got Congress to appropriate money to let the Secretary of the Interior negotiate for the Sioux land. A commission charged with promoting the scheme claimed to have gotten the requisite signatures of three-quarters of the Sioux men to ratify such a plan, but their methods were so questionable that the Senate established a committee to investigate. Henry L. Dawes, a Republican senator from Massachusetts, was chosen to head the probe. Dawes was a reformer who believed that the Indians must assimilate or they would die out.[3]

The commission ultimately decided that the Sioux opposed dividing the reservation, and the land scheme fizzled. But the committee's investigations had long-term implications. Senator Dawes listened to testimony from Indian agents who were determined to force Indians into the new American economic system and who believed that taking the Sioux land was the best way to do it. The Indian agent at Standing Rock, a stubborn, strong-willed reformer named James McLaughlin, was a representative witness for the committee. He told its members that the only way to solve "the Indian problem" was for the government to shove the Teton Sioux into the modern economy, weaning them from their traditional ways by turning them into farmers. The usual method of providing the Indians cash annuities, guaranteed by treaty, was a terrible idea. Indians, he argued, should be rewarded only when they did something for themselves, like building houses or plowing fields.[4]

Reducing the size of the Great Sioux Reservation, McLaughlin argued, was an essential step in Americanizing the Sioux. Only that would weaken their traditional hunting economy enough to make farming their sole option. The best way to make them take up the new economy was to destroy the old.[5]

Senator Dawes took this advice to heart. In 1887, he marshaled through Congress the General Allotment Act, a law designed to force Indians into an American way of life. This act, also known as the Dawes Severalty Act, abolished the system of providing tribes with large tracts of land to use as they saw fit. Instead, the government would provide individual Indian men with land for farming. The Allotment Act dramatically reduced the land available to tribes and destroyed their ability to live off game, which relied on unsettled land for its habitat.

Many supporters of this act simply wanted the Indians' land, but others believed that forcing Indians into the modern world was a kindness that would enable them and their children to have a future. In an era when many white and black Americans were landless, the idea of guaranteeing Indians land on which to farm seemed to many a generous gift. Indians who adopted the new ways were also offered American citizenship, a boon that had been previously denied them in 1868 with the ratification of the Fourteenth Amendment, which guaranteed citizenship to all other men born or naturalized in America, but withheld it from reservation Indians.

Far from being a boon, the Dawes Act was calamitous for the Sioux. Congress designed the law to push Indians into the free labor economy, but the eastern model wasn't economically viable in the Dakotas. The idea was that individual young men would work hard, make money, and hire others—spreading prosperity as everyone in the system moved up. But there was no place in this model for the Indians to start. Farming required mules, harnesses, plows, fencing, tools, and seeds to work the fields, as well as cows and pigs and chickens for the barnyard. Policy makers assumed Indians would either receive necessary supplies from government agents or would work for wages to raise money to buy them. But agents awarded the contracts for supplying the Indians to political friends who didn't fulfill them, and white employers wouldn't hire Indians.

Some Sioux did, in fact, try to farm, but those who tried discovered that it could not be done without supplies. Sitting Bull complained to investigators that the government had given him a job that was impossible with the tools he had. "You sent me here and advised me to live as you do," he said. "I asked . . . for hogs, male and female, and for male and female sheep. . . . I did not leave out anything in the way of animals that the white men have; I asked for every one of them. I want you to . . . send me some agricultural implements, so that I will not be obliged to work bare-handed."[6]

But even with the right instruments, dry farming on the prairies was a losing battle. Most eastern settlers who tried to put down roots in the Dakotas found the environment drove them quickly into despair. Water was short, hot summer winds seared crops, goods from the East were costly, mortgages mounted. Only the promise of a great crop that could clear a mortgage and put money in the bank kept desperate farmers borrowing and hoping.

Indeed, it turned out that the Indians' economy beat the American economy hands down on the dry prairies. Generations of Indian hunters had made the prairies perfect for grazing animals. Eventually, settlers also came to rely on animal herds, realizing that the only way to make the prairies profitable in the days before irrigation was by ranging cattle on them. Herding animals, though, requires far more land than farming does. By cutting Indian land into small parcels, government policies destroyed Indians' ability to practice the only economy that worked in the harsh environment of the Plains.

The Dawes Act reduced Indian landholding on the large scale as well as on the individual level. The reservation had twice the land necessary to give every household head in the Sioux bands an allotment. Seeing a chance to open more land to settlement, western developers and their supporters in Congress revived the plan to divide the Great Sioux Reservation. They wanted to take the "extra" land from the Sioux in a corridor through the reservation and sell it to railroad men and homesteaders for fifty cents an acre. Pushed off their range, the Sioux would relocate onto six reservations arranged around the existing agencies: Pine Ridge, Rosebud, Cheyenne River, Standing Rock, Crow Creek, and Lower Brulé, where they could gradually move to individual land allotments. The scheme's promoters offered to use some of the money they raised to establish a permanent fund to help the Sioux make the transition to farmers. The money would also enable the government to provide farm animals, tools, schools, doctors, and so on to the Sioux reservations.[7]

Congress approved the plan, but before it could be enacted, there was an obstacle to overcome. Under the Fort Laramie Treaty of 1868, three-quarters of the adult males in the tribe had to agree to the cession of land. This was the same requirement that had tripped up the Pettigrew plan five years before.

In 1888, the Secretary of the Interior appointed a commission to obtain Indian approval of the proposed cession. His ignorance of the Sioux showed in his choice of Captain Pratt of the Carlisle Indian School to serve as the commission's leader. As the hated head of the school that tore Indian children away from parents in order to crush the Sioux culture, Pratt had little chance of success. To make matters worse, he chose to start negotiations at Standing Rock, the home of Sitting Bull and the least likely of the Indians to approve of the cession.

Ironically, Pratt's unbending policies left room for a reformer more sympathetic to the Sioux to work against him in the land debate. Pratt and his supporters believed that children must be taken out of their culture and had insisted on educating them back East. Government officials had neglected the schools on the reservations that had been promised by treaty. Three years earlier, in 1885, Elaine Goodale, a young woman from Massachusetts, had toured the Great Sioux Reservation. Well connected although poor, and with a growing reputation as a writer, Goodale had taught Indians at Hampton Institute, where a few had come to study at the school organized for ex-slaves. She shared reformers' conviction that Indians must adapt to American society, or die out. Her tour of the reservation convinced her that the government had badly neglected its duty to encourage Indians into modern ways. It had not built the schools it had promised and, consequently, the Sioux clung to traditional practices. Goodale determined to move to Dakota Territory to teach, trying to lead the Sioux to "civilization" from the ground up.[8]

The next year, Goodale and a friend moved to the Lower Brulé agency and opened a school four days before Christmas. Goodale staunchly believed that the Indians must be "civilized" and Christianized, but she also loved the freedom of life in Dakota Territory. She liked the Sioux and worked hard to integrate herself into their world. She learned the Lakota language, slept in their tepees when traveling with them, mourned their dead, and occasionally took their side against government policies.[9]

At Lower Brulé, Elaine Goodale counseled the Indians to reject the land proposal. She wanted to see the government push the Sioux more firmly into farming and Christianity, but didn't see any advantage for the Indians in losing half their land at fifty cents an acre. Her fame as a writer meant that the Sioux who opposed the land deal invited her to private meetings and asked her to present their side of the story to the newspapers. Angry that his plan was breaking down, Pratt warned Goodale that she was a government employee and must support any and all administration policies. She retorted that her only interest was in what was best for the Sioux.[10]

Pratt's frustration reflected the futility of his mission. Goodale's opposition wasn't really necessary; even those few progressives willing to talk to the commissioners complained of the low price offered for the land. The commissioners gave up on getting the treaty signed even before they visited Pine Ridge, Rosebud, and Cheyenne River. Instead, they arranged for sixty-seven Sioux leaders to go to Washington in October to lay out their conditions for cession.[11]

The trip to Washington seemed to kill the proposal. The Sioux demanded a price of $1.25 per acre for their land, the same price the government asked for its own lands. This seemed outrageously high to the Secretary of the Interior; indeed, the Indians had probably asked for it to stop the land sale. Unable to convince the Sioux to sell, the Secretary of the Interior sent the delegates home.[12]

But November 1888 brought a change that meant the delegates' high price might not end discussion of a land sale after all. Voters put Republican president Benjamin Harrison into office along with a Republican Congress. The incoming Republican administration boded well for South Dakota settlers hoping to get Sioux lands.

Republicans and Democrats had fought for years over admitting new western states, with members of each party blocking the admission of states believed to favor the other. Republicans counted on Dakota and Washington Territories to be theirs, while the Democrats were pretty sure to have Montana and New Mexico Territories. In early 1888, congressmen had floated the idea of a compromise by which all four states would come into the Union together. But the election of Republican majorities in the House and Senate meant that the Democrats had to cut a deal with their opponents, and quickly, or the Republicans in the next Congress would simply admit their own states and no others.[13]

The Democrats got the best deal they could, but it was not a good one. On February 22, 1889, outgoing President Cleveland signed an omnibus bill that divided the Territory of Dakota in half. The bill also enabled the people in the new Territories of North Dakota and South Dakota, as well as the older Territories of Montana and Washington, to write state constitutions and elect state governments. The four new states would be admitted into the Union in nine months. This plan cut Democratic New Mexico out of statehood, and split Republican Dakota Territory into two new Republican states. Rather than the two new Republican and two new Democratic states that Congress had considered the previous year, the omnibus bill created three new Republican states and one new Democratic state that Republicans thought they could capture. In their eagerness to admit both Dakotas, Republican congressmen also ignored the uncomfortable fact that much of the land in the anticipated state of South Dakota belonged to the Sioux.[14]

Harrison's men were eager to bring new western states into the Union. They expected that the 1890 census would reveal such growth in the western population that the region would become a driving force in American politics. Admitting new states full of western Republican voters would dramatically increase the strength of the Republican Party in Congress. It would also change the number of electors in the Electoral College, altering the number of votes necessary to win the presidency. Harrison's men were only too aware that the 1888 election had been won only in the Electoral College, and they had every intention of weighting the College more heavily toward the Republicans before the election of 1892.[15]

Harrison's people made no secret of their intentions. *Frank Leslie's* expected that the Republicans could take Montana, and gleefully anticipated that the new western states would send eight new Republican senators to Washington, making the count in the Senate forty-seven Republicans to thirty-seven Democrats. The newspaper also pointed out that the changing balance of the Electoral College would stop the Democratic-leaning state of New York from determining the next president.[16]

South Dakota, though, could not be turned into a viable state unless the Sioux sold much of their land, and Congress set out to make that happen. On March 2, 1889, just a week after President Cleveland had split South Dakota off from North Dakota and authorized them each to organize a state government, the lame-duck Congress authorized the division of the Great Sioux Reservation into six smaller reservations. Desperate to get Sioux land for the nascent state of South Dakota, the incoming Republican administration was willing to offer higher land prices than the Democrats had. The new bill allowed for payment of $1.25 per acre for Sioux lands sold in the first three years after ratification; payment would be 75 cents an acre for the next two years, and 50 cents an acre thereafter. It also established a $3 million treasury fund invested at 5 percent for the benefit of the Sioux, an extra twenty years of educational benefits, and compensation to Red Cloud's Oglalas for the ponies the army had taken in 1876. Congress was determined to get the job done one way or another. It appropriated the extraordinary sum of $25,000 to be used to induce Indians to sign a treaty approving the bill.[17]

In April, Harrison named a three-man commission to secure the necessary Sioux signatures. On it, he placed two party hacks, former Ohio Governor Charles Foster and former Republican representative from Missouri William Warner. These were not qualified men—Foster justified his participation by reflecting that "the Indian is a queer character and pretty soon he will become extinct, so that if a man wants the experience of serving on an Indian Commission he has no time to lose."[18]

The strength of the commission was in the third member of the party, General George Crook, commander of the Division of the Missouri. With keen eyes, a thin, pointed nose, and wild whiskers that he wore in extravagant wedges on either side of his face, Crook was one of the nation's leading Indian fighters. Rather than being consumed by hatred of the people whose arrowhead he carried in his body, he worked to understand his adversaries. He had a temper but was generally reserved. When he did speak sharply, people hurried to get back in his good graces. Indians and officers both believed him to be strictly honest, and felt they could rely on his word. The Sioux knew Crook and respected him from the days of the 1876 campaign.[19]

In May, the commission set out from Chicago to get the necessary 4,259 votes out of 5,678 that would equal three-quarters of the number of Sioux men over the age of eighteen. On May 31, they arrived at

Rosebud, where a relatively calm atmosphere prevailed along with generally friendly relations between its agent and people.[20]

The Crook Commission's task would not be easy because most Indians opposed the treaty. They had seen too many treaties broken, annuities and provisions delayed or denied, and lands guaranteed to them "forever" slip from their control. To obtain the necessary signatures, the Crook Commission used every method its members could think of. At Rosebud, it produced feasts and exuded goodwill, but could get no signers until Crook made a number of personal promises that redressed old grievances. In 1876, the government had obtained the Black Hills by threatening to take away Sioux rations, and the Indians at Rosebud were nervous that the two would be connected again. They made Crook put in writing that this land cession would not have any affect on rations. For his part, Crook noted that anyone who refused to sign would be considered disloyal, a thinly veiled warning when it came from a man who had fought the Indians in the war summer of 1876. Between the promises and threats, the commission got three-quarters of the Brulé to sign, despite the adamant opposition of traditional leader Two Strike.[21]

Negotiations were harder at the other agencies. From Rosebud the commission went to Pine Ridge, where Red Cloud, old now and going blind, met Crook with warriors dressed for battle. He ignored them and proceeded to negotiate with other Indians at the agency for weeks, but succeeded only in getting progressive American Horse and some of his followers to sign. American Horse immediately declared he had been tricked, and the other Oglala leaders—Red Cloud; Young-Man-Afraid-of-His-Horse, the powerful and politically savvy son of Man-Afraid-of-His-Horse; and Little Wound, an older man who tended to be willing to work with his agent—wanted no part of the treaty.[22]

From there the commission went to Lower Brulé and Crow Creek, where the Sioux were willing to negotiate. The Indians there, in the middle of the stretch of land the settlers wanted, were worried that they were going to lose their land no matter what they did. They wanted simply to forge the best deal they could out of the situation. Crook promised them that if all their land got taken, they would be resettled on good land at Rosebud. He also made a number of personal promises on a wide range of topics to reluctant signers.[23]

Up the Missouri at Cheyenne River, the commissioners also got the required signatures, but how they did so is shrouded in mystery. The Minneconjous adamantly opposed the treaty. A number of them were relative newcomers to reservation life, having settled at Cheyenne River after coming back from Canada with Sitting Bull. The leader of the Cheyenne River Indians was a man named Hump, one of Sitting Bull's allies. Hump and his people wanted no part of farming, and clung to their old ways. They were so resistant to signing that Crook finally left in fury. He told the agent and an army officer who remained at Cheyenne River to do as they wished to get the signatures. In two weeks, they signed up everyone—even Hump—but left no record of how they did so.[24]

The commission used similarly heavy-handed tactics at Standing Rock, where the Hunkpapas opposed the treaty as fervently as the Minneconjous had. Even progressive chief John Grass was determined not to sign. The commission worked around his opposition by telling him that it already had enough signatures to take the land. This was not true, but Agent James McLaughlin echoed it in a secret meeting with Grass. If his people did not sign, McLaughlin warned, they would lose their land and get nothing for it. The agent also promised that Crook would get Congress to pay for ponies the army had taken from Standing Rock and Cheyenne River Indians in 1876. Grass agreed to support the treaty. The next day, as the Hunkpapas with Grass were preparing to sign, Sitting Bull and his people rode in, furious, from their camp on Grand River. He had not been told of the council, Sitting Bull said, and he demanded to address the meeting. Agency police held the chief and his men back while McLaughlin shepherded the rest of the men to the table to have their names recorded.[25]

Crook begged and bullied to get the signatures he needed. He insisted that the land agreement would not affect rations. He promised not to force Indians onto allotments until a majority wanted the land divided; he said he would try to get Indians rather than whites hired for agency jobs. He assured the Indians that he would see that the construction and funding of schools and gristmills, and the provision of farm animals, long ignored by government agents, would finally be accomplished. Crook used a number of tactics to divide the Indians, making presents to individuals, taking men aside for private conferences, and suggesting that those who held out would not get the same benefits as those who signed.

Crook also permitted the white husbands of Sioux women—known as squaw men—to sign, counting them as full-blood Sioux to reach the number of signatories necessary to adopt the measure.[26]

Later, Crook would insist that he had never promised the Indians anything, that he had only assured the Sioux that he would press for their concerns to be considered in Washington. But there was no doubt that the Sioux had signed only after receiving what they believed were his personal promises to see that the government would address long-standing Indian grievances.[27]

Crook was adamant that the Indians needed to sign, in part, perhaps, because he suspected that they would lose their land one way or another. While the Treaty of Fort Laramie had established that three-quarters of the Sioux men would have to approve changes to the Indian reservation, that requirement had been thrown out the window before. In 1876, the Sioux lost the Black Hills under a treaty approved by only a handful of chiefs under the threat of losing all rations unless they signed. Crook had reason to suspect that the government might do something similar in 1889, as pressure built to turn Dakota Territory into two new states. Only by signing could the Indians hope to receive anything for the loss of their land. Time was short. A constitutional convention had been called for July 4, 1889, in Sioux Falls to adopt a state constitution and prepare for the Territory to enter the Union.[28]

By August 6, Crook and his men had the requisite number of signatures. Traditional leaders disliked the deal the American government had handed them, but the majority of Indians had eventually agreed to sign. They did so for different reasons. Some signed after fervent assurances that the Indians would be paid for the land and for ponies surrendered a decade before, and that money and supplies guaranteed by treaty but often absent would be forthcoming. Some, like American Horse, signed because they saw a more prosperous future for their people—and themselves—if they worked with the government. American Horse was not widely popular with the Sioux, though, and was backed by only a small following, primarily of his kin. Others had signed in desperate hope and under duress. Eventually, even Gall, the man who led the charge against Custer at the Battle of the Little Bighorn, signed. "I have given my consent . . . my Indians have signed because I told them to after learning the Government could take our lands for nothing if it wanted to. The whites have now got our lands, and I hope they will be satisfied and let us live in peace in the future."[29]

Not everyone was willing to take this desperate gamble, though. Indians like Sitting Bull, and those younger men who didn't trust Americans or didn't want to give up their culture, clung to the world they had known as youngsters, when they supplied their own needs from the buffalo hunt, protected their own kin, rode over their wide territory, and lived as free men. In 1890, that way of life was only twenty years behind them; but with the decimation of the buffalo and the reduction of their hunting lands, it had vanished completely. Sitting Bull did all he could to defeat the treaty, and the signing disgusted him. In the end, even his old ally Gall had defected. When a reporter asked Sitting Bull what the opening of the reservation would mean for the Indians, the old leader replied bitterly: "Don't talk to me about Indians; there are no Indians left except those in my band. They are all dead, and those still wearing the clothes of warriors are only squaws. I am sorry for my followers, who have been defeated and their land taken from them."[30]

The 1889 land agreement brought disastrous changes to the Sioux. According to Congress, they had agreed to part with fully half their land. From now on, the different bands of the Sioux would be divided onto six different reservations, although about 2,000 of the 10,500 Brulé were entered against their will onto the rolls at Pine Ridge, where the Oglalas lived. While different groups would live on their own within the reservation boundaries, usually in log cabins along rivers or streams, they would have to come in to the agency for rations and supplies.[31]

Each agency was a little cluster of buildings, almost a town. At each, the government constructed a house for the agent and his family, a school, an office and living quarters for the agency doctor, a warehouse for the distribution of clothing and supplies, and perhaps a few houses for important Indian chiefs and others who were tied to the government. Traders and suppliers living locally also built their own structures for storing or selling goods to the Indians. Religious orders ran a church or chapel and perhaps put up other structures for worship. The wooden agency buildings stood up straight and square, alien on the rolling western hills.

• South Dakota Reservations •
Yellowstone R.
North Dakota
Bismarck
Heart River
Fort Abraham Lincoln
Fort Rice
Montana
Cannonball River
Standing Rock Agency
Missouri R.
Grand River
STANDING ROCK RESERVATION
Little Missouri R.
Moreau River
CHEYENNE RIVER RESERVATION
South Dakota
Cherry Cr.
Belle Fourche R.
Cheyenne River
Cheyenne River Agency
Fort Sully
Fort Pierre
Pierre
CROW CREEK RES.
BLACK HILLS
GREAT SIOUX RESERVATION
LOWER BRULÉ RES.
Wyoming
BADLANDS
White River
Missouri R.
PINE RIDGE RESERVATION
S. Fk. White R.
Rosebud Agency
ROSEBUD RESERVATION
Pine Ridge Agency
Wounded Knee
Fort Randall
Yankton
0 Miles 100
Niobrara R.
0 Kilometers 100
Nebraska
© 2010 Jeffrey L. Ward

At the agency, people worked, prayed, taught, studied, chatted, argued, and loafed. Teamsters moved supplies from the nearest railhead, their wagons rattling along behind horse teams as they pulled in to the agencies. Students tried to make sense of new clothing, new foods, and new ideas as they struggled over their books. Teachers, who were usually reformers determined to mold young Indians into modern Americans, cajoled and explained and probably lost their tempers. Chiefs and progressives who lived near the agencies tended their horses and farm animals, mended their fences, and tried to grow vegetables. Their wives nursed babies, cooked, and negotiated the two cultural worlds in which they lived. The agent either worked with or against his charges, depending on his temperament, as he tried to pull them into the modern world. On ration days, the agency buzzed with the influx of newcomers from the camps, and the atmosphere was cheerful. On other days, the agency doctor might be inundated with sick patients, and anxious relatives would spread their worry around the agency. Some days the agency might laze quietly in the summer heat.

A life that revolved around the agencies was a traumatic wrench for the Sioux, but eastern Republicans saw the cession of the Sioux lands as the rightful extension of the American economy westward. Easterners had been gazing longingly at those 11 million acres of land for years, and now they had them. For two months, prospective settlers had been camped on the eastern bank of the Missouri River waiting for the Sioux lands to become American lands. They cheered the news of the agreement and boasted that their friends would be coming along behind them. The *New York Times* predicted that the rush into the Dakotas would be even larger than the one into Oklahoma in April 1889, because the land in the Dakotas was of better quality and offered better prospects for success.[32]

Administration Republicans heralded the news of the land agreement and linked the "march of civilization" to economic prosperity for everyone. Every advance of civilization meant better crops, more traffic of goods and passengers on the railroads, and new businesses. They hastened to assure voters that the taking of the Sioux land had been accomplished under "the terms of the treaty made when the Indians were given the reservation," with no self-consciousness about using the word "given" in this context. While no one expected that the government would want to buy more land so soon, it noted, even "the Indians who . . . expected that they would rest quietly for the remainder of their lives, share in the amazement of foreign nations at the rapidity of the advance of our civilization."[33]

The Republicans also spun the organization of the Dakotas into states as the triumph of civilization over savagery. On July 6, two days after the South Dakota constitutional convention met, *Frank Leslie's* featured an article by a Republican railroad magnate and politician rhapsodizing about Custer "rough-riding over the unexplored Black Hills in search of the hostile Sioux" and explaining that mankind only advanced through dangers and bloodshed. Indeed, the glorious transformation of the Dakotas from wilderness to "happy and law-abiding settlements" was simply a continuation of the genius of America that had been set free by the patriots of 1776, the writer declared. A month later, another article in *Frank Leslie's* alluded to Custer once again to illustrate the steady march of civilization: "Many who even now are not of an age can recall the horror which followed the massacre of General Custer and his sturdy band of followers by the Sioux. The rapidity with which our material development progresses is revealed, in a remarkable way, by the fact that the scene of this bloody massacre is now about to be opened to settlement."[34]

While Republicans trumpeted their promotion of development and civilization, they were nonetheless forthright about the other agenda underlying their push to fill South Dakota with settlers. They made no secret of the fact they expected western Territories to support the Republican Party. In May 1889, elections for members of the constitutional conventions in the two Dakotas and Washington Territory had gone Republican. Montana went Democratic, but Republicans refused to accept that the people in the Territory leaned Democratic; instead they blamed the result on Democratic gerrymandering. In October 1889, congressional elections in North Dakota, South Dakota, and Washington confirmed that those Territories would come into the Union as Republican. *Frank Leslie's* counted the numbers: Republicans had garnered 169 seats to the Democrats' 161. Republican legislatures would also give six new Republicans to the Senate, which put the count in that body at forty-five Republicans and thirty-nine Democrats. *Frank Leslie's* reported the numbers, then explained what they meant: Republican supremacy in Congress was pretty much assured for the foreseeable future.[35]

Harrison's men were willing to manipulate elections and attack opponents to make sure this ascendancy would endure. When the Montana legislature threatened to go Democratic in 1889, Republicans simply threw out the Democratic votes, charging fraud. They did have to admit that a Democratic governor had won, although they insisted he had done so by fewer than three hundred votes. The governor, Joseph K. Toole, was so popular that he was reelected twice, but the Republicans tried to weaken him from his first day in office by constantly harping on what *Frank Leslie's* called his "arbitrary, partisan, we might almost say indecent official conduct."[36]

Montana might not have been firmly in the Republican camp, but South Dakota promised to be a Republican stronghold. The first South Dakota legislature met at Pierre on October 15, 1889. On the seventeenth, the legislators elected Republicans R. F. Pettigrew, a railroad promoter from Sioux Falls, and Gideon C. Moody, a machine Republican from Deadwood, as U.S. senators. The state was admitted to the Union on November 2, 1889. In honor of the occasion, Governor Mellette had had a state seal designed. The new seal carried the legend: "Under God the people rule."[37]

South Dakota did not come into the Union alone: In little over a week in November 1889, four new states entered the Union. On Saturday, November 2, President Harrison also proclaimed North Dakota a state. That Friday, November 8, he welcomed Montana to the Union, and the following Monday, November 11, he declared Washington a state.[38]

Just as they had planned in February, the Republicans had added three Republican states to the Union, and had come close to grabbing a fourth. The West was the key to maintaining national political power, and it looked as though Harrison's men had managed to claim the region for themselves. Republican dominance in the new western states, *Frank Leslie's* pointed out, would tip the scale of the parties, which had been perilously balanced for more than a decade. The votes of the new states would virtually assure the Republicans the presidency in 1892.[39]

On the reservations, it appeared that the dire predictions of the traditionalists who had opposed the land agreement were coming true. Opponents of the treaty had warned the signers that the whites were not to be trusted. Once they had taken the land, they would try to starve the Sioux to death. Crook and his negotiators had sworn that this was ridiculous, that rations had absolutely nothing to do with the treaty. Indeed, at Rosebud, Crook had put in writing his promise that the treaty would not in any way affect rations or the distribution of clothing and supplies, and he had made similar promises elsewhere. Crook was not lying to the Sioux—rations and the land treaty really did not have anything to do with each other on the government's account books. Nonetheless, just as soon as the treaty went back to Washington, food rations decreased.[40]

The business of providing the Indians with rations was a muddle of dishonesty. Twice a month since they had been assigned to agencies, the Sioux had packed up their belongings—their tents, tent-poles, bedding, clothing, frying pans, and pails—and traveled to the agency by horseback or wagon for rations. Once there, the Indians set up their tents, families visited, marriageable girls dressed in their colorful finery, people traded at the agency store. The procuring of the beef issue was the highlight of a ration day. On the day of the issue, the agents would indicate which of the wild long-horned Texas cattle were allotted for the different bands. The young men of the band would chase the beef on horseback to kill it, a custom that reformers desperate to "civilize" the Indians had long been trying to suppress, because they believed it made Indians remember the buffalo chase and disdain farming. Once the beef was killed, the chief of the band distributed the meat amongst the families. Soon cooking pots steamed with boiling meat while women cut the beef into thin strips to dry. Along with rations of flour, coffee, and other supplies, the dried meat would have to last until the next distribution day.[41]

According to the Treaty of Fort Laramie, the quantity of rations the Sioux received was determined by their population. But the reality was that the system of providing Indian rations was a macabre game in which both sides fudged numbers to try to get the best deal they could. Agents were required to provide a certain number of pounds of beef per person, but that number had been falling as officials had illegally cut rations over the course of the 1870s. By the early 1880s, the Sioux were receiving only about two-thirds of their legal allotments of beef.[42]

Contributing to the swindling of the Sioux was the fact that the treaty did not stipulate when the beef would be weighed. As a result it became standard practice for the cattle traders to sell beef to the agents in the fall, when the animals were at their maximum heft. Over a Dakota winter, those same beeves could lose up to a third of their weight, reducing the animals to skin and bone before they were distributed as Indian rations. Beef was not the only problem. Across the board, provisions were rarely adequate. Flour was often spoiled, clothing late or poorly made, and so on, down the whole list of provisions allotted to the Sioux by treaty.[43]

The Indians, in turn, had their own ways of fighting back against the inadequate supplies. They inflated their numbers by moving children from one family to another during population counts and hushing up the deaths of family members. This subterfuge meant that they managed to keep their rations at about what they should have been.[44]

This unsavory equilibrium suddenly tipped immediately after the Sioux accepted the 1889 land cession. Just weeks after the Sioux commission left South Dakota, government officials cut Sioux rations. There was not a direct connection between the treaty and the reduction in rations, although both were outgrowths of the Republican determination to push economic development in the West.

The decision to cut rations came from an official who had been appointed thanks to an alliance between Indian reformers and Republican politicians. Both groups believed that the Sioux must be pushed into the American way of life, although they had different reasons for this conviction. Reformers wanted to drag Indians out of their culture to save their souls and their lives; politicians wanted to get traditionalist Indians out of the way so Americans could have their lands for economic development. Because their goals were similar, they were able to agree on General T. J. Morgan as Commissioner of Indian Affairs when President Harrison took office. While this appointment seemed providential to reformers and safe to politicians, it quickly became clear that Morgan's tenure would be devastating to the Sioux.[45]

Morgan was a man after President Harrison's own heart. He had served under Harrison during the Civil War and was a staunch supporter of his former commander. He was also a fervent Baptist who shared reformers' zeal for forcing Indians out of their traditional ways into Christianity. Passionate also in his determination to turn the Indians into good American citizens, he went so far as to prepare instructions for the agency schoolteachers on how to tell the children to celebrate important American holidays: Washington's birthday, Decoration Day, the Fourth of July, Thanksgiving, Christmas, and February 8, the day that the Dawes Severalty Act had become law. He encouraged teachers to have the students sing patriotic songs repeatedly until they had memorized them. He also urged the teachers to use discretion. When they were dealing with students, they "should carefully avoid any unnecessary reference to the fact that they are Indians."[46]

Morgan's zeal to do his work properly provoked an immediate crisis on the reservations. The Treaty of Fort Laramie provided that the Sioux would be counted every year to determine the correct amount of rations. In 1889, Morgan had appointed A. T. Lea, an ardent reformer with no sympathy at all for the Indians, to count the tribes. Lea had shown up early in the summer, before the Crook Commission arrived, to begin his count. His presence during the negotiations had undoubtedly been a factor in the Indians' fears that the land cession had something to do with rations. In August, Lea sent his numbers to Morgan, claiming that there were almost 2,500 fewer Indians on Rosebud than had been drawing rations; he reported similar inflations at the other agencies. It is unlikely that his count was accurate. He probably did not go out of his way to make sure he found every single individual on the Great Sioux Reservation, while the Indians, who feared the census counts, worked to elude him.[47]

Morgan promptly scaled back the beef allotment to reflect the new count. He cut 2 million pounds of beef from Rosebud, a million pounds from the Pine Ridge allotment, and similar amounts from the other agencies. General Crook, who had staked his honor on his assurances that rations would not be affected by the new treaty, protested, but Commissioner Morgan was firm. In the interests of "civilization," he also forbade the Sioux from eating offal—the heart, liver, reticulum, and kidneys of the beeves. Although he could not have known it in these very early days of nutritional science, his command robbed the Indians of crucial vitamins and minerals that were not available from the muscle meat to which he limited them.[48]

Morgan hid behind Congress to argue that he could not restore the cuts once they were made. In the same act that had created the Crook Commission, Congress had cut $100,000 out of the usual $1 million appropriation for Indian affairs. This cut enabled Morgan to insist that he could not restore regular rations. It would take a special act of Congress to do so, he claimed, although there was money in Indian trust accounts that he did not suggest using. Of course, Congress was unlikely to approve a restoration of funds, despite its profligacy on statues and courthouses and pensions for voters. Having already acquired the Sioux lands and eager to force the Indians into the exciting economic development they insisted the West was enjoying, Republican congressmen were in no hurry to provide extra food for the Sioux.[49]

The reduction in rations came at an especially unfortunate time. Crops had been poor in 1888 and 1889, and while settlers and Indians both were suffering, the Indians were worse off than their American neighbors. They had been summoned to the agencies during the growing season of 1889 for extended talks with the Crook Commission, and while they were away cattle had broken down their fences and destroyed what little was growing. Now, having signed away their hunting lands but still far from seeing any profit from the deal, Indians found their rations reduced at a time when they had no stores to fall back on. South Dakota settlers whose crops had failed could cut their losses and move back East, but the Indians had no similar option.

The cuts exacerbated the angry divide in Sioux communities between traditionalists and progressives. Traditional leaders blamed the progressive Indians, the mixed bloods, and the squaw men for having convinced members of the tribe to approve the treaty, thereby bringing on the reduction in rations that the traditionalists had always said would follow. The dire predictions of those who had opposed the land cession were being fulfilled, it seemed, and they were not slow to point this out to those who had backed the treaty. At the same time, the government rewarded the leaders who had approved the cession with goods and new houses, leading opponents to accuse them of being bought. The progressives became outcasts, mocked for their stupidity and accused of betraying their people. Those who had signed the treaty, in turn, railed against the Crook Commission.[50]

Crook and the other members of the Crook Commission were furious, too. The Interior Department politicians who oversaw Indian affairs had undermined the commissioners' credibility by abrogating the promises they had made to persuade the Sioux to sign the treaty. The commissioners arranged for a delegation of chiefs to go to Washington, where they could explain their distress and reiterate the expectations under which they had signed the treaty. Crook hoped that, in the process, the Indians might be convinced that the reduction in rations had not, in fact, been related to the cession.[51]

Led by progressive American Horse, a delegation of Sioux took their complaints to the capital. They conferred with Secretary of the Interior John W. Noble on December 18, telling him that they had signed the paper only conditionally. They counted on the fulfillment of Crook's promises, including his assurance that the government would finally honor the provisions of the old treaties by building schools and mills and providing farm implements.[52]

Noble assured the delegates that he would honor those of the commission's deals that came under his control—hiring Indians instead of whites at the agencies whenever possible, pushing forward gristmill construction, and ending the prohibition on "innocent dances," by which they meant the Sun Dance. Only Congress, though, he said, could replace the money that would accomplish the most important items on the delegates' list. Without more funds, Noble told them, he could not restore the beef allowance. Nor could he make reparations for the ponies taken from the Standing Rock and Cheyenne River Indians in 1876. Only Congress could authorize the money that would improve the reservation schools and provide adequate farming tools.[53]

The delegation's visit to President Harrison was an honor but netted no more commitments. American Horse and the other progressives returned to the reservation with nothing but more promises.[54]

After two years of drought, the Sioux faced the winter of 1889 to 1890 with little food and a great deal of resentment. The long, cold South Dakota winter exacerbated both their hunger and their anger. Underfed Indians entered the season easy prey to the epidemic of influenza that was sweeping the United States—and much of Europe as well—that year. It was a particularly deadly strain that spread virulently. The *Medical and Surgical Reporter* concluded that 12,000 people had died in the seven weeks "the grip" lasted in the East, but the Philadelphia *Press* thought that was low; 5,000 people died in New York alone. *Harper's*

Weekly mused that: "Nothing is more striking and mysterious than the sudden diffusion of such a malady over the globe."[55]

It seemed less mysterious in South Dakota, where the Sioux watched their hungry children and elderly die of influenza, whooping cough, and measles. At Pine Ridge, home to 5,550 Indians, forty-five people died in a single month. Even those who avoided the worst of the illnesses suffered from worms, stomach ailments, and respiratory viruses. As Indians attended one funeral after another, they concluded that the leaders in Washington had not only stolen the Indians' land but actually now wanted them to die.[56]

While not deliberately launching a program of extermination, the administration certainly did nothing to stop the crisis on the reservations. Harrison Republicans made it clear that they would not be sad to see the end of the Sioux. In January 1890, *Frank Leslie's* complained that "Indian banditti and the white highwayman of the hills" had made western travel difficult, but rejoiced that "these robbers" would soon disappear as settlers took over the land. Republicans were already planning what they would do when the Sioux were out of the way. Word leaked out that South Dakota Senator Pettigrew was backing the construction of a railroad from Sioux Falls to the Pacific, even though the land through which such a railroad would have to run had not yet been opened for settlement.[57]

Like Pettigrew, President Harrison clearly thought of the Sioux as obstacles to be brushed out of the path to economic growth. The president ignored the commitments of Crook and his commissioners and threw open the reservation for settlement on February 11, 1890, although none of the outstanding promises to the Indians had been fulfilled. The Republicans were firm friends of the railroads, and of the railroad men who were pushing the tracks west. Prospective settlers were in the towns on the borders of the reservation, so restive that the weary soldiers assigned to keeping them from the reservation land begged for reinforcements. Harrison and his advisers had much more interest in helping the railroad men and prospective settlers than in honoring the government's commitments to the Sioux.[58]

News that President Harrison had declared the lands open reached the settlers in South Dakota on the afternoon of February 12. The town of Pierre, on the eastern edge of the cession, was turned upside down as men raced to be the first into the reservation. Stores closed and the town emptied in the party atmosphere. Lumber wagons rumbled across the frozen Missouri River into the reservation, taking with them all the wood available. Railroad surveyors arrived within hours, running their lines over newly staked claims. Tempers flared, voices cracked, fists swung. Still more and more wagons jolted into the reservation. By nighttime, there were houses where in the morning there had been nothing but prairie.[59]

And yet despite the tremendous enthusiasm of the early settlers, the drought and hard economic times on the plains meant that the expected land boom never really materialized. Word was beginning to spread through the East that South Dakota was not the agricultural paradise railroad promoters had promised. Within a year, events in the West would confirm that life there was desperately hard, and few easterners would choose to cast their lot in South Dakota.

But administration Republicans refused to admit defeat. In March, *Frank Leslie's* ran a celebratory story about a small town in South Dakota, "A TOWN BUILT IN TWELVE HOURS," it claimed. Within an hour of the afternoon announcement that the land was open, a "town-site company" was laying out streets. Carpenters began to put up buildings at once, and they worked through the night. By morning, a town had appeared. Wagons hauled in goods, and stores filled their shelves. This "magic city" bore the name "Sherman."[60]

While the land rush was not as successful as Republicans hoped, it was nonetheless devastating for the Sioux. They had lost almost half their land. No longer able to hunt for enough game to feed themselves, they would be dependent on the government for food. They had also lost what remained of their cultural autonomy. Even those who resisted farming were now tied to agencies, where the agents could supervise and circumscribe their lives. In return for the loss of their land they had received nothing. Crook had not been able to deliver on his promises, and because settlers didn't snap up Sioux acreage as government agents had said they would, its value plummeted. Only land that sold in the first three years would bring in $1.25 an acre; for the next two years it would be 75 cents an acre, and then it would drop to 50 cents an acre, the same low price that the Sioux had utterly rejected when the Pratt Commission had tried to get them to sell in 1888. After two years of stubborn effort to protect their lands, the Sioux had lost them, and had received virtually nothing in return.

The Sioux had little defense against what *Frank Leslie's* described as the morally and physically civilizing influences of settlement, and they soon lost their key advocate. At Chicago's Grand Pacific Hotel, General Crook died of heart failure on March 21, 1890. Red Cloud told Father Francis Craft, a Catholic missionary: "Then General Crook came; he, at least, had never lied to us. His words gave the people hope. He died. Their hope died again. Despair came again."[61]

With Crook dead, the Sioux gave up on earthly aid and turned to another world for assistance. In March 1890, Short Bull from the Rosebud Reservation and Kicking Bear from Cheyenne River, along with five fellow travelers, returned home from a trip to Nevada bringing back with them the news that a prophet had foretold a new era in Indian history. The prophet's name was Wovoka, and he had seen a world renewed—a world where Indians lived without whites, a land of plenty, a land where the dead lived again. Short Bull and Kicking Bear had seen and heard Wovoka, and they believed he was a divine messenger. They had returned to their people to encourage them to help usher in the new world Wovoka foretold.[62]

Short Bull and Kicking Bear's news was not unexpected. Arapaho and Shoshone visitors from neighboring Wyoming had brought rumors of an Indian prophet to Pine Ridge as early as 1888. By the summer of 1889, while the Crook Commission was angling for signatures, letters from western tribes confirmed that a prophet had emerged at the base of the Sierra Nevada Mountains. In the fall of 1889, with news of the ration cuts just sinking in to the Sioux tribes, Red Cloud called a council at Pine Ridge, where Young-Man-Afraid-of-His-Horse, Little Wound, and American Horse, as well as chiefs from Rosebud and Cheyenne River, discussed the news of a rising prophet. They decided to send a delegation over the western mountains and into the desert they vaguely knew lay somewhere beyond to learn more about the new religion.[63]

Around the time of the new year, eleven emissaries set out, heading ultimately for Walker River Reservation in Nevada, near the prophet's home. The travelers included minor medicine man Short Bull and

Mash-the-Kettle, both from Rosebud, and Kicking Bear from Cheyenne River. Some of the men were, or had been, traditionalists who resisted eastern incursions. Both Short Bull, a squat man with a pronounced squint, and Kicking Bear, whose tendency to carry his shoulders forward gave him an unsettled stance, had been with Crazy Horse in 1876. Kicking Bear was Crazy Horse's cousin.[64]

The men headed due west over the Wyoming buttes to the Wyoming Wind River Reservation, where the Shoshone and Northern Arapaho lived. There they met delegates from tribes similarly curious about the prophet. Five Shoshones, three Northern Cheyennes, and an Arapaho joined the expedition. The travelers then took the Union Pacific Railroad from Wyoming through Utah's dramatic Wasatch Mountain Range and north to Fort Hall agency in Idaho, where they stayed for ten days.[65]

Fort Hall Reservation was a central hub for Indian communication over the mountains and a critical center for information about the new prophet. The Bannock and Shoshone people at the reservation roamed across the continental divide. There they were in close contact with the Northern Paiutes, whose language they spoke, and from whose numbers the prophet had arisen. On the eastern side of the mountains, the Shoshone socialized with the Arapaho, who had a reputation for their devotion to religious matters and who had embraced the new faith from the first. Four railroads converged on Fort Hall, making it an easy place for northern Plains Indians to reach, while the nearby main line of the Union Pacific Railroad made it easy to travel far away, as well. It was from Fort Hall that news of the prophet had first come to the Sioux, and it was at Fort Hall that the travelers picked up the latest talk about him from Nevada. There they also found five Bannocks and Shoshones who were willing to come with them and interpret the Paiute language.[66]

From Fort Hall, the pilgrimage to Nevada to see Wovoka began in earnest. The growing band of travelers took trains south and then westward, into lands dramatically different than they knew on the plains. In Utah, they stopped for a day at a town on the Great Salt Lake itself, where they marveled, perhaps, that such a broad stretch of water supported no fish. Their agents had warned the Indians that the people they would meet on their travels were "bad people." By this they meant the Mormons who lived in Utah and Nevada, who were pariahs in the late nineteenth century, still tainted in outsiders' eyes by their practice of polygamy (which the church would not outlaw until September 1890). The Sioux travelers, who had had plenty of experience with the opinions of government agents, no doubt reserved judgment about this warning, and they were pleasantly surprised to find the Mormons they met easy to get along with. They did not drink or fight or behave badly, and they provided the pilgrims with food and railroad passes. They had heard of the new Indian religion and treated it with respect. When pressed by an agent later for details about his trip, one of the travelers responded with a dig: "I thought it strange that the people should have been so good, so different from those here."[67]

The travelers then passed through the Great Basin that lies in the heart of Nevada. There they saw a landscape unlike anything they had known at home. Nevada was a dry land, where most rain fell on the tops of the rugged mountains that ridged the dry plains, less on their sides, and still less on the gritty flatlands. The mountaintops boasted ancient bristlecone pines and white firs, and the mountainsides sported purple fields of the spiky penstemon flower and low white phlox along with sagebrush and the famous loco weed—whose neurotoxins made the cattle they poisoned act crazy. But the dry valleys could grow only yucca, cactus, and twisted Joshua trees in the two to eight inches of annual rainfall dropped by summer storms.[68]

The landscape shaped the economy, and thus the relationship between the Indians and the settlers. The harshly beautiful environment helped to protect Indians from whites' greed for land, for the settlers had no need to scoop up unproductive land along with productive tracts. Indians lived in camps among the scattered cattle ranches, working for ranchers in the summer and going back to their traditional ways in the winter, hunting, fishing, and gathering seeds and pine nuts. The Paiutes had managed to maintain their own culture with less direct interference, and they interacted with settlers on terms closer to equality than the Sioux could. The travelers from the South Dakota reservations were struck by what they saw: "All the whites and Indians are brothers, I was told there," one traveler recalled. "I never knew this before."[69]

In Nevada, the emissaries found a world where everything seemed strange and new. While their own world was a dreary predictable clash between two cultures, one ancient and one just made, the world of Nevada Indians seemed exotic and rich. As they meandered southwestward on one railroad line after another, they met Indians wearing American clothes of good quality, Indian women with their hair cut into bangs in the new fashion some called a "lunatic fringe," Indian men with their faces painted white with black spots. The visitors met Indians who shocked them by living in houses made not of buffalo skins or logs, as the Sioux had been forced to when the buffalo disappeared, but of woven reeds laced onto a framework of poles with sagebrush fiber. The Paiute Indians who inhabited these wickiups dressed in white man's clothing, spoke English, and earned wages, but they retained their native culture. They foraged off the land and ignored white consumer goods, using their earnings primarily to buy guns and ammunition, blending two worlds in a way the Sioux had not managed.[70]

Arriving at Pyramid Lake agency, near present-day Reno, in early March, the travelers found a strange land. The air was warmer than it would be at home in early spring. It smelled of brine, with angular gray-white rock formations jutting out of cobalt blue, salty water. People from fifteen or sixteen different tribes were congregating at the agency to learn about the new prophet, mingling in their different kinds of clothing, speaking different languages. It was a world of novelty and possibility, where anything could happen. It was a world where they were welcome and, it turned out, expected. Their hosts greeted them with the announcement that Christ had reappeared. He had told them to watch for the arrival of pilgrims from the north.[71]

He also sent word that he would meet the visitors at the Walker Lake agency, about seventy miles to the south, in two weeks. With his message, he sent a package of pine nuts for his visitors to share, a food the northern travelers had never seen before. For the next fourteen days, the travelers mingled with the others at Pyramid Lake, seeing cultures they had not imagined existed. One traveler recalled with surprise that the Indians at Pyramid Lake ate fish. This diet seemed to fascinate the meat-eaters of the plains, and they continued to refer to the Northern Paiute as "Fish-eaters." Perhaps this description was a translation of the name of the people at Pyramid Lake agency, who were known as Cui Ui Ticutta, or eaters of the cui-ui, a dark gray and white suckerfish endemic to Pyramid Lake. The cui-ui and the larger, pink and brown spotted Lahontan cutthroat trout made up the bulk of the Northern Paiute diet.[72]

Wovoka was a prime example of a man who had combined his traditional culture with that of the settlers who had begun to push into his land in the 1840s. He did not live at Walker River Reservation, where he planned to meet his visitors. He lived about forty miles to the northwest, in Mason Valley, where as a teenager he had found work with a rancher after his father died. The rancher, a man named David Wilson, had taken Wovoka into his home, given him his white name—Jack Wilson—and had introduced him to English and Christianity. When he was a young man, Wovoka married. Although he continued to work for Wilson after his marriage, he also respected the ways of his father, whom he described as a "dreamer" with powers that made him invulnerable.[73]

About four years before, when he was around thirty, Wovoka had begun to follow his father, leading his people in spiritual matters. His great revelation had come two years before as he lay ill with pneumonia during a solar eclipse. In a vision that combined Christian traditions with Indian aspirations, he saw God, surrounded by Indian ancestors, happy and young in a land full of game as it was before the settlers came. God told him that the Indians must live at peace among themselves and with the settlers, that they must work hard and forbear lying or stealing. To this peaceful state of mind, they must also add action. God gave Wovoka instructions for a five-day dance the people must perform periodically. If they did these things, the Indians would be reunited with their ancestors in a world where there was no sickness or death.[74]

God charged Wovoka to "take charge of things in the west, while 'Governor Harrison' would attend to matters in the east." He gave Wovoka control over the rain and snow, and told him to go out and teach his people.[75]

After the visitors had been at Pyramid Lake for two weeks, they set out on the seventy-mile trip to Walker Lake to meet the prophet. There, they joined a throng of other visitors, perhaps as many as a few hundred. When they arrived, they learned that Wovoka was not expected for two more days. On the morning of the third day, the visitors cleared all the brush and grass from a circle in front of the agency. They waited with growing anticipation and anxiety throughout the afternoon and into the dusk.[76]

Just before sunset, a few whites and a large number of Indians dressed in white people's clothes escorted Wovoka to the agency. Some of the visitors saw the prophet's band form a ring around the cleared space and build up a fire, so that Wovoka could be seen as he sat quietly on the edge of the grass. Others saw smoke descend from heaven, leaving behind a good looking man dressed in white man's clothes and moccasins. He was big, with broad cheekbones, a narrow jaw, and smooth black hair cropped in a straight line below his ears. The crowd held silent in the flickering light while Wovoka bowed his head under his white sombrero. At last he looked up. "My children, I want you to listen to all I have to say to you. I will teach you, too, how to dance a dance, and I want you to dance it. . . . When the dance is over, I will talk to you."[77]

Wovoka taught his followers the Ghost Dance. The Sioux visitors were certainly familiar with dancing, but this particular dance was novel to them. The traditions of the Paiute, which informed the Ghost Dance, were different from those of the northern Indians. The Sioux did not normally hold hands or move in a circle when they danced, but these things were central to the Ghost Dance. The dancers held hands and shuffled in a circle, singing special songs that heralded the return of the old world. As they moved together in the dark for hours, Sioux dancers could feel the rebirth of Indian unity through the hands they clasped on either side, their brothers and sisters joining with them in a sacred hoop.[78]

Also new to the Sioux men was the central feature of the dance: the trance into which participants fell. While visions were common in Sioux life, they were usually private experiences that a visionary would relate later. In the Ghost Dance, though, individuals fell from the circle in trances and, upon regaining consciousness shortly afterward, would tell others what they had seen. This gave the dance enormous power. Individuals danced in the hope of seeing deceased relatives, and when they did, the visions assured them that their loved ones were well and happy.[79]

After the travelers had danced for two nights, Wovoka explained to them his revelations. If the Indians would live in peace with the whites, stop quarrelling among themselves, work hard, and not lie or steal, they would be reunited with friends and relatives who had died. Illness, aging, and death itself would end. The ancestors would bring back the old world by herding game before them as they returned from the spirit realm. A new land would cover the old, ruined one, covering the whites and any Indian who refused to embrace the new doctrine.[80]

To bring this paradise on earth, Wovoka instructed, Indians had to dance the Ghost Dance on five successive days, repeating the sequence periodically until the new world came. He gave the visitors white paint and paint of red ochre from the nearby mountains to decorate themselves as they danced. He also told them to cut the head, tail, and feet off any buffalo they killed, enabling it to spring back to life. If the Indians did as he bade them, Wovoka assured his audience, the world would be renewed, probably in the spring of 1891, when a big flood would wash away all nonbelievers.[81]

Observers disagreed about whether Wovoka was a prophet or Christ himself, returned to earth, but at least some of the Sioux seeing him at Walker Lake apparently believed he was divine. Telling the audience that he bore wounds on his hands, feet, and back inflicted by white people, Wovoka explained that God blamed the whites for his crucifixion, and had sent his son Wovoka back to the Indians, since the whites were bad. If the soldiers tried to arrest him, he promised, he would open his arms wide and make them disappear, or the earth would swallow them.[82]

Not everyone was convinced of Wovoka's special relationship to God. Cheyenne visitor Tall Bull was one of those who asked Wovoka for some proof of his divine powers. Wovoka obliged, sitting on the ground with his sombrero between him and the skeptics. He waved eagle feathers over the empty hat and then pulled something out of it. The Cheyenne saw only "something black" in his hand and allowed as how Cheyenne medicine men could do as well. Believers watching the same event, though, saw Wovoka wave eagle feathers over his hat and, after he had taken his hand from the bowl of the sombrero, saw "the whole world" left behind inside it.[83]

While the Sioux travelers left no record of their conversion to the new religion, their later actions indicated that they were fervent about it. Shortly after meeting Wovoka, the Sioux pilgrims left the excitement and promise of Walker Lake to take the Ghost Dance back to their people. They found their faith proved on the way home by a series of miracles. They later recounted that on their journey they had met a man and a woman long dead, who were living in a fine buffalo-skin tepee. The decimation of the buffalo had put such homes out of reach for living Sioux. Then a herd of buffalo crossed their path, another rare sight on the ravaged plains. They killed one and, cutting off its feet, head, and tail, as Wovoka commanded, saw it come back to life. Wovoka also shortened their journey for them, they recalled, moving them closer to home while they slept after they had asked him for help in their travels.[84]

Their faith in Wovoka carried the travelers back to the bleakness of late winter in South Dakota. While they had been gone, hunger and disease had continued to stalk the reservations. The weather-beaten prairies promised spring but were not yet producing anything green to eat when the travelers got to Pine Ridge.

Word of their experiences and the promise of the new religion inspired the Sioux to call a council to hear the travelers' account of their adventure, but the initiative didn't get far at first. One of the Pine Ridge agent's men passed news of the excitement to Agent Hugh D. Gallagher, who threw three of the Pine Ridge enthusiasts into jail for two days. They refused to tell him what the ferment was about, but his antagonism curtailed plans for a council.[85]

Meanwhile, the Indians from other reservations had left Pine Ridge and headed home to their own people. At Rosebud, Short Bull and Mash-the-Kettle immediately began to tell their relatives about the messiah, causing the Brulés to neglect the fields they were supposed to be planting. The Rosebud agent, J. George Wright, who had been appointed only six months before, sent his Indian police to find out what all the fuss was about. They brought Short Bull and Mash-the-Kettle back to the agency, where Wright demanded they stop their agitation. They pretended to agree, then went farther away from the agency, where the police could not monitor them, and resumed their dancing.[86]

The Ghost Dance spread to the northern reservations. Kicking Bear went home to Cheyenne River and started the dancing among the Sioux there. With its promise of the old world's return, the Ghost Dance was especially attractive to the Cheyenne River Minneconjou. Some of the converts had been with Sitting Bull in Canada and had been settled on the reservation less than a decade before. They welcomed the news that their old way of life was coming back. Afraid that the agent and the Indian police would try to stop them, they danced sixty miles away from the agency, out of their reach. Kicking Bear needn't have worried; the agent didn't think the new religion would amount to much.[87]

And it seemed as though he might be right. The Sioux caught the religious fire only briefly before it flickered out. Kicking Bear and his followers summoned other Sioux to a council at Cheyenne River to learn the Ghost Dance, but the agents at Pine Ridge and Rosebud refused to let the Oglalas and Brulés on those reservations attend. The hostility of agents Gallagher and Wright weakened the religion among the Pine Ridge and Rosebud Indians generally. Their flagging enthusiasm dampened the fervor of the Minneconjou at Cheyenne River, too. Kicking Bear, probably disgusted at his people's apparent neglect of spiritual matters, went to visit a properly religious folk, the Arapaho in Wyoming. It seemed the Sioux had failed him in their ultimate indifference to the new religion.[88]

In the late spring of 1890, life on the reservations resumed its usual course. Fields were planted, and the season promised well. But some of the local settlers had noticed the new Indian religion. On May 8, 1890, an article in the *Chadron Democrat*, the newspaper in the town closest to Pine Ridge (although it was actually located across the border in Nebraska), noted that a messiah had appeared among the Indians in Montana. A week later the paper's editor, Charles W. Allen, published a longer article about the Ghost Dance, clearly based on the accounts of the travelers. While Allen made fun of the new religion, his article noted a new aspect of the movement that made settlers uneasy. According to Allen, the root of Ghost Dancing lay in the belief the Christ had abandoned the white men because of their wickedness, wickedness especially evident in their theft of Indian land. They had taken the land and promised to pay for it with provisions, but instead were starving the Indians. By their actions, the whites had given up their right to salvation. Now Christ was coming to save the Indians and, Allen said, "kill off all the whites."[89]

Despite the growing calm on the reservations, rumors of an Indian uprising reached Washington in early June. The Commissioner of Indian Affairs wrote to ask the agents if such a rumor could be true. No, they each answered. There were indeed rumors of a messiah in the West, but they predicted that the religious enthusiasm would run its course and expire when the promised millennium failed to materialize.[90]

The agents at Standing Rock and Rosebud did, however, use this opportunity to complain about the men on their reservations who were exercising an "evil influence." Men like Crow Dog at Rosebud and Sitting Bull at Standing Rock had opposed the 1889 treaty and continued to needle the progressives who had backed it, especially when, as they had predicted, rations had been cut. Politicians' fears of an uprising might provide the excuse the agents needed to exact revenge on the traditionalists whom they perceived as stirring up discord.[91]

Standing Rock agent James McLaughlin took the lead in trying to get rid of the traditionalists. He hated Sitting Bull for his attachment to the old ways, and suggested this would be a good time to have him arrested, although he had no crime to charge him with except his refusal to accept the new order of things quietly. While there was no planned uprising, McLaughlin wrote, there were "malcontents" at the agencies who refused to accept modernity and were trying to hold their people back. They were slowing down the Indians' progress. Removing a handful of traditionalists like Sitting Bull would end all the trouble, he predicted.[92]

It was not a crime, however, to dislike government policies, and the Commissioner of Indian Affairs did not to attempt to have the powerful traditionalists arrested. Still, the brief flirtation of the Sioux with the Ghost Dance in the spring of 1890 combined with the antagonism of the agents to plant seeds that would bear poisonous fruit. Agents equated Ghost Dancers with traditionalists, who were famous for their hostility to American expansion, the same hostility that had, in the past, left hundreds of people dead. While the agents dismissed the danger of the Ghost Dancers, other Americans would not.

By June, it seemed like the Ghost Dance had run its course. Warm weather and spring rains had given Indians more faith in this world and less need for divine intervention. Crops promised well for those that had managed to get seed wheat—an easier proposition for reservation Indians, to whom it was provided, than for settlers, who had to borrow to buy it because their own crops had been too poor the previous year to give them a surplus for seed. Beginning in May, regular storms had brought rain to the plains just in time to nourish the new crops. Both Indians and settlers faced the summer with hope.[93]

Western promoters bristled with renewed confidence, insisting that farmers still complaining about poor conditions had brought their problems on themselves. With the promise of bumper Dakota crops, they claimed, farmers had indulged in foolish extravagances. They had gone into debt to buy expensive harvesters, and then had left them in the fields in all weather to rust. They had wasted their money on expensive goods and fancy foods, living better than they had ever dreamed of before. They had spent their cash down to the last penny, boosters claimed, making them unable to ride out poor seasons. The problems of farmers on the Plains were wholly of their own making. Any hardworking farmer in the Dakotas could succeed. The trick was to avoid profligacy.[94]

This rosy optimism was short-lived. In July, hot winds swept the Plains. Relentlessly, they burned up the promise of the spring. Vegetable gardens were the first to bake. Then the crops withered and died. Finally, even the native hay crop turned brown and dry.[95]

Indians and settlers alike were hungry and desolate. Elaine Goodale, who had become a school inspector, visited the reservations in the heat of the summer. She saw the Indians' pitiful gardens shriveling in the hot winds. Everyone was gaunt and exhausted, she recorded, even the young men. But the heat took its worst toll on infants and the elderly. They died. Brokenhearted mothers mourned their dead babies.[96]

Farmers suffered in the heat, too. Their crops died; they couldn't pay the mortgages on their farms or the notes on their machinery. Slowly, they, too, began to starve. Settlers who had come to the Dakotas from the East either organized to demand relief from the government or turned around and went home.

Indians, though, had no political influence and no choice but to stay. They were bewildered, an observer noted, by the political machinations that had brought them to such distress and offered them no relief.[97]

Rather than helping them, in fact, it appeared the government had plans to make things worse. The census that had begun the previous summer and had resulted in such a disastrous cut to rations was under way again. The Indians were afraid of the count, and rightly so. Census agent A. T. Lea opposed providing food to Indians, and his earlier work had brought the Sioux to the brink of starvation. The Indian Commissioner and the administration were both openly advocating that the government cut Sioux rations further and spend money instead on books, plows, and farming tools to make the Indians self-sufficient. This plan made great sense to anyone trying to move the Sioux into the American economy, but it did not fit either the needs of the Indians or the environment of the Plains.[98]

The Sioux refused to cooperate with the census count. Some bands refused to be counted, others threatened to bolt to agencies to which they hoped to be transferred, and still others, angry at the land cession, moved as far away from their agencies as possible and called for others to join them. To keep the Indians tractable during the census count, Secretary of the Interior John Noble called in the army. Soldiers camped outside of Pine Ridge and Cheyenne River Reservations in the summer of 1890.[99]

The presence of troops on the reservations sounded an ominous note for the starving Sioux. It might be time to turn to another world for help. This one had surely turned bad.

CHAPTER 4

Managing the West

FARMERS AS WELL as Indians were uneasy in South Dakota in the burning summer of 1890, and their restlessness upset the administration. Crops were withering and dying, leaving farmers hungry and short of cash while prices for food and consumer goods remained high. To the dismay of many western Republicans who expected the government to act in their interests, the administration seemed not to care about their plight. Harrison's people were firmly in the corner of eastern industrialists, and the core issue for businessmen, the issue above all others, was the tariff. Harrison's men were determined to give industrialists the tariff they wanted, even if it squeezed the suffering farmers. Before the election, Republicans had promised to revise the tariff as soon as Congress convened in December 1889, and Republican farmers had willed themselves to believe that the anticipated revisions would help them. But by the following summer, congressional leaders had made it clear instead that the revision would reflect the desires of businessmen. Western Republicans, like many other party members, were increasingly unhappy with the Republican administration, and their allegiance was wavering.[1]

Administration men had made their governing ideology clear as soon as they had taken office. When congressional Republicans began to organize the House of Representatives in December 1889, they indicated that the machine wing of their party would run roughshod over the rest of the representatives. For Speaker of the House, they elected Thomas B. Reed, a tall, heavy-set man with a baby face and a rapier wit delivered in the Down East drawl he acquired in his native state of Maine. He was the ultimate party man. In charge of making committee assignments and enforcing rules, Reed consistently interpreted things to favor administration Republicans. Occasionally, he even invented rules to silence opponents and make sure his people could push their policies through the House.[2]

By February 1890, his partisan caprices infuriated even moderate Republicans. *Harper's Weekly*, a Republican magazine, complained that "under the discretion of a relentlessly partisan Speaker," the House was attempting "to do business without rules."[3]

Under Reed and his men, tariff reform would be undertaken by committed protectionists without any input from representatives of the farming or laboring constituencies that were eager for lower rates. Reed stacked the House Committee on Ways and Means, which would write new tariff legislation, with hard-core pro-business party cronies. The thirteen-member committee would have two New Yorkers, while Reed cut the entire agricultural South down to a single representative. At the head of the committee he placed William McKinley, a Harrison stalwart. The rules of the House meant that, as head of the Ways and Means Committee, McKinley would also sit on the Rules Committee, helping his colleagues tinker with procedures to help control tariff debates. On the same day that *Harper's Weekly* complained that the House was doing business without rules, *Frank Leslie's* assured readers that the tariff would be reformed by its friends, who would work quickly and thoroughly. The result would be a new law that would be satisfactory to protectionist Republicans, the paper promised.[4]

Despite *Frank Leslie's* unbridled enthusiasm, however, the administration was facing a genuine challenge to tariff revision. By the spring of 1890, the economy was sliding into a recession that some people—even some Republicans—worried was about to become a serious depression. Wages had dropped over the course of 1889 and in the beginning of 1890 showed every sign of continuing to slide. Workers' distress was part of a larger business slump. Each week, the stock market refused to show an uptick no matter what the administration promised would happen with a firmly pro-tariff policy.[5]

Privately, Harrison and his cabinet officers were anxious. The tight money market worried them for both economic and political reasons. Although the administration refused to acknowledge it, Republican economic policies had created a hazardous level of speculative investment in western railroads as well as the dangerous inequalities of wealth that were driving the nation into a panic. Publicly, however, Harrison's Republicans resolutely refused responsibility for the troubles and blamed an assortment of other culprits for the economic downturn. Regulations hurt business, they insisted; the Interstate Commerce Law that regulated railroads was "communism." The Democrats were at fault, they said; complaints about the tariff were making businessmen nervous. The problem was volatile foreign markets, they suggested. They even complained that bad weather kept investors from trading.[6]

Harrison's men refused to admit their economic policies had anything to do with creating the trouble, but they were incredibly eager to fix it. Their solution was higher tariffs. They insisted that more protection for American industry would permit more businesses to grow, and those new businesses would hire more workers. Once employed, workers could begin the climb to prosperity, earning higher wages according to their worth. While higher tariffs did not explicitly address the problem of slipping wages, they were nonetheless the key to an upward spiral for all Americans, Republicans maintained. In February 1890, *Frank Leslie's* predicted that Harrison's promise to protect the tariff would give businessmen confidence and make 1890 the first year of a new era of extraordinary prosperity. It told readers to "Watch and see."[7]

But the administration's tariff policy flew in the face of the opinions of a growing majority of Americans. Those suffering in the faltering economy were more enthusiastic about lowering the tariff to make goods cheaper than they were about waiting and watching for an economic miracle. As the economy continued to suffer and businessmen continued to profit, anti-tariff forces gained momentum.

Democrats pushed tariff reform aggressively. On December 31, 1889, the Massachusetts Tariff-Reform League invited Congressman Roger Q. Mills of Texas, chief sponsor of the Mills Bill of 1888, to speak at its annual dinner. Although the rhetorical flourishes in his speech made a coherent argument elusive, Mills managed to communicate that high tariffs promoted monopoly, destroyed competition, and slowed consumption by keeping prices high. Americans needed foreign markets to sell their surplus, and they should not worry about the competition of foreign goods, because their products were the best in the world. High tariffs were a product of big manufacturers' "sordid greed and selfishness," which stifled American genius. To reform the tariff and restore American greatness, Mills called on "a race of men who severed a continent from despotism and dedicated it to free men, free government, free institutions, free thought, free speech, free labor and free trade." The event gave tariff reform "a splendid boom," according to the *Boston Globe*. Two hundred of New England's leading men attended, and a reference to ex-president Grover Cleveland, the front-runner for the 1892 Democratic presidential nomination, "brought everybody up like an electric shock, and a scene of the wildest and most deafening enthusiasm ensued."[8]

Far more dangerous to the Harrison administration than Democratic enthusiasm was the fact that moderate Republicans were also swinging away from it on the issue of protection. *Harper's Weekly* had begun to argue that high tariffs were a sort of welfare for business, leading to the very sort of centralized government that Republicans should oppose. High tariffs created treasury surpluses, which bred "extravagance, corruption, and jobbery" as politicians spent profligately to keep themselves in office. Even worse, it seemed a short step from high tariffs to "socialism or communism," for if the government could protect businesses at the expense of laborers, it would only be a question of time before labor interests demanded the same government protection.[9]

Worried about the growing strength of anti-tariff forces by the fall of 1889, Harrison Republicans sought to undermine popular support for free trade. They admitted that antitrust sentiment was stirring up politics, but they insisted such sentiment was ill informed. *Frank Leslie's* argued that business competition was actually more dangerous for the people than monopoly—although it didn't explain why—and claimed that if one-third of those businesses still operating could be absorbed by the other two-thirds, those left would better serve their customers and workers both. To counter the pernicious forces of tariff reform, the newspaper suggested that trust officers should give stock to hostile legislators to buy their support. It also called for the men who managed trusts to push reporters to write stories explaining that business combinations served the public good. Pro-tariff men were creative in their propaganda efforts. In the fall of 1889, protectionists made it a point to celebrate the hundredth anniversary of the nation's first tariff bill, which had been signed by President Washington, although the nature of late nineteenth-century tariffs was radically different than those of a hundred years before.[10]

Pro-tariff Republicans not only attacked the policies of the free traders, but also made personal attacks on the individuals who wanted lower tariffs. They impugned the loyalty of Democratic free traders, charging that Democrats who backed the Mills Bill were from the states that had supported slavery before the Civil War and could not shake their fondness for the institution. Tariff reformers from the South either wanted to turn white workers into slaves, or were so woefully ignorant that they didn't understand finance. Anyone who needed proof of their backwardness on that score had only to look at the Confederates' financial failure, *Frank Leslie's* chortled.[11]

Protectionists were hostile to all Democrats, but the majority of their venom was reserved for Grover Cleveland, who they feared might win again in 1892. According to pro-tariff Republicans, Cleveland was a broken old man who wanted the office for the spoils it would bring. He was a liar. He was a glutton who ate so much he was gaining twenty-five pounds a month. "The fat of his neck lies over the collar of his shirt and coat in three heavy folds," *Frank Leslie's* alleged.[12]

The Republicans' relentless attacks on their opponents did not manage to sway voters' growing belief that the administration was out of touch with what was happening in the nation. Mrs. Harrison had drawn up plans for a $700,000 extension of the White House with conservatories, winter gardens, and a statuary hall, "so as to make it a fit home for the Presidential family." *Frank Leslie's* thoroughly endorsed the initiative: Russell Harrison editorialized that it was "shameful" for the head of the nation to be forced to live in cramped quarters, although observers noted that the cramping came from the fact that the president's extended family—including Russell Harrison's wife and child—had moved into the White House with the president and first lady.[13]

The Harrisons weren't the only Republicans to complain about the confines of their luxurious lifestyle while the rest of the country went broke. Speaker Reed's wife added her two cents, complaining that the $5,000 annual salary of a representative was inadequate, even though it was five times more than most Americans made. She explained that political families needed more money because their expenses were so high. Politicians' wives, for example, had a social position to keep up; they had to have suitable gowns and a carriage, and every woman knew just how expensive those were.[14]

As the weakening economy threw urban laborers out of work and the brutally hot summer of 1890 baked dry the gardens of the Sioux and fields of western settlers, anti-Republican sentiment spread. By the summer of 1890, the administration realized that name calling and cheery promises of prosperity were not enough to quiet the growing clamor against the tariff. Pro-tariff Republicans knew that they had to solidify their power to keep control of the government. Turning their eyes to the upcoming midterm elections, and with the presidential election of 1892 on the horizon, they planned an aggressive campaign to rig the electoral system to the Republicans' advantage.[15]

Ballot reform was the first item on the Republican agenda. Americans had been flirting with the idea of cleaning up the voting system for a number of years. Their inspiration came from the other side of the world, where in 1856 Australians had adopted a secret ballot in place of public voting. Reformers in America wanted to purify elections by adopting a similar system. Republicans adopted the language of ballot reform in 1890, but their real goal was to skew the vote toward their candidates, not to purify the system.

In the nineteenth century, American voting was much more public than it is today and was largely controlled by party leaders. Ballots were printed by the political parties, and listed only the names of each party's own candidates. A voter did not have to mark the ballot, and he couldn't "split the ticket," voting for some of his party's candidates but not others. He simply handed his party's ballot to a voting official in a public place crowded with onlookers, often a saloon. To make certain an illiterate voter couldn't be duped into voting for the wrong party, and to guarantee that he couldn't promise to vote one way but then quietly switch, parties color-coded their ballots. Everyone knew how a man voted, and votes were often for sale—either indirectly, as party bosses brought whiskey to the polls and made sure supporters got jobs from cooperative employers, or directly, with cash bribes. The system was wide open for abuse, and party officials constantly charged their opponents with bribery, stuffing ballot boxes, illegally throwing out votes, miscounting, and so on.[16]

The voting system implemented in Australia, and increasingly popular in America by 1890, promised to clean up this system. It would make voting secret and limit participation to men who could read, those citizens who, reformers presumed, would vote intelligently rather than at the behest of a party machine. Under the new program, government officials rather than political bosses would prepare a single ballot, which would be used by all voters. Men would mark the ballots in private voting booths, in a polling place designed solely for that purpose, rather than in a saloon or other public gathering place. After the ballots were marked, government officials would gather them, count them, and report the results.

Massachusetts adopted the secret ballot first, in 1888, and the next year nine other states followed suit, adopting most of the tenets of the Australian ballot, although they each had their own quirks. In 1890, still more states undertook to reform their voting systems.[17]

But the new idea was not universally popular, by any means. Political bosses didn't like it, of course, nor did the owners of the establishments that had previously been used for balloting. Opponents complained that the secret ballot would disfranchise the illiterate, take too long as voters pondered their decisions, and create great confusion.[18]

Still, many Americans gravitated toward the idea that the voting system must be cleaned up. Few were principled advocates of pure elections, though. Most wanted to purge elections of voters who supported the other party. In discussions of ballot reform, members of both parties criticized the corruption of the ballot, but each pointed to the transgressions of the other side. By 1890, with Democrats increasingly comfortable that they enjoyed the support of the majority of Americans, cries for ballot reform came primarily from Republicans, and they were increasingly shrill.

Republicans focused their attention on two areas: New York City and the South. While people who lived in upstate New York tended to vote Republican, New York City almost always went Democratic. The Democratic city government was notoriously corrupt. Politicians from the Tammany Hall political machine distributed public contracts to friends in business who, in turn, hired immigrants and struggling workers. These men voted to keep the Democratic machine in power.

Tammany's tight grip on New York City's voters made Republicans furious. It was bad enough that immigrants and other workers determined the policies of the city rather than the men who paid the taxes that funded those policies. Worse, though, in the minds of national leaders anyway, was that the vote in New York City often determined the outcome of a presidential election. When the city's votes swung the state into the Democratic column, Republican candidates had a hard time making up the difference in the Electoral College.

By 1890, New York had not yet adopted a ballot reform measure. Blaming the Democrats for the lack of a new law, Republicans demanded ballot reform. Stemming the Democratic tide in New York City would almost certainly guarantee Republican victories, *Frank Leslie's* speculated.[19]

The other area of Republican focus on ballot reform was the South. Southern African Americans overwhelmingly voted Republican, but the number of them who made it to the polls had been dropping steadily since Democrats had taken over Southern state governments in the 1870s. Southern Democrats had a number of tactics to keep black men from voting, all of them discriminatory, and some of them deadly. There were many Americans—both white and black—who honestly wanted to protect black rights. There was no getting around the fact, though, that increasing black attendance at the polls would also help the Republican Party. Indeed, administration Republicans claimed that Southern Democrats only won national office when they suppressed the black vote, and they insisted that the election of 1884 had been a defeat of the true will of the people, as Southern Democrats terrorized potential black voters and kept them from the polls. Republican officials believed that if they could increase black voter turnout in the South, they could turn Southern Democratic states Republican, as they had been in the first years after the Civil War.[20]

From the time Harrison was elected, Republicans positioned themselves as defenders of oppressed African Americans in the South with the goal of getting Congress to protect black voting. There was never any doubt that the Democratic southern state governments would be unwilling to adopt any ballot reform that would benefit their states' black voters, but Republicans hoped to convince Americans that Congress should step in. *Frank Leslie's* repeatedly ran stories of white attacks on the Southern black population, insisting that white Southerners celebrated the murder of blacks. It extolled the progress made by African Americans in the South, and suggested that any Republican politician who did not want to protect the rights of unfortunate black men in the South should be driven out of office.[21]

Republicans who backed the federal protection of black suffrage in the South grandly claimed that the fate of the nation hung on the issue. Nothing else compared with it "in its relation to the welfare of the people, the perpetuity of our free institutions, and even of the Republic itself," *Frank Leslie's* announced. The administration's rhetoric on the issue of black suffrage was stirring, but its actions belied those grand words.[22]

Harrison's men were hardly principled proponents of black voting. They relied on racist cartoons to attract white voters and, when opponents charged that they were promoting black equality, they strongly denied any interest in racial equality. "There are no Republicans known to us who wish to see the social relations of the Southern States determined by any other considerations than those of mutual inclination, which determine them in the Northern States and elsewhere," wrote *Harper's Weekly* in the brief period when it backed the administration on this issue.[23]

There is no doubt that black voters needed protection, but there is also no doubt that most of the Republicans promoting the idea were interested in the votes rather than the voters. Their policy proposals revealed the gap between their language and their plans. The administration insisted on the rights of African American men to vote for members of Congress, but declined to protect their right to participate in state or local governments, the entities that most affected their lives. When Southern whites complained that Republicans were trying to resurrect the worst days of Reconstruction, a time they inaccurately recalled as one when whites were "humiliated" under a government elected by black voters, *Frank Leslie's*, the voice of the administration, reassured them. Southern states would always control their own affairs, it said. Congress was only interested in the election of members of the House of Representatives.[24]

Harrison's men insisted that if immigrant voting in New York City could be curtailed and black voting in the South assured, a long-term Republican ascendancy would be guaranteed.[25]

In mid-March 1890, Republican Congressman Henry Cabot Lodge of Massachusetts proposed a bill to implement national ballot reform. His bill would require the secret ballot in federal elections and place federal marshals at the polls upon the request of five hundred voters. This would allow angry New Yorkers and disfranchised black Republicans to ask that their elections be monitored by Republicans rather than the Democrats dominant in their local governments. Each polling place would also have clerks of both parties to make sure all voters were legitimate. The measures would have the effect of suppressing immigrant voting in New York and supporting black voting in the South. *Frank Leslie's* was honest about what it liked about the plan: it would dramatically increase the number of Republicans in the House of Representatives. The paper warned that party members would be "fatally remiss" in their duties if they did not push the matter.[26]

The urgency of creating more Republican votes became clear only weeks later. In mid-March elections in New York, voters replaced a number of Republican municipal governments, including those in Buffalo, Binghamton, Ithaca, Middletown, Newburg, Oswego, Schenectady, and Watertown, with Democratic ones. The *New York Times* reported that voters were tired of the Republicans' obvious use of the government for partisan ends and were drifting away from the party. *Frank Leslie's* disagreed, insisting that the elections were not a referendum on Harrison's administration. It blamed instead Republicans who hadn't bothered to vote and claimed that "the great mass" of New Yorkers were well satisfied with Harrison's administration.[27]

The next month, town elections in Indiana and Ohio also went Democratic, but *Frank Leslie's* clung to the idea that the results had nothing to do with the president. The paper blamed Democratic gerrymandering and Republican apathy for the party's losses, maintaining that Republican voters would uphold the party in more important elections. Claims that Democratic gains were a rebuke to the Harrison administration were "too absurd to deserve serious mention," wrote Harrison's son, sounding a little desperate.[28]

In late April, Massachusetts senator George Frisbie Hoar introduced to the Senate a new bill that demonstrated party members' heightened anxiety after the recent election results. The measure put partisan practicality above the principle of pure elections. It would place elections under federal supervision if one hundred voters asked for it, and provided for a detailed chain of command for federal voter oversight. In essence, it would guarantee that Democratic state election officials could be marginalized by federal officers appointed by the administration. These federal officers would undoubtedly favor Republicans at the polls and in later election disputes. Astonishingly for a measure designed to promote "ballot reform," the new proposal dropped any provisions for the Australian ballot, focusing only on guaranteeing federal oversight of the existing system.[29]

When a Republican caucus in June blended the two plans, what emerged had the critical features of Hoar's version (although, confusingly, the Federal Elections Bill would continue to be called the Lodge bill). With opposition to their policies mounting, Republicans no longer pretended to want fair and clean elections. Now they made it clear they simply wanted to win.[30]

Democrats instantly cried foul at this version of election "reform." They were not alone, though; moderate Republicans bridled at it, too. The independent Republican *New York Times* stated that the bill was designed simply to promote the partisan schemes of the Republican leaders and to provide scores of patronage jobs to potential voters. Harrison's men were desperate, the *New York Times* pointed out. The recent elections had shown that they had lost their hold on some of the Northern states. Without garnering more votes from the South, they would lose control of the government.[31]

Administration Republicans defended their bill by ratcheting up the rhetoric about the dangers of voter fraud. They warned that it was imperative to guarantee the purity of elections, because if citizens had any doubts on that score, they would revolt. At the very least, they would lose faith in government, and form posses to uphold the law. In language that seemed to incite the very action it purported to abhor, Lodge warned that fraud was a deadly peril because it led the defrauded voters to resort to violence.[32]

The administration was determined to pass the Federal Elections Bill before the midterm elections in November 1890. All summer, administration Republicans insisted the measure was the only thing that could save American government from being stolen by corrupt Democrats. In the House, Speaker Reed forced the bill through by shutting down debate and using the party lash freely. But apocalyptic rhetoric and the administration's high-handed silencing of congressional critics only strengthened the Republicans' opponents. In the hot summer of 1890, tension between Republicans and Democrats grew. Worse for the administration, though, was that the fight over the Federal Elections Bill had swung more moderate Republicans into the opposition camp. It was clear they would have to try a different approach to bolster their numbers.

Skewing election results by manipulating ballots was proving harder than the administration had hoped, but there was another way to increase the Republican majority in Congress. Congress could simply create more western states, as it had the year before when it welcomed Montana, Washington, North Dakota, and South Dakota into the Union. Adding states helped the Republicans by strengthening their power in the western Territories, which were clamoring for statehood despite their low population numbers. If the Republicans backed the statehood movements, they would increase the loyalty of voters there. And each new state would send representatives to Congress. The one congressman each would send to the House of Representatives was good, but far better were the two senators each would contribute.

In 1890, the administration turned its gaze toward Wyoming and Idaho. Since Wyoming had boasted a population of fewer than 21,000 in 1880, it was a stretch to argue that it was ready for statehood, but the Republicans were adamant it should join the Union.[33]

They also wanted Idaho. In March, *Frank Leslie's* rhapsodized about the region: Idaho had 86,000 square miles of territory and, according to the paper, that land was "magnificent" for grazing, mining, timbering, and hunting. People were pouring into the Territory, *Frank Leslie's* claimed, asserting that Idaho would come into the Union with a population of more than 150,000 people. This, too, was a stretch; Idaho Territory had had a population of fewer than 33,000 in 1880 and had grown only to about 88,500 by 1890. Nonetheless, *Frank Leslie's* told readers that Idaho had as much promise of growth and prosperity as any state that had ever been admitted to the Union. "Welcome Idaho!" it concluded. The Republicans were in such a hurry to admit Idaho that they bypassed the normal procedures of state admission, permitting the Territorial governor to call for volunteers to write a constitution, which voters approved only months later.[34]

In May 1890, the process of building a secure Republican majority in Congress began when the Senate seated two machine Republicans from the new state of Montana, which had been admitted to the Union the year before. They brought the number of senators to eighty-four, forty-seven of whom were Republicans. This gave the Republicans a safe majority of ten, *Frank Leslie's* noted.[35]

Democrats did not let the move to admit Wyoming and Idaho pass without a fight. They pointed out that there was no argument for Wyoming and Idaho statehood that did not apply to Democratic New Mexico and Arizona, and the Republicans weren't pushing the admission of those Territories. "The picking out of the two Territories and plucking them into the Union by the ears looked like an operation that was not to be justified by any sound principle of statesmanship or of public necessity, and that only found justification in the minds of its promoters by the fact that they were thus increasing their political influence in the next presidential election," a Democratic representative charged.[36]

Shamelessly, Republicans painted their western enthusiasm as statesmanship rather than partisanship. They accused Democrats of being the partisan ones when they opposed the admission of the new states. In incendiary language, Republicans accused Democrats of refusing to admit any state unless it pledged allegiance to the Democratic Party. Democrats were ignoring "the prosperous and growing communities of the great West" and were keeping westerners from their full rights as American citizens, argued *Frank Leslie's*. These same westerners had "rescued our Territories from barbarism," the paper claimed, and had laid the foundation for states that were enormous in area, resources, and potential. Indeed, it crowed, Democratic opposition to admission of the new states virtually guaranteed that their voters would support the Republicans.[37]

On July 3, 1890, Wyoming and Idaho were admitted to the Union after a vote that followed strict party lines. Administration Republicans were elated. But Democrats and moderate Republicans were not enthusiastic. The Democratic *Boston Globe* pointed out that both new states together had a population of "a fair sized congressional district in Massachusetts," but they would be represented in Congress by four senators and two representatives. The *Boston Globe* angrily suggested that, once the Republicans were done admitting all the nation's "trackless wastes and uninhabited territories as States," party members could keep finding more senators by subdividing existing Republican states. They should also, it advised sarcastically, cut Alaska into a number of new states. "To be sure, there are very few inhabitants there, but that is no obstacle whatever to Republican statesmanship," its editor sneered. "A few Republican families are enough for a State."[38]

Although it was a Republican paper, the moderate *Harper's Weekly* did not share the administration's joy at the prospect of the new states. It pointed out that the admission of the new states badly skewed congressional representation. The 105,000 people of Wyoming and Idaho, it complained, would have four senators and two representatives. The 200,000 people in the First Congressional District of New York, in contrast, had only one representative. It also pointed out that there were fifteen wards in New York City that had populations as large as the population of Wyoming and Idaho put together. To get their additional Republican senators, the Harrison administration had badly undercut the political power of voters from much more populous regions, a maneuver that did not seem to serve the fundamental principle of equal representation in the republic.[39]

The administration didn't just focus on getting new western voters, it also tried to win back the allegiance of the existing ones. Republicans actively cultivated voters in the West. Ignoring the poverty there, they reiterated their vision of agricultural prosperity for the region. Calling the West "Uncle Sam's Farm" to suggest, as they said, the potential wealth of the land, they reminded voters that western land had been made available to them by the Republicans' "wise and beneficent" public policy of moving farmers westward.[40]

To counter the growing anger of farmers that they had been duped into moving to a region where they couldn't possibly make a living, Republicans suggested an answer to the region's terrible drought conditions. What the dry prairies needed, they said, was improvement by the new science of irrigation. In February 1889, the Senate appointed seven men to a select committee on Irrigation and Reclamation of Arid Lands. Chaired by William Stewart of Nevada, the committee was charged with visiting "various parts of the arid region," which included California, Arizona, New Mexico, Colorado, Wyoming, Idaho, Utah, Montana, eastern Washington Territory, Nevada, and Dakota Territory—and investigating "the whole subject of irrigation in its economic, commercial, and political aspects." It would report when Congress reconvened in December. *Frank Leslie's* promised that the committee would produce "a flood of light" upon the "reclamation" of the dry prairies. It predicted that legislation to promote irrigation would follow soon.[41]

Administration men did not stop at redrawing the map of the country and cheering on westerners to ensure their party's ongoing ascendancy. They also implemented a host of others measures to attract voters before the midterm elections and to keep them for the 1892 presidential election.

Republicans manipulated the census of 1890 to favor Republican districts. The Constitution requires the government to count the population of the country every ten years, and then to apportion the members of Congress according to that count. The census of 1890 was a wonderful opportunity for Republicans. First of all, it gave them approximately 47,000 patronage jobs to distribute, sending census takers all across the country to count their neighbors. Then, these Republican appointees would overcount prospective Republicans, like African Americans in the South and white rural residents in Republican districts, while undercounting likely Democrats, especially those in cities like New York City. A skewed count could significantly reapportion congressmen in favor of Republicans, and everyone knew it. In September 1890, *Frank Leslie's* cheerfully reported that an early report from the census director showed an increase in the American population to 64 million, and projected fifteen more Republican congressmen to the Democrats' additional seven. It noted that this would translate into a majority—a small one, but still a majority—in the Electoral College in 1892.[42]

Republican congressmen also tried to sway the upcoming elections by funding projects that put money into the hands of voters and reminding them of the Republican Party's glorious service to the country. Over the course of the spring, Congress appropriated millions of dollars for public buildings. In May, the Senate approved a $300,000 statue of

General Ulysses S. Grant and a $50,000 "heroic size" statue of Lincoln's Secretary of War Edwin Stanton. These monuments were designed to emphasize the Republicans' successful prosecution of the Civil War (just as recurring images of William Tecumseh Sherman and Ulysses S. Grant in Republican papers were designed to do).[43]

Congress also requisitioned funds for constituencies most likely to vote Republican. In June, Congress passed the Dependent Pension Act, which gave pensions to disabled soldiers, their wives, and their children. The new law would bring the number of pensioners from about 675,000 to 970,000, and the annual appropriations would rise from $81 million to $135 million. Money would flow to former soldiers and their families in time for the 1892 election.[44]

So extravagant were the Congressmen that by midsummer newspapers started to grumble about deficits. Aware that the plan to bolster Republican voters might well backfire if the administration appeared profligate, President Harrison eventually took out his veto pen, nixing some of the proposals for grand public buildings in small towns, where it was hard to argue there was pressing national public interest.[45]

Notably, the generosity of the Republican Congress stopped dead when it came to nonvoters. When a House committee called for pensions for army nurses, *Frank Leslie's* objected that the plan would impoverish the treasury and would involve far too many people. Of course, Congress also chose not to spend any money to fund the agreements General Crook had made with the Sioux.[46]

Republicans were using every tool at their disposal to increase their chances of winning, even as they insisted that it was the Democrats, not they, who were manipulating the system. Partisan politics ruled the day, *Frank Leslie's* announced in March. Then, in an astonishing comment coming from the Harrison administration, the editors admonished: "It behooves the citizen, regardless of party affiliations, to think of the calamities that must in the end result from the intensifying of party feeling and the subordination of right and justice to the desire to advance party success."[47]

Despite—or perhaps because of—the Republicans' cynical machinations, the public mood continued to swing away from the administration in the late spring and early summer of 1890. By July,

Democrats were euphoric about their chances for the fall elections, if only they could keep Republicans from rigging the vote in the South. That was a big if, of course, but the Democrats had their own strengths. The election would turn on the Republican administration's reputation for running the government solely for the benefit of their business cronies—a reputation it was doing little to dispel.

Those suffering in the poor economy hated the Harrison administration, which seemed to be drifting ever further from ordinary Americans. The president spent the summer rusticating in New Jersey in a twenty-room "cottage" on the sea given to his wife by John Wanamaker and other wealthy friends who were trying to promote Cape May Point as a Christian summer resort. President Harrison celebrated his fifty-sixth birthday there on August 20, when he received a handsome plate of solid gold from supporters in California. Meanwhile, his son Russell was living the life of a rake, hanging out on Coney Island with W. J. Arkell, who, along with tobacco king Pierre Lorillard and financier August Belmont, the two premier horse-racing aficionados in the country, was negotiating to buy the famous Saratoga Racetrack.[48]

While President Harrison relaxed by the sea, the plains were drying up and distressed farmers were shifting away from the Republican Party. In the summer of 1890, political reform burned across the dry prairies as westerners abandoned the party of Lincoln. Western farmers had by now endured five years of increasing hardship as the increased rainfall that had encouraged settlement on the Plains in the mid-1870s had reverted to more typical weather cycles of hot, dry summers and harsh winters. Droughts had first hit hard in 1886, and cattlemen had watched their herds die off on the overgrazed grasslands. Farmers stood by helpless as their crops baked in the hot winds that could ruin a field of corn in two days. "This would be a fine country if only it had water," a hopeful farmer said in a western joke. "Yes, and so would hell," was the punch line.[49]

Winter provided no relief. The snows took their toll on both the underfed animals and the weakened settlers. The horrific winter of 1886, when snow fell from November to April and the winds drove it into drifts a dozen feet deep, killed between 30 percent and 85 percent of the cattle on the Plains. The winters continued hard. In January 1888, the Schoolchildren's Blizzard hit during the day, when children were in their schoolhouses, and killed five hundred people from Montana through Nebraska and the Dakotas.[50]

By 1889, western farmers were literally starving. Men who had believed they were the backbone of the nation and that they would thrive if only they worked hard were desperate, hopeless, frustrated, and angry. They began to band together to take back American government from big business, demanding that instead of fostering industrial development alone, Congress must shape laws in such a way that farmers could prosper, too. Since the mid-1880s, farmers' organizations had pressed the government to stop catering to big business, and during the Harrison administration, these groups, known as Alliances, took off. They complained of eastern capitalists who crippled farmers with a gold standard and then sucked them dry with high-interest mortgages, of railroad barons who charged enormous prices to get grain to market, of middlemen who skimmed the profits of farming into their own pockets. By the end of 1889, a thousand farmers a week from the dry Plains were joining the Alliances; Kansas alone had 130,000 members.[51]

Alliance members wanted the government to take action that would bolster the economic position of farmers. They called for the treasury to coin silver as well as gold to increase the money supply. An expanded currency would make it easier and cheaper for farmers to borrow, and because silver mines lay in the West, silver coinage would likely reduce the power of eastern bankers in western markets. Alliance farmers also wanted to break the monopolies of railroad magnates by nationalizing at least one of the major railroads. They pushed for the government to impose income and real estate taxes to narrow the wealth gap in the country. Various state Alliances called for local governments to buy and distribute seeds to impoverished farmers, and they pulled farmers together in cooperatives to buy goods and sell products without middlemen. Finally, they hoped to end machine politics once and for all by inducing the nation to adopt the secret ballot.[52]

As early as February 1890, *Frank Leslie's* noted that western Republicans were restive because Harrison was doing too little for them (although it said they were being unreasonable). By March, observers pointed out that farmers were becoming the most important power in western politics. If disaffected Republicans and western farmers joined forces and supported a new political organization, they would be formidable indeed. By May, pro-Harrison Republicans in the West were worried that that merger was under way. Alliances were backing their own candidates for office. If these third-party tickets pulled voters from the Republicans, as seemed likely, they could easily hand western states to the Democrats. At the very least, they would hold the balance of power in those states, and could demand candidates and policies that Republicans would have to honor. By June, *Frank Leslie's* admitted that farmers were taking control of western states, and it thought a political realignment in the West was "likely." It worried that the first casualty of that readjustment would be the protective tariff.[53]

The Alliance fire burned especially strong in South Dakota. There, Alliance men had tried to work with Republicans in 1889 and early 1890, but then machine Republicans had made a backroom deal that had cut out Alliance candidates for the Senate. Throwing the Alliance a federal judgeship instead, they had given the first senatorships from the new state to two machine Republicans, Richard F. Pettigrew of Sioux Falls and the unpopular Gideon C. Moody of Deadwood. Angry over this deal, since they had expected one senator to come from their ranks, Alliance members in South Dakota bolted from the Republican Party in June 1890 and organized as an independent political party.[54]

In the summer of 1890, South Dakota Republicans held the machinery of state power, but they knew their constituency was in danger of slipping through their fingers. Republican leaders across the nation also saw their voters abandoning the party in what became known as the "Alliance Summer" of 1890. New Alliances sprang up in one Plains state after another and, to the dismay of Republican officials, many of them joined forces with labor parties. While farmers wanted easier credit and cheaper transportation and laborers wanted higher wages and better working conditions, both groups shared a conviction that big business controlled the government. They demanded that the government stop privileging industrial development and level the economic playing field.

The Alliances, working in tandem with labor parties, posed a formidable challenge to the Republican Party. In July, the Republicans in Arkansas decided not even to produce a state ticket; they just endorsed the Union Labor ticket. In Minnesota, the Farmers' Alliance and United Labor Party nominated a joint state ticket denouncing the protective tariff and calling for silver coinage to inflate the currency, the secret ballot, prohibition of child labor, equal pay for women, and arbitration to settle labor disputes. In August, the Farmers' Alliance opened a "mammoth literary bureau in Washington" to distribute political tracts, and Republican newspapers in the West felt obliged to abandon the idea of protectionism. By September, westerners of both parties were trying to court Alliance men by nominating farmers for state tickets. Alliances united with organized labor for political action felt sufficiently emboldened that they began to make plans to run their own presidential ticket in 1892.[55]

The Republicans were on the defensive. To assuage angry voters, prominent party members embarked on a propaganda campaign, asserting that everything the party had done was for the good of the country. Reed might have been a bit heavy-handed with his iron-fisted control of the House of Representatives, they admitted, but under him Congress had acted decisively to get things done that the Democrats would have blocked if Reed had let them. After all, the Republicans had accomplished a great deal since the Civil War, they reminded voters, in an obvious attempt to rest on their wartime laurels. Likewise, Republicans argued that the controversial Federal Elections Bill was designed to protect Northern voters. If it passed, it would guarantee that white Southerners could not gain extra power in Congress by counting African Americans as members of the population and then refusing to let them vote. And the census? "No one in his senses can believe for a moment that the census has been made upon any other than straightforward business principles" insisted *Frank Leslie's*. As for the tariff, which was being debated in Congress, well, it might not have provisions that benefited farmers yet, but it would surely get some before a final bill was approved.[56]

But mounting western anger could not be soothed by rhetoric alone. Western farmers and wage laborers were determined to stop government from doing the bidding of industrialists. It was clear that something concrete had to be done to calm popular anger at the trusts. If not, the people would take matters into their own hands, electing Democrats or Alliance members to Congress, and the tariff that protected business would be in serious jeopardy. Administration Republicans could not bear to see the tariff weakened. In the early summer of 1890, they concluded they must at least nod to some of westerners' demands.

Senator John Sherman, the chairman of the Senate Finance Committee and an adamant supporter of the tariff system, spearheaded the initiative to undercut the western insurgency. That Sherman would lead the administration's charge against westerners showed just how desperate he was to protect the tariff. Sherman found himself in a strange position in the summer of 1890. He was a founder of the Republican Party but was at odds with the men who ran the administration. He had watched as President Harrison worked closely with machine politicians like William McKinley and James G. Blaine, whom Harrison named Secretary of State. Meanwhile, Sherman—more senior and more experienced—sat ignored in the Senate. But now, despite his dislike of President Harrison, he felt obliged to help the president pacify the West. Sherman was determined to preserve the tariff system he had helped to design during the Civil War.

To undercut protests that the government worked for business to the detriment of ordinary Americans, Sherman shepherded two bills through Congress in the spring and summer of 1890. The first was a measure to break up trusts. For years, tariff reformers had argued that the best way to end monopolies was to lower the tariff and thus increase competition. Determined to protect the tariff, Sherman tried to undercut popular anger at the trusts by breaking them up directly.[57]

The antitrust measure was more public relations than an actual attack on trusts. In March, the Senate sent Sherman's initial bill to the Committee on the Judiciary, which watered it down so badly even Sherman derided it as a humbug designed only to placate westerners. The bill that emerged from the committee was a very general and vague set of provisions that made it illegal for businesses to combine in order to restrict trade. Since it never defined what restricting trade meant, though, the measure was essentially toothless. It left the door wide open for courts to give great leeway to business combinations. When the bill came up for a vote in the Senate in April, Republican senators signaled that they perceived the bill as both necessary and harmless to business. Fifty-one senators voted in favor and only one voted nay. The House also passed the bill with only one negative vote, and Harrison signed it into law on July 2, 1890. Much to Sherman's chagrin, it became known as the Sherman Anti-Trust Act.[58]

Part of the impetus for passing the antitrust measure was likely the unexpected revolt of western senators against the administration's hard-money currency policy in mid-June. Westerners had called for silver coinage since the recession of the 1870s, when they had taken a stand against easterners' rigid adherence to the gold standard. Western demands for the coinage of silver had only increased with the troubles of the late 1880s. Silver coinage and the inflation it would create were enormously popular in the cash-starved West. Democrats had never been entirely comfortable with inflation but had also never been firm adherents to the Republicans' hard-money policies. They had begun to take some political cues from the growing Alliances and were beginning to champion the cause.

Republican senators were aware they must put their names to a silver coinage measure or else give the Democrats a perfect issue to attract westerners to their standard. Republicans had been mulling over new coinage legislation in a rather desultory way when, in mid-June, Senator Preston B. Plumb of Kansas introduced a measure that provided for the free coinage of silver, with sixteen ounces of silver equaling one ounce of gold. With the price of silver cheap and dropping thanks to the new lodes, this measure would dramatically inflate the currency. Other Republican senators from the western states backed Plumb's revolt and joined Democrats to pass the bill.[59]

Horrified that even the conservative Senate was willing to cave in to western demands for inflation, Sherman led an eastern Republican effort to water down the westerners' inflationary measure. While Sherman admitted that a large majority of the Senate favored the free coinage of silver, he was not willing to permit such an attack on the Republican hard-money policies that he had helped design. Sherman was the senior member of a conference committee of House and Senate members that reported a new silver coinage bill.

The committee's new measure undercut the inflationary potential of the Plumb bill's coinage provision. Sherman's bill provided that the treasury would buy 4.5 million ounces of silver every month, and then issue treasury notes in small denominations that could be redeemed in coin—which would likely be gold—to pay for the purchase. This measure would support the market for silver, but prevent it from flooding the country as currency. Essentially, it simply provided that the government would buy silver and store it in the treasury. Under the guidance of McKinley at the head of the Committee on Ways and Means, the House passed the compromise silver bill. The Senate did so as well, and Harrison signed it into law on July 14, 1890. Republican politicians hoped the Silver Purchase Act, together with the antitrust law, would calm western anger at the administration.[60]

In the summer of 1890, Republicans defending the administration's economic policy fought back against their western opponents. They aggressively criticized farmers' complaints, insisting, first of all, that hard-working farmers were doing just fine. Western farmers weren't really heavily in debt, *Frank Leslie's* reported in June. Reports of high mortgages that farmers couldn't pay were the false claims of demagogues and free traders. Such charges were "a libel upon the thrift and economy, as well as upon the honesty and intelligence of the Western farmer." These accusations were doubly unfair, it claimed, because they suggested that the western states were barren and infertile—obviously untrue, since everyone knew the West was a paradise.[61]

Republicans also attacked the westerners who complained about eastern capitalists. Western diatribes against eastern moneylenders were "demagogical 'rot' of the worst kind," complained *Frank Leslie's*. After all, it was northeastern money that had funded the settlement of the West. Eastern bankers had put up the cash for the railroads, as well as for the tools and provisions that settlers needed to get started. "What would the West and South be but for the money-lenders of the East and Northeast?" *Frank Leslie's* demanded.[62]

Above all, farmers had no cause to complain about the tariff, Republicans insisted. If farmers were in trouble—and they were not, for the most part—they were suffering from a worldwide depression in agricultural prices sparked by overproduction, not from the tariff.[63]

Those few farmers who were indeed in debt were to blame for their own troubles, administration Republicans claimed. They didn't understand their own interests, and tried to farm with too little capital. This meant they had to borrow more than they could afford. To pay back their loans, they had to sell their products immediately in a depressed market, rather than waiting for better prices. Farmers would have agreed with this analysis, although they would have blamed their lack of capital not on themselves, but on the dry plains and on the Republican economic policies that kept grain prices low and prices for everything else high.[64]

Financial foolishness wasn't the farmers' only sin, however. Republican lawmakers claimed that they had "extravagant notions," and too high a standard of living. Farmers had abandoned the rag carpets of twenty-five years before in favor of imported rugs. They disdained pork and potatoes for fancier fare like beef and chicken. Rather than good, old-fashioned hoecake, they indulged in angel food cake, with its extravagant recipe that included a dozen eggs.[65]

Ultimately, the farmers were lazy. According to Republicans, the farmers' political agitation revealed nothing more than the desire of uneducated and selfish men to have the government take care of them. Farmers' Alliances demanded "a sort of paternal Government." It was simply un-American.[66]

The Republicans went so far as to deny the weather reports. The West was not arid and impoverished, they insisted. In November 1890, *Frank Leslie's* ran an article titled "The Black Hills: An El Dorado of Health, Wealth, and Picturesque Scenery." The mountains were lovely for tourists, it claimed, and far below them lay an agricultural paradise. There were green hills with browsing herds, valleys with meandering streams, and fields of ripening grain. Towns nestled in the mountains and foothills, and in the distance visitors could see a winding river as it made its way to the ocean. The Black Hills were the "Garden of the Dakotas." Suggesting that the article was intended to promote a South Dakota railroad, it informed readers of which railroad lines could take them to this earthly paradise.[67]

Nowhere was the prosperity and progress of the West more evident than in the Sioux regions of South Dakota. In June 1890, *Frank Leslie's* ran illustrations of miners and cattlemen fending off fighting Indians, but celebrated those Indians who had adopted white ways. In July, it noted the graduation from Boston University Medical School of Charles Alexander Eastman, who long ago had been Santee refugee Ohiyesa, fleeing from Minnesota to Canada with his uncle.[68]

In September, *Frank Leslie's* was willing to let the whole Sioux nation represent the Republican development of the West. "PROGRESS

AMONG THE SIOUX," announced the paper. Ignoring that, in reality, the Sioux were starving, sick, and disheartened by the fall of 1890, it celebrated "wonderful changes" among the Sioux in recent years, and commended missionaries and the government for their effective work. Their efforts had raised the Indians "from the depths of degradation and idleness to their present advanced state." Schools were established and effectively bringing the children to civilization, it reported, and the students were bright. A few "hostiles" continued to resist American ways, but as a whole, the Sioux nation had advanced to become one of the most enlightened tribes in the great Northwest. The government had built comfortable houses for Indian families and had hired white men to teach them to farm. Republicans predicted that, if they continued at the current pace, most of the Sioux would be "entirely self-supporting" in only a few years.[69]

And yet despite their propaganda efforts, even Harrison's men had to recognize privately that westerners were suffering. In September, Republicans in Oklahoma Territory reaffirmed their loyalty to the administration and thanked the president for his wise policies. This vote of confidence, though, could not obscure that westerners were in terrible trouble, and administration men knew of the suffering. On the same day that the Oklahoma men commended the president, the Acting Secretary of War dispatched troops "to investigate the condition of the citizens of Oklahoma, claimed to be destitute," reminding the commanding officer: "It is desired that no publicity be given to this order."[70]

By the late summer of 1890, President Harrison had become keenly aware that he had to shore up the western wing of his party in the face of Alliance bolters. Warnings had been pouring in from all quarters. As early as July, a Republican in California had warned him that "the leading Republicans of Arizona . . . have recently felt that they were largely ignored at Washington," and counseled him that it would be a good political move to invite to the White House two prominent Arizona men visiting Washington. In August, Republicans in charge of the upcoming midterm elections begged the president not to antagonize Alliance men when he made government appointments.[71]

President Harrison took action. He sent his son, Russell Harrison, back to Helena, Montana, where the younger man had an interest in the *Helena Daily Journal*, to try to sway Montana politics. The president also embarked on a tour of the West himself in October (in a railroad car supplied by Mr. Pullman himself), ostensibly to attend an army reunion, but with an eye to bolstering Republican support there. Although he privately complained that "the 'dear public' [has] demands upon me that are inexorable. . . . It will be a tiresome trip and I . . . dread it," the president could not ignore the dozens of importunate letters that had been pouring in from frantic western Republicans over the course of the past two months. As a supporter from Colorado wrote: "Your personal interest in our people may be like the saving movement in the turning point of a crisis battle: the sight of the General's inspiring!"[72]

The trip was not a great success. While President Harrison wanted to placate starving farmers, it seemed he did not sympathize with their plight. In Topeka, Kansas, he told an audience that a year of poor returns should not ruin their hopes for the future. Life was made up of averages, after all, and on average, they would do fine. "Kansas and her people have an assured and happy future," he declared, giving small comfort to people who could not figure out how they would put food on the table until the next year's harvest. Still, *Frank Leslie's* told readers that westerners had loved the president, proving "his great popularity with the masses of the people." Democrats disagreed. Westerners had shown "a curious absence of enthusiasm" for the president's tour, the *Boston Globe* reported.[73]

The summer of 1890 had proven to voters that the Harrison administration was dangerously out of touch with the problems in the nation. Republicans had enacted legislation that its sponsors argued would help people by breaking up trusts and buying up silver, but Democrats and suffering farmers and workers recognized that the new laws made no meaningful reforms to the policies that were causing such distress. Worse, it seemed Republicans refused to acknowledge the reality of the suffering on the plains, asserting instead that all was well there and blaming drought-stricken farmers for their own plight. Despite the Republicans' angry defense of their policies and denunciation of their opponents, the November elections threatened to hand the party serious losses. This would leave it badly weakened for 1892, unless it could somehow rebuild its voter base.

To recoup their political losses, the Republicans turned to their signature issue: the tariff. From the time of President Harrison's election, pro-tariff forces claimed that his victory was a mandate for strong protection. This was wishful, for he had barely squeaked into office, lacking a majority of the popular vote even after the generally popular President Cleveland had vetoed a bill to provide pensions for hundreds of thousands of Civil War veterans. Nonetheless, President Harrison's advisers maintained that he had a mandate. The people demanded a strong protective tariff, *Frank Leslie's* insisted.[74]

In late summer and early fall of 1890, administration Republicans pushed a new tariff bill, arguing that such a law was the only thing that could bring wavering voters back to the fold. On the one hand, a new tariff would mend the faltering economy by raising tariffs on certain items, which would protect new businesses and put laborers back to work. On the other hand, revising the tariff would let congressmen drop tariff rates on other items, so the price of some consumer goods would sink. With the economy reviving and prices falling, the administration's popularity would surge. It sounded like a win-win scenario to Harrison's men, and they pressured congressmen to move forward quickly on a new tariff bill.[75]

Republicans had begun their efforts to produce a new tariff in the spring of 1890. A subcommittee of the House Ways and Means Committee, with administration stalwart William McKinley at its helm, was charged with preparing a bill. It set out to wade through the duties on a dizzying array of products, trying to determine which could be lowered. But 1890 was the year of the midterm elections and businessmen howled that their enterprises would be badly hurt if tariffs were lowered to permit competing European products into the market. They reminded the congressmen of how much money they had given to Harrison's presidential campaign, and suggested that future donations depended on the maintenance—or even raising—of tariffs. *Frank Leslie's* tried to downplay business's influence on the bill by claiming that the subcommittee was being careful to protect farming interests, but in an era when the United States exported most of its agricultural products rather than importing them, this reform offered little benefit to farmers.[76]

On March 31, McKinley reported the subcommittee's bill to the full Committee on Ways and Means. Although they knew pro-tariff men were pressuring the members of the subcommittee, advocates of tariff reform were still shocked when they saw the shape of the proposed bill. Far from reforming the tariff, the new measure raised rather than lowered tariffs overall. While the rates of some items had gone down, rates on everyday articles like lime, plaster, tin plate, cutlery, woolens, and shotguns had gone up. Horseshoe nails had jumped from a rate of 47 to 76 percent. Every conceivable domestic industry had been protected from foreign competition by guaranteeing that imported goods would be more expensive than ever before. This meant, of course, that consumers would have to pay higher prices, a burden that they could not sustain as industrial employers slashed their wages.[77]

Opponents attacked McKinley, who had chaired the subcommittee and, as the head of the Committee on Ways and Means, would also sponsor the bill. Once again, he and his cronies were simply using the apparatus of the federal government to build a Republican ascendancy. The shape of the bill proved that "MCKINLEY'S PICKPOCKETS [were] PAYING A PARTY DEBT," the *New York Times* charged.[78]

In mid-April, opponents' outrage grew more acute. In the few hours before McKinley reported the unpopular bill from the Ways and Means Committee to the House, it acquired a dramatically increased duty on sugar. Not coincidentally, the committee had changed the duty after its members had had a conference with members of the Sugar Trust. The price of Sugar Trust stock jumped dramatically when McKinley introduced the tariff to the House, and the *New York Times* reported that the sugar men, who had just made a killing, were "jubilant."[79]

While the industrialists and business tycoons who were bankrolling the Republicans liked the new bill, no one else did. Eastern importers were apoplectic over it, for it would almost certainly put them out of business. Merchants and small businessmen also hated the new tariff proposal, which would raise prices and make it difficult for them to compete with the trusts. Western Democrats and Alliance members resented the higher prices it would cause at a time when they were already near ruin. Even many Republicans disliked it, not only because of its higher tariff rates, but also because they abhorred the administration's use of government systems to build partisan advantage. Westerners demanded the bill be rejected, Alliance members threatened to defect to the Democrats if the measure weren't thrown out, and moderate Republicans carped at the administration's abuse of power. With dislike of the new tariff bill building only six months before the 1890 midterm elections, Democrats promptly suggested they would try to replace the new tariff bill with the Mills Bill of 1888, and proposed an even larger free list than that bill had provided.[80]

The outpouring of anger over the bill was overwhelming but, astonishingly, administration Republicans refused to budge, insisting that objections to the proposed bill were misguided or hyper-partisan. The tariff alone could rebuild the economy, they insisted, and with it the fortunes of the administration.

With the help of Speaker Reed's iron fist, McKinley maneuvered the Republican bill through the House in May. McKinley launched debate over the measure with a two-hour speech on May 7 that gave a standard defense of protection. The development of the economy depended on the protection of its industries, he insisted. High tariff walls were "indispensable to the safety, purity, and permanence of the Republic." Administration Republicans lauded his speech and demanded the bill's early passage. Although other observers dismissed the speech as rather lack-luster, *Frank Leslie's* reported that when McKinley sat down, the Republicans applauded at length and mobbed him to shake his hand. "Vote! vote!" men called, suggesting that they wanted to push the bill through.[81]

Certainly Speaker Reed wanted to move it along. He permitted only ten days of discussion on the measure. In mid-May, he cut off debate. On May 21, after a morning of absolute chaos, with members packed into the House chamber shouting amendments, yelling to demand votes, interrupting each other, and talking over each other three or four at a time, the House passed the measure and sent it to the Senate. The vote had been along party lines except that two Republicans—one from Louisiana and one from Arkansas—crossed over to vote with the Democrats. The Republican side of the chamber burst into cheers and applause when their victory was announced. So did the Democrats on the other side. "You may rejoice now, but next November you'll mourn," shouted one across the aisle.[82]

McKinley laughed at this sally, convinced that the administration was in the right. And, sharing his conviction, Harrison's men kept up the pressure on the lawmakers to maintain the bill's momentum. "HURRY IT THROUGH!" demanded administration newspapers. Uncertainty about the tariff was responsible for "unsettling business interests and stagnating trade," *Frank Leslie's* contended, and its passage would calm the financial crisis.[83]

But passing the bill in the Senate was not as easy as passing it in the House. The Senate split over the measure, with westerners leading the opposition. They demanded that the Senate Finance Committee justify, in writing, every single change in the tariff schedule, a requirement that would delay passage of the bill indefinitely. While the Finance Committee prepared its schedules, Congress passed the Sherman Anti-Trust Act and the Silver Purchase Act to placate westerners. Their efforts did not pay off. As the summer got hotter, voters around the country protested the tariff bill. Nowhere were the protests more emphatic than in the West.[84]

Then, on July 15, a bombshell suddenly upset the balance of the tariff struggle.

Staunch Republican Secretary of State James G. Blaine broke with the administration to side with the westerners. Blaine wrote a public letter denouncing the McKinley Tariff. He pointed out that it closed the United States off from foreign markets. This would do nothing for farmers, who needed to be able to ship their wheat and pork abroad to the burgeoning markets of South America and Asia. What America needed was reciprocity agreements, not trade walls, he wrote.[85]

Blaine made this shocking move for reasons of his own. He strongly advocated cooperation between North and South America and worried that high tariffs would destroy his dream of a pan-American trading sphere. At the same time he brooded that House Speaker Reed was eclipsing him at home—both were from Maine—as well as in the leadership of the national party. Throwing a spanner in the works of the McKinley Tariff could accomplish two goals: it would help establish trade reciprocity with the rest of the Americas and at the same time slow down Reed's rise to prominence.

Blaine's apostasy infuriated the editors of *Frank Leslie's*. Republicans had promised a new tariff, the paper railed, and failing to produce one was criminal. Rejecting the McKinley Tariff would do incalculable harm to the nation's industrial and commercial interests. But many Americans—even Republicans—were willing to back Blaine. The levels of protection in the bill were just too high, and the methods Reed and McKinley had used to pass it just too high-handed. The *New York Times* chortled that Blaine was a bull in a china shop, and cheered him on. With his standing as a senior statesman in the party, Blaine had made it legitimate for any Republican to break ranks with the increasingly unpopular administration.[86]

The fight over the McKinley Tariff revealed deep political rifts in the country. Democrats opposed the administration, of course, but even many Republicans were fed up with Harrison's people. Their unease with the administration's partisanship became active opposition over the bill. By mid-July 1890, moderate Republican newspapers had begun to attack President Harrison and his men. *Harper's Weekly* rejected the claim that in winning the 1888 election President Harrison had received a mandate to pass a higher tariff. Rather, it said, Harrison had been elected by "corruption." Manufacturers and others had poured money into the campaign and had bought votes. [87]

The *New York Times* agreed that Harrison's men had gone too far with the McKinley Tariff. Republican leaders had stolen the 1888 election, the editors argued, and the success of that scheme had convinced Republican leaders that, so long as the moneyed men were behind them, they needn't pay any attention to the public will. The purpose of the McKinley Tariff bill, the *New York Times* said, was to guarantee a permanent fund that Republicans could use to buy elections.[88]

July had brought a number of occasions that showed the dictatorial bent of the administration, and moderate Republicans highlighted them with scorn. Speaker of the House Reed had forced his colleagues to pass the Federal Elections Bill the same way he had pushed the tariff bill. He had cut off debate to move the bill to a vote and had applied the party whip brutally to get the unpopular bill through. When Senate Republicans tried to follow Reed's lead and cut off debate, they drew fury. Refusing to permit debate on something as important as a national election bill suggested that its supporters were up to no good, warned *Harper's Weekly*.[89]

Harper's Weekly also blamed the Republicans for the passage of the Silver Purchase Act. The same inflation that would help western debtors would hurt eastern workers and capitalists, lowering real wages and devaluing capital. Many easterners worried that the law was the beginning of an inflationary policy that would dangerously unsettle the nation's finances, and they resented the western congressmen who had pushed the measure. *Harper's Weekly* pointed out that the westerners marshaled the power they did only because of Republican political machinations. Republicans had rapidly created six new western states solely for party advantage, and the silver act had passed only thanks to the votes of the new western Republican senators. "Admitting States to the Union should be regarded as an act of vital national interest, and not as a mere game of party," the paper complained.[90]

By the end of August, attacks on the Republican leaders were no longer limited to complaints about specific pieces of legislation. Instead, sweeping indictments condemned the entire administration. Claiming to speak for "a great body of Republican, Democratic, and independent citizens" who were eager to see the defeat of the administration's transparent power mongering, the editors of *Harper's Weekly* complained that congressional Republicans had deeply injured the party. It lumped the Republicans' signature measures into one pattern of wrongdoing. The pension bill was virtually a raid upon the treasury, nothing more than a way to buy Republican voters. Worse was the House's passage of the McKinley Tariff, which was not necessary for revenue, and which had split the party between machine Republicans and intelligent Americans who wanted laws that benefited everyone. Worse still was the Federal Elections Bill. It was a startling measure that overturned the American system of local control of elections, and put them under the control of partisan federal agents. Opponents of the measure were not, as Republicans charged, in favor of the repression of black voters. Rather, they feared the solution even more than they feared the problem. Aware that they no longer had a moral hold on their countrymen, it charged, Republicans were straining legal bonds to hold on to their fading power.[91]

Virtually nothing the administration did was immune from criticism. The census was a particularly sore point. The Civil Service Reform League accused the administration of giving jobs to party workers regardless of their abilities, and noted accurately that people were generally dissatisfied with the census process. In mid-October, *Harper's Weekly* reported that people all over the country were complaining that the census takers were "conspicuously unfit." Some could not even add. What else could be expected, it asked, when politicians appointed employees with regard only to their party loyalty? Indeed, the census numbers in New York City, at least, were so skewed that the mayor asked for a recount on the grounds that the count disagreed so dramatically with records kept by the Board of Health.[92]

Opponents of the administration went after individuals as well as policies. *Harper's Weekly* took on Speaker Reed. His will was law, it claimed. He inflamed Republican partisans by his constant insistence that there was only one way to look at an issue, and that was his way. The Republicans, he claimed, were all virtuous and patriotic citizens, while Democrats were treasonous. Yet, to advance the Republicans' agenda, he was willing to manipulate rules, force through bills, and stifle debate, all the time claiming he was obeying the mandate of the country. He had thrown out time-honored precedents and demolished valuable traditions.[93]

The *New York Times* went after President Harrison directly. His "pathetic" presidency revealed "the utter failure of the great hopes of a small mind, with large opportunities, [and] entire confidence in itself. . . ." When Harrison was nominated for president, no one believed he would actually be able to do the job. Then he was elected, thanks to corporate money and corruption, and while no one thought he would be great, many were willing to hope he would be at least an average sort of president. As soon as he took up the post, though, he began to insist on his own "dull, obstinate, narrow" way, ignoring or perhaps even defying the advice of congressional leaders. His only leadership quality was stubbornness and, rather than using it in the service of intelligence and integrity, he used it solely to advance his own agenda, which was "narrow, selfish, trivial, [and] often mean." The newspaper's final verdict was damning: "By the peculiarities of his personal character, his petty selfishness, his unworthy nepotism, his dull conceit, and ungraciousness . . . with others, he made himself as thoroughly disliked as any President we have ever had."[94]

By mid-August, administration leaders recognized that they were in trouble. Their efforts to pass the Federal Elections Bill had stalled in the Senate, and there seemed to be no hope the measure would pass. The McKinley Tariff was also drifting in the Senate, and protesters across the nation kept up agitation to make sure it stayed adrift. Republicans had succeeded in pushing through a number of initiatives—the Anti-Trust Act and the Silver Purchase Act, for example—but they had not managed to paper over the growing rift between westerners and the Republican establishment. Democrats and Alliance members in the West were attacking the administration. Moderate Republicans had abandoned the administration and seemed, if anything, even more hostile than the westerners. With fewer than three months before the midterm elections, the administration had to do something quickly.

President Harrison and his men decided to double down on the tariff. They gave up trying to pass the enormously unpopular Federal Elections Bill. New York had recently passed its own secret ballot law, taking away one of the Republicans' key arguments for their own bill. And few Americans liked the Republican measure that promised to defend black voting only for congressmen and that seemed to be driven by party members' determination to control the government. So President Harrison's men abandoned the Federal Elections Bill and put all their energies into turning the McKinley Tariff bill into law.[95]

They threw everything they had into getting the tariff bill through the Senate. Administration men flayed restive western Republicans with the party whip to keep them on the right side of the tariff vote. They publicly chastised anyone who strayed. When Senator Plumb of Kansas voted with the Democrats on several proposed amendments to the bill, *Frank Leslie's* warned him of the dangers of "erratic infidelity to party obligations." In contrast, administration men lauded the party faithful. *Frank Leslie's* approvingly called attention to the course of Iowa's Senator William B. Allison, who admitted he didn't like everything about the bill but said he was willing to vote with the party rather than to stand by his own judgment. His vote, the paper maintained, was a rebuke to some of his "impetuous and thoughtless colleagues" who would do well to follow his example.[96]

By September, eastern and western Republican senators had called a truce over the tariff, recognizing that it was suicide to go into an election split over their signature issue. To neutralize the threat posed by Blaine and his allies, the Senate added to the bill a lukewarm reciprocity measure permitting the president to drop tariffs on raw materials if other countries did the same. Moderates declared themselves happy enough, although some grumbled that this was simply a meaningless sop to western voters.[97]

Administration Republicans also tinkered with the details of the bill to insure the support of key lawmakers. Tariff managers jockeyed the tariff duties to placate westerners, but their efforts only emphasized the gulf between manufacturers and farmers. In late discussions on the bill, Senator Moody of South Dakota demanded protection on tin to protect the fledgling tin mines in the Black Hills of South Dakota and Wyoming. But while the measure would prop up western mining interests, it would actually hurt western farmers and eastern laborers. Farmers and workers ate from tin cans, carried tin lunch pails, used tin kitchen utensils, and ate on tin plates. The proposed doubling of the duty on tin made opponents of the tariff howl that the price increase would enrich owners of tin mines and manufacturers of tin pails, while anyone who used the pails would pay the price. But Moody, who was, after all, a firm supporter of the administration, got the tariff on tin and supported the bill.[98]

An even bigger sticking point for westerners was a proposed tariff on binding twine. Farmers resented the high costs they paid for all of their supplies, but nothing hit harder than the cost of this staple. Only with binding twine, which reapers used to tie up shocks of grain, could farmers use machinery to cut their crops. Without it, they would have to return to old-fashioned hand harvesting, which was backbreaking and terribly slow. But the Jute Trust—a trust that Southern farmers already hated for its control over the bags that held cotton—held a monopoly on the important twine.

The tariff bill had put binding twine on the free list, but to protect the Jute Trust, the Senate added tariff duties on imported cording. Western senators then balked at the bill. Nine western Republican senators won a public rebuke from President Harrison when they pledged to oppose the bill unless binding twine was put back on the free list.[99]

Western lawmakers were in a difficult position, caught between the demands of the pro-business Republicans and the threat of the pro-farmer Alliance movement back home that was cutting through Republican constituencies like a scythe. While they were expected to do their party's bidding, they also had to deal with impoverished voters. They could not force an across-the-board tariff cut, but they simply could not let the price of binding twine rise.

Party leaders lowered the proposed tariff on binding twine slightly and then put enormous pressure on the western senators to vote for the bill. Ultimately six caved in, saving the bill. But three held their anti-tariff line: Preston Plumb of Kansas, Algernon S. Paddock of Nebraska, and Richard Pettigrew of South Dakota. Furious at their apostasy, *Frank Leslie's* darkly predicted that their constituents would "settle the score with them." The senators might just as easily have made that same prediction to the administration. The fight over binding twine revealed that western voters no longer supported the Republicans' signature measure, and that their opposition was strong enough to force lawmakers to break party ranks on this critically important vote. Republicans had created new western states to be staunchly Republican allies, but the Senate vote on the McKinley Tariff indicated that they would have to court those states with something besides a promise of economic development if they were to continue to support the administration.[100]

On September 30, 1890, the Senate passed the new tariff, and President Harrison signed it into law on October 1. In the face of broad popular demand for tariff reduction, the new law raised tariffs to the point that average duties were about half of a product's value.

Congressmen did not wait around for national reaction to the bill. They adjourned for the session immediately after passing it. But Democratic congressmen snarled at their cheerful opponents and summed up the past months. The entire congressional session had been run "by revolutionary methods, and as such will be notorious in history," one charged. Republicans had helped their business friends and actively injured the laboring interests of the country. "Partisan and class legislation has been the session's distinguishing characteristic." The connection between the election and the tariff was also very clear to observers; the *New York Times* called it "the campaign contributors' Tariff bill." The Harrison administration had secured broad business support, but at an immense cost to its reputation.[101]

The new tariff law put enormous stress on an economy that was already fragile. Consumers were outraged. Prices rose as soon as the bill passed, even on goods that were already in stock. Department stores sent circulars to their clients, warning them that prices were going to rise further because of the McKinley Tariff. This was partly a ploy to increase immediate sales, to be sure, but in the pre–World War I era of advertising, people were likely to believe what vendors told them.[102]

The threat of rising prices forced the tariff to the forefront in the 1890 election season. Women, who frequented the new department stores and shopped to feed and clothe their families, counseled their husbands to vote Democratic in the hope that a Democratic Congress would repeal the new law and lower tariffs. For their part, Democrats had been advocating tariff reform for years and were happy to promise that, if elected, they would reverse the Republicans' course. Republicans countered by accusing those complaining about higher prices of being greedy, refusing to pay a little extra to help keep workers' jobs at home.[103]

By November, the leaders of the American Protective League were reduced to begging the president to say or do something to prop up public opinion in favor of protection. They lamented the widespread charges that the new tariff would raise prices. Such "mis-statements" had "shaken the faith of many of our former friends." They asked the president, whose words could reach even the remotest corners of the nation, to speak on the virtues of the tariff. Such reassurance would renew the courage of protectionists and help the Republicans to face the upcoming election with confidence.[104]

As the election approached, the Republicans tried to court voters with promises that the new tariff would restore prosperity. The stock market had refused to rally all year, but in October, *Frank Leslie's* business columnist announced: "WALL STREET—BETTER TIMES AHEAD." Famous financier Jay Gould, the paper claimed, thought the economy was healthy and that "a long period of prosperity" stretched in front of them. And he was not the only one who thought so, *Frank Leslie's* claimed. Many of "the oldest and most sagacious men in banking and business circles" agreed. The newspaper suggested that Americans could expect to have a very merry Christmas, indeed.[105]

And what was responsible for the coming prosperity? The McKinley Tariff. *Frank Leslie's* explained that, thanks to the new tariff, "the most experienced financiers" predicted that the nation was on the verge of the greatest prosperity the nation had ever known. The economy would pick up in a year, or maybe even less. When it did, *Frank Leslie's* claimed, people would realize that "President Harrison's Administration has been, as we predicted it would be, a business administration, intended primarily to promote the welfare and prosperity of the American people."[106]

Belying this cheery news, though, was persisting business stagnation. Ten pages later in the same issue, the editor wondered what on earth was going on with Wall Street. Business was booming, railroad earnings were up, and money was in demand, he claimed, but stocks were nonetheless selling at a drastic discount. *Frank Leslie's* offered up one reason after another for why the market was not booming, at one point blaming the closing of a New York rope factory on the westerners who got the duty on twine reduced.[107]

Repeatedly forced to acknowledge that the economy was continuing to slow down, *Frank Leslie's* finally snarled that the trouble was not the Republicans' fault. "Whatever politicians may say regarding the recent financial stringency specially felt in Wall Street, the truth remains that it cannot justly be charged to the present or to the late Administration's policy." No, the administration was not responsible for the recession—just the opposite. The administration was responsible for the McKinley Tariff, which would soon make business boom again.[108]

CHAPTER 5

A Season of Desperation

THE DETERMINATION of Harrison's men to attract western voters made them turn their attention once again to the South Dakota Sioux reservations. One of the most important tools administration officials had for cementing an election victory was their ability to put Republicans into political appointments. If they placed in office men who could spread government contracts to people willing to vote Republican, they could solidify political support. Harrison and his men had distributed appointments cannily and aggressively since the moment they took office, and by the fall of 1890 were working harder than ever to find lucrative jobs for political allies. They did not overlook some of the plum positions in the administration: Indian agency jobs in the West. But their enthusiasm for political appointments created a crisis in South Dakota. They made appointments only with an eye to winning the midterm elections, not to ameliorating the suffering on the reservations. Pushed together, the politically appointed agents and starving Sioux sparked a conflagration.

The West was particularly amenable to the juggling of appointments for political advantage because it had a long history of federal control. Unlike the older eastern states, the new western states had spent a generation as Territories. Since federal officials appointed Territorial officials, who were usually beholden for their jobs to a single congressman or senator, these states had a political culture of patronage, cronyism, and party hacks that dwarfed that of the East.[1]

The job of Indian agent was a prime position, for agents had at their disposal tens of thousands of dollars worth of contracts to feed and clothe their charges, as well as contracts to build agency mills, schools, warehouses, and so on. Under previous administrations, Interior Department officials had insisted that Washington must control appointments to the Indian agencies because the agents chosen by local congressmen were so corrupt. But Harrison's administration very deliberately moved away from the idea that Indian agents should be under the control of the federal government. Instead, they adopted what they called "Home Rule," a policy that let state politicians name Indian agents.[2]

Home Rule was terrible for the Indians. State officials would simply hand out the lucrative agency appointments to local political supporters. The quality of Indian agents plummeted: the new agents were men who were out of work and money—or they wouldn't need the appointment in the first place—and were unlikely to be skillful administrators. And because they were local appointees, bred of a culture that was determined to get Indians out of the way of American development, the new agents had no sympathy for their charges.

The policy had immediate consequences for Pine Ridge Reservation. At the request of South Dakota senator Richard Pettigrew, who had once referred to a Sioux man as a "fierce buck [who] follows the war path with butcher knife in one hand and reeking scalp in the other," the lucrative position of agent for the Pine Ridge Reservation went to Daniel F. Royer just before the 1890 election.[3]

It would have been hard to find a worse Indian agent than Royer. A fellow Republican enthusiastically described him in a newspaper article as "a man of positive qualities and good executive abilities," but this was a charitable view indeed. Royer might have been good at drumming up votes for the Republican Party, but he had few other skills. He was a failed medical man and a pharmacist, and it is possible that the drug addiction that came to haunt his later days was already afflicting him in 1890. If he was indeed still clean, though, he was nonetheless a weak man who knew little of Indians.[4]

Royer's first day on the job was October 9. It was a terrible time for a new agent to take over at Pine Ridge. The Ghost Dance had not won strong adherents among the Sioux in the spring, but the searing summer winds had fanned the flames of religious hope. The hot wind baked not only the little gardens the Indians had planted, but even the native grasses, destroying the hay crop. Illness swept the camps of the undernourished Indians, leaving Elaine Goodale shocked at the "gaunt forms, lackluster faces, and sad, deep-sunken eyes" of her Sioux friends.[5]

With nowhere else to turn, the despondent Sioux had embraced the promise of a messiah. In August, the Ghost Dance movement swept Pine Ridge, probably ignited by Kicking Bear, who returned from Wyoming with news that the Arapaho were already dancing and talking with their dead. The report rekindled interest in the Ghost Dance. Pine Ridge Indians, who had suffered such a terrible mortality rate during the previous winter and now faced more food shortages, fervently wanted to hear that their dead loved ones were happy and that Ghost Dancing could bring back the herds that once sustained the tribes.[6]

The dance spread rapidly through the traditionalist camps. It was no accident that the Pine Ridge Ghost Dancing began at Big Road's settlement on Wounded Knee Creek. Big Road had fought with Crazy Horse and had led the Oglalas who had fought against Crook and Custer. Later he had fled to join Sitting Bull's people in Canada. Traditionalist Indians were angry at progressives over the land deal, and traditionalists were far more likely than progressives to gravitate toward the Ghost Dance. While Big Road's people joined the movement, Red Cloud, back at the agency, did not. But while he had converted to Catholicism some time before, he had not relaxed his determination to oppose government control of his people. He told them they should dance if they wished, no matter what the agent said.[7]

From Big Road's camp, the dance moved west to No Water's camp near the mouth of White Clay Creek, north of Pine Ridge agency. There, the hungry and angry Sioux seemed to emphasize a different part of the Ghost Dance than Wovoka apparently had. They changed Wovoka's rather gentle doctrine of the ancestors bringing back the old world by herding the game with them as they returned from the spirit world. In their version of the dance, the Sioux saw the present world destroyed either in a flood, a fire, or a landslide. While the Indians would be unharmed by this cataclysm, the settlers would be drowned, burned, or buried. Moving in a circle holding hands, the dancers would sing:

Father, I come;
Mother, I come;

Brother, I come;
Father, give us back our arrows.

Still, the dancers were not hostile to American observers. Our description of the Ghost Dance at White Clay Creek comes from a Pine Ridge teacher, who had driven out with a party of sightseers to watch the dance take place.[8]

By the end of August, there was a camp of two thousand or so Ghost Dancers gathered on White Clay Creek, eighteen miles north of the agency. The dancing had led to a serious confrontation between the Pine Ridge Sioux and their agent. They had taken up arms against Agent Gallagher and twenty police officers when they came in force to break up the dancing. Knowing that he was about to be replaced by a Harrison appointee, the Democrat Gallagher decided to leave the problem to his successor.[9]

Royer inherited a tense situation. "Dr. D. F. Royer our new agent took charge this week," wrote interpreter Philip Wells to Standing Rock agent James McLaughlin in October, "but I think he has got an elephant on his hands, as the craze had taken such a hold on the Indians before he took charge." Wells was not too worried, though: "As yet I have all hopes he will be able to stop it without any serious trouble."[10]

Wells's confidence was misplaced. Royer was the wrong person to try to stop the Ghost Dance movement.

The dancing on Pine Ridge quickly spread to three of the other Sioux reservations. In September, the movement had traveled from the Oglalas at Pine Ridge to the Brulés at Rosebud. Short Bull had been silenced at Rosebud in the spring, but in September, Short Bull, Two Strike, and Crow Dog began the dances again. The Brulés had had no strong chief to replace Spotted Tail after Crow Dog had assassinated the great leader in 1881 in an unsuccessful attempt to gain political control over the tribe. The modest Two Strike, who tended to do what Crow Dog urged, led many of the Brulés by 1890. Others, though, did not trust his judgment. While there would eventually be at least 1,800 Brulé Ghost Dancers, not all the Brulé followed Two Strike into the movement. Still, by September, the dancing on Rosebud was well enough established to prompt the agent to try, unsuccessfully, to stop it.[11]

By late September, the movement had also moved north to the Minneconjous at Cheyenne River Reservation. Hump and Big Foot, who had led the Minneconjous' opposition to the land agreement, encouraged the Ghost Dance. Hump had been a good friend of Crazy Horse and an important leader in the battles of 1876. His band of almost six hundred people lived sixty miles west of the agency on Cherry Creek, while Big Foot's people were eighty miles west of the agency on the Cheyenne River. Both camps were dancing the Ghost Dance.[12]

In late October, Cheyenne River agent Perain P. Palmer, another one of Senator Pettigrew's appointees, called Big Foot and Hump to the agency to talk about the movement. Big Foot, who was famous as a negotiator, chatted willingly, but refused to stop the dancing. Instead, he complained that the new reservations were far smaller than the Minneconjous had been promised, and told the agent his people were simply ignoring the boundary lines. Hump was "sullen and had nothing to say," Palmer reported. He had lost his influence by signing the land treaty, and was trying to recoup his position by backing the Ghost Dance, the agent figured. For this reason, Palmer concluded that Hump was "the most dangerous character on this agency." He wanted to destroy Hump's influence over his people by having him taken off the reservation. As soon as men like Hump were gone, Palmer told his supervisors, their followers would stop intimidating "the Christian and well disposed Indians," and the Sioux would adapt more quickly to the modern world.[13]

The agents were unable to slow the spread of the Ghost Dance. By October, Sitting Bull was curious about the new religion. He asked his agent if he could travel from Standing Rock Reservation, where he lived, to visit the Minneconjous on neighboring Cheyenne River Reservation to learn more about it. When the agent denied permission, Sitting Bull instead invited Kicking Bear to visit his village at Grand River and explain the Ghost Dance to the Hunkpapas there. Kicking Bear arrived on October 9 and started the dance among Sitting Bull's people.

The agent at Standing Rock, James McLaughlin, who hated Sitting Bull and the traditionalists, sent Indian police to throw Kicking Bear out of Standing Rock. Instead, the police came back more than half convinced of the truth of the new religion. Although the officers had not managed to arrest Kicking Bear, Sitting Bull promised to send him home anyway, and did so. But he insisted his people had the right to continue dancing if they wished.[14]

McLaughlin blamed his nemesis Sitting Bull for the strength of the traditionalists among the Hunkpapas. In mid-October, he complained to the Indian Commissioner that the chief "is a man of low cunning, devoid of a single manly principle in his nature or an honorable trait of character." McLaughlin described Sitting Bull, a skilled warrior famous for his wisdom, as "a coward [who] lacks moral courage . . . a polygamist, libertine, habitual liar, active obstructionist, and a great obstacle in the civilization of these people." And therein lay the rub. McLaughlin loathed Sitting Bull because he led what the agent called the "worthless, ignorant, obstinate and nonprogressive" Indians. These were the men who had objected to the 1889 land cession and who resisted the agent's plan to "civilize" them. McLaughlin wanted Sitting Bull arrested and removed from the reservation.[15]

McLaughlin's hatred of Sitting Bull was out of the ordinary, but his frustration reflected the same irritation that the agents at Pine Ridge, Rosebud, and Cheyenne River felt. Try as they might, they could not squelch the Ghost Dance. McLaughlin was experienced and powerful. If he was frustrated, things did not bode well for the inexperienced Royer at Pine Ridge.

While agents on four of the reservations fretted over the Ghost Dance, its influence was actually fairly limited. The Sioux at Crow Creek and Lower Brulé Reservations never caught the Ghost Dance enthusiasm as fervently as the Sioux at the other reservations. While some Indians there danced, the agents at those reservations always stayed comfortably in control of their charges. Crow Creek and Lower Brulé largely stayed isolated from the crises of the next two months.[16]

Even on the four reservations most affected, not all the Sioux embraced the Ghost Dance. Elaine Goodale, traveling around the reservations in her new job as school inspector, found the Ghost Dance in full swing when she reached Standing Rock in October. She believed that the movement had been adopted only by those who had never joined the church or attended school. "Educated and Christian Sioux scorned the whole matter," she recorded. Goodale estimated the Ghost Dancers at only 10 percent of the population. McLaughlin agreed that only the traditionalist faction of the Hunkpapas had joined the new religion, and blamed the excitement entirely on Sitting Bull.[17]

Although the movement was limited, Republicans began to see it as a political opportunity. In mid-October, a South Dakota newspaper tried to make political hay out of the Ghost Dance movement. It printed the report of a local man who blamed the trouble at Pine Ridge on the Democrats. The problem, he said, was that the Indians at Pine Ridge had regressed back to savagery under Democratic agent Gallagher. A lazy man who was rarely around, according to the report, Gallagher had "allowed the Indians to do about as they choose." What they chose, the paper reported, was to "leave their children and stock to care for themselves and spend their time in dancing and wild religious orgies," during which they profligately ate their cattle, undermining government attempts to make them good farmers. This article was picked up by at least one other Republican newspaper farther east.[18]

Fortunately, the papers noted, a solution was at hand. The new Republican appointee taking over as Indian agent at Pine Ridge would fix things. Daniel Royer would be a strong agent who would straighten the reservation out just as soon as he cleaned up the sad mess left by the Democrat. When Royer assumed control, the local informant assured readers, "things about the agency will put on a different face."[19]

The newspaper report was correct in one regard: Royer did transform the agency almost as soon as he took over. But rather than justifying his fellow Republicans' faith in him by improving conditions there, under his leadership the situation deteriorated with breathtaking speed. The Sioux accurately named Royer "Young-Man-Afraid-of-Indians."

Royer's own inadequacies were exacerbated by his lack of supervision. While Royer was starting at Pine Ridge, the Commissioner of Indian Affairs, T. J. Morgan, was on a tour of the southwestern Indian agencies. He had left the business of the Office of Indian Affairs to his assistant until his return at the end of the year. The acting commissioner, R. V. Belt, was left to manage Royer and the growing trouble, but was nervous about doing too much on his own. He did tell Royer to forbid any further Ghost Dancing, but when Royer passed on the message to the Indians as soon as he took office, they ignored him. The nervous and incompetent agent leapt to a dramatic conclusion about what needed to be done. After less than a week at his new job, Royer told the

Indian Office on October 12 that he might need troops to keep order on Pine Ridge. Interior Department officials, though, had fought long and hard to keep control of Indian affairs, and wanted no part of admitting they needed the army to keep order. On October 18, Belt urged Royer to use persuasion to get the chiefs to stop the dancing. Royer continued to try to talk to the Indians interested in the Ghost Dance, and they continued to ignore him.[20]

Fortunately, it seemed, Royer and Belt had backup nearby. General Nelson Miles had been appointed Commander of the Division of the Missouri after the death of General Crook. Since the problem fell within his Division, he was the chairman of a commission charged with evaluating the claims of the five hundred or so Northern Cheyenne at Pine Ridge that they should be resettled with their kin in Montana. To adjust this situation, he went to Pine Ridge at the end of October. En route, he gave an interview to a newspaper reporter assuring the public that any future Indian outbreak was unlikely. The army was well equipped to handle disturbances, and new railroads enabled officers to congregate troops quickly. Still, he cautioned, Indian affairs should always be handled with great care.[21]

It was not until he arrived at Pine Ridge that Miles heard of Royer's troubles. The general worked to calm the worried agent. The two men called the Oglalas to council, where Royer told them again that they must give up the dance. The Ghost Dancers, led by the aged Little Wound, responded that they wanted Royer to write to the president and tell him they would not.[22]

Rather than obeying commands to stop exploring their new religion, the Pine Ridge Indians explained to General Miles why the Ghost Dance was so important to them. They detailed their crushing circumstances and suggested that the agents had been little help. They hoped that Miles, whom they believed was fair and honest, could do something. Red Cloud told General Miles that he was glad the general had come. "It is like a person coming out of darkness into light to meet a good man," the chief told him. Little Wound said the new religion was the only way the Indians had to address their poverty and desperation. He had been a progressive himself, but had turned to the Ghost Dance because his daughter was dying from lack of food and medical care. Little Wound told Royer and Miles that the dance permitted Indians to "be Indians again as they once were," and that "he wanted his people to be Indians and live like Indians and not try to live and act like white people."[23]

Little Wound's words did not change Miles's opinion that the Ghost Dance was harmless. He told Red Cloud that he had no objection to the new religion and that the Indians could dance if they wished. He brushed off Royer's panic with the assurance that the Ghost Dance would fade away on its own.[24]

The Indians had been happy to see Miles, but his nonchalance about the Ghost Dance movement had done nothing to shore up Royer's credibility. A day after the meeting, the agent tried again to convince the chiefs that they must stop the dancing. They laughed at him and told him they would "keep it up as long as they pleased."[25]

All this was too much for Royer. After the meeting with Miles, he scribbled a long and frantic letter to Acting Commissioner Belt in Washington. "I was sent here to advance these people as fast as possible on the road to self support and to suppress as far as it is in my power any inclination on their part toward taking backward steps," he wrote. But he claimed that as many as two-thirds of the Oglalas supported the Ghost Dance, making his work impossible.

The words continued to tumble out of him headlong: the Oglalas were defying the law, threatening the police, and taking their children out of school. Royer was shocked to discover that if he sent the police after the children, their parents would fight rather than handing them over. The "crazy Indians" were "tearing down more in a day than the Government can build up in a month."

Royer wanted troops and he wanted them soon. He had the support of George Sword, American Horse, and Young-Man-Afraid-of-His-Horse, he claimed, and these experienced warriors had told him it would take six or seven hundred soldiers to suppress the dance. "If the ghost dance is stopped there is some hope for these Indians and if it is not stopped these people will be backward until they reach the savage mark of the [eighteen] sixties," he warned.[26]

Back in Washington, the politicians at the Interior Department had no intention of giving up control of Indian affairs to the army if they could possibly help it. Rather than asking military officials to send soldiers to Pine Ridge, Belt detailed James A. Cooper, a Special Indian

Agent who had been with the Cheyenne Commission, to stay at Pine Ridge to reinforce Royer. With luck, Cooper would be able to lend some authority to Royer's negotiations, and the reservation would calm without military intervention.

While the relationship between the agent and the Oglalas at Pine Ridge deteriorated, a similar crisis was shaping up on neighboring Rosebud Reservation. To a large extent, the problems on Rosebud resulted from the same sort of political machinations that had plagued Pine Ridge. On Rosebud, Harrison's men had removed an agent the Brulé had respected because they wanted his place for a South Dakota Republican. Secretary of the Interior Noble had refused to appoint a candidate favored by reformers but, under pressure, he had eventually given the job to J. George Wright, the son of the man the reformers had wanted for the position. The Brulés liked the younger Wright, but when census agent Lea claimed there were 2,500 fewer Brulé than had been drawing rations, Wright had been accused of exaggerating the population of the reservation to get more food. He had been suspended pending an investigation.[27]

Wright's replacement, Special Agent E. B. Reynolds, a Republican reformer only recently arrived from Indiana, staunchly opposed the Ghost Dancers and recoiled from the Indians. His letters to Acting Commissioner Belt showed a man who was trying to make the best of things at Rosebud, but he had no funds to improve conditions for the hungry Indians. When he tried to impose agency rules, the Brulés simply ignored him. Their disdain increased his frustration and fear. Reynolds complained that the Brulés pestered him every day about their need for food. When he couldn't provide any, they openly butchered and ate cattle that had been provided as breeding stock. Then he tried to arrest them for killing cattle against orders, but they defied him. "They had better die fighting than to die a slow death of starvation," they told him. The new religion promised they would come back to earth after it had been renewed with buffalo and game, so they had no fear of death.[28]

Reynolds was alarmed when he heard rumors that the Brulé were buying guns and ammunition. The Indians were probably preparing to hunt for food, but Reynolds interpreted the Brulés' actions through his fear that they were plotting the "annihilation of the white man." He believed they were stocking up on weapons not to hunt, but to kill settlers.

The shortage of agency money created another situation that heightened the agent's fears still further. Brulé men who had delivered wood to the agency should have been paid in cash, but Reynolds had none. Instead he gave them IOUs, which, of course, the hungry Indians couldn't use for anything. It seems likely that the Brulés were frustrated at the agent's apparent bad faith after their hard work, and they probably lacked conviction that the government would ever pay them. Certainly they had a long list of government promises that had gone unfulfilled. So they tried to sell the IOUs to traders, at about a third of their face value, for cash. When they did so, the agent believed that the Brulés were selling at such a loss only because they were desperate to arm for a brewing war.[29]

Like Royer at Pine Ridge, Reynolds panicked. In early November, he reported to Belt that the Brulés were trading everything they owned for guns and ammunition. He begged for troops. An Indian outbreak was imminent, he insisted, and could be sparked inadvertently at any time.[30]

Between the antics of Royer and Reynolds, the Brulé Ghost Dance leader Short Bull, who had met Wovoka himself when he had traveled to Nevada, was fed up. At the end of October, he spoke to a group of Indians at the Pine Ridge Reservation. Whites were interfering too much with the new religion, he said. His time as a leader of the Ghost Dance movement seemed to have convinced Short Bull that he was, himself, the son of God. Wovoka's prophecy had promised the new world would come in the spring of 1891, but Short Bull advanced the time of the approaching cataclysm from the next spring to "the new moon after the next one, or about December 11th." Short Bull told the Brulé that believers must gather at Pass Creek, the boundary between Pine Ridge and Rosebud, to await the coming of the new world.[31]

Short Bull knew full well that the gathering of the Indians would alarm the agents, and he warned his listeners that the soldiers might come. He assured the Ghost Dancers that they did not have to worry about the troops. God would protect them. The Sioux Ghost Dancers at White Clay Creek had recently adopted special clothing to wear in their ceremony: loose dresses or shirts of white cotton, painted in blue and red and decorated with the moon and stars. Short Bull told his followers that these shirts would be imbued with magic. He promised his followers that the special shirts would protect them from the guns of the soldiers sent to stop the Ghost Dance. "My father has shown me these things," he told them.

> If the soldiers surround you four deep, three of you, on whom I have put holy shirts, will sing a song, which I have taught you, around them, when some of them will drop dead. Then the rest will start to run, but their horses will sink into the earth. The riders will jump from the horses, but they will sink into the earth also. Then you can do as you desire with them. Now, you must know this, that all the soldiers and that race will be dead. There will be only five thousand of them left living on the earth. My friends and relations, this is straight and true.[32]

Short Bull's speech seemed to justify the agents' fears. Royer and Reynolds passed word of it back to Washington as evidence that it was only a question of time until the Indians rose up and began to kill settlers. But their view was skewed by their fear and by the Indians' refusal to starve quietly. The Ghost Dance movement was gaining adherents, but even on Rosebud, where there wasn't a strong leader to work with the agents to preserve peace like Red Cloud did on Pine Ridge, it still didn't capture the whole tribe. Meanwhile, the agents were trying to stop the movement with commands, rather than addressing the desperate need of the Indians in ways that might offer them a future in this world, rather than limiting their hopes to the next. For their part, the Oglala and Brulé Ghost Dancers had little to lose by joining a religion that offered food, prosperity, and a world without government agents.

Despite the panic filtering back to the Interior Department, the administration continued to emphasize that its western policies were ushering the Indians into a productive and full citizenship. In late October, *Frank Leslie's* ran the story of a "full-blooded Sioux, John Fastman," who had been named to a federal grand jury at Sioux Falls, South Dakota, and insisted: "It cannot be said that the American Indian is not coming into the possession of the rights of manhood."[33]

The Indian School at the South Dakota Pine Ridge Reservation. After the Civil War, Americans were eager to spread their new economy across the western plains, but it did not blend easily with the traditional culture of the Sioux. *Denver Public Library, Western History Collection, John C. H. Grabill, NS-285*

Republican Senator John Sherman. Sherman worked hard during and after the Civil War to craft policies and pass laws that would nurture American industry. Such policies ushered in a business boom that benefited men like him, but whose prosperity rested on an increasingly impoverished working class. *Photographic reproduction by Cydney Ambrose Photography*

General Nelson A. Miles. Miles was related by marriage to John Sherman and his brother General William Tecumseh Sherman and shared their determination to push American development west. Stationed on the western frontier after the Civil War, he came to prominence fighting the Sioux after the 1876 Battle of the Little Bighorn and went on to become one of the nation's most famous Indian fighters. *Photographic reproduction by Cydney Ambrose Photography*

Gall, Hunkpapa Sioux. Gall helped to repulse General Custer and his men when they tried to subdue the Sioux at the Battle of the Little Bighorn. But by the 1880s, even Gall had been forced to accept life on a reservation. In 1889, he signed an agreement opening up much of the Great Sioux Reservation for white settlement. *Denver Public Library, Western History Collection, D. F. Barry, B-903*

Sitting Bull, Hunkpapa Sioux. Sitting Bull led Sioux resistance to the U.S. Army from the time of the Civil War until he surrendered in 1881. Settled on the Great Sioux Reservation in 1883, Sitting Bull refused to sign the agreement that ceded Sioux land to white settlers. He became a symbol of traditional resistance to American society. *Denver Public Library, Western History Collection, D. F. Barry, B-119*

Harvesting on the Oleson farm, Brookings, South Dakota. In the late 1870s, settlers began to pour into Dakota Territory, carving the prairies into fields. *Copyright © Colorado Historical Society (Detroit Publishing Co. Scan #20102803)*

Ox teams in Sturgis, Dakota Territory. False-fronted stores and oxen harnessed to wagons promised prosperity to the region. *John C. H. Grabill, Library of Congress Prints and Photographs Division*

Pine Ridge agency. In 1889, the government divided the Great Sioux Reservation into six smaller reservations organized around the old agencies. Pine Ridge agency lay near the Nebraska border. *Denver Public Library, Western History Collection, X-31494*

Rosebud agency. To the east of Pine Ridge lay Rosebud Reservation, its agency tucked among the hills. *Denver Public Library, Western History Collection, W. R. Cross, X-31725*

Dr. Charles Alexander Eastman. Eastman, a Santee Sioux educated in eastern schools, arrived at Pine Ridge to become the agency doctor just as troubles began to escalate between the Ghost Dancers and the new agent, a political appointee frightened of Indians. *National Anthropological Archives, Smithsonian Institution, 02908602*

Elaine Goodale. Goodale was an eastern reformer who came to the Great Sioux Reservation to teach at an Indian school. She was a critical observer and participant in the events of late 1890. *Rockwood, Sophia Smith Collection, Smith College*

Chief of Pine Ridge police George Bartlett and Sioux police officer pose with Indian family in front of a cabin and a tepee on Wounded Knee Creek at Pine Ridge. Reformers like Eastman and Goodale hoped to help Sioux families make the transition from their traditional culture to that of modern America. *Denver Public Library, Western History Collection, C. G. Morledge, X-31387*

View overlooking General John R. Brooke's Second Infantry camp north of the Pine Ridge agency. In October 1890, the new agent at Pine Ridge begged for troops to put down the Ghost Dancers. While army officers insisted the dancers posed no danger, politicians in Washington obliged the agent. *Denver Public Library, Western History Collection, X-31412*

View overlooking Sioux tepees and United States Cavalry camp on the Pine Ridge Reservation. Army officers tried to divide "loyal" Sioux from Ghost Dancers by ordering the Sioux to their agencies. Sioux families gathered near the Pine Ridge agency, but there was much contact between people at the agency and those at the Ghost Dance camps. *Denver Public Library, Western History Collection, C. G. Morledge, X-31314*

Reporters pose in front of tepees at Pine Ridge agency. When the army mobilized, reporters rushed to Pine Ridge, but things there remained quiet as General Brooke tried to coax the Ghost Dancers back to the agency. The bored reporters invented lurid stories and killed time posing for photographers. Left to right are: C. H. Cressey (*Omaha Bee*); William Fitch Kelley (*Nebraska State Journal*); Major John Burke (manager of Buffalo Bill's Wild West Show); an identified Native American man; Alfred Burkholder (*Chamberlain* [SD] *Gazette* and *New York Herald*); and Charles W. Allen (*Chadron Democrat* and *New York Herald*). *Denver Public Library, Western History Collection, C. G. Morledge, X-31438*

Seventh Cavalry. The Seventh Cavalry was ordered to South Dakota to prevent an uprising. Its men were not well-disposed to the Sioux because, under General George A. Custer, the Seventh had been destroyed by the Sioux at the 1876 Battle of the Little Bighorn. *Denver Public Library, Western History Collection, A. G. Johnson, X-31483*

View of the ravine at Wounded Knee. On December 29, 1890, the surrender of a band of Ghost Dancers who had traveled from Cheyenne River to Pine Ridge sparked a massacre. When the firing broke out, Sioux ran for shelter in a ravine while women and children tried unsuccessfully to escape in wagons. *Denver Public Library, Western History Collection, X-31468*

View of the council area, Wounded Knee. On January 1, 1891, Lieutenant Sydney A. Cloman, First Infantry, rode his horse among the frozen bodies of the Sioux killed at Wounded Knee. Soldiers had carted their own dead and wounded back to the Pine Ridge agency on the day of the fighting, but a blizzard kept them from gathering the Sioux. When men returned to the scene of the fight two days later, Indian bodies were frozen and twisted in the snow. *Denver Public Library, Western History Collection, Northwestern Photographic Company, X-31421*

Gathering the dead at Wounded Knee. A burial detail from Pine Ridge Agency counted and buried the Sioux left on the field. After stripping the bodies of mementos, they piled them on a wagon to cart them to the hill where the artillery had fired down at the Indians during the fight. *Denver Public Library, Western History Collection, Northwestern Photographic Company, X-31464*

Burying the dead at Wounded Knee. Men in charge of the burial threw the bodies into a trench, dug in the frozen ground on the hill. Soldiers and civilians pose for a photographer around the trench of dead, frozen Sioux. *Denver Public Library, Western History Collection, Northwestern Photographic Company, X-31292*

Interior of Holy Cross Episcopal Church at the Pine Ridge agency. Dr. Eastman placed grievously wounded Sioux on the floor of the Episcopal chapel, cushioned with hay and wrapped in blankets. Here soldiers and a Sioux man stand near wounded Sioux as they lie beneath the Christmas decorations Eastman and Goodale had put up only days before. *Denver Public Library, Western History Collection, A. G. Johnson, X-31471*

General Nelson A. Miles and Buffalo Bill at Pine Ridge Reservation. Miles arrived at Pine Ridge to oversee the surrender of those Sioux who had fled the agency in panic after the massacre at Wounded Knee. He and Buffalo Bill posed for a photographer in front of an army camp, Buffalo Bill pointing something out to the general with his left hand. *Denver Public Library, Western History Collection, John C. H. Grabill, NS-56*

Sioux Delegation, 1891. General Miles arranged for a delegation of Sioux to go to Washington to explain the dire circumstances on the reservations to President Harrison and other administration officials. The talks came to nothing. The back of the photograph identifies the people here as: "TOP ROW, 1. Zaphier, 2. Hump, 3. High Pipe, 4. Fast Thunder, 5. Rev. Cha[rle]s Cook, 6. P. T. Johnson, MIDDLE ROW, 1. He Dog, 2. F. D. Lewis, 3. Spotted Horse, 4. American Horse, 5. Maj. Geo[rge] Sword, 6. Lewis Shangreau, 7. Bat Pourie[r], BOTTOM ROW, 1. High Hawk, 2. Fire Lighting, 3. Little Wound, 4. Two-Strikes, 5. Young Man Afraid Of His Horse, 6. Spotted Elk, 7. Big Road."
Denver Public Library, Western History Collection, X-31799

Red Cloud's house at Pine Ridge agency. Two women stand with Red Cloud outside the chief's home. Red Cloud had led the Sioux against the army after the Civil War, but signed a peace treaty in 1868. Once settled on the Great Sioux Reservation, Red Cloud tried to help the Sioux negotiate a path into American life. *Denver Public Library, Western History Collection, X-31410*

Red Cloud's bedroom, Pine Ridge agency. *Denver Public Library, Western History Collection, C. G. Morledge, X-31433*

Red Cloud, Oglala Sioux. Red Cloud had been forced to accept the inevitability of the loss of his lands, but he recognized the terrible toll of the American economy on those it did not benefit. At the end of his life, he concluded sadly: "I wish there was some one to help my poor people. . . ." *Denver Public Library, Western History Collection, X-31326*

In contrast to *Frank Leslie's* promotion of Republican western policy, though, administration officials were starting to worry that they had a big problem on their hands in South Dakota. Only days after *Frank Leslie's* boast about the integrated grand jury, Harrison asked Secretary of War Redfield Proctor to organize an investigation into what was going on in South Dakota. Worried by Royer's cries for help, the president ordered the Secretary of War on October 31 to take all necessary precautions to prevent an outbreak, including stationing troops in the vicinity in case they were needed. He also asked that General Miles or Brigadier General Thomas H. Ruger, commanding officer of the Department of Dakota, go to Standing Rock and report what he found.[34]

Miles was concentrating on the Cheyenne in Montana, whom he considered a far greater threat than the Sioux, so it was General Ruger who set off for Cheyenne River and Standing Rock. When he arrived in early November, the agents at both the reservations assured him that, with the soldiers at nearby forts in reserve in case of an emergency, they could control their Indians. Ruger increased security at Cheyenne River by ordering more infantry to Fort Bennett, near the Minneconjous there.[35]

At Standing Rock, General Ruger agreed that Agent McLaughlin and Lieutenant Colonel William F. Drum, the commander of nearby Fort Yates, had things under control. They told Ruger that they could maintain calm so long as Sitting Bull was removed from the reservation. They wanted to put off arresting him until the winter turned colder, though, to prevent his men from protecting their chief. McLaughlin convinced Ruger that the Standing Rock Indian police could make the arrest, with Drum's soldiers supporting them if necessary.[36]

Once he had dispatched Ruger, President Harrison put the Indian problems in South Dakota to the back of his mind. He and his men had other things to worry about. Election Day, November 4, was fast approaching. In preparation for it, Republicans ran through their talking points. They insisted on the sanctity of the tariff and pushed the Federal Elections Bill, although they reiterated their own dislike for black Americans and reassured Southerners that election protection would absolutely not apply to local elections. They reminded voters that they were responsible for the Dependent Pension Act. Their most important mission, though, was to persuade westerners to vote Republican. In the West they were quiet about the tariff, and directed Republican speakers to remind voters of all that they had received already from the administration and all that they could continue to expect. Russell Harrison also begged the president to let a railroad company build through an Indian reservation in Montana. The construction would bring jobs and money to the suffering state. "This matter must be attended to at once, as it will have a bad effect on our campaign if it is not." Only such a deal could swing Montana into the Republican column, he counseled.[37]

As nervous as they were privately, Republicans insisted in public that their prospects in the election were "very favorable."[38]

And yet, despite all their propaganda, redrawing of the electoral map, and endless catering to wealthy donors, the Republicans got hammered in the 1890 midterm elections. They had argued for preserving their economic system despite the fact that it was clearly failing a great many Americans, and they had manipulated the political system to do it. But the voters were not fooled.

Angry voters took away the Republicans' slim majority in the House and handed their opponents a majority of more than two to one. New York City, so crucial to the party's success and the focus of so much Republican attention, went heavily for the Democrats. Rising prices there, blamed on the new tariff, infuriated workers and even middle-class homeowners, and as it turned out, New York's new secret ballot did not hurt the Democrats as badly as the Republicans had hoped. (They actually worried privately that more of their voters were stymied by the new system than Democrats were.) William McKinley himself, sponsor of the tariff, went down in defeat in Ohio.[39]

Moderate Republicans as well as Democrats celebrated the verdict as a popular condemnation of the abuses of the Harrison gang, but most observers chalked up the Republican loss to the McKinley Tariff. By increasing rather than decreasing tariff rates, the new law seemed to prove that the administration served big business to the detriment of everyone else. As soon as the tariff had passed, observers recognized that the election would be a referendum on whether or not Americans liked the new law. The Republicans' overwhelming defeat delivered the answer. "It seems that about nine-tenths of [voters] were out of humor with the McKinley bill, and the remaining one-tenth were disappointed concerning the distribution of patronage," wrote Elliott Shepard, a leading Republican operative, to President Harrison's private secretary.[40]

Republicans, not surprisingly, went on the defensive. Some contended that the tariff was delayed too long and hadn't had time to make a positive impact on the economy. Others claimed the loss had nothing to do with the tariff at all. Harrison himself seemed sad and confused, blaming the defeat on a variety of local issues and declaring that the tariff was not to blame. He insisted that the Democrats had not, in fact, gained any permanent ground.[41]

In the weeks after the election, as results trickled in, *Frank Leslie's* mounted a spirited—if desperate—defense of the tariff, running article after article about its benefits. It blamed higher prices on the storekeepers themselves, who, they said, had used it as an excuse to raise prices—even on goods they had purchased before the McKinley Tariff went into effect. The tariff, the paper insisted, was not to blame for the malaise of the national economy; rather, the new law promised to make the economy even healthier than it already was. Still, the stock market stubbornly continued to deliver bad news. As it did so, *Frank Leslie's* added another culprit to blame for the downward trend: it was the London market that was depressing the American economy.[42]

But the real reason for the defeat, claimed Harrison Republicans, was that Americans had not been sufficiently willing to let the administration run things. Across the board, administration Republicans blamed the party's defeat not on their own increasingly unpopular program, but on those people, moderate Republicans as well as Democrats, who refused to adopt the administration's program wholesale. Moderate Republicans had rallied too late to the McKinley Tariff; Democrats had obstructed the Federal Elections Bill. Democrats had attacked the census only to slow down the necessary reapportionment that would have benefited Republicans. Had these things gone into effect as the administration had wanted, the Republicans would have won resoundingly, *Frank Leslie's* maintained.[43]

In an exasperated outburst, *Frank Leslie's* even went so far as to blame the outcome of the election on the stupidity of voters:

> It is utterly amazing, in view of the trouble the newspapers took to explain again and again the practical workings of the Ballot Reform law in this State, that thousands of intelligent voters did not know how to vote. In nearly every district in the State men were found who did not understand the workings of the law and who were out of patience with its provisions, and who sometimes finally refused to vote. Nobody with a grain of common sense, who takes a daily or a weekly newspaper, had an excuse for not knowing precisely how to handle his ballots on election day.

It certainly wasn't *Frank Leslie's* fault, the self-righteous editor concluded. Evidently, "people who take the papers do not always read them."[44]

Westerners were the worst when it came to misunderstanding their own interests, according to *Frank Leslie's*. Like most eastern observers, the editors of *Frank Leslie's* were stunned by the power of the Alliances. The farmers' political movement had swept through the West "like a wave of fire," as *Harper's Weekly* put it, and the election results shocked Republican organizers. Alliances had worked quietly, through new and local newspapers that old party machines had largely ignored. They had drawn a surprising number of votes.[45]

Alliance voters had created a dramatic political shift in the West that dangerously threatened Republican power. State governments all over the West would have new officials beholden to Alliance voters. The Alliance had carried almost the whole state ticket in Kansas and had a majority of the legislature there. Alliance men held the balance of power in the Minnesota and Illinois legislatures, and had carried South Dakota. In Nebraska, they had split the Republicans, thus giving the governorship of the state to a Democrat. The same split in Iowa gave the state legislature to the Democrats.[46]

The power of the Alliances stretched to Washington. Alliances had elected five of Kansas's seven congressmen, and two of Nebraska's three. By splitting the Republicans, they had helped Missouri and Iowa elect a Democratic delegation to Congress. Ultimately, Alliance members would control fifty-two votes in the next Congress, forcing it to take up the issues of land, money, and transportation that eastern Republicans wanted to avoid. It was also virtually certain they would force Congress to revisit the new tariff law.[47]

Republicans could see that western disaffection might well bleed enough support from them to throw the next presidency to the Democrats. One of the Alliance's key issues was the tariff, and Republicans were well aware that the frontrunner for the 1892 Democratic nomination was tariff reformer Grover Cleveland. Harrison told a supporter that the Republicans could well deal with the Democrats in 1892, but could not handle the Alliances. "If the Alliance can hold full one half of our Republican voters in such states as Kansas and Neb[raska] our future is not cheerful." *Frank Leslie's* hoped that the 1890 election results would encourage Republicans to come together before 1892, and encouraged Republicans to remember that "this is an Administration to swear *by* and not *at*."[48]

The best way, still, to affect the 1892 vote was by weighting the vote toward Republicans. But Republican plans to do just that came under attack immediately after the election. Early reports of the census count drew widespread complaints that the census agents were either incompetent, Republican operatives, or both. The count looked so badly skewed that even Republicans privately disparaged it.[49]

While the administration vociferously defended the census, a congressional investigation reported at the beginning of December that the numbers were gravely wrong. The census superintendent retorted that those charging a deliberate miscount "are either reckless demagogues or ignorant partisans, who judge the actions of others from the standpoint of their own moral capacity and mental incapacity, and who are neither willing nor capable of investigating and understanding the facts for themselves." *Frank Leslie's*, of course, continued to defend the census. But by this time even many Republicans admitted the whole enterprise had been a disaster.[50]

After the election of 1890, Republicans hung onto power only through their lock on the Senate. There, their earlier manipulation of the electoral map had paid off. Thanks to the admission of the new states (and the heavy-handed replacement of the Democratic senators from Montana with Republicans) the Republicans had four more senators than their opponents did. Or so it appeared immediately after the election.[51]

But even in the Senate, the Republicans had a problem. Their economic and political strategy depended on the protective tariff. Newly elected Democratic and Alliance representatives threatened to repeal the McKinley Tariff and pass true tariff reform, and it looked likely that a Democratic president in 1892 would stand by them even if Harrison could hold them off for the next two years. The only way for the Republicans to protect the tariff was to control the Senate. But three of the senators that made up the Republican majority there—Plumb, Paddock, and Pettigrew—had voted against the McKinley Tariff. And, jubilantly supported by the voters in their western states, they continued to oppose it. Ultimately, the survival of the McKinley Tariff hung on one vote—that of a senator from South Dakota.[52]

South Dakota senator Gideon Moody had been up for reelection, and Republicans believed they had held his seat, but they would not be certain until January, at least. In the nineteenth century, senators were not elected by a popular vote but were chosen by the state legislature. This meant that the real fight for control of the Senate took place within states, as politicians worked to get their own men elected to the legislature so they could pick the party's senatorial candidate. (It was this need to control the legislature that made Abraham Lincoln debate Stephen A. Douglas in towns across Illinois in 1858 in his quest to unseat Douglas and become an Illinois senator.) Indeed, one of the reasons that Harrison supported "Home Rule" for Indian agencies was to enable senators to distribute lucrative posts effectively to the local men who could help them hold their positions. National officials were far less effective at the state-level patronage game—they could easily miss local nuances and give positions to the wrong people.

Before the election, Republicans in South Dakota downplayed fears that the Alliance would siphon voters from the party, certain that they would hold on to the state government. They were wrong. In the 1890 elections in South Dakota, Republican defections to the Alliance and even to the Democrats hurt the party badly. Arthur C. Mellette, the Republican governor, won, but he received 20,000 fewer votes than he had only the year before. Together, the Democratic and Alliance candidates received more than 42,000 votes while Mellette marshaled only 34,000. The Alliance candidate lost to Mellette by only about 10,000 votes.[53]

Even worse were the poll results for the state legislature. In the state's short history, South Dakota's Republican politicians had sided with the machine wing of the Republican Party rather than with its moderates, making them vulnerable to attacks by the Alliance. The senator who had drawn the longer term when the state came into the Union, Richard Pettigrew, was not vulnerable in 1890, but the reelection of his colleague, Gideon Moody, depended on a Republican legislature. The state had been bitterly contested, and the vote was very close. Coming out of the election, initial reports placed the legislature firmly in the Republican column, but then news leaked out that a ballot box in Sioux Falls had been broken into and ballots "tampered with." Rumors of other irregularities quickly followed. Democrats and Alliance members demanded recounts and insisted that a fair count would prove their candidates had won.[54]

Suddenly the legislature of South Dakota was in play for all parties—and with it South Dakota's second Senate seat. If local election boards declared that Republicans had actually won, the legislature would be Republican and Moody, an administration supporter, would be returned to the Senate to bolster his party's withering ranks. The Republican program for the nation, including high tariffs and measures to increase Republican voters, would be protected. If the local boards counted in Democrats or Alliance legislators, though, the legislators would back a hostile senator.

Moody's reelection was vital to the national Republican Party, and that reelection was in grave jeopardy. By mid-November, it appeared that the Republicans had lost the South Dakota legislature and party members would have to hope that they could work with the Alliance to elect Moody. But the South Dakota Alliance dashed those prospects. In late November, it held a convention and adopted a platform that called for loyalty to the Alliance above any other organization. It castigated the Republicans for their spending on "unneeded and extravagant public buildings and unearned services, and not one dollar . . . for the advancement of the industrial enterprises" of South Dakota.[55]

It was clear that the Harrison administration had to do something to prop up its power in South Dakota before the legislature met to pick the state's new senator. If it could just convince local election boards that the Republicans were better for the state than Democrats, they would undoubtedly be willing to count in the Republican state legislators, who, Republicans maintained, had won the election in any case but who might be counted out unfairly by Democrats or Alliance men. The trick would be to encourage South Dakota settlers to think well of an administration that increasing numbers of them had grown to loathe.

As the winter approached and more Sioux embraced the Ghost Dance movement, their actions increasingly worried the agents at Pine Ridge and Rosebud. By November, the agent at Cheyenne River Reservation to the north was also concerned. There, Big Foot and Hump continued to encourage the Ghost Dance. On November 4, Cheyenne River agent Palmer reported to Belt that he could manage the dancers there with the help of the Indian police so long as the army could remove Hump. Palmer told Belt that he had sent Christian Indians to stop their kin from converting to the new movement. Together with the missionaries, the Christian Indians were doing good work, he reported.[56]

After visiting the Ghost Dancers at Cherry Creek a few days later, though, Palmer's tone abruptly changed. The dancers would not let him or his police approach the camp, he reported. Worse, rather than talking Ghost Dancers out of their religion, many of the Christian Indians had joined them. The agent also reported a rumor that Sitting Bull, at nearby Standing Rock Reservation, was preparing to fight, along with all the warriors at the Ghost Dance camps. Indians were selling cattle and "using all their available means" to buy Winchester rifles and ammunition, he wrote. Shifting rapidly from rumor to certainty, he told Belt that "if these rifles could be taken away from these hostile Indians all farther trouble [sic] would be managed by the Indian Police but as long as Winchesters are among these Ghost excited Indians the Police are powerless and can do nothing. No offences can be punished and the Indians do as they please."[57]

At the same time to the south, at Pine Ridge, Royer was growing increasingly frightened. His support, even among the progressives, was fragile. Red Cloud was still the leader of the Oglalas and was not encouraging the dancers, but by now he was an old warrior whose failing vision forced him to rely on younger men. George Sword was trying to do as the agent wanted, but had little confidence in him. The progressives American Horse and Young-Man-Afraid-of-His-Horse, along with three or four other chiefs, were trying to support Royer, too, but they had lost authority within the tribe since the land agreement debacle. Opponents of the treaty were gaining ground.[58]

Consolidating power were traditionalists Little Wound and Big Road, both of whom had joined the Ghost Dance and now had a following Royer estimated to include 350 to 400 fighting men (or "bucks," in his racist language). An older man with graying hair and an earnest gaze, Little Wound seemed to be in charge of the Ghost Dancers, Royer noted, describing him as "one of the most influential Chiefs among the Sioux of this Agency and . . . the most stubborn, head-strong, self-willed, unruly Indian on the reservation." Another candidate for leadership at Pine Ridge was hot-headed Jack Red Cloud, who looked like his father but, no matter how hard he tried, would never be the man his father was. He spent his energy desperately trying to live down that shortcoming, acting militantly to attract followers.[59]

In early November, Royer told Acting Commissioner Belt that there were four Ghost Dancing camps at Pine Ridge. One was on White Clay Creek with about 600 dancers, led by four men including Jack Red Cloud. One was on Porcupine Creek with about 150 dancers led by three minor chiefs. One was on Wounded Knee Creek with about 250 dancers led by three men including Big Road, who had spoken for his people since his days with Crazy Horse. The fourth was on Medicine Root Creek with about 500 dancers led by Little Wound.[60]

As he felt himself losing control over his agency, Royer's missives to Washington became increasingly alarmist. By mid-November, he was begging Belt to permit him to come to the capital to explain in person just how bad things were on the reservation. Belt relayed Royer's plea to Secretary of the Interior Noble, who turned it down, curtly responding that "in these troublesome times the agent should remain at his agency and do his duty."[61]

Observing the contending factions at Pine Ridge in early November was the new Pine Ridge doctor, Charles Alexander Eastman. From

1872 to 1890, Eastman had worked his way from the mission school at Flandreau through western preparatory schools and on to Dartmouth College and Boston University, where he earned his M.D. in June 1890. He had come a long way since his boyhood days as Ohiyesa, when he had fled from the Santee affair in Minnesota in 1858.[62]

Hired by the government to be the agency physician at Pine Ridge, Eastman arrived in early November, as the troubles on the reservation were escalating. Educated and friendly with the eastern Indian reformers, he was a firm Christian who hoped to see the Sioux leave their traditional ways. But he was also fluent in Lakota, understood Sioux culture, and was sympathetic to the Indians' plight.

At the agency, Eastman reported to rudimentary quarters furnished only with a desk and two wooden chairs. The office had a sort of ticket window through which previous doctors had passed out pills and potions to waiting Indians rather than actually examining them. He set about getting the layer of fine Dakota dust out of his four rooms—a bedroom, a sitting room, an office, and a dispensary—and meeting the many patients who simply wanted to get a look at the "Indian white doctor."[63]

The Indian reformers and the Christian Indians on the reservation welcomed Dr. Eastman enthusiastically. Within days, Eastman attended a tea party given by the wife of the Episcopal missionary, Reverend Charles Smith Cook, a Yankton Sioux educated at Trinity College and Seabury Divinity School. At the party, Eastman met Elaine Goodale, who was at Pine Ridge to inspect the schools there. While Goodale was generally reserved and dignified in company, she and Eastman talked of their dedication to the Sioux, and clearly they were attracted to each other. "I might as well admit that her personality impressed me deeply," Eastman later recalled.[64]

Almost immediately, Eastman got caught up in the trouble at Pine Ridge. George Sword, now the head of the Pine Ridge Indian police, warned Eastman shortly after his arrival that Royer wanted the Ghost Dancers to stop dancing. But Sword was afraid "the people will not stop. I fear trouble, kola [my friend]," he told Eastman. Royer weighed in soon after, telling Eastman, "We have a most difficult situation to handle, but those men down in Washington don't seem to realize the facts. If I had my way, I would have had troops here before this."[65]

Concerned at the thought of troops coming to Pine Ridge, Eastman consulted Reverend Cook, and the two men concluded that the religion would die of its own accord so long as troops were not brought in to stop it by force. Days later, Sword reappeared to explain that the Ghost Dancers just wanted to be left alone. But Royer had ordered the police to move all government employees and their families to the agency. Sword was afraid that meant he was preparing for the arrival of troops. With soldiers on the reservations, anything could happen.[66]

Military men agreed with Eastman and George Sword that Royer's demand for troops was the wrong way to resolve the problems on the reservations. Indeed, when it came to Indian affairs, military officers almost always sided against the politicians at the Interior Department. There had frequently been tension between the military and politicians in America, but the postwar years had tightened the strain.

At the end of the Civil War, congressmen had divided the nation's military system in half. They had put a commanding general in charge of the army's actions and the Secretary of War in charge of its administration, including supplies. Army staff reported to the Secretary of War rather than the commanding general. Politicians liked this division for two reasons: it prevented the army from becoming an entity separate from civilian control, and it enabled politicians to dole out patronage positions to reinforce their political clout. Military men hated it for the same reasons. It enabled staff to forge political ties and exercise power in Washington, while it left military men dependent for the supplies to carry out their orders on politicians and their cronies, who might or might not be any good at the jobs to which they had been appointed. The political import of army staff positions was not insignificant. The quartermaster general had more than ten thousand civilians working for him, and the Army Corps of Engineers handled construction projects worth tens of millions of dollars. Politicians worked to protect their control over this civilian "army."[67]

The ongoing battle between army officers and politicians had always been most heated over the proper approach to Indian management. Since the 1870s, military officers had insisted that they should control Indian affairs, but politicians had successfully resisted their demands. If political appointees mismanaged their work, though, the military got stuck with the dangerous job of fighting angry Indians. While politicians refused to give up their power, military men resented that politicians' mistakes could cost soldiers their lives.

Interior Department officials were very protective of their control of Indian affairs, and that protectiveness would hamper the administration's ability to handle the situation on the Sioux reservations. In Harrison's administration, Secretary of the Interior Noble did not get along with Secretary of War Proctor. As a consequence, Noble communicated his messages, regardless of their urgency, along strict departmental chains of command, slowing their transmission by days. Any message that an agent wanted to send to an army officer had to be transmitted from the agent to Acting Commissioner of Indian Affairs Belt, who would then send it to the Secretary of the Interior. Noble would then transmit it to the Secretary of War, who sent it back down his own chain of command.

The army maintained a similar communication structure. General Miles had to send his missives to the Adjutant General, who would send them up the line to General Schofield, the Commander of the Army. Schofield would generally show them to the Secretary of War in person. Proctor would then send the messages over to the Secretary of the Interior, who would transfer them down to his underlings. The entire process often took several days.

Except for the agents and officers in the field, all the people who needed to see these messages were in Washington, D.C. The complicated chain of transmission meant that government officials often took several days to respond to imperative requests, or wasted time devising solutions to circumstances that no longer existed. The struggles in Washington developed a life of their own, divorced from what was actually happening in South Dakota.

General Miles was a staunch proponent of military control over Indian affairs. Under his direction, military men in 1890 worked hard to prove that they, rather than politicians, should be in charge of Indian affairs. Officers stationed at the forts in South Dakota and generals overseeing the Department of Dakota and the Department of the Platte had firsthand experience with the Sioux and the agents who oversaw their welfare. These officers denied that the Indians were rising up. Instead, they blamed the troubles in South Dakota on mismanagement of the Sioux by the politicians at the Interior Department. They urged remedies for the suffering of the Indians, and assured their superiors that the Ghost Dance movement would fade if the Indians were only treated fairly.

In early November, a group of 102 Brulé men from Rosebud weighed in on the side of the army. They wrote to President Harrison to complain that when they had given up the Black Hills, "you told us in that Treaty that . . . we could get food just like the soldiers." They had not, though, and were starving. They begged for food. The letter, undoubtedly composed under the supervision of an army officer, went on with a dig at politicians: "Please let us have a soldier for our Father (Agent)," rather than a political appointee. A memorandum accompanying the petition, written by an officer, listed the Indians' grievances, from missing rations and drought to rigged scales that added twenty-five pounds to beef weights.[68]

An army investigation produced more evidence against the politicians in the Interior Department. After seeing the Brulé petition, his superior officer asked Captain C. A. Earnest to poke around a bit at Rosebud Reservation when he inspected ration cattle there to get a sense of what was going on. Earnest chatted with various people while he was at Rosebud, and on November 12, reported confidentially about the situation there. He told his superior officer that the Indians were generally disaffected. The year's crop of wheat, corn, oats, barley, and vegetables had utterly failed because of the drought. Then rations had been cut, and the Secretary of the Interior had recently ordered Indians to stop eating the offal that was so important to their diets, believing that different eating habits would help "civilize" them.[69]

The Indians' list of complaints continued. Congressional delays of appropriations meant that annuities were late, so Indians couldn't buy sugar and coffee. Sioux freighters were not being paid. The summer's prairie fires had burned off the winter pasturage, and the Sioux were worried that the winter beef would be emaciated before it was killed. Agent Wright had been suspended because Lea's census count suggested that he might have deliberately inflated the number of Indians who needed rations, and the Indians were "sullen" and discontented because they "have great confidence in this officer."[70]

The Ghost Dance, Earnest explained, was a product of this extreme disaffection. Agent Wright had left it to disappear on its own, but busybodies had threatened the Indians to hasten the movement's end, telling them that if they didn't stop the soldiers would take away their ponies. Originally, the dancers had not contemplated violence, Earnest said, but this threat "gave the Indians 'war hearts.'" Still Earnest did not expect trouble. He believed that everything would settle down over the winter as soon as the Indians got supplies and, with luck, Wright was reappointed. As a final jab at the agents, he pointed out that, for all their fears, they had neglected to provide the Indian police at the agency with ammunition, while all the other Indians had plenty.[71]

Earnest's report went to his superiors, then traveled east to Washington.

Agent Royer had no patience for the military officers' caution and criticism. He was losing control of his reservation. On the same ration day that Earnest wrote his description of Rosebud, predicting a quiet end to the dancing once the problems there were addressed, Pine Ridge Indians openly challenged Royer's authority. Their revolt convinced him that an uprising was imminent.[72]

On November 12, Indians from across Pine Ridge Reservation converged on the agency for the distribution of meat and the short rations allowed them. After the food had been handed out, a man named Charging Hawk (or Little) went into the council room of the Sioux leaders where a meeting was taking place. The meeting included both progressives, like American Horse, and traditionalists, including Jack Red Cloud. Charging Hawk was wanted by the agent for some minor infraction—perhaps killing cattle, although some accounts just call him a "troublemaker." Royer ordered Lieutenant Thunder Bear and his police to arrest him. But when they tried to take Charging Hawk into custody in the council room, he drew a knife on them. The traditionalists in the council, men like Jack Red Cloud, protected Charging Hawk from the officers. More Ghost Dancers ran to the melee and held the police at gunpoint outside the council room, threatening to kill them.[73]

At the sound of the uproar, Charles Eastman had run from his office adjoining the council room. Just as he got near enough to see what was going on, the progressive American Horse, dressed in white man's clothes, stepped up and berated the traditionalists:

> Stop! Think! What are you going to do? Kill these men of our own race? Then what? Kill all these helpless white men, women and children? And what then? What will these brave words, brave deeds lead to in the end? How long can you hold out? Your country is surrounded with a network of railroads; thousands of white soldiers will be here within three days. What ammunition have you? What provisions? What will become of your families? Think, think, my brothers! This is a child's madness.

His words had the opposite of their intended effect on Jack Red Cloud, who shoved a cocked revolver into American Horse's face. "It is you and your kind who have brought us to this pass!" he shouted. American Horse turned his back on Jack Red Cloud, entered the council room, and shut the door. The crowd drifted away.[74]

That night the drama continued. Late in the evening, American Horse and his wife, along with Captain George Sword, Lieutenant Thunder Bear, and most of the Indian police, dropped in on Charles Eastman. What should they do, they asked, if forced to choose between the Ghost Dancers, people of their own blood, and the government to which they had pledged their loyalty? The doctor counseled them all to work to keep the peace. But, if they had to cast their lot on one side or the other, he and the rest of them had to stand with the government, to which they had sworn a solemn oath.[75]

American Horse was still nervous, afraid that one of the younger traditionalists might attack him, so he and his wife prepared to spend the night in Eastman's spare room. As soon as they were settled, Royer called Eastman to the agent's office. There, the doctor found Royer, the chief clerk, and a visiting inspector, deep in conversation. Royer and the other white men insisted that the attack on the Indian police had been deliberately planned, and speculated that the Indians were plotting to massacre whites next. Eastman demurred, telling Royer that there was absolutely not a general uprising, and that calling for troops would force the Ghost Dancers to fight. Royer called in Reverend Cook, the missionary, who agreed with Eastman. Royer then sent for George Sword, Thunder Bear, and American Horse, all of whom agreed with the agent. Royer had made a pretense of getting advice from them, Eastman later recalled, but he had already determined that he must have soldiers to restore order on Pine Ridge.[76]

Royer continued to call for troops and, in the wake of the standoff between American Horse and Jack Red Cloud, his begging took on a new urgency. On November 13, Royer wrote a frantic and often incoherent letter to acting commissioner Belt. "The condition of affairs at this agency when I took charge, whether intention or not, [sic] were to render my administration a failure," he began. No one was listening to him, he complained, and the "condition of affairs is growing from bad to worse." He related the events of the day before, then added a sequel in which a reader can almost hear his voice squeak in outrage. Charging Hawk had just told the agent that he had four weeks to fire the police officer that had tried to arrest him. If Royer didn't fire the man, Charging Hawk said, he could expect trouble. Rather than taking orders from Royer, the Indians at Pine Ridge were now giving them. His evident loss of control was pushing Royer over the edge. "The police force are overpowered and disheartened. We have no protection and are at the mercy of these crazy dancers." Again he begged to come to Washington, and this time he added a threat: "I do hope you will grant my request or let the blame rest where it belongs."[77]

Royer was frustrated by the apparent foot-dragging of the politicians in the Interior Department, but in fact Belt and Noble were working hard in Washington to get Royer the troops he claimed to need. Unwilling to admit that their policies might be wrong or their agents poorly chosen, they embellished the stories of just how dangerous the Indians were, and freely suggested the use of force against them. On November 7, Noble had advised President Harrison that it would require considerable military force to stop the Ghost Dancing. In the case of Hump and Big Foot, he urged: "It may be best to have a force of soldiers sufficient to arrest and watch these Indians for a time, but if it is attempted, it should be done with firmness and power so great as would overwhelm the Indians from the beginning."[78]

The following day, November 8, Belt forwarded to Noble the frantic letter that Rosebud's special agent Reynolds had sent on November

2, in which he claimed the Brulé wanted to annihilate the settlers. Explaining Reynolds's letter to the Secretary of the Interior, Belt asserted that the Indians at Rosebud were extremely disaffected and troublesome because of the Ghost Dance, and their anger had been aggravated by low rations. According to Reynolds, Belt said, traditionalist Indians were defying the Indian police. If the traditionalists were to be prevented from gaining complete control over the agency, the agents must have troops to back them up. An outbreak was imminent.[79]

As the communications from the South Dakota reservations worked their way higher and higher in the government, they became increasingly detached from reality. Cheyenne River agent Palmer had reported vague rumors that Sitting Bull was going to war and that local Indians were selling their cattle to buy ammunition. When Belt passed Palmer's message up the line to Noble, the rumors had become fact. The Indians "are selling their cattle and buying Winchester rifles," Belt wrote. "The police are powerless and can do nothing, no offenders can be punished, and the Indians do as they please." He also turned the rumor of Sitting Bull's rebellion into reliable information that the chief's whole band was preparing for war. "There is no doubt," he wrote, "that all the hostile Indians at all the dancing camps are preparing to defy the authority of the Department." When Noble sent the message to Secretary of War Redfield Proctor the next day, he reduced the uncertainty of the original message even further. In the hands of Interior Department officials, a suspect rumor had become a substantiated uprising.[80]

By mid-November, Belt was requesting that the Secretary of the Interior forward the increasingly alarming reports from the reservations to the Secretary of War. In mid-November, Belt repeated to Noble Royer's missive about "crazy dancers," and warned him that the situation at the agency was "very critical." Hostilities could break out at any moment, he insisted. It was not safe to leave the agency unprotected. He begged Noble to convince the Secretary of War to engage the military. Belt's goal, he said, was to avert an Indian uprising and to demonstrate to the Sioux that they must respect "the authority of this Department and its agent."[81]

By this time, Belt and Noble were not the only members of the Interior Department lobbying administration officials for military intervention. Another member of the Commission on Indian Affairs sent the same information about the "crazy dancers" directly to President Harrison, telling him that Agent Royer wanted troops to arrest the Ghost Dance leaders and disarm the rest of the Indians on the reservation.[82]

Over the course of fewer than two months in the fall of 1890, the Ghost Dance movement had transformed. It had reignited in late September as a religious response on the part of the Indians to dire conditions on the South Dakota Sioux reservations. But when inexperienced agents were unable to stop the dancing, they began to see Sioux adherence to the Ghost Dance as preparation for an uprising. By mid-November, the messages they sent to Washington foretold a war. As the messages simplified in their retelling up the ranks of Washington officials, they virtually promised one.

The president wanted the army's views on the apparent crisis. He had been busy with appointments and the devastating election and, while he had undoubtedly been paying close attention to the South Dakota election results, had paid scant attention to events on the Indian reservations. Nonetheless, it was a striking fact that, for all the agents' complaints, they seemed alone in their panic. No settlers had written in terror, no governors had begged for help, no newspapers in South Dakota had mentioned an uprising. Was there really any danger? President Harrison conferred with Commanding General of the Army John Schofield, asking him to find out Miles's views on the subject.[83]

President Harrison's request for information from Schofield was not as pure a fact gathering exercise as it would have been in the days when army commanders like Sherman had resolutely insisted upon their independence from the Secretary of War. Early in his career, Schofield had been a proponent of that independence, but he had spent the post–Civil War years deep in political intrigue rather than on battlefields. At eastern desk jobs, he had lost his commitment to the separation of the military from the civilian side of military affairs.

When he had become the Commander of the Army in 1888, Schofield had found a new way to negotiate the long-standing clash between his office and the War Department. A longtime political operator himself, Schofield simply stopped fighting for autonomy and declared himself subordinate to the Secretary of War. This let him influence the decisions of the Secretary of War, who was willing to listen to his opinions because he no longer saw the military head of the army as a rival. At the same time, though, it gave Proctor, a staunch Republican politician, ultimate control over military decisions. This was an outcome that Schofield, who shared Proctor's political leanings, didn't mind. It also meant, though, that the Commander of the Army could make no suggestions that were uninfluenced by politics. If anyone were going to speak for the army, it would have to be General Miles.[84]

As they conferred on the best approach to the problems in South Dakota, President Harrison and his men undoubtedly had in mind the administration's political problems in the West, and in South Dakota in particular. They desperately needed to assuage western anger and to court South Dakotans who would soon be instructing their state legislators what to do about naming a new senator. Administration men who had spent the last several months weighing every appointment, every contract, and every potential voting issue in the West simply must have considered what the apparent Sioux crisis could mean for their party's chances in the region. And they knew that western voters liked military intervention in Indian issues. Troops brought contracts and government money into the chronically poor West, money that would be most welcome in the current economic depression there. Troop deployment would also show that the administration was looking out for the settlers, promoting their welfare as it had indicated it would do when it pushed so hard for western development. Such discussions would have taken place without records, but it is impossible to imagine that they did not happen.

In any case, when Schofield asked Miles for information on November 13, it seemed clear that the president was already leaning toward military intervention. General Schofield told General Miles that the president wanted to know what military measures should be taken to prevent an outbreak and "insure due submission of the Indians to the authority of the Government." The president had also sent the communications from the agencies and from Belt and Noble to the Secretary of War. "The situation seems to me to be serious," wrote Harrison. It was imperative to maintain the authority and discipline of the agents. Equally important was to guarantee that the lives and homes of settlers were never put into peril. The military must take "adequate and early" steps to prevent such a danger. The president instructed Proctor to ready troops and to make sure that there were enough of them "to be impressive and, in case of resistance, quickly and thoroughly efficient."[85]

But the president had not irrevocably decided on war. He asked Miles for information about necessary military measures, but also asked the War Department to send a high-ranking officer to investigate the situation on the reservations. Then he put off Secretary of the Interior Noble, telling him to get his agents to separate the traditionalists from the progressive Indians and to avoid forcing any issue that might cause an uprising until the military could be put into place.[86]

Despite the push for war in Washington, General Miles remained calm about affairs on the Sioux reservations. He placed his subordinates on alert, but he was not overly concerned. He was still convinced that the political appointees, who had virtually no experience, were misreading the situation. In a message back to General Schofield on November 14, he obliquely reiterated that his own superior knowledge of the Indians gave him perspective that the inexperienced agents, new to Indian reservations, lacked. Miles pointed out that he had spent considerable time among the Sioux, Cheyenne, and Crow, and that he knew Red Cloud, American Horse, Young-Man-Afraid-of-His-Horse, and others personally. Miles agreed that the situation was "serious," but insisted it was not yet dangerous.[87]

In fact, Miles pointed out, General Ruger's fact-finding tour was bringing good news. Ruger had just telegraphed his impressions of Standing Rock. He had reported that many of the prominent men were opposed to Ghost Dancing, and expressed loyalty to the government. The "Messiah craze" affected about two hundred men and their families, "mostly from Sitting Bull's band, who are opposed to civilizing methods." Ruger dismissed the idea of an uprising during the winter, although he thought that, if the movement did not wane before the spring, discontented warriors would likely gain a following and make trouble if they weren't stopped. As a precaution, Ruger had called for an additional company of infantry at Standing Rock, which Miles had provided.[88]

Two days later, on November 16, Ruger sent a telegraphed message from Cheyenne River in a similar vein. About nine hundred people, mostly Minneconjous, were dancing under the leadership of Hump and, to a lesser extent, Big Foot, he wrote. But only about two hundred men older than sixteen were involved. While they were "sullen," they had made no threats against the agent or agency employees. Ruger would leave some troops from Fort Meade in the area, but he foresaw no trouble at Standing Rock or Cheyenne River.[89]

Ruger was less sanguine about things at Pine Ridge. He had heard that more Indians there had joined the Ghost Dance than at other reservations. The agent there had lost control and, on the orders of the Commissioner of Indian Affairs—presumably this meant Acting Commissioner Belt, not Morgan—had asked Ruger directly for soldiers to back him up. Ruger recommended that troops "strong enough to overawe the Pine Ridge Indians" be sent to the Pine Ridge agency as soon as convenient.[90]

The problem, if there was a problem at all, seemed to be at Pine Ridge alone.

On Pine Ridge, Royer was firmly convinced he was on the brink of a catastrophe and that no one was listening to his prescient warnings. On November 15, he telegraphed Belt again, furious that the president had ignored his demand for troops. "Indians are dancing in the snow and are wild and crazy," he wrote. "I have fully informed you that the employes [sic] and government property at this agency have no protection and are at the mercy of these dancers. Why delay by further investigation? We need protection and we need it now, the leaders should be arrested and confined in some military post until the matter is quieted and this should be done at once."[91]

Royer decided to take matters into his own hands. He was fed up with the seemingly cavalier attitude of General Miles and General Ruger. Although South Dakota was in the Department of Dakota, which Ruger oversaw, on November 16 Royer sent a telegram to Brigadier General John R. Brooke, commander of the Department of the Platte, who oversaw matters in nearby Nebraska and Wyoming. Royer apparently did this with the approval of his own superiors in the Interior Department. In the telegram, Royer begged Brooke for military support. "Indians are wild and crazy over the ghost dance," Royer wrote, and he and the police were overmatched. "Will your Department take immediate action to suppress this most dangerous craze? Dancers defy law and order. Commissioner of Indian Affairs has directed me to report promptly and fully to you. We are at the mercy of these crazy demons. We need the military and need them at once."[92]

Brooke's response indicated that he was taken aback by Royer's telegram. He asked if any overt acts had prompted Royer's cry for help. "A number of overt acts have been committed," Royer fired back. He told the story of Charging Hawk and the knife, claiming that more than two hundred Indians had rushed to Charging Hawk's assistance. The Indians threatened him and only the older warriors had kept them from burning all the government buildings and supplies. Royer insisted: "We need protection and we need it now. The Indians are buying all the ammunition they can get and are well armed. Delay is dangerous."[93]

On November 16, Brooke sent these extraordinary telegrams on to Miles with some skeptical observations. Royer had only mentioned one serious challenge to his authority, Brooke wrote, and that challenge had been quelled by the older men, who still seemed to have considerable influence. He suggested he had too few troops to do much good on the reservations without significant reinforcements, but if troops were to go in, they should go to both Rosebud and Pine Ridge at the same time.[94]

Miles forwarded Brooke's communications to Schofield who, in turn, sent them to the Secretary of War several days later. But by the time Proctor saw Brooke's comments events had overtaken them. On November 13, Noble had sent Royer's panicked telegram about "crazy dancers" on to Secretary of War Proctor "for such action as the War Department and the military authorities think necessary." Then Proctor had passed it back down his chain of command to Schofield, the Commander of the Army. In turn, Schofield forwarded it to Miles on November 17, and wrote: "You will please take such action as the circumstances require, if in your judgment immediate action is necessary."[95]

General Miles had staunchly denied that there was an Indian uprising and maintained that there was no need for additional troops on the Sioux reservations. But the fact that Commander of the Army had just placed squarely in Miles's lap the responsibility for managing Indian affairs in South Dakota changed everything. First, and perhaps most important, Miles had no intention of getting stuck with the blame if an uprising actually occurred. Second, he recognized that here, finally, was an opportunity to wrest control of the Indian agencies from the Interior Department once and for all. Together, these two opportunities—preventing an Indian uprising and commanding a mobilization that would prove how important the army was to the nation's safety—should be Miles's ticket to yet more fame, even, perhaps, to the presidency.

On November 17, Miles ordered troops into Pine Ridge and Rosebud reservations.[96]

The mobilization of soldiers into South Dakota served President Harrison and his administration well. South Dakota settlers would be protected against an Indian "uprising," and army mobilization, always popular in the West, would boost the local economy in the weeks before South Dakota legislators elected a senator. And the call to send in troops had come from General Miles. If something went wrong, Harrison's political officials had someone else to blame.[97]

CHAPTER 6

Once Set in Motion . . .

THE DECISION to send troops to South Dakota was a complicated one for General Miles, and required him to balance two countervailing agendas. On the one hand, he understood the Sioux, and had a long history with them. He had hunted the fighting bands down after the Battle of the Little Bighorn. In admiration and vexation, the Sioux called him "Bear Coat" because, unlike most other army officers, he was willing to dress in heavy bearskins and fight in the subzero temperatures of a northern Plains winter. Miles had seen Indians on the warpath—and in late fall of 1890, he believed that there was no current danger of a Sioux uprising. If the government would only dump the corrupt system of agency patronage, live up to its treaties, and give the starving Indians what they were owed, then the rising tension would surely dissipate.

On the other hand, Miles had a career to look out for, and also an abiding concern about the nation's commitment to the army. The Ghost Dance crisis had emerged in the context of a long-standing struggle between politicians and military men for control of the army, and of Indian affairs, which had begun once the Civil War ended. One of the reasons military men in general—and Miles in particular—hated political interference in army affairs was their belief that civilian meddling with Indians had been an utter failure. For Miles, putting the army in charge of the South Dakota reservations advanced his goal of giving military men precedence over civilians in military affairs, especially in that special preserve of politicians, the Indian agency.[1]

It was no secret that politicians stuffed the Indian agencies with political appointees who were, more often than not, corrupt and indifferent to the needs of their charges. Eventually, the abused Indians broke out and started killing local settlers, at which point the military men were called in to risk their lives to restore order. When they did so, usually under appalling conditions, they were hampered by War Department bureaucrats who failed to produce supplies and who knew so little of actual war they issued stupid orders. Miles had encountered this problem early on—he had complained of the War Department's "criminal neglect" when he was chasing the Sioux in early 1877. If only bureaucrats had provided him with the food and supplies he desperately needed to maintain his forward march, he grumbled, he could have defeated the Sioux months earlier. But the reformers were even worse, most army officers thought. Every so often a wave of contrition would sweep over the Interior Department, and its officers would place at the agencies reformers who were determined to lead the Indians gently into farming. Their efforts were inept and ineffectual, officers thought, actually moving civilization backwards as the Indians ignored them and retained their own culture.[2]

But for Miles, the decision to send troops into South Dakota represented more than merely an opportunity to assert the army's precedence over politicians. Mobilization was about the military's very survival. Undoubtedly, the deployment was Miles's way of illustrating that the army was still vital to American security.

Army officers in general and Miles in particular worried that the nation was allowing the army to fall into neglect. Bounded by Mexico and Canada, countries that were generally not a great military threat in the nineteenth century, the American government had only developed a strong army to fight the Civil War, then maintained it—at greatly reduced levels—to fight the Indian wars. With the Indian threat all but dissolved after the 1876 Battle of the Little Bighorn and the subsequent rounding up and removal of all Indians to reservations, to many the army once again began to seem superfluous. In the last two decades of the nineteenth century, as the western Territories joined the Union as states, the frontier itself seemed to have disappeared. Indeed, the director of the 1890 census famously commented that he would not discuss the movement of the nation's frontier line in his report because "there can hardly be said to be a frontier line" any longer.[3]

As the army came to seem less and less essential, the public and politicians both began to call for strengthening the navy instead. In the post–Civil War drive to cut the budget, Congress had slashed funding for the navy, leaving naval officers and the navy establishment drifting for decades. They chafed under their inaction and eagerly fed the growing interest in international expansion that rose by the late 1870s. In 1882, twenty-three-year-old Theodore Roosevelt gave American navy promoters a boost when his book *The Naval War of 1812* refuted traditional histories of that war and argued that the navy had been key to the American victory. In 1890, the president of the U.S. Naval War College, Alfred T. Mahan, produced his own classic work, *The Influence of Sea Power Upon History, 1660–1783*, which argued that naval power was the critical element in any nation's rise to greatness. It became one of the most influential books of its age.

The oceans, particularly the Pacific, were highways to new markets, making them essential to late nineteenth-century American and European economic growth. By the 1880s, Western countries were expanding aggressively into the Pacific Ocean, and England, Russia, Germany, and America were jockeying for supremacy there. Asian markets were essential to American companies' economic growth, and businessmen had been urging support for their efforts, both through subsidized steamship lines and through naval protection on the shipping lanes, for decades. By the 1890s, they also wanted coaling and supply stations for ships traveling between the west coast of the Americas and the east coast of Asia, and naval protection against an international blockade. European nations had similar plans.[4]

Promoters of a strong U.S. navy had received a dramatic boost in 1889, when international intrigue in the Pacific had come to a crisis over Samoa. The South Pacific island was an ideal coaling station for American ships en route to Asia. In the mid-1880s, Germany helped to overthrow the local leaders, then installed a government that favored German commercial interests over American and British businesses. In 1888, warships from America and England steamed into Samoa's Apia Harbor and faced off against the German warships there. Only a March hurricane prevented an international war—but it brought immense destruction in its own right. Smashing into Samoa, it destroyed all the German warships, all but one of the British, and two of the American—the *Trenton* and the *Vandalia*—while forcing the sailors on the USS *Nipsic* to run the ship aground to keep her from sinking. America lost four officers and forty-six sailors when the two ships foundered.[5]

The Samoan debacle reinforced the arguments of those who wanted a stronger navy. The United States had actually obtained rights to a harbor and a coaling station in Samoa in 1878, but the navy had paid so little attention to the island that Germany was able to take over without opposition. Then, when American ships had finally deployed to protect the nation's interests in Samoa, the old vessels had fallen apart in the hurricane, leaving the weak navy further debilitated. In contrast, England's newly built HMS *Calliope* had safely ridden out the storm. The disaster illuminated the deplorable condition of the navy, *Frank Leslie's* asserted, and proved that Congress had to make "liberal appropriations" for new ships, armaments, and coastal defenses.[6]

Americans of all parties got behind rebuilding the navy, and Harrison's men adopted it as one of their key issues. For administration Republicans, building the navy and protecting the coast had two significant benefits. It would advance international business by protecting Pacific shipping. It would also spend down the budget surplus, which was running over $100 million a year and which the Treasury Secretary kept down to about $50 million only by buying up U.S. bonds as quickly as possible. Getting rid of the surplus would remove the free-traders' key piece of evidence that the tariff was unnecessarily high. In November 1889, *Frank Leslie's* speculated that defenses on the Pacific coast would cost at least $40 million, which would eat up the entire surplus. This only proved that the nation had abundant uses for all the money the government received from tariffs.[7]

As soon as he took office, President Harrison lined his administration up behind the naval project. In his first message to Congress in December 1889, he advocated using the treasury surplus for coastal defenses and improvements to rivers and harbors. He also called for liberal subsidies for American steamship lines and for developing the American merchant marine. Congressional Republicans, especially those from coastal states, jumped at the opportunity to endorse this idea. As soon as Congress got down to work, a staunch Republican senator from Oregon outdid *Frank Leslie's* projection of $40 million. He introduced a bill to spend $126 million over the next twelve years for coastal defenses. The editors of *Frank Leslie's* liked it: "We have a surplus revenue; we need coast defenses, and the expenditure of money will stimulate trade and business."[8]

The redirection of federal funds away from the army and toward the navy threatened all senior officers with reduced commands, but it was especially troubling to Nelson Miles, who had presidential ambitions. Miles was a touchy man, jealous of rivals and obsessed with self-promotion. Connected by marriage to the wealthy and powerful Shermans, he had good reason to think he might be able to parlay his military career into the presidency. He was a Civil War veteran, a longtime army officer, and the Indian fighter famous for bringing both Sitting Bull and famous Apache leader Geronimo to the authorities after other men had failed. A presidential bid was certainly within his reach, but to make it happen, he had to keep himself visible, carrying out popular policies.

Continuing to claim that Ghost Dances posed no threat on the reservations would not do the trick, especially if he were wrong and settlers lost their lives. Mobilizing the army to guarantee there was not an uprising would. Miles did not believe that the Sioux were dangerous; he believed they were hungry and frustrated by the government's refusal to honor its obligations. But President Harrison had forced him to choose between the Sioux and his hopes for a political future. Adding to these considerations his anxiety about the nation's commitment to the army, General Miles came down on the side of what was best for him and, it seemed, the nation as a whole.

On November 20, George Sword shook Charles Eastman awake at dawn. "Come quick!" he shouted. "The soldiers are here!" Eastman recalled: "I looked along the White Clay creek toward the little railroad town of Rushville, Nebraska, twenty-five miles away, and just as the sun rose above the knife-edged ridges black with stunted pine, I perceived a moving cloud of dust that marked the trail of the Ninth Cavalry."[9]

The army had begun its largest mobilization since the Civil War.

One hundred seventy horsemen and two hundred infantry marched into Pine Ridge Reservation. At the head of the column were Brigadier General John R. Brooke of the Department of the Platte, who had greeted Royer's call for help with skepticism, along with Agent Royer and Special Agent James A. Cooper. The troops were well armed, in this case with two Hotchkiss cannons—a light mountain gun that fired explosive 1.65-inch caliber shells—in addition to their rifles. They were biracial, with three troops of the Ninth Cavalry Regiment, the black soldiers wearing buffalo coats and muskrat caps, riding in front of four companies from the Second Regiment and one from the Eighth Regiment. And they were well organized. They marched to the west of the agency and pitched their tents on a plateau from which they could survey the ground below them.[10]

The arrival of the troops did not take the Indians by surprise. News of their coming had already spread across the reservation, leaving anxious Sioux to speculate wildly about what was going to happen. Indian scouts stood on their ponies on every hilltop around the military encampment, watching the soldiers.[11]

The coming of the troops may not have caused surprise, but it did create chaos. Brooke ordered the people of Pine Ridge to gather at the agency, under the oversight of the troops, forcing Indians to make a frightening choice, casting their lot either with the army and the agent or with the Ghost Dancers. He encouraged compliance by placing a military guard at the Oglala boarding school on the agency and locking one hundred students inside. This gave their fathers—most of whom were chiefs or leaders—a strong incentive to do whatever he asked. Those who had sided with the agents all along chose to obey Brooke's order. They put up their tepees to the south and west of the agency.[12]

The presence of troops and the order for Sioux to gather at the agency weakened the progressive chiefs at the very time army officers needed their influence. Progressive leaders, who in the past had been honored by the government with nice houses and who had been able to build herds of ponies and cattle, were reduced to living in cloth tepees near the soldiers. Red Cloud, an old man now and almost blind with cataracts, worried that the army had come to steal his horses, the way they had in 1876. The men in his band ostentatiously set a guard around their four hundred ponies. To observers, it must have seemed that even Red Cloud no longer enjoyed the favor of the government.[13]

For those who had joined, or even simply flirted with, the Ghost Dance, the decision about whether or not to go to the agency was much more difficult. They longed to stay true to their people and to their new religion, which promised salvation if they believed and destruction if they did not. But they also worried that the agents and the army might punish them for having transgressed in the first place. Families were torn apart as people tried to guess whether staying in the Ghost Dance camps at Medicine Root, White Clay, Porcupine, and Wounded Knee creeks was a better decision than going to the agency. (For others, the choice was obvious: Jack Red Cloud, a fierce Ghost Dancer only days before, suddenly became a "friendly" and stayed at Pine Ridge, where it's likely he calculated that his famous father could protect him.)[14]

While many men left their homes and took their families to the agency, a number fled in the other direction—just how many is unclear, but most likely somewhere in the hundreds. They gathered under Little Wound's leadership on Medicine Root Creek. Those who left the agency were considered "hostiles," although Elaine Goodale pointed out that they had committed no hostile acts and had fled only out of fear.[15]

Goodale herself was at Pine Ridge because Brooke had also called all government employees to the agency to keep them out of harm's way. Many whites in and out of government service obeyed. Teachers, farmers, missionaries, traders, and so on, joined the "crush," as newspaperman Charley Allen put it, at Pine Ridge.[16]

At the same time Brooke's soldiers were marching into Pine Ridge, troops arrived at Rosebud, throwing that reservation into confusion, too. The Brulés were especially nervous about soldiers since they associated troops with unprovoked violence. The Brulés on Rosebud still remembered the surprise attack by soldiers in 1855 that had left Spotted Tail in prison, grievously wounded, and his wife and daughter hostages. With no strong leaders to intercede with authorities on their behalf, they greeted the arrival of soldiers with trepidation.[17]

Even before the soldiers came in, some of the Brulé had begun to move toward Pine Ridge. They had heard rumors that the soldiers were on their way, and the news encouraged them to move to Pass Creek, to join Short Bull where he and his people were awaiting the coming of the new world.

When the soldiers actually appeared, the Brulés began to leave their homes in larger numbers and in haste to rendezvous at the Ghost Dance gatherings on Pine Ridge. As the army rode into Rosebud as many as 3,500 Brulés fled, some out of fear, some from religious conviction. One group followed Two Strike and Crow Dog to Big Road's Ghost Dance camp on Wounded Knee Creek. The rest of the Brulés joined Short Bull's camp at Pass Creek. This larger band then moved up the White River from Rosebud to the mouth of White Clay Creek.[18]

The sudden influx of people to the Pine Ridge camps forced the Ghost Dancers to cross the government directly for the first time. Short of food, and unable to feed this large crowd that had suddenly come together, Ghost Dancers killed government cattle for food. They also stole cattle, horses, and supplies from the nearby cabins of the Indians who had gone in to the agencies. They still did not threaten white homes or settlers, but their plundering of Indians who had sided with the government put them at odds with government agents.

With the arrival of the troops, settlers and local government officials suddenly begged for protection. Until the soldiers had come into South Dakota, there had been no sign of worry about an Indian uprising from local settlers, not a single complaint from a newspaper, not a worried telegram from a public official. But as soon as the troops were on the reservations, the wires suddenly hummed with telegrams and letters rushed eastward begging for more government action.[19]

South Dakota governor A. C. Mellette was first in line, eager to show voters that he would protect them. He telegraphed General Miles on November 26 that a cattle rancher with a large spread, "a very cool courageous man," expected an uprising very soon. According to Mellette, twelve men armed with Winchesters and laden with ammunition had stopped by the man's ranch on their way to join Short Bull's band. They were surly and defiant, Mellette reported. One said that "he had seen the time when he used to beat out the brains of children and drink women's blood, that the time is coming when they will do it again." Miles sent this telegram on to Washington.[20]

Local citizens also called on Washington for help. On November 25, men gathered together in Chadron, Nebraska, just over the border from South Dakota, and demanded government action to suppress the Sioux.

The government had invited them to the border of the Sioux reservation, they wrote, and they had bought their lands with the implied promise of military protection. Threats of Indian outbreaks both put them in danger and slowed the development of the region, "thereby depreciating and jeopardizing our property, and virtually defrauding us of vested rights." They wanted the government to restore their confidence by taking steps to stop the Indians from rising once and for all. It was unreasonable to allow "savages" to be "armed to the teeth" in the new state; the settlers wanted the government to punish the leading Indian "criminals" as traitors, anarchists, and assassins—that is, with death. They called for disarming the Indians and taking away their horses, giving them instead oxen trained to the plow. Signing these stinging resolutions were five men, including a young lawyer recently arrived from the East, E. S. Ricker. On November 26, they sent the resolutions directly to Secretary of War Proctor.[21]

The deployment of troops to the reservations had panicked the Indians and convinced Americans that South Dakota settlers must be in danger. Having created the fear of an Indian uprising, politicians in Washington and military officers in the field would have to find a way to resolve the crisis. Their task would be made harder by the fact that they thoroughly disagreed about how to proceed.

The agents had succeeded in getting the army to come to the reservations, but the arrival of the troops would launch an even more heated fight over who should control Indian policy. To the military men, the answer was obvious. They had once again been called in to clean up a mess caused by the politicians, and they intended to act as they saw fit. Rather than doing the bidding of the agents—who hoped for numerous arrests—the officers immediately set about to calm the situation. In telegrams, Miles repeatedly told Brooke that he had been sent there not to fight, but to support the loyal Indians and to make sure the traditionalists did not cause trouble. He left the particulars of the mobilization up to Brooke, but made one critical warning: "One thing should be impressed upon all the officers, never to allow their command to be mixed up with the Indians or taken at a disadvantage." Miles knew that it was essential to keep soldiers and Indians scrupulously separated during military maneuvers to avoid disastrous surprises.[22]

Within days of arriving at Pine Ridge, army officers made it clear that they intended to take firm control of the agencies, pushing aside the agents and wresting control of Indian affairs from the Interior Department. Brooke telegraphed to Miles that he had permitted the agent to appear to retain control but that he would not curtail rations to force good behavior as agents had suggested. The Indians had real grievances, Brooke wrote, and were starving. He wanted additional rations and demanded that the Indians' just claims be addressed immediately. Miles sent the telegram on to Washington and launched more ammunition at the Interior Department, adding: "General Brooke's recommendation that sufficient food be supplied should be granted at once, and in the future he should have absolute general control over these agencies."[23]

Miles's demand that Brooke officially be put in charge of Pine Ridge made its way through the usual complicated channels in Washington. Secretary of War Proctor called it to the attention of Secretary of the Interior Noble, and eventually it went up to President Harrison. In a frosty message written by his private secretary, the president insisted that Noble fix the problems on the reservations called to his attention by the military and the 102 Rosebud Brulé men who had written to him begging for relief three weeks before.[24]

In Noble's exhaustive replies to Proctor and President Harrison on November 25, he defended the actions of the Interior Department and rejected the idea that the army should assume control of the Indian agencies. Noble's defense showed that Interior Department officials would protect their turf by refusing to accept any blame for what had happened. Instead, they would insist they had acted appropriately, and that any trouble on the reservations was solely the fault of hostile Indians. Noble also addressed the many complaints Captain C. A. Earnest had reported to his superior officer two weeks earlier after his inspection at Rosebud.

Noble tried to refute every accusation that military men, especially Captain Earnest, had made against the agents and the Interior Department. He enclosed in his letter to the president a memo from Acting Commissioner Belt responding to Earnest's letter, and drew from that same information in his letter to Proctor. Noble declared that the Interior Department could not increase rations because Congress had not appropriated money for more beef. The Commissioner had requested an additional appropriation of $100,000, but his request was sitting untouched in congressional committee. In any case, the reduced rations were really the right amount of food; previous issues had been far too high because of the Indians' deceitfulness in exaggerating their numbers. As for the demand that the Indians stop eating offal, the Commissioner had forbidden the practice in the interests of their civilization. He would consider modifying the order but indicated that a change was unlikely. Eating offal was "a filthy habit serving to nourish their brutal instincts." Noble addressed Earnest's last few points by explaining that the Commissioner was sending Wright back to Rosebud immediately, and was furnishing ammunition to the police force.[25]

In the letter Noble enclosed to the president, Belt went on to defend the Office of Indian Affairs from its army detractors. He objected strongly to Miles's repeated requests that Brooke be given control over the agencies. In a rather shocking about-face, he downplayed the idea of an Indian uprising and suggested that the army was only on the reservations as a precaution. "I have not considered from the beginning of this excitement that there was any serious danger of an outbreak," Belt wrote, noting that there had been no attacks on settlers and no sign of any to come. Without army interference, the dance would die of its own accord, he said. The army was necessary only because the Indians were too excited to listen to the Pine Ridge agent's orders, and if he forced them to comply with "proper regulations" there might be a disturbance. This uneasiness alarmed settlers and loyal Indians, making it prudent to have soldiers around in case there was threat of an outbreak.

The army should be subordinate to the Interior Department, Belt indicated. Soldiers should back up the agents, but not interfere with their management of the reservations. There was no more reason for the military to take control of the agencies than for it to take control of the South Dakota government, he declared.[26] Noble made it clear he backed Belt, and was going to push back hard against General Miles's effort to put the military in charge of the reservations. He warned Secretary of War Proctor that he was preparing another communication on that topic.[27]

Noble had no intention of taking orders from soldiers, and every intention of commanding them. While Miles wanted to calm the tensions on the reservations by feeding the Indians adequately and addressing their legitimate complaints, Noble believed that the only way to achieve peace was to force the Sioux to submit to the agents' authority. Just as soon as troops arrived at the agencies, Noble told Belt to ask the agents which leaders should be arrested. Special Agent E. B. Reynolds at Rosebud wanted to be rid of twenty-one men, including Short Bull, Two Strike, and Crow Dog. Standing Rock agent James McLaughlin named his enemy Sitting Bull and five of his men for removal before the next spring, but cautioned against arrests until winter. The weather was still warm on the reservation, and Indians could fight back against officers taking their leaders. The agent for Crow Creek and Lower Brulé wanted no arrests at all; he said all was quiet and his Indian police had everything under control. Belt passed all this information to Noble with a polite disclaimer. Soldiers should only make the arrests if the military agreed the troublemakers should be removed for the good of the agencies, he wrote, but he left no doubt that he expected the arrests to take place. He asked Noble to send Proctor the list of Indians to be arrested, which Noble promptly did.[28]

The question of how to proceed against the Sioux was becoming so intensely politicized that it was time for President Harrison to take a stand. The president, along with Secretary of War Proctor and Commander of the Army Schofield, sided with the politicians at the Interior Department, although Harrison made it clear that he was irritated with Noble for letting the Sioux agencies slide into such a mess. Miles had initially planned not to send in many troops. He told Brooke the soldiers were at Pine Ridge only to keep the peace, and that sending in too many of them would create more harm by frightening the Indians into stampeding away from the agencies. But Schofield, Proctor, and President Harrison saw the military mission differently. Schofield told Miles not to move against the Ghost Dancers, but to build up the troops and prepare for a long winter encampment and an eventual spring campaign.[29]

Just why the administration was keen on a long military occupation of the South Dakota reservations is unclear, for Harrison's men debated their options in person and left no records. A line in a telegram from Schofield to Miles suggests something about their motives, though, looked at in the context of the dire political straits in which the administration found itself in late November of 1890. After instructing Miles not to plan to move against the Ghost Dancers until the spring, Schofield pointed out that the troops coming from far away could not bring with them all the horses, equipment, and supplies they would need. Schofield ordered Miles and his staff officers to get everything the soldiers needed locally, "by contract or otherwise." Schofield sent a copy of this telegram to the Adjutant General, who oversaw military contracts.[30]

As Miles had always complained, Washington officials were ignoring conditions on the ground and were arguing for what made sense in their own political calculations. While army officers were trying to solve a crisis without loss of life, Harrison and his men were pressing for the authority of their agents to be upheld by military action. And they were willing for the effort to take many months. The mobilization might be miserable for the soldiers wintering in South Dakota, but it would comfort South Dakota voters with valuable contracts to provide food, horses, and equipment for the encamped soldiers.

While politicians argued in Washington, the trains thundered to railheads near the reservation, bringing carloads of troops who marched into the lands around Pine Ridge and Rosebud. Within two weeks of the first troops tramping into Pine Ridge, soldiers from as far away as Kansas and New Mexico found themselves on railroad cars clacking toward South Dakota. The telegraph wires strung on poles beside the train tracks hummed, and operators rapidly tapped out messages in Morse code as commanders even put troops in California on alert.[31]

The general flood into Pine Ridge turned a sleepy agency—which boasted only the bare agency buildings, a supply station, and a few stores—into a bustling military town. Dust and horses on dirt tracks became columns of men in blue uniforms marching to the tinny sound of military bands. Horses and mules pulled pack trains, wagons, artillery, and ambulances. Ultimately, some five thousand troops would be stationed at the agency, with another four thousand or so scattered on the other reservations and in the lands between them—fully a third of the U.S. Army.[32]

Most of the soldiers were not well disposed toward the Sioux. Among the arrivals at Pine Ridge was another troop of the Ninth Cavalry, this one under the command of Major Guy V. Henry. Once at Pine Ridge, he took control of the entire squadron of the Ninth. Henry was not impartial toward the Sioux; he had been shot through the face, from one cheekbone to the other through the top of his mouth, at the Battle of the Rosebud in 1876.[33]

Other unfriendly soldiers were arriving as well. From Fort Riley, Kansas, came the entire Seventh Cavalry, rebuilt after the Battle of the Little Bighorn. Six of the unit's officers had fought under Custer, and the Seventh Cavalry was now under the command of an officer who had served with Custer during the Civil War. That officer, Colonel James W. Forsyth, was the same man who had been assigned in place of Cump Sherman to train the military regiment John Sherman had raised in 1861. After the war Forsyth had had a long military career, most of it spent in one administrative position after another. He had commanded the Seventh since 1886, through four calm years. This mobilization, though, promised real war, and Forsyth and his men were undoubtedly eager for action.[34]

While the troops poured into Pine Ridge, Brooke continued to negotiate with the Ghost Dancers in an attempt to draw them back to the agency. To tempt them, on November 27, Thanksgiving Day, he ordered a large beef issue and allowed the Sioux to hunt the animals from horseback, as they preferred, rather than receiving them already butchered. While seemingly benevolent, Brooke's order permitted him to see how well the men were armed. The men who ran down the beeves revealed that they each had a weapon, and some of the other men also showed guns. But Brooke was not overly concerned. When Short Bull, Two Strike, and Little Wound, the leaders of the three main Ghost Dance camps, all drifted into the agency for the celebration, he made no effort to have them arrested.[35]

Instead, Brooke talked to Little Wound, trying to gauge the true purpose of the Ghost Dancers. On November 29, Brooke called Little Wound and the chief's friend and former agent Valentine T. McGillycuddy, along with Agent Royer and Special Agent Cooper, to a conference. Little Wound insisted that the religious movement was a reaction to legitimate grievances. The officials asked Little Wound if he was a Ghost Dancer. He replied that he was too old to dance himself, but believed that movement was probably a good thing. If the promise of a new world was false, the religion would die on its own, but for his part, he was willing to wait and see. And, he pointed out to Brooke, the arrival of troops had strengthened rather than weakened his belief in the coming of a golden age. If the whites were not afraid that the Messiah was coming to make the Indians strong again and give them back their land, why had they sent soldiers to stop the dance?[36]

Despite his enthusiasm for the new religion, Little Wound was not hostile. Officers perceived him as one of the most dangerous of the Pine Ridge Ghost Dance leaders, and Little Wound blustered he would maintain his camp on Medicine Root Creek. He had only come to the agency to see his old friend McGillycuddy, he said. But when it came time to go back home, he elected to stay at the agency instead.[37]

The comings and goings of the Ghost Dance leaders reflected the fluid boundaries between the agency and the camps. There was no clear division between the agency "progressives" and the "hostiles" who refused to be brought in. The lines between different groups of Indians, soldiers, scouts, and reformers were blurry. Brooke had ordered that no Sioux could cross the picket lines around the agency after 4:30 in the afternoon, but there was plenty of movement between the agency and the people at Wounded Knee and White Clay creeks earlier in the day. Indian families were divided between the camps and the agency and individuals traveled between the two, keeping each informed of the events at the other.[38]

Indian scouts also moved back and forth between the camps and the agency. Miles had ordered a dramatic build up of Indian scouts with the intention of co-opting the Indians. Providing them with regular paychecks and government authority would go a long way to ending troubles on the reservations, he believed—a point members of the Sioux delegation had tried to make to Interior Secretary Noble in December 1889, when they asked for the government to hire Indians rather than whites on the agencies. Miles had told Brooke to put together two troops of Indian scouts, and within a week, there were forty scouts around Pine Ridge. Progressive Oglalas and Cheyennes began to work for Brooke. So did experienced mixed-blood scouts like Philip Wells and the famous "Big Bat" and "Little Bat"—Baptiste Pourier and Baptiste Garnier—along with James H. Cook, who had good friends in both the Indian camps and the agencies. These men hung around, their pay of thirteen dollars a month a welcome addition to the depressed reservation economy. Almost all of the scouts spoke Lakota and were well known in the Indian camps; they traveled back and forth to bring messages to Little Wound and Short Bull, and to the people with them. They were the central link between army officers and the Indians, and their missions and translations would determine the outcome of Brooke's attempt to make peace.[39]

Indeed, not just scouts, but many old-timers who had worked or fought with the Sioux in the past, came to Pine Ridge. Even former agent McGillycuddy wandered around from time to time, checking things out for Governor Mellette and grumbling angrily that the agency he had managed with dispatch had come to such a pass under such a foolish agent.[40]

Adding to the circus atmosphere of the agency was Major John R. Burke, the press agent and general manager of Buffalo Bill's Wild West Show. Former scout William F. Cody—aka Buffalo Bill—had started his Wild West Show in 1883 as a way to bring the frontier to eastern audiences. With its cowboys and Indians, shooting and roping, staged battles and reenacted historical scenes, it had become the biggest entertainment event of the era. Buffalo Bill made a great point of hiring Indians to present his "authentic" histories, but Indian reformers hated that Buffalo Bill's Wild West Show paid Indians to show off their "savagery." On the show's recent European tour several Sioux had died, most of them in accidents. Reformers had lodged a complaint with reformer T. J. Morgan at Indian Affairs, charging that Cody was abusing his Indian employees. Buffalo Bill had returned to America from the European tour in mid-November and, great showman that he was, had taken a hundred Indians to Washington, where they testified that they had been well treated. Hiring his manager to look after the continued well-being of his employees was a public relations ploy by Buffalo Bill to make sure he could continue to hire Indians without interference from reformers.[41]

Installing Burke at Pine Ridge to look after the welfare of the show's former employees meant that Cody would have a ringside seat at the unfolding drama. Coming by often to check in with his general manager, Cody was just one of many old scouts hanging around the scene in search of excitement. And he would have plenty, soon enough.[42]

Brooke was irritated by the motley crowd at Pine Ridge, but his gentle approach to the crisis appeared to be working. By November 26, the Brulés left at Rosebud were all quiet. The next day, Miles reported to

Schofield that, according to Brooke, the resolve of the disaffected Indians was weakening by the hour. Little Wound and Short Bull had both had come in, Miles reported, and Little Wound's followers were on their way. So were Short Bull's followers, estimated at about 2,500 people. Big Road was still out, but he had behaved well in the past and was not nearly as dangerous as Short Bull, Miles reported.[43]

Miles's cheerful report was not, however, completely accurate. Little Wound had indeed come in and would stay with his people at the agency, but after the Thanksgiving Day beef issue. Short Bull and Two Strike had slipped away. Miles wanted to prove that the army could handle Indians much more easily and efficiently than the agents could, but the recalcitrant Ghost Dance leaders were thwarting him. Miles was starting to grow impatient.

The threat of an Indian uprising and the mobilization of the army out West were a boon to newspaper editors, stuck in the dull news cycle after the midterm election. They raced to get reporters—either their own or local stringers—out to South Dakota and into the Pine Ridge agency. "Please send Herald Short dispatches each day about Indians" telegraphed *New York Herald* editor James Gordon Bennett to Charley Allen of Nebraska's *Chadron Democrat*. "If any serious matter or engagement with troops want good graphic story earliest possible moment." The *New York Herald* hired three local men to send reports from Pine Ridge, and other newspapers followed suit. As the days passed, more reporters came, until by early December there were about fourteen reporters steadily at Pine Ridge, with others drifting in and out.[44]

Once there, though, the reporters were confronted with a problem: there really wasn't much of a story to tell. Brooke had been told to prevent a war, not provoke one. Rather than marching off to battle, he had set about planning how to bring in the Ghost Dancers. It was clear to reporters that the officers didn't consider the Ghost Dancers much of a threat. "Army officers frankly admitted that 'the army doesn't know what it is here for,'" Elaine Goodale recorded. And even if anything dramatic was happening, the journalists were unlikely to hear of it—Brooke was not well disposed toward the reporters, and he refused to tell them anything. And so, as the days passed, the reporters and soldiers cooled their heels while General Brooke sent emissaries to the camp on Wounded Knee Creek, where Two Strike, Short Bull, and Kicking Bear gathered with their people, promising food and leniency if they would come in to the agency.[45]

Sent to report on a story that wasn't there, reporters invented one. Writing on the long planks of the counter of the agency store after the business closed for the night, they constructed copy out of rumor, or even out of whole cloth. Charley Allen, Will Kelley of the *Nebraska State Journal*, and the other reporters spent their days gambling, swapping rumors, "chaffing one another, making aimless turkey-tracks or penciling crude sketches," Allen recalled. They joined forces with the photographers eager for exciting pictures to sell, staging pictures of hand-to-hand combat with compliant Indians posing as hostile warriors. To while away the time, the reporters wrote stories to amuse themselves, interviewed each other, and sent sensational copy back East.[46]

The columns the reporters filed were electrifying, describing Indian murders and atrocities and predicting an imminent battle. Allen remembered that C. H. Cressey of the *Omaha Bee* "had a penchant for lurid, long-drawn-out stories. . . . His favorite pastime [was] grabbing thrilling rumors and converting them into something he considered a 'scoop' on his rivals, though . . . they more nearly resembled puffballs." On November 19, reporter Charles Seymour arrived in Rushville, Nebraska, on the same train as Cressey. He sent a column off to the *Chicago Herald* as soon as he got off the train, before he had time to do anything but pick up local rumors. "REDSKINS WILL FIGHT," his headline roared, "PREPARED TO MEET THE TROOPS."[47]

The newspaper stories exacerbated tensions among the Indians. At the camps, many of the Sioux had English-speaking friends read the newspapers to them, and were alarmed by stories claiming that the army was ready to march against them. One of the mixed bloods at Pine Ridge read the incendiary reports in the white newspapers to his Indian family and friends, "with the effect that the Indians were scared and driven to confusion, fear and disorder," reported one of civilians working for the army. Brooke's scouts, coming and going between Pine Ridge and the camps, reported that the people in the camps were uneasy and arguing among themselves about what to do. Many were preparing for war, others wanted desperately to return to the agency. It was growing colder, and food was limited to the cattle they could take from the homes of their own people who had taken shelter at the agency.[48]

At the end of November, the Ghost Dancers split. Most of the Oglalas, led by Big Road and Little Wound, came in from their camps to settle around the Pine Ridge agency. The Brulés left in the Ghost Dancing camps went the other direction. Around November 30, the two biggest bodies of Ghost Dancers joined together before striking off to the north. Two Strike's people moved down Wounded Knee Creek from their camp near Big Road's village. About the same time, the body of Ghost Dancers with Short Bull and Kicking Bear moved down White River from their camp at White Clay Creek. The two groups met at the mouth of Grass Creek and turned north.[49]

The group began to move toward the Badlands. In these ancient spires and valleys of sandwiched volcanic rock and the sediment of eons, banded in pinks and grays with oases of green grass, stood a place called the Stronghold. It was a plateau with two springs and good grass, located between White River and Cheyenne River, and was accessible only by a land bridge that stretched off another plateau now known as Cuny Table. Three hundred feet above the plains, with water and forage for cattle, Kicking Bear and Short Bull believed they could hold out against the U.S. Army if they had to. As they moved west from Wounded Knee Creek, they took the cattle from the agency herd camp about thirty miles away. They moved up White River, then turned north to the Stronghold.[50]

Newspaper stories from the reporters at Pine Ridge did not really do much reporting of facts. What they did was to provide an incendiary narrative that politicians back East could use in their protracted battle to control the American government.

While newspaper readers far from the reservations were warned that an Indian war was imminent, the reality was that settlers living with the Indians weren't very worried. Elaine Goodale reported that she traveled from Standing Rock to Pine Ridge over the wildest parts of the reservations in November without anything but cordial relations with the Indians. She continued to work among them as she always had, "I visited the homes as usual and talked freely with everyone I met. I was received with the familiar kindness and treated to pounded meat with cherries and other native delicacies."[51]

Even settlers who did not enjoy such cordial relations with the Sioux were nonchalant. When a courier arrived at midnight on November 24 to tell ranchers Henry P. Smith and his brother J. B., who owned the Oar Lock Ranch on the north bank of the White River, that the Indians might be coming to fight, Henry ignored the message. He had heard so many such reports, he would believe in an attack when it happened. He went out the next day to cut fence posts. When armed Rosebud Indians on their way to Pine Ridge camped near his ranch and the fields they needed for hay, Henry and his brother, along with another rancher, rode into their camp and warned them to be careful with their fire so it didn't get out and burn the fields. The white men were not frightened of their visitors. The Indians claimed they were going to fight, but the ranchers dismissed their threats as a bluff to spook the new agent. Afterward, Smith and his neighbors were cautious, but remained relatively unconcerned about the threat of an Indian war. Occasionally, they traveled without even remembering to carry guns with them. On December 6, Smith recorded, "We are, as far as news is concerned, better off than the so-called reading-public, who are continually stuffed with reports exagerated [sic] beyond measure."[52]

Back East, newspapers turned the wild reports coming from the vacuum at Pine Ridge into two distinctly partisan narratives. Democratic newspapers and Republicans fed up with Harrison tore into the administration's handling of the Indians. With the military men so vocal in their complaints about the Interior Department's management of Indian affairs, editors had rich material from which to draw. Opposition newspapers also quickly picked up the criticisms levied by the Indians of Rosebud, who had petitioned the government begging for rations because they were starving. There would be no disturbance at all in South Dakota, the opposition papers argued, if the Republicans had not put such incompetent appointees into the Indian agencies and had honored legitimate treaty obligations.[53]

Opposition newspapers echoed Miles, but went further than he did in their public denunciation of the politicians controlling the Indian agencies. "The Indians' only complaint is that they don't get enough to eat," the *Boston Globe* reported. They were not marshaling for a fight;

they realized that fighting would be suicide. They were running, the newspaper insisted, because they were panic stricken at the overwhelming force brought into the reservations. *Harper's Weekly* also wrote in this vein, but went on to use the Sioux crisis to hammer home its disgust with the administration's manipulation of the political system. "The chief source of the difficulty is politics," a column read. Indian affairs should be governed by honesty and efficiency. Instead, agents were chosen according to their tariff views and power to corral votes. The Indian question would be a national disgrace as long as the nation's relations with the tribes were controlled by men whose only goal was to promote the fortunes of a political party.[54]

Opponents of the administration accused it of pushing a policy deliberately designed to goad the Sioux into fighting. Provoking the Indians into a last stand, the *Boston Globe* charged, would justify the insistence of administration men that their policies were correct. The *Globe* ran this piece right above an AP story featuring a version of the letter from staunch Republican governor Mellette to Miles, in which the governor quoted a big-time cattle rancher to foretell an Indian uprising. In the letter, the governor requested that Miles establish posts at Chamberlain and Forest City and ship a thousand more guns, with their ammunition, to Mellette for distribution to settlers. This seemed a clear indication of the administration's desire to provoke a war. It followed this observation with a warning: "The soldiers are slowly but surely drawing a cordon about the reservation, and when this has been accomplished some sort of a blow will be struck by the government. . . . The Sioux nation will soon be held in a vise of sabers and carbines, and if any attempt is made by them to burst from their fetters they will be cut to pieces."[55]

The attacks on the administration spurred President Harrison and his men to defend their policies. They launched a flurry of public activity to push back against their critics. In their drive to justify their actions, though, they intensified, rather than defused, the crisis in South Dakota.

The administration began its offensive by refuting the charges laid at its door by military officers. While opposition papers tended to echo the officers, administration papers borrowed heavily from the defenses the agents and the Interior Department were throwing up to deflect blame for the crisis. Sometimes they argued there was no problem on the reservations and that Miles was stirring up trouble for his own career. Other times they argued that there was, in fact, a terrible uprising, but it had nothing to do with the inadequacy of Republican appointees or policy. Rather it was the doing of the old Indian traditionalists, who either hated whites or wanted to regain power after losing it to progressives, or who were just troublemakers.

Different men bore the brunt of newspapers' accusations, but the one most often blamed for causing the crisis was none other than the famous Sioux traditionalist, Sitting Bull. *Frank Leslie's* called Sitting Bull, "the So-Called High Priest of the Indian Messiah Craze," and reported that he was deliberately fomenting disaffection among the Sioux. It explained the seemingly sudden reemergence of the old chief by claiming that his disturbing influence had lately increased dramatically.[56]

The charges were most unfair. In reality, Sitting Bull was not a strong adherent of the religion and was doing his best to be fair both to the Ghost Dancers and to the progressives. He had tried repeatedly to go into the trance of the Ghost Dance and had not succeeded, but he wanted to believe. When Agent McLaughlin tried to convince him that the messiah was a hoax, Sitting Bull proposed that the two men travel together to check out the messiah and see who was right. It was hardly the proposal of a man bent on violence. Even had he been inclined to fight, his band of Hunkpapas on Grand Creek only numbered about three hundred, including women and children. Usually about a quarter of such a band would be men of fighting age, meaning that there were probably only about seventy-five warriors amongst them.[57]

Despite the old man's conciliation, administration Republicans found that raising the memory of Sitting Bull's days on the warpath was a perfect way to deflect attention from the Democrats' insistence that the administration was to blame for the entire mess.

There was little Sitting Bull could do in retaliation for these misrepresentations, but on November 21, the administration incautiously attacked someone who could—and would—fight back. Rather than couching the Interior Department's actions in terms of Indian policy, an administration man made a personal attack on General Miles. An item leaked to the *Washington Evening Star* claimed that "a prominent army officer" was exaggerating the Indian crisis to strengthen his presidential chances. "Miles is predicting a general Indian war and virtually asks that the command of the entire army be turned over to him. He wants to create a scare and pose as the savior of the country. . . . He is one [of] the most ambitious men in the army and he is pulling the wires shrewdly." Miles, of course, had been downplaying the danger of a Sioux uprising, not exaggerating it, and he was furious at this story.[58]

Miles demanded the person who had planted the story be tracked down, but Schofield and Proctor dragged their heels. Although it wasn't confirmed until a month or so later, Schofield and Proctor may well have known right away who planted the story—Colonel Chauncey McKeever, a member of the Adjutant General's Office. He had had access to the telegrams pressing a reluctant Miles to mobilize against the Indians, but was nonetheless willing to suggest that the general was the one manufacturing the crisis for political gain. If Schofield and Proctor, both staunch Harrison men, did in fact know the identity of the leaker they would have been loath to pursue it for fear of directing yet more attention to Harrison's unfortunate patronage appointments. It was also quite likely that they did, in fact, fear Miles as a presidential contender against the unpopular Harrison. And so they did nothing, while whispers about Miles's exaggerations and presidential ambitions circulated and Miles's fury mounted.[59]

Recognizing their strength in Washington, Interior Department officials pushed for control over the military's actions in South Dakota. Acting Commissioner R. V. Belt was convinced that the Office of Indian Affairs should be in charge of maneuvers on the reservations. He demanded that the military support the agents and issued one suggestion after another for the troops.

Thrilled that the soldiers were finally on Pine Ridge and Rosebud, the agents now demanded that the troops help them establish their authority. On November 27, Royer fired off a telegram to Belt, claiming that the friendly Indians all agreed that there would be an outbreak in the spring. To prevent it, he wanted the president to order Brooke to arrest all the Ghost Dance leaders—a list of sixty or seventy men—and to disarm all the others on the reservation. He insisted the arrests must be made immediately, before the Indians received rations, because as soon as they had supplies, they would go home again and would be harder to round up. Special Agent Cooper sent his own telegram to the

Commissioner, agreeing that the army should arrest and imprison "the violators of the law" and disarm the others.[60]

Belt sent these telegrams to Interior Secretary Noble, endorsing the idea that hostile leaders should be arrested whenever military authorities thought it could be done with the least danger. He also wanted all firearms taken away from the Sioux. The peaceable Indians could just give their guns to their agent, with assurances that either the guns would be returned or Congress would appropriate money to make them reasonable compensation, Belt wrote.[61]

This scheme would require the support of the troops, of course—but no army officer who knew anything about the Sioux would want to participate in such an incredibly incendiary plan. The Sioux depended on their guns for food and protection, and guarded them zealously. Trying to disarm them would provoke a full-blown battle. Probably aware that the Secretary of War would reject this request out of hand, Noble sent the correspondence directly to President Harrison for his "consideration, and for such action as you deem it deserves."[62]

Belt began to push the agents to take better control of the agencies, using the army to back them up. On the same day he suggested that the president order army officers to arrest sixty or seventy men at Pine Ridge, he ordered Royer to tell the Indians who had fled from Rosebud to Pine Ridge to go home, and the agent at Rosebud to tell all his missing Indians to return to Rosebud. Belt clearly expected these demands to fail in the short term. Royer had no control over anyone at Pine Ridge, so no one would be returning home on his command, and the telegram to the Rosebud agent planned for failure by also ordering him to write down the names of anyone who did not obey. But Belt was not concerned about long-term failure. The agents had no power on their own, but Belt expected the army to enforce the agents' demands. With the troops behind them, the agents would be able to assert authority over the Sioux.[63]

Belt was eager to use soldiers not just to establish the agents' authority, but also to do the agents' bidding. On November 28, the agent at Crow Creek and Lower Brulé discovered a Ghost Dance on White River at Lower Brulé. He had his police arrest nine of the dancers and put them in the agency jail, but he reported to Belt that the jail was now full. This presented a problem, since he thought that there were many more Ghost Dancers still left on White River and there would undoubtedly need to be more arrests. He needed more jail space. Belt forwarded this information to Noble, and asked that it be transmitted to the Secretary of War with a recommendation that the nearest military officer move the arrested Indians from the agency jail to a suitable military post for safe-keeping. As agents continued to arrest troublemakers, Noble wanted army officers to take charge of them and hold them in military custody. In effect, Belt wanted the agents to be able to use the military officers as jailers.[64]

Noble endorsed this idea in a note to the president. He even added to it the idea that the troops could police the property of friendly Indians, which was sometimes attacked by the unsettled bands. But here even Noble recognized that his civilian agents might be overstepping the boundary of what was proper in their orders to the military. "My communications are to you, Mr. President, as I desire to avoid anything like direction from this Department to the Honorable Secretary of War," Noble wrote stiffly.[65]

Meanwhile, Miles's management of the war reflected his own growing frustration. The recalcitrance of the Ghost Dancers and the slow progress toward a resolution irritated him, and he determined to bring in the Ghost Dance leaders and end the standoff once and for all. He was angry at Interior Department officials, who insisted on controlling the Indian agencies and were making such a mess of them. He was even angrier at the sly accusations of Washington politicians that he was exaggerating the Indian threat for his own aggrandizement, accusations his superiors were making no effort to squelch. To end the conflict quickly, advance the primacy of the military, and defend his political future, General Miles dramatically escalated the conflict in South Dakota.

Brooke was negotiating with the Ghost Dancers in the Stronghold, and the signs looked promising for success. On December 3, Brooke sent Jack Red Cloud and a popular Catholic missionary to negotiate with the dancers. They convinced a number of the Ghost Dancers, including Two Strike, to come to a conference at the agency. At the conference on December 6, the Indians denounced the census that had so drastically cut their rations, and made a list of their other complaints. Brooke told them that their grievances could be addressed after they surrendered. The conference did not yield a solution, but it did reveal that the Stronghold Indians were short of food and supplies, and that Two Strike was willing to consider bringing his band in.[66]

When the Sioux returned to the Stronghold, thirty-two of the Pine Ridge Indians and a popular mixed-race scout went with them to persuade the Ghost Dancers to come in. Their first attempt to talk the dancers into surrendering failed. After a two-day Ghost Dance, though, during which it is probable that the scout and the Pine Ridge Indians negotiated quietly, Two Strike and Crow Dog suddenly announced that it was time to return to the agency. Short Bull exploded. The Indians should stick together as brothers, he insisted, and Brooke's promises of leniency were lies—the Indians would end up in jail. He turned on the scout who had split the Ghost Dancers: "I know he is a traitor; kill him; kill him!" The camp broke into a melee. In the end, though, Two Strike had won the day. Short Bull and his people agreed to join the trek back to the agency.[67]

Once the older men restored order, the entire camp—including Short Bull and his people—packed up and moved toward Pine Ridge. Short Bull changed his mind after a few miles and refused to go any further. Two Strike and his people, though, continued on their way, grievously weakening the Ghost Dancers at the Stronghold. On December 12, Brooke reported to Miles that the camp had broken, and Two Strike and his people were coming in.[68]

As Brooke coaxed the Stronghold men to return to the agency, Miles was chipping away at the Ghost Dancers on the northern reservations by bringing in their leaders. Hump, from Cheyenne River, had scouted for Miles during the Nez Perce campaign of 1877, and the general knew that the chief trusted Captain Ezra P. Ewers, who was now stationed in Texas. Miles ordered Ewers up to South Dakota and sent him to talk to Hump, who was, indeed, willing to listen to his old friend. Hump and most of his band left their camp and moved, as requested, to Fort Bennett.[69]

The strategy worked well enough that Miles was encouraged to try it again. At a banquet in Chicago on November 24, Miles and Buffalo Bill, who had campaigned together against Sitting Bull in 1876, discussed the crisis. Sitting Bull had worked for Buffalo Bill in his Wild West Show in the mid-1880s and the two had gotten along. Cody had given Sitting Bull a horse that the chief prized, and Cody was confident that he could bring his old employee in to the military authorities without incident. Miles was willing to give it a try. He scribbled a note on the back of a calling card authorizing Cody "to secure the person of Sitting Bull and deliver him to the nearest com'g officer of U.S. Troops."[70]

Buffalo Bill arrived at Fort Yates on November 28 and planned to head out the next day, with eight companions, for Sitting Bull's camp at Grand River. When Standing Rock agent McLaughlin learned of his arrival, he immediately telegraphed Belt in high dudgeon, demanding that General Miles's order be rescinded. McLaughlin claimed that he wanted the order overturned because it was "unnecessary, and unwise, as it will precipitate a fight which can be avoided." But the next day, after he had been unable to prevent Cody from setting out, he gave his true reasons for trying to thwart the mission. In a rant to T. J. Morgan, McLaughlin said he wanted to make very clear "the fact of my never asking for military assistance in making arrests and my protest against military interference." He could handle his Indians, he insisted, and wanted to continue to "encourage industrial pursuits and stimulate civilisation [sic]."[71]

Although he did not yet know it, McLaughlin's protest worked. His telegram of November 28 had gone straight to the president. Immediately—the day before McLaughlin's second protest—Secretary of War Proctor had sent a telegram to General Miles in Chicago, with the astonishing news that the president himself, who had deferred to Miles over whether or not to send the troops into South Dakota in the first place, was now willing to override Miles's plan for arresting Sitting Bull. "The President thinks any arrest of Sitting Bull or other Indian leaders should be deferred," Proctor telegraphed on November 28. "If any order for arrests have been made you will suspend them for the present and communicate your views to the Department."[72]

At Standing Rock, McLaughlin stalled Cody by sending him out on the wrong trail to catch Sitting Bull. By the time Cody figured out he had been tricked and rode back to the agency, McLaughlin had a telegram from Washington canceling Cody's authority to go after the chief. Buffalo Bill left and went back to Chicago, where he submitted a bill for $505.60 for his transportation and expenses.[73]

The rescinding of his order to Buffalo Bill was the last straw for Miles in his struggle with the Interior Department. The politicians there had created a crisis with their incompetence, then undercut him repeatedly when he tried to fix it. They had accused him of exaggerating the Indian threat to advance his political standing. If no one else was going to defend him and stand up for the military, Miles was going to do it himself.

On November 28, Miles launched his own salvo against the politicians he blamed for the troubles in South Dakota. Previously, he had stood firm that the Indians did not pose a real danger, but with a message to General Schofield about conditions in the new state, he changed his tune. Suddenly the Indians were a terrible threat—the worst Indian threat ever—and the deplorable condition of affairs in South Dakota was almost entirely the fault of poor management by the administration.

Miles's report to General Schofield laid the blame for the South Dakota troubles squarely on the politicians in the Interior Department. The army had subjugated the tribes, he began his statement, but then the Indians had been turned over to civil agents, who were changed as often as presidents came and went, and who were usually inexperienced. Under such political appointees, the Indians had become dissatisfied with their conditions and were willing to go back to war to solve their difficulties. Miles advocated for the continued strength of the army, calling it an "erroneous and dangerous delusion" to think that railroads and settlement had ended Indian wars. Indeed, warriors could live better on cattle than they formerly could on buffalo, and horse farms would guarantee they could stay mounted. They remained a serious threat, he insisted.[74]

Miles tried to undercut the argument that he was exaggerating the troubles for his own purposes. "Danger is imminent," he warned. The Indians were more unhappy than they had been for years, and they were hatching a plot more comprehensive than ever before—more comprehensive, even, than the infamous uprisings led by Tecumseh and Pontiac in the late eighteenth and early nineteenth centuries. He estimated those affected by the messiah craze at 30,000, and put the Sioux willing to fight at about 4,000, with another 6,000 who needed to be watched. Four thousand Indians could make an immense amount of trouble, he warned. Far fewer than that had been involved in the brief Santee uprising, yet they had killed more than five hundred settlers.

Miles blamed the crisis on reduction in rations and on delays in providing what few rations there were, which had created starvation conditions. He mentioned crop failures and, of course, the Ghost Dance. He reported as fact the rumor that Sitting Bull had sent emissaries to other tribes, whose men had been involved in the "Custer Massacre" and the Minnesota and Fetterman "massacres." According to Miles, Sitting Bull had urged his old allies to gather arms and ammunition and to join together near the Black Hills in the spring. "The facts . . . are beyond question," he wrote, and the government must respond with "the most positive and vigorous measures." Newspapers across the country picked up and printed the highlights of Miles's report.[75]

The general left Chicago on the evening of November 28 to take his arguments directly to Washington. There, Miles launched his own newspaper war against Interior Department officials. "These hostiles have been starved into fighting, and they will prefer to die fighting rather than starve peaceably," Miles told reporters. He hoped the problem could be solved without bloodshed, but suggested that such a happy ending wasn't likely. Political mismanagement had laid the groundwork for an outbreak that would cost the lives of a great many brave men and destroy the homes of hundreds of settlers. The *New York Times* commented that "the disagreement between the Interior and the War Departments," revealed most clearly by the Buffalo Bill incident, "is one of the most interesting features of the affair."[76]

The newspapers jumped on Miles's report, spreading his accusations to weaken the administration. The day after Miles released the document, an article in *Harper's Weekly* warned readers that Miles and other officers feared "such an Indian uprising as has never been known," and offered the gist of Miles's argument. It went on to attack the administration's handling of the Sioux, quoting from another opposition paper, the *New York Herald*:

> In the mean time the rations promised by the government have not arrived and the Indians are starving. They have little or no clothing to

> protect them from the bitter cold, and just food enough to keep them hungry all the time. These wards of the republic are cheated out of the food which has been promised, but when they complain, or in very desperation rise in revolt and commit an outrage, they are shot down like dogs, and word is sent to "the Great Father" at Washington that the only good Indian is a dead Indian.

Harper's Weekly condemned the Harrison administration for putting party loyalty above competency in Indian affairs and praised the command of Miles—a man who understood and sympathized with Indians. In a separate article a week later, it continued to promote Miles's position. It published artist Frederic Remington's laudatory account of traveling with the general, who was, according to the overweight artist, always pushing his men to great exertion, always out front. Miles was always a leader, Remington wrote, unlike the old political men of the army who sat at desks in the East, hindering the work of younger men.[77]

By mid-December, *Harper's Weekly* had upped the ante. It suggested that Miles's report did not go far enough. The "one constant reason for the Indian troubles . . . is the causeless change of agents . . . because politicians must reward their henchmen," it wrote. The paper laid responsibility for the trouble squarely on the president and the Secretary of the Interior, who treated the Indian service as party spoils. "We teach the Indians to distrust us," it lamented, "and when they naturally turn against us we destroy them." Even the *New York Tribune*, usually a reliable administration supporter, stood firmly behind Miles, defending him against the charges that he was exaggerating the situation.[78]

Miles's campaign against the Interior Department paid off. On December 1, he won three major victories. First, Secretary of War Proctor wrote to the general to explain away President Harrison's countermanding of Miles's order, assuring Miles that such interference would not happen again. The same day, the Secretary of the Interior was forced to advise the Acting Commissioner of Indian Affairs that the agents must do what the army said. While he tried to save as much dignity as possible, assuring the agents that they would still control the schools and other functions of the agency, the central message was humiliating. For the present, he wrote to the agents, they must obey the orders of the army officers on their reservations. According to an army officer interviewed by the *Washington Post*, the order "virtually turns over the absolute control of the Indians to the military."[79]

Miles won the fight over Indian rations, too, at least temporarily. Belt and Noble had steadfastly maintained that the Sioux had plenty of food, even declining to use money in the tribes' permanent fund to buy food until Congress increased the Indian appropriation, because there was not an "absolute" necessity—the Indians were not actually starving, they insisted. But on December 1, Noble had to tell the Commissioner of Indian Affairs to distribute more rations.[80]

Fighting back from this loss of face, Interior Department officials defended themselves and almost desperately insisted that the Indians, not politicians, were to blame for the troubles. The day after Miles got control of the Indian agencies, Belt forwarded to Noble a letter written by Census Agent Lea, offering a defense of the agents and blaming the Indians for all the troubles on the reservations. Lea wrote that his work had taken him into every Indian habitation and that he had had a "splendid opportunity" to observe Indian life. He was completely unsympathetic to the Indians' plight. They had plenty of food, Lea wrote. He had asked them if their rations were sufficient, and, he reported, they all said yes.

The problem, in his opinion, was that the "unprogressive" Indians were improvident. They set a cooking pot out in the morning and shared with everyone who stopped by. The same was done with coffee and bread. "Those who are most gluttonous in their natures eat up their rations often a day or two before issue day, but they never go hungry. They know who the most provident are, and live off of them until rations day." "Hunger has nothing to do with the present trouble upon Pine Ridge reservation," Lea declared unequivocally. The problem was that the "old bucks" were restless, power hungry, influenced by "designing whites," and suffering from "pure cussedness." They backed the Ghost Dance because it would give them "an opportunity to regain their lost titles."[81]

Noble endorsed Lea's extraordinary missive. Lea was better informed than military officers, the Interior Secretary claimed, for officers only saw the Indians gathered at the agencies away from their homes. Lea's account should outweigh those of the army men. Noble pointed out that Lea confirmed the position of the Interior Department: that the

Sioux were not starving, though many of them suffered from hunger because they were improvident, not because they lacked sufficient food.[82]

The fight between the administration and its opponents over Indian policy was not simply an internecine fight within a small administrative bureaucracy. It inflamed Congress, too, just as soon as the lame-duck session reconvened on December 1, 1890. Recently elected Democrats and Alliance men would not come to Washington until the following December, but the Democrats were newly confident in their denunciations of the Harrison administration. The Indian crisis gave them devastating ammunition against the president. They had been complaining for two years that the administration's policies were injurious to all but their wealthy supporters. Now they had poignant proof of just how harmful those policies were.

The injection of a fight over the Sioux into congressional debates was as unwelcome to Republicans as it was relished by Democrats. Republicans were fighting a holding action. They needed desperately to bolster their party before the Democrats and Alliance members arrived in the next Congress. If they didn't pass the Federal Elections Bill before the 1892 election, they could expect to lose the White House to a Democrat who would reverse their high tariff policy. The president urged his party to continue to push his agenda and to "take no backward step" at the coming session of Congress before the Democrats took over.[83]

As soon as the Senate convened, Senator Hoar of Massachusetts tried to push the Federal Elections Bill—now dubbed the Force Bill—but Democrats ignored his agenda and started a fight over the Indian crisis. Republican senators introduced two appropriations requests for South Dakota: one from Noble to buy rations and one from Proctor to buy guns for South Dakota settlers.[84]

In response to the proposed appropriations, Democrat Daniel Voorhees from the anti-tariff farming state of Indiana took the floor to deliver a withering attack on the Harrison administration. Building from Miles's statement that the Indians had been starved into fighting, Voorhees condemned "the 'niggardly, parsimonious, dishonest, criminal policy' which had brought on an Indian war and endangered the lives of thousands of men, women, and children." The speech was devastating. The administration's Indian policy was "a crime in the sight of God and man. . . . Instead of sitting here debating election bills and force bills and providing the issuance of arms to the States of the Northwest for their protection, we should be hurrying anxiously, eagerly, to provide for feeding these starving people. . . . In some of the branches of the government, or perhaps in more than one, there is a blood guiltiness that will have to be answered for."[85]

Massachusetts senator Henry L. Dawes, Chairman of the Committee on Indian Affairs and the staunch Republican and reformer who had sponsored the Dawes Severalty Act, tried to defend the administration. Dawes claimed that Sitting Bull and Red Cloud—both of whom were old men, one of whom was virtually blind—were behind the troubles. Complaints of starvation were just an excuse for Sioux warmongering, he insisted. The Indians' problems were caused by the fact that they had left home to fight. If they had stayed at home and farmed, they would have plenty of food, he said in a shocking display of either ignorance or indifference to the drought on the plains.[86]

Dawes insisted that the administration had handled the Sioux situation perfectly. It had been cutting supplies to make sure the Indians had to work to feed themselves, and those who had done so had plenty of food. The Indians had to have it impressed upon them that they could no longer live by hunting and fishing. Indeed, they needed to understand that everything that defined traditional Indian life had gone, never to be recalled. Utterly ignoring that rations were partial payment for their cession of lands, Dawes insisted that the Indians' threat to fight was merely an attempt to extort more food out of the government so they would not have to work for a living. Machine Republican senator Gilbert Pierce of North Dakota, who had lost his seat in the last election, backed Dawes. The Indians weren't starving, he scoffed; they were "better fed apparently" than the skinny Voorhees.[87]

Voorhees retorted by implicating the Republicans' western policy in the Sioux debacle. Senator Pierce and his constituents simply lusted after the Indians' lands, he charged. He reminded the Senate that "there are . . . people who die in this matter. The screams of mothers are to be heard. The wail of children is to be borne on the gale. . . . Soldiers . . . both privates and officers, will bite the dust in this miserable war, brought on by . . . the starving of Indians into fighting."

Voorhees's sensational comments instantly appeared in the press. Belt, meanwhile, threw up defenses, leaking the letter of Special Census Agent Lea to the papers. Both sides of the debate were playing out in the newspapers, and the Democrats had the upper hand. The administration had been defending its policies since the summer of 1890, and had taken a bad hit in the fall elections. Now, as opponents piled on, attacking their economic policies, the Sioux crisis had given the Democrats a concrete and poignant illustration of just how devastating the administration's misguided policies had been.[88]

The next day, Voorhees continued the attack. The Senate passed a joint resolution to provide arms for settlers in South Dakota (after expanding it to include North Dakota settlers, too), but the senators also took up the argument over what was really going on in South Dakota. Voorhees quoted extensively from an interview that former Ohio governor Charles Foster, a member of the Crook Commission, had given to the prominent Democratic newspaper the *Cincinnati Enquirer*. Foster had thrown his weight emphatically behind Miles and the army. The Indian troubles could have been easily avoided, he said. "The whole matter has been brought about by a combination of bad policy and the incompetence of some officials." Foster lambasted the administration for reducing Sioux rations during two years of crop failures, and Voorhees again insisted that what the Indians needed was food, not military intervention.[89]

Dawes countered by blaming Red Cloud and Sitting Bull for the crisis again, using Agent McLaughlin and census taker Lea as his sources of information. Astonishingly, Dawes went so far as to dismiss Miles's assessment of the situation because he had been stationed on the West Coast for a few years before his recent promotion. General Miles had no personal knowledge of the condition of things, he asserted, while Lea was a man "who has been on the ground for fifteen or twenty years, and who has the confidence of all political parties." This comment was unintentionally ironic—it was common knowledge on the reservations that the army officers were quite well informed, while the reformers and politicians were always misled about local circumstances. Dawes got the last word in the day's Senate debate, but it was hardly a convincing one: "The government of the United States has been in the main dealing as fairly and as honestly with the Indians as has been the dealing of man with man in this country," he insisted.[90]

Clearly aware that the situation in South Dakota was a liability, administration men continued to try to convince listeners they were doing a good job. A few days after this exchange, Dawes produced a series of documents that he claimed exonerated the administration, including the Lea letter. He begged the Senate to print his documents for the public, to make sure the record was clear.[91]

Dawes gained no traction. Voorhees continued to hammer at the administration, scoring hit after hit simply by reiterating the points Miles had been making for weeks. When Dawes again insisted that Miles wasn't a reliable source, Voorhees retorted that the general was more reliable with his life on the line "than Senators sitting here trying to . . . shield official delinquency, incompetency, or something worse." Voorhees accused the administration of trying to "hide and cover."[92]

Behind the scenes, members of the Interior Department furiously continued to defend themselves and pushed back against the idea that they had contributed to the Indian crisis. To discredit Miles, they insisted that he was either senile or had "a Presidential bee in his bonnet" when he sent Buffalo Bill to arrest Sitting Bull. They accused Cody of being drunk when he arrived at Fort Yates, and congratulated themselves that he had been stopped before he made it to Grand River.[93]

The Republicans' weakening position in the nation became evident when senators turned back to the Federal Elections Bill after finishing their fight over the Sioux. Alliance members declared that they would not support the Republicans' elections measure. This meant that, if the administration forced the bill through without somehow placating the western members, the newly elected Alliance members in western legislatures would refuse to work with Republicans when it came to picking senators. Pushing the elections bill to gain Republican voters in the South could actually decrease the numbers of Republican senators in the short term. This could doom the McKinley Tariff. It was a dilemma.

Back at Pine Ridge, Elaine Goodale and Charles Eastman found their own way to show their disdain for the administration. "We were practically under martial law," Goodale complained. "Like the missionaries I resented the soldiers and was deeply sympathetic with the Sioux. . . . The whole situation was intolerable." Trying to calm the nervous Indians around the agency, most of whom were Christians, they decided to have a number of small Christmas parties, complete with gifts. They set up a Christmas tree and wove garlands of cedar to hang in the wooden chapel. They took up a collection to buy oranges and candy, and practiced singing carols.[94]

Events in the tense camp had thrown Goodale and Eastman together a great deal, and under the Christmas tree they had decorated together for "our people," Eastman proposed marriage. Goodale accepted his proposal. Her later account of the exchange suggested that her decision was not motivated purely by love for the young doctor. "The gift of myself to a Sioux just at this crisis in their affairs will seem to some . . . unnatural," Goodale reflected, but "it followed almost inevitably upon my passionate preoccupation with the welfare of those whom I already looked upon as my adopted people." The decision to marry Dr. Eastman meant that Goodale "embraced with a new and deeper zeal the conception of life-long service to my husband's people," she later recalled.[95]

General Miles's report and his statements to the press about the danger of an uprising were misleading. By early December, the Ghost Dance movement was coming apart. Its leaders were surrendering to officers, and the men at the Stronghold were entertaining the idea of returning to Pine Ridge. As the dancers began to submit to government authority, army officers came down more harshly on the ones who still held out. Just as the movement started to crumble, tensions escalated.

On December 9, after talking with his friend Captain Ewers, Hump brought most of his people in to Fort Bennett. Their defection weakened the Minneconjou dancers at Cheyenne River. They left Big Foot disillusioned and eager to abandon the Ghost Dance if only he could find some way to do so without losing his authority over the younger adherents of the religion in his band. Big Foot gave up the Cherry Creek camp, where the band had been dancing, and moved his people back to their homes on the Cheyenne River.[96]

The army had established a camp of observation, dubbed Camp Cheyenne, near Big Foot's village. Days after Big Foot's return from Cherry Creek, a new commander was assigned to the camp to observe him. Big Foot spent two days there getting to know the officer. Lieutenant Colonel Edwin V. Sumner and Big Foot got along. Big Foot impressed Sumner by his readiness to obey the officer's orders. He promised to stay at home and assured Sumner that he and his band were on the side of the government. Big Foot, a talented negotiator, made "an extraordinary effort to keep his followers quiet," Sumner reported. He noted the tractability of Big Foot's band to General Miles, who telegraphed it to Washington.[97]

While Cheyenne River and Pine Ridge were calming, Standing Rock remained a hot spot. As Republican newspapers had blamed him for the trouble in South Dakota, Sitting Bull had become a national scapegoat for the unrest. He was a popular target for those angry over years of hostility between Indians and settlers. From Augusta, Georgia, on December 8 came a letter warning Sitting Bull that if the military authorities didn't get him, about "20 or 30 of us Georgian 'Corn-Crackers'" would come cut off his leg and beat his brains out with the bloody end of it. Less graphic but no less adamant, *Frank Leslie's* blamed the entire mess in South Dakota on Sitting Bull, and highlighted the terrible threat that Miles was gradually bringing under control with U.S. troops.[98]

The tension between Miles and McLaughlin, and between McLaughlin and Sitting Bull, made the old chief an easy scapegoat in those two long-standing feuds as well. Both McLaughlin and Miles remained determined to bring Sitting Bull in, but each wanted to be in control of the operation.[99]

Miles was furious that McLaughlin had thwarted him before, and he determined to bring Sitting Bull in himself this time. On December 10, he ordered General Ruger to arrest Sitting Bull. Miles made it clear he was angry that the officers at Fort Yates had allowed McLaughlin to ruin his previous arrangement with Buffalo Bill. Miles told Ruger that the commanding officer at Fort Yates should consider it his special duty to secure Sitting Bull, and should remember that McLaughlin was under his direction, not the other way around. Ruger passed this order on to Colonel Drum at Fort Yates on December 12.[100]

Once again, though, Drum worked through Agent McLaughlin. He and McLaughlin agreed to arrest Sitting Bull on December 20, using the Indian police rather than troops. This was a ration day, when most of his people would be away from the camp and thus unable to cause trouble for the police. Troops would stand ready nearby as backup, but the actual arrest would be at the hands of Sitting Bull's own people.[101]

When their plans were in place, Sitting Bull inadvertently forced Drum and McLaughlin to advance them by several days. McLaughlin had stationed one of his trusted Indian police officers, Lieutenant Henry Bull Head, at the Grand River settlement to watch Sitting Bull. Bull Head reported to the teacher at the Grand River school, who spoke enough Lakota to understand Bull Head and pass his information to McLaughlin. On December 14, the teacher wrote to the agent to report that Sitting Bull had held a council the previous day. He and his men discussed a letter the chief had received from Oglala leaders at Pine Ridge. They had asked Sitting Bull to travel south to that troubled agency, and Sitting Bull's people had decided that he should go. The chief had written to McLaughlin to ask permission, the teacher wrote, but "if you do not give it, he is going to go anyway; he has been fitting up his horses to stand a long ride."[102]

Bull Head wanted to arrest the chief immediately, before he slipped away. The teacher wrote to McLaughlin to say that if he wanted the arrest made, he should tell Bull Head right away.[103]

McLaughlin wrote to Lieutenant Bull Head to prepare to arrest Sitting Bull early on the morning of December 15, while troops stood nearby to help if needed. As the troops moved nearer to Grand River to wait in readiness, Bull Head sent messengers to the agency police, who were living at their homes, to meet at his house. The messenger who came for police officer John Loneman told him sadly that he guessed they were about to arrest Sitting Bull. Loneman had been at the Custer fight and had fled with Sitting Bull's band to Canada, but he "had reformed, from all heathenish, hostile and barbarous ways," he said, once McLaughlin had favored him with an agency job. Loneman and the messenger gathered other officers as they rode the thirty miles to Bull Head's home. There, the assistant farmer for the district translated their orders into Lakota for them, since none of them spoke English.[104]

Nervous and sad at their assignment, the forty-three police officers spent the night telling war stories. They were siding with the Americans, arresting one of the greatest leaders their people had ever known. Sitting Bull had seen the Hunkpapa through the days of American invasions, then, together with the legendary Crazy Horse, had held the

Sioux lands against the army until 1876. He had marshalled the Sioux against Crook and Custer at Rosebud and Little Bighorn. Even when forced onto a reservation, he had held as tightly as he could to traditional Sioux ways. Sitting Bull's era was over, these younger men recognized, but they still revered him. It was no wonder they stayed up all night, reassuring themselves with boasts of their own great exploits.

As dawn approached, Lieutenant Bull Head led the men in prayer. Then they saddled their horses and rode off. Their mounts jogged along on slippery trails with owls hooting and coyotes howling—warning them to beware, one of the officers commented. About a quarter of a mile from Sitting Bull's village they stretched into a gallop and, according to Loneman, "rode up as if we attacked the camp." Two of the officers ran for the corral to catch and saddle Sitting Bull's favorite horse, the one Buffalo Bill had given him. Most of the other police scattered around the settlement, and four went to the house. "It was still dark," Loneman remembered: "Everybody was asleep and only dogs which were quite numerous, greeted us upon our arrival and no doubt by their greetings had aroused and awaken[ed]" the people from their beds.

Bull Head, Red Tomahawk, and Shavehead knocked at the door of Sitting Bull's cabin, while Loneman guarded their backs. Reflecting his longtime policy of keeping his door open for all, Sitting Bull invited them in. "I come after you to take you to the Agency," Bull Head told him. "You are under arrest."[105]

Initially, Sitting Bull was willing to cooperate. "Let me put my clothes on," Sitting Bull answered, "and go with you." One of his wives brought his clothes and he dressed, but the delay had given his supporters time to emerge from their cabins to rally to their leader. They started to rail at the police. "Here are the 'ceska maza'—'metal breasts,'" sneered Catch-the-Bear, referring to the metal badges the police wore. "[J]ust as we had expected all the time. You think you are going to take him. You shall not do it." He turned to the others and bade them "Come on now, let us protect our Chief." The Hunkpapas crowded around Sitting Bull, while the police warned them not to cause any trouble.

All of a sudden, Sitting Bull changed his mind about going with the police. His son Crow Foot had interfered. "You always called yourself a brave chief. Now you are allowing yourself to be taken by the Ceska maza," he told his father. The tribal leaders were grooming Crow Foot to be a chief, and the boy had been much influenced by their advice and opinions. Sitting Bull was quite fond of his son, and Crow Foot's comment seemed to change his mind. "Then I will not go," he announced.[106]

Bull Head ordered Sitting Bull not to listen to anyone, while Loneman implored the chief not to let the others lead him into trouble. But Sitting Bull continued to resist. When he still would not go with them, Bull Head and Shavehead took his arms and started to drag him, while Red Tomahawk shoved from behind. The women and children cried while the men berated the police, but they offered no harm to the officers, Loneman later recalled. Once outside, though, in the heat of the struggle, Loneman remembered, Catch-the-Bear pulled a gun from under his blanket and shot at Bull Head, with whom he had a long-running personal feud, wounding him in the side. Loneman ran toward the group and scuffled with Catch-the-Bear for the weapon. He jerked the gun away from Catch-the-Bear and clubbed him. He fell. As Loneman and Catch-the-Bear struggled, Lieutenant Bull Head, who was still hanging on to Sitting Bull, fired a bullet into the chief. Red Tomahawk, behind him, shot again. Sitting Bull, the man who had led the Hunkpapa for thirty years, fell.

The great chief of the Sioux was dead, in front of his own cabin, killed by another Sioux. The enormity of his death would overshadow the rest of American history, but no one could take the time to mourn him properly right then. Sitting Bull's death sparked chaos. His followers ran for the timber where they could fire at the police from shelter. The police took refuge in the sheds and corrals by the cabin, knocking the chinks out from between the logs and firing through the cracks. The troops that were supposed to reinforce the police didn't show up.

When the shooting stopped, six of Sitting Bull's supporters were dead. The police gathered their own four dead and three wounded in Sitting Bull's cabin, while one of the officers set off to find the missing army reinforcements.

The police were angry—at their situation, at Sitting Bull's people, and at themselves. The inside of Sitting Bull's cabin was covered with strips of cream-colored muslin, tacked to the logs to brighten the room. As the police sat inside, recovering from the battle, one noticed that the curtain in the corner was moving. Loneman raised it. "There stood Crow Foot and as soon as he was exposed to view, he cried out, 'My uncles, do not kill me. I do not wish to die.'" "Do what you like with him," Bull Head told the police bitterly. "He is one of them that has caused this trouble." The police opened fire on Sitting Bull's young son. "I do not remember who really fired the shot that killed Crow Foot," Loneman said. "Several fired at once."

About this time the missing soldiers appeared. Rather than reinforcing the police, though, they ignored the white flag in front of the cabin where the officers were holed up. They fired on their allies with a cannon. Finally dissuaded from shooting at the Indian police they were supposed to be supporting, the soldiers rushed into the camp and looted it, taking souvenirs.[107]

With Bull Head out of commission, Red Tomahawk took over. He sent the police officers home, telling them they had discharged their duty and could sit out the rest of the Ghost Dance campaign. Loneman rode back to his house. Before reuniting with his wife, brothers, sisters, and mother, he cleansed himself in a sweat bath and burned the clothes he had been wearing. The next day he took his family to the agency and reported to Agent McLaughlin.

McLaughlin had already heard the news from Grand River and had jubilantly written about the fight that day to his superiors in Washington. While it was sad to lose so many of the agency's noble and brave police officers, he wrote, he rejoiced in the death of Sitting Bull, who had so retarded the progress of the Sioux. He was especially gratified that Sitting Bull's own people had sided with the government and brought the old chief down.[108]

McLaughlin greeted Loneman in the same spirit. "He laid his hand on my shoulders, shook hands with me and said: 'He [A]lone is a Man, I feel proud of you for the very brave way you have carried out your part in the fight with the Ghost Dancers.' I was not very brave right at that moment," Loneman remembered. "His comment nearly set me a crying."[109]

CHAPTER 7

The Massacre

SITTING BULL'S death shattered the détente between the troops and the Sioux on the reservations. The murder of one of their most famous leaders convinced Ghost Dancers at Standing Rock and Cheyenne River that government officers planned to exterminate them. They tried, frantically, to figure out how best to position themselves to survive a coming assault by the huge numbers of soldiers recently moved to the region. General Miles, in turn, interpreted the Indians' terror as the precursor to an uprising. Still convinced that his old enemy Sitting Bull was at the root of the government's problems with the Sioux, he determined to arrest anyone connected with Sitting Bull or his band.

As the troops moved into the Grand River settlement, Sitting Bull's people fled in panic. They ran south from Standing Rock Reservation to join their relatives at Big Foot's village on the Cheyenne River. Big Foot had abandoned his advocacy of the Ghost Dance, although he still had strong adherents of the religion in his settlement. His reputation as a negotiator and peacemaker made his village seem like a safe place for the refugee Hunkpapas to find shelter and a way back into the good graces of the government.

Big Foot's skill as a negotiator was in demand at Pine Ridge, too. Red Cloud, No Water, Big Road, Calico, and Young-Man-Afraid-of-his-Horse had recently promised one hundred ponies to Big Foot if he would come to Pine Ridge and make peace there.[1]

But for the moment, Big Foot's people had more immediate concerns. In mid-December, the chief and his band had moved from their village to the mouth of Cherry Creek to a place of issue to draw rations.

They carried the supplies back home, then on December 17, unaware of the fight at Grand River, they went about their normal preparations for the winter. They visited Lieutenant Colonel Sumner to tell him they were going to collect their annuities at Fort Bennett and to reiterate that they were friendly. He gave them his blessing, and they closed up their houses and started their trip down the Cheyenne River to the fort.[2]

Sumner saw Big Foot's trip to pick up annuities as confirmation that he had managed to swing his band out of the Ghost Dance movement and back into the column of government supporters. Sumner was well aware this shift had been a delicate operation. The younger men in the band still embraced the new religion and rejected government authority. But Big Foot had coaxed them into a trip to pick up their annuities, signaling that they were willing to resume their old relations with the government. Sumner made a point of showing the chief great respect and support, trying to strengthen his hand in the struggle over the younger Minneconjou Ghost Dancers.[3]

General Miles, however, thought differently. Miles was determined to have army personnel end the Ghost Dance standoff once and for all. He was angry that McLaughlin had botched the arrest of Sitting Bull yet again—killing the chief this time—and wanted to have the army break the Ghost Dance by arresting all the Indians associated with it. He wanted to mop up the Ghost Dance escapees from Grand River. And he wanted to arrest Big Foot, the last Ghost Dance leader on either of the northern reservations still living outside military control. No sooner had Sumner wished Big Foot a good journey than the general received a telegram that rejected his previous favorable accounts of the chief. "It is desirable that Big Foot be arrested," a telegram from Ruger's headquarters read. There were not enough troops nearby to capture him, but as soon as it was possible, Ruger would likely order his arrest, he wrote.[4]

Miles was determined to arrest Big Foot not only to take control of all the Ghost Dance leaders, but also because he knew that the refugees from Grand River were running to join Big Foot's band. He was convinced that the men who had been with Sitting Bull were hostile and dangerous, and would tip back into hostility any groups who sheltered them. While these two impulses were initially separate, in the next few days they would come together to create the image that Big Foot and his band were enemies of the government.

Ruger's telegram impugning Big Foot arrived at Camp Cheyenne only hours before Sumner received another piece of bad news. He heard that Sitting Bull's men from Standing Rock were on their way to intercept the Minneconjous with the plan of diverting them to join the Ghost Dancers at the Stronghold. Sumner fired off a number of telegrams to his superiors. While he suggested hopefully that Big Foot's band had traveled too far by this time to be in the path of the Hunkpapa refugees, he also promised to try to cover all of the many trails the Indians might take south to the Stronghold. Still, as he noted, the country was huge. He wrote plaintively that he would capture Big Foot's entire group if he could find it, but it seemed like a hopeless task: there were too many trails, the Indians knew them all and would avoid the soldiers, and they would probably travel at night anyhow.[5]

While Sumner stewed over this new information at Camp Cheyenne, Big Foot was also confronted with a different situation than he had expected when he set off for Fort Bennett only days before. Big Foot was not, in fact, hostile to the government, but his loyalty was challenged the day after he left his village when he heard for the first time of the catastrophe at Grand River.

On December 18, Sitting Bull's nephew and a friend arrived at Big Foot's camp, the nephew with a bullet in his leg. They told Big Foot that the chief had been killed and that his people had fled to the mouth of Cherry Creek, where they were stranded without food or shelter. Big Foot sent ten men to verify the story and, if it were true, to bring the refugees back with them to his camp where they could be fed and sheltered. Dewey Beard, a twenty-nine-year-old man traveling in Big Foot's band with his parents, brothers, wife, and newborn son, was one of the ten men tapped to go. He was likely chosen because he had traveled to Canada with Sitting Bull's people after the Battle of the Little Bighorn and had friends and kin among the refugees.[6]

Beard and his compatriots rode up the river, where near Hump's village at Cherry Creek they found about three hundred of Sitting Bull's people. The women were huddled around fires mourning, singing death songs, and crying over the deaths of Sitting Bull and the others killed. The men sat in council with Hump, who was now working for the army and who wanted to take Sitting Bull's people to the agency.[7]

Hump was not pleased to see the visitors, who announced they had come to take Sitting Bull's people to Big Foot. Hump was convinced that Big Foot's men were still fervent Ghost Dance adherents and were plotting to launch a war. Hump was now a government man, and had the zeal of a recent convert. He threatened to kill the ten emissaries and promised that he would send soldiers to attack Big Foot's band. He refused to let any of the Standing Rock Hunkpapas go with Beard and his friends, although some of the younger men wanted to.

The Indians at Hump's camp were split over their future course. Hump had emphatically cast his lot with the government, but he had led his people in the Ghost Dance until recently, and many of his people were not as willing to abandon the new religion as he was. Not all of Hump's people accepted his dictum that they stay on the side of the soldiers, especially after what had happened to Sitting Bull. When the ten emissaries from Big Foot left to go back to their camp, about twenty of Sitting Bull's people went back with them. En route, they passed a traveling group of Hunkpapa refugees who turned toward Big Foot's camp rather than Hump's settlement. The next day, about thirty more of Hump's people also joined Big Foot's band. The forty or so hungry and ill-supplied Hunkpapas looted a store near the camp for food, clothing, and material for tents, confirming military suspicions that they were hostile.[8]

The rest of the Hunkpapas and Minneconjous took their chances with Hump and the army. They surrendered on December 22 and were taken to the Cheyenne River agency, shipped down the Missouri, and imprisoned at Fort Sully. As it turned out, they were the lucky ones.[9]

While Beard and his companions rode down the Cheyenne River to Big Foot's camp, Hump's scouts were riding in the other direction, to Sumner at Camp Cheyenne. There, they warned Sumner that Big Foot's men were spoiling for a fight and were sheltering some of Sitting Bull's hostile Hunkpapas. This information seemed to prove the accusations in the telegrams Sumner had received in the days since Big Foot had left for Fort Bennett. Sumner started down the river with fifty men and two Hotchkiss cannons, chasing after the traveling Minneconjous.[10]

Late on December 20, Sumner's command caught up with Big Foot's band, and the next day, Big Foot brought two refugees from Grand River to the general to reassure him that the Indians were still friendly. Sumner angrily demanded to know why Big Foot was offering hospitality to the refugees from Sitting Bull's band, to which Big Foot pointed out that he could hardly let his cold, hungry, tired kinsmen and friends perish. Sumner accepted the explanation. He was shocked at the condition of the two refugees with Big Foot. They were, he said, "so pitiable a sight that I at once dropped all thought of their being hostile or even worthy of capture."[11]

Big Foot was eager to indicate that he was friendly to the government. He was nervous about Hump's threat to send soldiers, especially since his scouts had told him that Ruger had dispatched troops. The soldiers were to keep Big Foot's Minneconjous from making a break for the Stronghold, but with the news of Sitting Bull's death only days old, the Minneconjous were understandably wary of approaching troops. Big Foot made a point of reassuring Sumner that he was on the government's side.[12]

Sumner told Big Foot that his people must return to their homes, and Big Foot was happy to comply. On December 21, the soldiers escorted Big Foot's band to a new camp near Sumner's soldiers, who surrounded them with a guard. Sumner reported that he had 225 Minneconjous—men, women, and children—and thirty-eight Hunkpapas, fourteen of whom were warriors. Sumner ordered eight beeves killed, and the soldiers and Indians feasted.[13]

Big Foot and Sumner each wanted to believe that they had resolved the conflict between the Indians and the soldiers, but in fact tensions between their own men erupted dramatically on the trip back to Camp Cheyenne. On December 22, Sumner ordered a march back to the camp at the mouth of the Belle Fourche River. He separated the Indian women and children, traveling in wagons at the head of the column, from the men on horseback behind, and guarded the whole group with cavalry. Early in the day, two wagons got tangled in a fence gate. An officer who had been berating the Minneconjous all morning dismounted and began to shout at the women as they tried to clear the mess. An angry relative of one of the women confronted the officer. "I am still living; I don't like to see my relations abused by a white man." He threw off his coat to fight. The officer remounted and rode off. As he did so, the young men broke from the back of the column and rode to surround the wagons. The soldiers lined up with guns pointed at the oncoming men, and the women panicked, thinking they were about to be killed. The Indian men fell back into line.[14]

Big Foot still tried to pretend things were fine. When Sumner asked what had happened, Big Foot dismissed the question with a laugh. "Nothing the matter; some old women screamed."[15]

But the tensions between the Minneconjous and the soldiers could not be dismissed, and they sparked a major breach between Big Foot and Sumner. The route to Camp Cheyenne took the column near Big Foot's village. As they approached it, angry and uncooperative, the horsemen rode off toward their cabins. The women in the wagons begged to follow. Big Foot told Sumner that he was willing to go on to the army camp, but "there will be trouble in trying to force these women and children, cold and hungry as they are, away from their homes. That is their home, where the Government has ordered them to stay, and none of my people have committed a single act requiring their removal by force."[16]

Sumner realized that he had little choice but to let them all go to their village. Trying to force the entire band on to Camp Cheyenne would result in bloodshed. Separating Big Foot out and taking him along with the Hunkpapas wouldn't work, because Sumner understood that Big Foot was the only reason the younger men were cooperating at all, and if the chief weren't there it was impossible to guess what they would do. And he couldn't take the Hunkpapas alone because, he realized, he couldn't tell the Standing Rock Hunkpapas and the Minneconjous apart. Stumped, he let the Minneconjous go home and told Big Foot he and the Hunkpapas could go with them, even though he knew that his superiors wanted Big Foot arrested. Sumner trusted Big Foot when he promised to bring the Hunkpapa refugees to Camp Cheyenne by noon the next day. Sumner telegraphed to Miles that "they seem a harmless lot, principally women and children."[17]

The Minneconjous went home with their Hunkpapa guests, and the soldiers returned to Camp Cheyenne. There, Sumner received a telegram from General Miles that put him in a tight spot. Miles wrote in haste of a rumor that several hundred Indians were coming down from the north. Miles ordered Sumner to take his prisoners to Fort Meade, being careful to make sure they did not escape, and then to watch for the rumored warriors.[18]

Sumner, of course, didn't have any prisoners, and he had to come up with a plan quickly. He decided to wait until Big Foot and the Hunkpapas showed up by noon on December 23, and send them off to Fort Bennett while he guarded against the rumored Indians coming from the north. But on December 23, noon came and went with no sign of Big Foot. Sumner was eating dinner in preparation for moving out with his men toward Big Foot's village when a local cattle rancher named John Dunn showed up to sell some butter to the general. Dunn was married to a Minneconjou woman and knew Big Foot's people. Sumner hired him to go down to the village himself and to tell Big Foot's people that, since they hadn't come in to Camp Cheyenne, they had to move to Fort Bennett. He was going to send fifteen soldiers to escort them. He would, he said, enforce the order with troops if they didn't move by noon the next day.[19]

Communicating partly through his own knowledge of Lakota and partly through an interpreter named Felix Benoit, Dunn managed to panic the already nervous Indians. Stopping in at Big Foot's house, he found the chief in bed. Dunn told the chief that Sumner wanted to know why he had broken his promise to come to Camp Cheyenne that day. Big Foot replied that he was sick but would go the next day. Dunn told Big Foot that his people must go to Fort Bennett, and that Sumner was sending an escort to make sure they went.[20]

By this time, the warriors had gathered in Big Foot's house. Exactly what Dunn told Big Foot's people next is not clear. Either Dunn threatened them to get them to move quickly or the Minneconjous were so afraid of soldiers they misheard his information about the escort, but somehow the Minneconjou got the idea that Sumner was coming with a thousand soldiers to arrest all the men. If they resisted, the soldiers would fire on them. By the time Dunn and Benoit left the village the Indians were rounding up their ponies and throwing together their belongings. Dunn and Benoit were satisfied that the Indians were packing up to go to Fort Bennett that very evening, and they conveyed that information to Sumner. But at 7:00 that night, Sumner's own scouts reached the village and found it deserted.[21]

The Minneconjous had not gone toward Fort Bennett. In panic, they fled from their village about nine miles southeast into the hills up Pass Creek (called Deep Creek by the settlers), where they debated what to do. They sat in council the night of December 23. Big Foot tried to convince his men that they should go to Fort Bennett as they had been ordered. They disagreed. Go to Pine Ridge as the Oglalas had asked him to, they insisted. Slip away from what was probably a trap, get the ponies that had been offered, and take shelter with Red Cloud, who was on decent terms with the authorities.[22]

Big Foot reluctantly agreed. When a scout from Sumner's camp arrived around midnight, Big Foot gave him a message for Sumner. Tell him I want to go to Bennett, he said, but my people want to go to Pine Ridge, and I will lead them there.[23]

Sumner had calculated wrong, and he knew he was in trouble. As soon as he had heard that Big Foot's village was deserted, Sumner had fired off a telegram to Colonel Eugene A. Carr, commanding the Sixth Cavalry, whose men were riding through the country between the Pine Ridge and Cheyenne River Reservations. Sumner ordered him to intercept the band while he guarded against the Indians from the north.[24]

The next day, Miles's wrath descended on him. In a telegram, Miles dismissed the rumor he had previously reported about Indians coming from the north and castigated Sumner for losing Big Foot and the Hunkpapas. "Big Foot has been defiant both to the troops and to the authorities, and is now harboring outlaws and renegades." In a telegram shortly after the first, Miles added: "Your orders were positive and you have missed your opportunity. Endeavor to be more successful next time." Sumner had no choice but to take his command back to Fort Meade without any prisoners, an embarrassment that his men slyly taunted him about for months.[25]

General Miles was livid at Big Foot's escape. He believed Big Foot's people were hostile, and he had intended for the military to succeed where McLaughlin had failed. Most important, though, he worried that they would derail the peace negotiations that were under way to bring in the remaining Sioux in the Stronghold. General Brooke had repeatedly sent delegations from Pine Ridge to the holdouts, using men who had strong contacts with both sides, men like Jack Red Cloud and various scouts, to persuade the Ghost Dancers there to surrender. Two delegations had been turned away with shouts and gunfire, but the last one had returned in mid-December to report that the Ghost Dancers were ready to come in.[26]

Big Foot's escape created a problem. His trail from Pass Creek to Pine Ridge led toward the Stronghold. If Big Foot's apparently hostile band crossed the path of the wavering holdouts, they could stiffen their resistance and sabotage the entire peacemaking mission. Keeping the Minneconjou band from the Stronghold seemed crucial.

Meanwhile, back East, Sitting Bull's murder gave more ammunition to critics of the administration. Democratic representatives called for an investigation into Sitting Bull's death, asking under what authority the government had killed him. The resolution they proposed demanded that the House investigate the entire Sioux affair, including whether or not the government's neglect of its treaty obligations, especially in the case of rations, had had anything to do with the turbulence in South Dakota.[27]

General Miles also continued to hammer on the politicians in Washington, demanding that they address the Indians' legitimate complaints. After discovering that the suppliers who were supposed to provide winter clothing for the Sioux were waiting until the river froze so they would not have to pay water freight charges, Miles telegraphed Schofield to demand once again that army officers be put in control of the agencies, then badgered the War Department to rectify the clothing situation at once.[28]

Miles directly rebutted Senator Dawes's outrageous statements from the Senate debate. He sent a telegram to Senator Dawes on December 19 refuting the points in the senator's congressional speech and pointing out that Congress had been in session for two weeks, and had not yet managed to confirm the promises the Crook Commission had made. It would be the work of a few hours to fulfill these promises and appropriate the money to feed the starving Indians. Miles recommended, again, that the military be put in charge of the reservations.[29]

The same day, he reiterated to General Schofield that politicians simply must fulfill the nation's treaty obligations. The military could not solve the nation's problems with the Indians, he insisted; only Congress could. Crops had failed in the western drought, and starving Indians were increasingly disaffected. If Congress did not live up to its promises, hostility to the government would only grow.[30]

Miles was launching his own offensive against the way the government had handled the Sioux, but his determination to reduce the role of politicians in Indian affairs did not meet with enthusiasm in the administration. One might have expected the Commander of the Army to support Miles, but rather than taking his side, General Schofield deferred to his political colleagues. He forwarded Miles's demand for military control of the agencies to Secretary of the Interior Noble, the man responsible for distributing patronage on the reservations. Noble had, of course, worked hard to preserve the prerogatives of his department in the face of Miles's opposition. Although Miles wanted to remove politicians from Indian management altogether, Schofield weakened his proposal to try to make it palatable to the Interior Department. Schofield suggested to Noble that Miles's plan could be accomplished without disrupting the work of the agents—hardly what Miles was after—and asked for Noble's approval.[31]

The increasingly voluble criticism leveled at the administration for its mismanagement of Indian affairs prompted a reaction at the highest levels. While his days were focused overwhelmingly on patronage and economic issues, President Harrison took time out to prepare notes for a speech on the topic. The speech was never delivered, but in his notes the president argued that the Indians were not starving, and that while Congress's neglect to pass legislation fulfilling the promises of the Crook Commission might be unfortunate, "white men having just claims suffer in the same way."[32]

Other administration Republicans also pushed back against critics. They insisted that Sitting Bull had gotten his just desserts, and that the Indians bore the blame for the crisis. If anything, *Frank Leslie's* said, the government had been too kind. It had been a "great mistake" to let the Indians keep their tribal culture. The "savages" should have been "treated as other irresponsible persons are treated by every civilized community," forced to support themselves and take personal responsibility for their actions. As it was, they threatened the settlements with "violence, rapine, and plunder." "It is not true that the Indians have been starved," the editor snarled. "They have been liberally fed; worse than all, they have been treated like spoiled children, and allowed to purchase fire-arms and ammunition, to go on with their hostile demonstrations, to combine their forces, and finally to threaten the border settlements with their bloody vengeance. It is time to call a halt in our weak, foolish, and sentimental Indian policy. Let the Indian be treated as well as the white man, but no better."[33]

Harrison's men defended Sitting Bull's murder. Lest anti-administration forces get some traction by pointing out that Buffalo Bill could have arrested Sitting Bull without bloodshed, *Frank Leslie's* insisted that Miles had "incautiously and injudiciously" sent the scout without properly deputizing him. Commander of the Army Schofield applauded Sitting Bull's death. By sending the hostile Indians on the run, it would help to make it clear who was friendly and who was hostile, he said. Senator Pettigrew told reporters that the chief's demise would quiet the reservations by removing a leading troublemaker. A few members of the House Committee on Indian Affairs resolved that "the dispensations of Providence are always wise and beneficent; therefore . . . we coincide with the course of Providence in the removal of Hon. Mr. Sitting Bull, and offer our congratulations to his widows and orphans."[34]

Miles's efforts to force the administration into better treatment of the Indians went nowhere. President Harrison and his men were determined to break the opposition of the Sioux and force them to submit to governmental authority before they would consider ameliorating the Indians' dire circumstances.

Back in South Dakota, it seemed that the army had almost achieved the goal of Indian submission, although there was still plenty of room for a misstep. Many of those in the Stronghold had returned to Pine Ridge, and the holdouts were wavering. The uncertainty in the equation was Big Foot's band.

Beginning on the night of December 23, when Sumner had sent his telegram, Carr's freezing men patrolled the area between the Stronghold and Cherry Creek, but they could not find Big Foot's Minneconjous. In fact, the Indians had passed to the east of the troops. On the first night and day of traveling, December 23 and 24, they had traveled an astonishing fifty miles. But in the afternoon of the second day they had to get through the Badlands Wall, a hundred-mile rock formation dividing the northern grasslands from the southern plains, which lie two hundred feet below the land to the north of them. Big Foot's people discovered that the pass they intended to take had washed out, and the

The Cheyenne River and Big Foot's Journey to Pine Ridge/the Stronghold

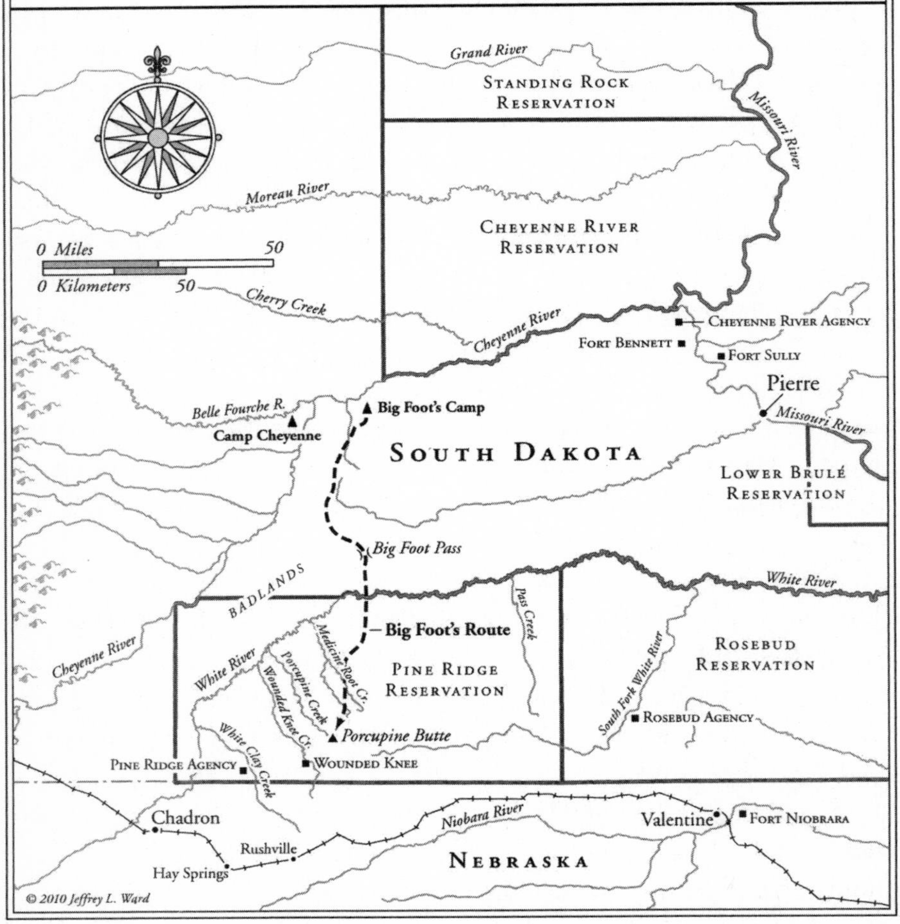
Grand River
Standing Rock Reservation
Missouri River
Moreau River
Cheyenne River Reservation
0 Miles 50
0 Kilometers 50
Cherry Creek
Cheyenne River
Cheyenne River Agency
Fort Bennett
Fort Sully
Pierre
Missouri River
Belle Fourche R.
Camp Cheyenne
Big Foot's Camp
South Dakota
Lower Brulé Reservation
Big Foot Pass
Badlands
White River
Pass Creek
Big Foot's Route
Cheyenne River
White River
Medicine Root Cr.
Porcupine Creek
Wounded Knee Cr.
Pine Ridge Reservation
South Fork White River
Rosebud Reservation
Rosebud Agency
White Clay Creek
Porcupine Butte
Pine Ridge Agency
Wounded Knee
Chadron
Niobara River
Valentine
Fort Niobrara
Rushville
Hay Springs
Nebraska
© 2010 Jeffrey L. Ward

men had to use axes and spades to get the wagons through it. The weather was sunny, but the wind blew "raw and cold," Joseph Horn Cloud remembered.[35]

By nightfall on the twenty-fourth, the illness Big Foot had complained of back at the village had turned into pneumonia. The next day, Christmas day, they made only eight miles. Big Foot sent three messengers to Pine Ridge to tell the Oglala chiefs he was sick and traveling slowly, but was on his way. The next day they made only four miles. Unprepared for the Indians' snail's pace and still convinced that Big Foot and his band were going to the Stronghold, the army continued to search for them. The cavalry ranged across the land to the west of the band, desperate to find the Indians, while four troops of the Ninth Cavalry under Major Guy Henry were stationed to cover all eastern entrances to the Stronghold. But they found no one.[36]

The Minneconjous would soon be General Brooke's problem. Brooke knew that Short Bull, Kicking Bear, and the other Ghost Dancers were on their way in from the Stronghold, and he was anxious to make sure nothing interfered with his delicate negotiations. Big Foot's people and the Hunkpapas, if indeed they were hostile, could well convince the Ghost Dancers not to surrender, destroying all his carefully executed plans. He was adamant that that could not happen.

At Pine Ridge, General Brooke heard from the Oglala chiefs on December 26 that Big Foot was on his way to the agency. Brooke sent three telegrams to Miles, promising that there would not be any more mistakes with Big Foot once they found him. Brooke promised to disarm the Minneconjous, hold them, and take their horses, as ordered. He sent out Major Samuel M. Whitside with Troops A, B, I, and K of the Seventh Cavalry, and a platoon of artillery with two Hotchkiss cannons, to intercept the band.[37]

Whitside and his men camped near the trading post at Wounded Knee Creek. From there, Whitside sent out scouts to search the draws around Wounded Knee and Porcupine creeks for the Minneconjous. General Brooke had promised twenty-five dollars to the first man to spot the Indians, and the bored reporters had upped the ante to fifty. As the scouts scoured the countryside, the soldiers set up a system of mirrors to communicate with Pine Ridge. On the twenty-seventh, a message from Brooke urged Whitside: "Find [Big Foot's] trail and follow, or find his hiding place and capture him. If he fights, destroy him."[38]

Big Foot was now desperately ill and was camped thirty miles to the north on Red Water Creek. Two of his scouts rode in from Pine Ridge to tell him that soldiers were waiting for him on Wounded Knee Creek. The chiefs at Pine Ridge suggested he should turn east to avoid them before cutting down to Pine Ridge. He was too sick, Big Foot replied. Rather than avoiding the soldiers, he would head straight to their camp. In any case, the scouts had told him that the holdouts at the Stronghold had given up and would come in to Pine Ridge on December 29. Kicking Bear and Short Bull were hoping that Big Foot would bring his negotiating skills to Pine Ridge at the same time to smooth their surrender.[39]

On the twenty-eighth, Big Foot's people made it to Porcupine Creek by midday. As Big Foot's advance men rode down the slope to the creek, they found four army scouts, including Baptiste Garnier, a good-natured, athletic man who went by the nickname of Little Bat, watering their horses in the stream. Big Foot's men grabbed the bridles of two of the scouts and took them to their chief. Big Foot asked the scouts to tell the officers at Wounded Knee that he and his people would be on their way to the army camp after they ate. When the scouts returned to the army camp and reported to Whitside that Big Foot was coming toward them, Whitside immediately moved out to meet the Minneconjous with 235 soldiers, along with two Hotchkiss cannons.

Big Foot's people finished their meal and began moving toward the soldiers with trepidation, aware that they must be in some amount of trouble for running away from Lieutenant Colonel Sumner at Camp Cheyenne. Still, they had no intention of fighting, and figured to brave their way to talk to the troop commander. As they moved forward over the top of the hills on the western side of Porcupine Creek, Dewey Beard's brother Joseph Horn Cloud later remembered, "they saw a cloud of dust rising and when they had descended on the other side the soldiers had also come over the hills from the west." To their dismay, the soldiers took up battle lines, the cannons ranged in front of them.[40]

Big Foot was huddling in blankets in the bed of a wagon. He counseled his nervous men to ride straight toward the soldiers. He had his own wagon taken to Whitside, who saw that he was indeed terribly sick.

Blood dripped from his nose onto his blankets and into pools on the floor of the wagon. Whitside demanded that the Minneconjous come with him to Wounded Knee. Big Foot wheezed that that was fine; after all, that was where he was headed anyway. Then he would go on to Pine Ridge, where he was expected to help make peace. The two men shook hands. Whitside had Big Foot transferred to an army ambulance. It would be more comfortable than the rough wagon on which he had been jolting for the ride to the army camp.[41]

An uneasy calm descended as the procession turned back to Wounded Knee camp. Whitside sent word to General Brooke that he had Big Foot and his followers—120 men and 230 women and children—in custody. Whitside asked that the rest of the Seventh Cavalry be sent to Wounded Knee for support. Brooke sent Troops C, D, E, and G of the Seventh, commanded by Colonel James Forsyth. He also sent a platoon of Light Battery E, First Artillery, with two additional Hotchkiss guns.[42]

Despite the promising news from Whitside, Brooke was still cautious, determined not to let Big Foot's people escape and hinder the surrender of the Stronghold warriors. Brooke ordered Whitside "to disarm Big Foot's band, take every precaution to prevent the escape of any; if they fought to destroy them." He also sent a troop of Indian scouts.[43]

Brooke was optimistic that Big Foot's people were safely captured. In a telegram, Brooke suggested to General Miles that, once they were disarmed, the Indians should stay under Whitside's eye at Wounded Knee until they could be moved to the railhead at Gordon, Nebraska, to be shipped to Omaha. "All right," Miles replied. "Use force enough. Congratulations."[44]

Escorted by the soldiers, Big Foot's band straggled into the Wounded Knee camp late in the afternoon. The Indians wended their way along the dusty road that ran down the slope to the east of the creek before it crossed the water, passed the store and the post office, went by the rows of army tents, ran southward along a dry ravine, then turned west toward the agency. They refused to camp in the army tents that the soldiers had been ordered to pitch for those who had no shelter, and instead set up tepees in a half circle to the south of the army tents and the north of the dry ravine. The destitute Indians then settled down to eat the three hundred rations Whitside had distributed. Whitside settled Big Foot into an army tent equipped with a camp stove on the northern edge of the Indian encampment, to the south of the main body of the army tents.[45]

Whitside remained wary. He set up the camp to ensure that he would not be surprised by a sudden outbreak. He ordered the artillery to place the Hotchkiss guns on the hill opposite the tepees, where the artillery commander, Lieutenant Harry L. Hawthorne, and his men could shoot down on them if necessary. Troops of soldiers were stationed around the prisoners.[46]

And still soldiers poured in to guard the Indians. The reinforcements from Pine Ridge arrived around 8:30 at night, bringing the two additional Hotchkiss guns. Colonel Forsyth, who assumed command from Whitside, had his men camp to the north of the army tents. By midnight on the twenty-eighth, there were 470 soldiers divided into eight cavalry troops, one company of scouts, and four Hotchkiss guns guarding about 350 cold hungry, exhausted, frightened, and angry Sioux men, women, and children.

Such a strong military presence to guard so few Indians—who were mostly destitute women and children at that—gave the military men confidence that their mission was over. With the knowledge that the Stronghold standoff had ended and that Big Foot's men were captured, the army men celebrated the close of hostilities. A trader from Pine Ridge had brought a keg of whiskey out with Forsyth, and the officers toasted the end of their successful campaign. They drank convivially as the night wore on.[47]

No one enjoyed the evening more than Colonel James Forsyth. Overseeing the surrender of the Minneconjous was an honor for him. He was a Civil War veteran with a long military career, most of it spent in one administrative position after another. He had commanded the Seventh since 1886, but the previous four years had been calm ones. This was real action—although without much danger—and Forsyth was undoubtedly enjoying it along with his officers, who liked their commander. The off-duty soldiers were also celebrating, but more quietly. They, too, had found whiskey, but were drinking it secretly, for they weren't supposed to have it at all.[48]

The Sioux were not so relaxed. They were well aware that new troops had come in, and worried about what that might mean. Ten or twelve of the men sat up all night talking over affairs with Little Bat in the tent the scouts were using, set up near the tent where Big Foot lay struggling to breathe. Others also sat awake and uneasy. Dewey Beard, whose brothers, father and mother, and wife and son were with him in Big Foot's camp, later remembered that he was unable to eat that night, and had not even tried to lie down to sleep until morning light. "There was great uneasiness among the Indians all night—were fearful that they were to be killed—were in doubt, did not know what was to happen. The soldiers were stationed all around them, and this was a feature that added to their alarm."[49]

The soldiers were up at reveille on Monday, December 29, and clustered around their fires on a fine South Dakota morning for hardtack and coffee. They were a mixed group. While their officers had been with the Seventh for years—six had fought with Custer—the soldiers were much less experienced. Most had never been in battle before, and a fifth of them were new recruits, including thirty-eight who had joined the regiment only two weeks before, when it had already arrived at Pine Ridge.[50]

The soldiers ate their breakfast and prepared to move the Minneconjou band to the Pine Ridge agency. It was there they expected the real story of the day to unfold: the holdouts from the Stronghold were going to arrive. What was happening at Wounded Knee seemed minor compared to that. As the soldiers ate, a detail distributed rations to the Indians, who were uneasy at the presence of so many troops, and anxious to move on to the agency.[51]

Forsyth had been charged with disarming the Indians, but with his overwhelming numbers he expected no difficulty. To remind the Minneconjous that resistance would be suicide, Forsyth placed his troops on all four sides of the tepees, up in the hills and along the plains, so that no soldier was more than three hundred yards from the Indian camp. Then he sent Little Bat and another scout to tell the Indian men that they were wanted in council in the area between the army tents and the cluster of tepees. While the men were in council, the women should hitch the teams to the wagons and be ready to leave, the interpreters told them.[52]

Arranging the council was easier said than done, however. Big Foot was too sick to talk much to his people, and the men, dressed in their

Ghost Dance shirts, kept drifting back and forth between the tepees and the council area. There were also visitors wandering around to watch the proceedings. Teamsters, army support, and merchants and settlers who had come from the agency in buggies stood at a distance behind the army officers. Three newspaper reporters also wandered around the tepees, examining the surrendering Minneconjous to pick up details for stories they would send out later.[53]

The council finally came together at eight or nine. The men sat in two half circles in front of Big Foot's tent, a number of young boys alongside them. The older men defended their presence by explaining that they had proved their bravery and had been recognized as men. Forsyth let the boys stay.[54]

The youngsters might have been recognized as men, but they were still children at heart. Charley Allen remembered seeing them "in numbers playing about the tents like little children around a country schoolhouse." Some were indeed schoolchildren; a number of schoolboys from Pine Ridge were traveling with Big Foot's band to return to their homes after visiting relatives on Cheyenne River, George Sword recalled.[55]

Once the council finally gathered and grew quiet, Forsyth ordered the men to surrender their weapons. His demand caused deep consternation. Their guns were vital to the Sioux, used for both hunting and protection. A good gun was also quite expensive, and an object of pride. No one was keen on handing over such a valued and valuable part of his lifestyle. When Forsyth ordered twenty Minneconjous to bring out the guns, the men began to mill around again, moving back and forth between the tepees and the council area. The men returned with twenty-five old guns—Springfield rifles, muzzle loaders, first-model Henry and Winchester rifles, old Spencer carbines—and insisted that these were all they had. Many of the men refused to sit down again; they stood with their wives, who had finished packing the wagons, behind them. The Minneconjous were anxious, but not panicked. Allen noted that eight or ten boys in their school uniforms were playing leapfrog at the southeast edge of the standing Minneconjou men.[56]

Forsyth was angry that more guns had not been surrendered, and in his confidence in the strength of the soldiers, he forgot Miles's chief tenet that commanders must scrupulously keep their soldiers separated from Indians. He had Big Foot, who was still bleeding from the nose, brought out of his tent and set on the ground, planning to have him make his men produce their guns. Forsyth also demanded that the men stop milling around. He brought the soldiers closer, and as the Indian men moved into the council area, the soldiers prevented them from going back out. One hundred and six men ended up in council, while the remaining fourteen were elsewhere, some working with the horses and wagons, some, perhaps, staying in the tepees.

As the men were corralled into the council, Forsyth demanded that the interpreter, Philip Wells, who had arrived with the scouts the night before, tell Big Foot to instruct his men to give up their weapons. Wells was a forty-year-old mixed-blood scout who was fiercely loyal to Forsyth and to the American government. He had translated for the army when Sitting Bull had surrendered in 1881 and had been employed by the government on the Sioux reservations, in one capacity or another, since 1882. In 1889, Wells had been the official translator for the Crook Commission. Wells represented the government with enthusiasm, lecturing his full-blood relatives ad nauseam on their backward ways.[57]

When Wells told Big Foot to order his men to give up their guns, the chief obliged. He told his men to bring out their weapons, but they told him they already had. When Wells relayed this information to Forsyth the officer called Big Foot a liar and said he would send soldiers to get the guns. "All right, let them do it," Big Foot answered. "Boys, do not be mad; let them do it," he told his men.[58]

Forsyth sent his soldiers to clean the weapons out of the Indian camp. He ordered Captain Charles A. Varnum and Captain George D. Wallace to take a detail of four soldiers and two interpreters into the tepees to search for firearms and steel-tipped arrows. Wallace told John W. Butler, a packer for the pack train, to come with him. Accompanied by Little Bat and John Shangreau, the men searched the tepees. While the soldiers searched, Forsyth was delivering a harangue to the Indians through Philip Wells about "their duplicity and their faithless disregard of promises." They listened sullenly. Bored by the tirade, newspaperman Charley Allen joined the searchers.[59]

The Sioux were, in fact, hiding additional weapons, mostly clubs or cooking knives, but also some valuable guns. At the first tepee, Butler passed a new war club out to Wallace, who tucked it under his arm and announced he would keep it and hang it in his office. As the men searched the tepees, they passed the guns they found to the soldiers standing outside. The officers numbered the guns and put them in two piles, one at each side of the camp. Wallace told Butler he could have one of the expensive guns, and borrowed the packer's knife to mark it for him.[60]

The detail continued to rifle through the dilapidated tepees, digging through sleeping robes and blankets and searching the women, some of whom who were trying to hide firearms. As the women moaned, the soldiers gathered up anything metal, "scissors, long awls, knives of any kind, cartridges and shells . . . butcher and case knives and axes," as well as hidden guns. They dragged the packed bags out of the wagons and dug through them. The men tried to push their way through the cordon of soldiers to reach their families, but the soldiers shoved them back.[61]

By this time, Forsyth and the Indians were furious with each other, and what happened next illustrates that hatred, as well as, perhaps, a mistranslation. The Sioux understood Philip Wells to say that Forsyth had ordered the Indian men to stand before the soldiers, then told the soldiers to empty their guns, hold them to the Indians' heads, and pull the trigger. If indeed Forsyth ordered such a demonstration, he might have intended it to prove that the government was powerful but merciful. He concluded: "After this you will be free. Afterwards you will go to the Agency and I will give you nine beeves," Joseph Horn Cloud remembered. It is also possible that Forsyth simply wanted the Indians to pass before the armed soldiers, and they misunderstood him.[62]

Whatever Forsyth's intention, even his officers were shocked by his martial theatrics. Captain Wallace sent Joseph Horn Cloud to tell the women not to worry about the wagons, but to saddle the horses instead, ready to flee. "There is going to be trouble; for that officer is half-shot," he warned.[63]

The Sioux men were outraged by Forsyth's latest demand. Dewey Beard and Joseph Horn Cloud remembered the cries of anger as the men moved around: "Now he sees we have nothing in our hands so he talks this way." "We are not children to be talked to like this." They were men, not cattle, they said, and they would not be killed like dogs. "We are people in this world."[64]

Big Foot urged his men to be calm. There were women and children and old men to be protected. The Indians could not afford to bring on trouble.[65]

As the warriors muttered and protested, Good Thunder, a medicine man dressed in a Ghost Dance shirt, began to go through the motions of the Ghost Dance. He moved around in a circle, stooping to pick up dirt and throwing it into the air. With all the activity, no one paid him much attention, but he appeared to counsel the younger men to submit to Forsyth's demands peacefully: "Do not be afraid and let your hearts be strong to meet what is before you; we are all well aware that there are lots of soldiers about us and that they have lots of bullets; but I have received assurance that their bullets cannot penetrate us. The prairie is large and the bullet will not go toward you but over the large prairies and if they do go towards you they will not penetrate you." When he finished dancing, Good Thunder squatted down with the others.[66]

But when the search of the tepees turned up only thirty-eight guns, mostly old and fairly useless, the furious Forsyth escalated his demands yet again. Determined to assert his authority over the surrendering Indians, he forced the men submit to a personal search. Philip Wells explained this to them but added his own commentary about their unacceptable behavior, as was his wont, leaving the Indians confused and angry. The older Indians lifted their blankets to prove they were unarmed, but the younger men showed no intention of participating in the search willingly.[67]

Their wrath at Forsyth was not the only reason the Indians refused to cooperate; the younger men had indeed hidden guns under their blankets. Forsyth had Whitside and Varnum work together, disarming the men one at a time. They turned up two rifles and ammunition on two of the first three men they examined.[68]

As Whitside and Varnum were searching the young men, a deaf Indian, Black Coyote, insisted he would not give up his gun. He couldn't see why he should—he had done nothing wrong. His Winchester had been expensive, and he did not want to give it up. He had heard about the soldiers pointing their guns at the Indians' heads, and "said he did not want to be killed; he was a man [and] was raised in this world."[69]

Tense and on edge by now, two or three soldiers jumped Black Coyote from behind and began to struggle with him for possession of the gun. Other soldiers leveled their weapons at Black Coyote while the men wrestled. Suddenly, Little Bat shouted: "Look out! Look out! They are going to shoot!" Elevated at a forty-five-degree angle toward the east, Black Coyote's gun went off, firing into the clear blue sky.[70]

With the report of the gun, all hell broke loose. Forsyth screamed: "Fire! Fire on them!" The soldiers fired a volley, mowing down the men, women, and children in the council area. Their bullets took down a number of the soldiers across from them, too, who were returning their fire. The pattering whine of bullets sounded like canvas tearing, like hail, like rumbling thunder.[71]

Teamsters holding the horses dropped their ropes and dived behind wagons for cover as the tied horses instinctively bunched together. Visitors who had come to see the disarming whipped up the horses hitched to their buggies or ran to take shelter in the store up the road to the southeast, as bullets snagged the spokes of their buggy wheels. In front of the tepees he was searching, Captain Wallace fell dead from a blow of the war club he had collected as a souvenir. Little Bat, who was a noted runner, took off for the scout camp, leaving newspaperman Allen and the other searchers to follow behind him at a dead run. Reporter Will Kelley saw a warrior coming at him with a tomahawk. He grabbed a rifle from a soldier who had fallen near him and shot his attacker, then joined the general fighting.[72]

One tall young man had spent the morning listening to Wells's harangues and "Philip's voice had made his heart bad toward him." The warrior had given in his gun, but had kept a knife. "When the crash of many guns came as if ignited by a single spark," he tried to stab Wells, but Wells parried the blow with his gun, and the knife nearly severed the end of his nose instead. The Indian stumbled on a body as he tried to reach Wells again, and fell by a soldier who was on his hands and knees, wounded. The young man took up the soldier's gun and ran for the ravine that ran behind the tepees.[73]

Smoke from the gunpowder obscured the field; Dewey Beard could see only the brass buttons of the army uniforms as he ran to the soldiers' line to wrest a gun from one of them. He seized a weapon from a young soldier and then stabbed him to death in the kidney, while soldiers firing at him killed their own comrades on his other side.[74]

• The Wounded Knee Battlefield •

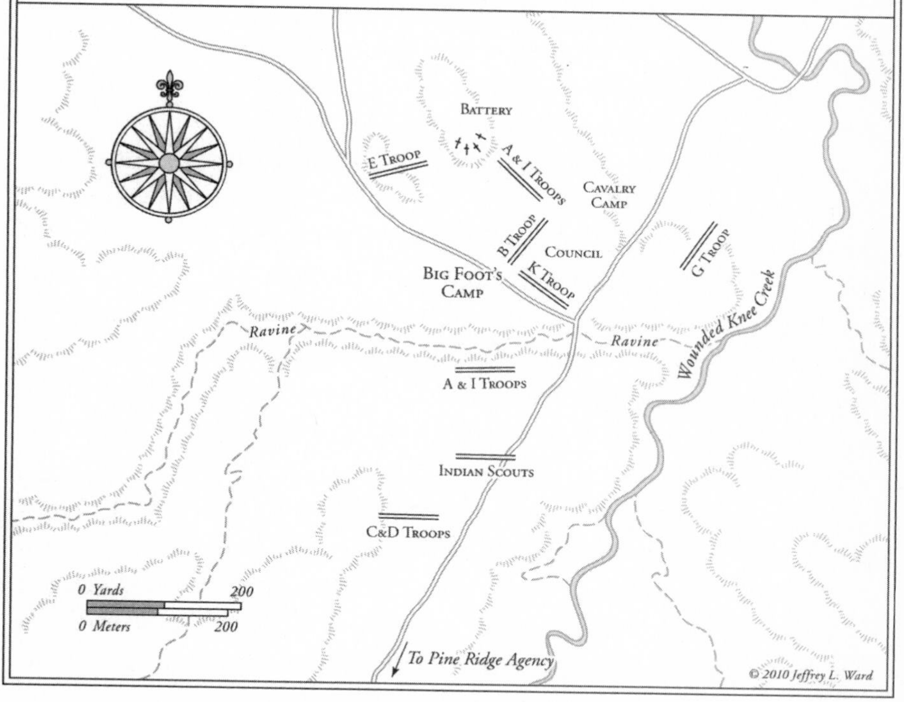

As soon as the firing started, those not in the council clearing ran for cover in three main groups. Men, women, and girls, some holding babies, from the eastern end of the camp took off northeast on the agency road toward the post office and store or ran to cover in Wounded Knee Creek. Women and children in the northwestern part of camp jumped into the wagons that were hitched and loaded behind the tepees. They also fled down the road but in the opposite direction, heading northwest where the road cut at a 90-degree angle around the rise where the artillery stood. Women and children from the far southern part of camp ran to the south for cover in the ravine.[75]

The men on the field—packers, horsemen, observers, reporters, police—recalled the bloody slaughter: "They run in every direction and the soldiers followed them and killed them while they run and some of them sat down on the ground and did not try to do anything." "I saw a boy and a girl, probably 8 or 10 y[ear]s old, running from the field in a southeast direction toward the creek, and I saw two soldiers drop down each on one knee, and taking a knee and elbow rest of their pieces, kill these little children who, when hit, carried by the momentum of running, went rolling over."[76]

Badly outgunned, the men and boys in the council area fought briefly, then they too turned and ran through the Indian camp toward the ravine behind it. One man in a Ghost Dance shirt ducked into the scouts' tent. The scouts had left their guns there that morning in the hope that their willingness to move about unarmed would reassure the nervous Minneconjous. Now, the man hiding in the tent could use those same guns on the soldiers and the scouts themselves.[77]

Dewey Beard was the last man to escape into the ravine. He had been hit in the leg, but managed to shoot a soldier in the chest to win his way to the ditch. As he worked his way into the ravine, soldiers were shooting all around him. "The soldiers' shots sounded like firecrackers and hail in a storm," he remembered. "A great many Indians were killed and wounded down in there." Beard himself was hit a second time above his knee. Getting farther into the ravine, weakening from loss of blood, he saw "many little children lying dead." "Now when I saw all those little infants lying there dead in their blood [I felt] that even if [I] eat one of those soldiers it would not appease [my] anger." When his own gun jammed he took that of an older man; when he ran out of ammunition, he borrowed a belt of cartridges from a man shot through the jaw. As he lay hidden, "I looked down the ravine [and] saw . . . women, girls and little girls [and] boys coming up, I saw soldiers on both sides of the ravine shoot at them till they had killed every one of them."[78]

Wounded again himself, he moved up the ravine looking for his wife, his son, and his parents. He found his mother stumbling along, badly wounded. Oddly, she was swinging a soldier's revolver. As Dewey stood near, soldiers on both sides of the ravine took aim at her and shot her down. Firing at the soldiers in retaliation, he continued on up the ravine, leaving her body behind. Farther along Beard found two of his brothers, both badly wounded, one fatally.[79]

Meanwhile, the artillery posted on a rise to the north of the council area opened fire on both groups of Indians fleeing on the road. Officers ordered the troops on the northwest to bring down the horses, but to avoid shooting the women and children. Their orders were moot; from a distance everyone looked like a fighter to the raging soldiers. The Hotchkiss cannons took out anything the soldiers thought was an escaping warrior. When nine women tried to get away to the southeast in a wagon, the soldiers turned a cannon on them. After the battle, one of the men who went to look at the wagon remarked that of what was left of the nine people in it: "You about get enough out of what remains to make a funeral." In their eagerness to shoot into the ravine, the artillerymen also fired shells into the ranks of their own troops, grouped near its edge.[80]

As the Indians in the ravine made a final stand over the bodies of dead and wounded women and children, the soldiers maneuvered a Hotchkiss gun into a position where it commanded the depression. As the soldiers strafed the ravine with the deadly cannons, Beard tried to give heart to the few remaining men who could fight. "Get the bow and arrows and shoot at them; the white people are afraid of arrows."[81]

But Beard's desperate rally was doomed. An army teamster who was on the battlefield recalled: "A searching fire was kept up on the Indians who were lying low in the gulch; whenever and wherever one was seen to move, as they often did in shooting at the troops, a shell would be dropped where he was which either killed him or hunted and chased him out; he would spring right up and march toward the soldiers singing the death song, and was quickly killed by the watchful soldiers."

Sporadic firing continued until noon, as hidden warriors would give away their positions by shooting. The soldiers would maneuver the cannon into position for an accurate hit, and fire.[82]

As the bullets rained down on them, some Minneconjous in the ravine managed to flee to safety either toward the store or toward the agency, or to the south of the ravine. Dewey Beard escaped and found his brother, Joseph Horn Cloud. Cloud had been gathering up the frightened horses and giving them to refugees to help them escape. Believing all his family had died, he had come back to the ravine to return to the fighting. Finding a family member alive convinced Horn Cloud to abandon his suicidal mission. He helped the badly wounded Beard onto a horse, and the men fled to White Clay Creek.[83]

Beard and Horn Cloud were lucky to survive, for the soldiers were using their rifles to pick off those who had escaped from the center of the firefight. They almost shot reporter Charley Allen. Finally too exhausted to keep running, he had tried to walk to shelter, only to find that he was in the line of fire of a troop of soldiers shooting at the Indians. When he dropped to crawl, the soldiers mistook him for a Minneconjou and shot to kill. Then the Hotchkiss cannon started up, and as the rifles fell silent, Allen, unscathed, stood up and walked toward the soldiers. They met him "with hearty handclasps and congratulations in not having been killed by one of them."[84]

Recovering from the shock of his ordeal, Charley Allen chewed a plug of tobacco and headed to the council area. The cannons continued to fire into the ravine, and, he later recorded, "desultory rifle shots could be heard at short intervals, aimed wherever a blanket was seen to move regardless of what or who might be under it."[85]

The wagons that had been called to Wounded Knee to transport Big Foot's band to Pine Ridge agency had arrived, and the civilian drivers were talking with their friends who had been in the fighting. Philip Wells called out to the wounded in the council area: "These white people came to save you and you have brought death on yourselves."[86]

He called out for survivors to give themselves up and be saved. Even though the Sioux had launched a battle, he said, "white people are merciful to save the wounded enemy when he is harmless; so, if some of you are alive, raise your heads; I am a man of your own blood who is talking to you." Flat on his back in front of his tent, wounded, Big Foot was one of those who lifted his head. As he did so, soldiers who had not understood Wells's Lakota instructions and who believed that the Indians were feigning death to lure rescuers within striking range, shot him in the back. From where she had been standing by his tent wrapped in a red blanket, Big Foot's heavyset, middle-aged daughter ran to her father. As she reached for him, a lieutenant grabbed a gun from the hands of a nearby soldier and shot her, too, in the back. She fell dead by her father.[87]

Queasy and faint, Charley Allen settled himself on a box with his pipe. He concluded that "those boys of the Seventh Cavalry were too excited to think of anything but vengeance." He had only begun to regain his composure when a group of soldiers discovered the man who had taken refuge in the scouts' tent, and who had been shooting from it when he could. A soldier slit the back of the tent with his knife. The man inside shot at him, his bullet tearing through the flesh in the soldier's shoulder. The troops opened fire, strafing the tent. Then they set matches to it. It burned away quickly, revealing the dead man lying on a blanket on a pile of hay.[88]

This was the last death in the council area. After forty minutes of carnage, officers began to shout, "Cease fire!" The men took up the call. When the shooting had stopped, Allen walked among the bodies. "On reaching the corner of the green where the school boys had been so happy in their sports but a short time before, there was spread before me the saddest picture I had seen or was to see thereafter, for on that spot of their playful choice were scattered the prostrate bodies of all those fine little Indian boys, cold in death." They could not have escaped the first volley from the soldiers, Allen surmised. "They must have fallen like grass before the sickle."[89]

Although a cease-fire had been proclaimed, not all of the day's deadly work was done. The cavalry hunted down and shot those who were trying to escape into the hills. The horsemen were effective. An old man and two boys were found killed by gunshots three miles from the Wounded Knee battleground. George Bartlett, the captain of the Pine Ridge Indian police, watched as two soldiers ran down five women. "[A]s soon as they saw they were being followed by the soldiers they sat down on the hill and faced them and the soldiers killed all five of them. When they saw they were going to be slain they covered their faces with their blankets and awaited death." Some of the soldiers scalped their victims.[90]

As the firing moved off into the hills, relative calm settled on the army camp. Scouts called to the wounded in the ravine that they would be rescued if they stopped shooting. Eventually they did, and rescue parties began to bring up survivors. Wounded Minneconjou women, girls, and children, some with their bones protruding from their skin, hobbled to the wagons with the help of soldiers. There were no boys; they were with the men, either on the run or dead in the ravine. The soldiers took their own casualties off the field, too. Officers ordered them to make stretchers, using tepee poles and saplings from the creek, to carry the twenty-five dead and thirty-seven wounded troops to the waiting wagons.[91]

As soldiers moved the wounded, the civilians and unemployed soldiers wandered aimlessly around the firing ground. Charley Allen saw a man carrying a Sioux gun he had taken as a souvenir. He wanted one, too. Walking to the spot where the guns that had been taken from the Indians that morning were still piled in a stack, he asked a soldier guarding them if he could have one. The soldier told him to help himself, and he took a serviceable Winchester from the pile.[92]

In his quest for a relic of the battle, Allen noticed that Forsyth and Whitside were not celebrating their apparent victory. They "were deep in earnest conversation," he recorded, "realizing the magnitude of the grave responsibility that had suddenly fallen upon them." Forsyth had been charged with accepting the surrender of three hundred or so destitute Indians, few of whom were warriors. He had overwhelming military support to enable him to do so without alarming the Ghost Dancers coming in to the Pine Ridge agency from the Stronghold. Instead of the clean process his superiors had expected, he had just presided over the deaths of twenty-five of his own men and the wounding of thirty-seven more. An untold number of Sioux had perished, too, and the wounds of those being led away suggested that ultimately few would survive. Forsyth had expected an easy surrender that would add to his honor. Instead, he had created a disaster.[93]

Serving a reading public rather than a superior officer, the newspapermen did not see the day's events that way. They repaired to the store where they wrote dispatches about the morning's events. The only nearby telegraph office was in Rushville, Nebraska, so the articles went out by courier as a batch. The reporters took turns having their copy go out first over the telegraph lines. On the night of December 29, it was Will Kelley's turn. He told the world that the Indians had attacked brave soldiers at Wounded Knee. "Before night I doubt if either a buck or a squaw out of all Big Foot's band will be left to tell the tale of this day's treachery. The members of the Seventh Cavalry have once more shown themselves to be heroes in deeds of daring."[94]

Back in Washington, General Schofield was happy to believe the newspaper reports of the event at Wounded Knee. The day after the battle, he sent a telegram to Nelson Miles instructing him to congratulate "the brave 7th Cavalry for their splendid conduct." Miles picked up the telegram in Chadron, Nebraska, as he passed through the town on the last day of 1890. He was shifting his headquarters from Rapid City to the Pine Ridge agency, a move he had launched just before midnight on the thirtieth, as sketchy reports from Wounded Knee alarmed him.[95]

Miles was aghast when he arrived at Pine Ridge and saw the scale of destruction. On January 1, he replied to Schofield that Forsyth's actions "will undoubtedly be the subject of investigation." He explained: "It is stated that the dispositions of the 400 soldiers and 4 pieces of artillery were fatally defective; large numbers of troops were killed and wounded by fire from their own ranks, and a very large number of women and children were killed in addition to the Indian men." A great many soldiers had been killed along with the Indians. Twenty-five of Miles's own men were dead, including Captain Wallace. Another thirty-seven were in a field hospital, wounded, along with two civilians who had been injured in the fighting. Also in the field hospital were fifteen Indians who were either so terrified or so bitter they would not let white men touch them.[96]

Because the field hospital had not been large enough to accommodate all the wounded Indians, Charles Eastman and Elaine Goodale were tending thirty-eight other injured Sioux in the Episcopal Church. On the twenty-ninth, the church had been full of mixed-blood refugees fearing Sioux reprisals for the massacre. But late that night, Reverend Cook had gone outside and found army wagons full of badly wounded Sioux women and children, along with a few men, huddled in bloody rags on bare wagon boards. They had been forgotten when the soldiers had unhitched the horses and then led the animals away to be tended and bedded down. Cook had sent the refugees in the church to a nearby house, summoned agency Indians to help him tear out the pews, and laid the victims in two long rows on the floor. They were placed on armfuls of hay and blankets borrowed from sympathetic agency workers.[97]

All that night Eastman and the others nursed the wounded, who were, as Goodale later recalled, "all pierced with bullets or terribly torn with pieces of shell, and all sick with fear." Most of their injuries were infected, and by the time Miles arrived on the thirty-first, the victims were dying. As she nursed the Sioux, Goodale noted the chilling juxtaposition of the Christian imagery in the church where the victims lay with the reality of the massacre. She recorded that "joyous green garlands still wreathed windows and doors, while the glowing cross in the stained glass window behind the altar looked down in irony—or in compassion—upon pagan children struck down in pagan flight."[98]

The next day, a blizzard of fiercely cold wind carrying snow struck in the afternoon. The Sioux at Pine Ridge worried that there might have been some Indians left alive on the battlefield, now perishing in the storm. The next day, Eastman volunteered to lead an expedition of about a hundred people, including ten or fifteen white men, reporters, and a photographer, to see what they would find. They set out through the inch or two of fresh snow that covered the ground, leading wagons to carry back any survivors.[99]

Fully three miles from the battleground they found the first body—a woman killed as she ran. From there on, bodies scattered the ground before them. Eastman's companions found friends and relatives and began to wail and mourn, singing death songs. In the council area, they found eighty bodies, and they fanned out from there, examining the bodies to see if anyone still lived. Some had. Eastman found a year-old baby girl, unhurt, a living but badly wounded elderly man, and an old blind woman who had crawled under a wagon. He discovered more injured victims holed up with corpses in a log shelter. It was clear that some of the Indians who had fled had come to the battlefield on the previous day, for a number of bodies had been taken away, and some of the wounded had been covered with blankets. Mindful that he was a government employee, Eastman's report of what he came upon at Wounded Knee was clipped, clinical. He recorded the horrors he found in the most detached words he could muster.[100]

Others could not recount what they saw without heart-wrenching details. The head of the Pine Ridge Indian police, George Bartlett, was one of those who had been told to go see if there was anyone alive on the firing ground. He saw piles of dead, and they would haunt him for years. Women and girls, always women and girls, mothers and daughters. "In some places there were five and six squaws in a pile and in one pile of squaws was that Indian baby alive—right in the bunch of squaws that were frozen stiff and cold." A little girl was in the middle of a pile of seven or eight dead women, frozen around the child. The searchers pulled her out. Other Indians were lying where they fell. "Women and children were lying dead among the slain and in great numbers," another searcher remembered. "In one place three women, the inference being that they were a mother and two daughters, were lying, the mother on her back, and the daughters across her chest. In another place was an old gray haired mother who evidently died in great agony, her hands clutching the grass, lying upon her back, and her daughter with her own child in her arms lying across her chest—all dead." "Saw a girl ab[out] 16 y[ears] old lying dead about 20 paces from the main camp. By her side lay her school case in which she carried her pencils and pens & penholders," a third searcher recalled. One of the men picked it up and gave it to a friend as a souvenir.[101]

As Indian scouts watched the searchers from the hills, Eastman rode back to the agency to get soldiers to escort the wagons, carrying only seven survivors, home. The procession of the desperately wounded, frozen victims reached the Pine Ridge agency on the same day that Miles did.[102]

The next day twenty civilian contractors would return to Wounded Knee, along with photographers and reporters, to bury the dead. While photographers took images of the twisted corpses frozen into the drifted snow, two men appointed to tally the dead Indians counted 184 in the council area.[103]

The men wandered around the firing ground and took souvenirs: objects from the tepees and Ghost Dance clothing. Philip Wells and another interpreter each cut a Ghost Dance shirt off a victim. One of the shirts they took was sewn with a sinew fringe. It was decorated with blocks of color around the neck, and covered in dots that were probably stars. The shirt had a bullet hole with a charred edge almost in its center and was partly burned. They surmised it came from the man who had died when the soldiers burned the scouts' tepee. W. A. Birdsall, there to bury the dead, saw Big Foot's body, stretched out in his agency-issued dark gray overcoat. He stooped and took a whetstone and a knife out of Big Foot's pocket.[104]

It was too late in the afternoon to dig a grave in the frozen ground, so the burial party spent the night in the trader's store and the next day fulfilled their gruesome assignment. It took all day to finish. While some hacked a trench out of the top of the hill on the site where the artillery had stood, others piled the frozen bodies on wagons. Then they drove the wagons to the trench and threw the victims in. One of the men kept count of the Indians buried in the mass grave. There were 146, he said: 24 old men, "to[o] feeble to fight"; 6 boys between five and eight years old; 7 babies under two; 7 old women; and 102 men and women over age ten.[105]

Big Foot's was the fourth body dumped into the grave.[106]

The wounded soldiers and dead Indians were only one of the reasons Miles was furious with Forsyth. December 29 had been supposed to mark the peaceful end of the Indian trouble. Instead, it had launched the fighting that Miles had tried so hard to avoid. The massacre at Wounded Knee aborted the surrender of the Stronghold Ghost Dancers. Kicking Bear, Short Bull, and their people had been only a few miles from Pine Ridge when news of the fighting had reached them. They promptly changed their minds about surrendering and rode about seventeen miles up White Clay Creek. They were not alone in their flight. The news that soldiers were firing on unarmed men, women, and children also panicked Two Strike's Brulé Sioux. They had been camped near Red Cloud's cabin at the agency since they came in themselves only two weeks before. Goodale remembered that when news of the attack came, "they were wild with fear. Their white camps melted away like snow in the sun. The brown hills were instantly alive with galloping horsemen, the loaded wagons following them." Some of the young men briefly shot at sentinels around the agency and tried to set fire to agency buildings before they left.[107]

Along with some Ghost Dancing Oglalas, including No Water, Big Road, and Little Wound, about three thousand people fled from Pine Ridge. As they ran, they swept Red Cloud and his wife from their cabin. Red Cloud later claimed to have been abducted, but the almost blind old man—or his wife—might have shared the panic and figured that they were better off with the fleeing Jack Red Cloud and the young warriors than remaining by themselves at the agency. They had concrete reasons to be afraid, since they had already come under fire at Pine Ridge. When the Indians had shot at the agency, someone there had fired back at Red Cloud's house. An officer barely stopped soldiers who had set up a Hotchkiss cannon from doing the same.[108]

Soldiers expected retaliation for the Wounded Knee massacre, but most of the Sioux simply ran. Some young men went to the tattered Wounded Knee camp to attack the soldiers there, but others fled to the northwest, down White Clay Creek. Near No Water's empty village, the fleeing Brulé and Oglala met with Kicking Bear, Short Bull, and their people, coming in from the Stronghold. The news of what had happened to Big Foot's Minneconjous convinced the Stronghold bands that giving themselves up would be suicide. About four thousand people, a quarter of whom were warriors, camped in the hills four miles east of White Clay Creek, twelve miles or so from the agency. They were crying, singing death songs, dancing the Ghost Dance. Throughout the night, refugees from Wounded Knee straggled into the camp, their ghastly wounds all the proof the Sioux needed that fleeing from the soldiers had been the right decision.[109]

At the camp on White Clay Creek, refugees from the battle took stock of how many of their kin had died. Joseph Horn Cloud managed to get his wounded brother to the camp. There Beard found out that seven of his relatives had made it out alive—five brothers, one sister, and his three-week-old son, Wet Feet. Six others had been killed. Beard lost his wife, his parents, two brothers, and a cousin who lived with the family. Three months later, Wet Feet died, too. Beard blamed the death on the massacre. "This child was nursing its dead mother who was shot in the breast; it swallowed blood, & from this vomited and was never well, was always sick till it died."[110]

When Miles arrived at Pine Ridge, Two Strike's Brulés and some Oglalas, including Red Cloud, had run away, but the agency was hardly deserted. Since the massacre, Christian Indians had been pouring in to shelter in its buildings. Everyone at the agency expected reprisals for the murder of Big Foot's people. The extent of attacks had been the pot shots and attempted arson of the twenty-ninth, but those inside the unprotected buildings fully expected a general assault on the agency.[111]

Illustrating just how thoroughly Forsyth had botched things was the fact that another party of Indians also coming in on the twenty-ninth had been disarmed peaceably by their Indian leader and had arrived without incident. A group of Sitting Bull's Hunkpapas, who had broken off from Big Foot's Minneconjous when they fled toward Pine Ridge, had come to Pine Ridge with Standing Horse, an Oglala who had found them and convinced them to surrender. But Forsyth's massacre had almost made them slip off, too. As they rode down from the hills to Pine Ridge, a scout from the Oglala party that had gone to bring them in, a man named Last Horse, stumbled onto the Wounded Knee battle ground. Standing Horse had planned to camp at Wounded Knee that night, but Last Horse quickly relayed word that the Hunkpapas would stampede if they came to the battlefield. The ground was covered with bodies, and the very air stank of powder. Standing Horse told his charges that there were troops in their way, and that they would have to swing into the sand hills to avoid them. They entered the agency on the night of the thirtieth from the south.[112]

Forsyth had bungled another military operation, too. The day after Wounded Knee, about fifty Brulés scouting to see if General Brooke was launching an attack set fire to a log cabin near the Holy Rosary Catholic Mission, known as the Drexel Mission, about four miles from the agency near White Clay Creek. Brooke sent out the Seventh to make sure the mission itself, where refugees, mostly mixed-bloods, had taken shelter, wasn't under attack. Although Forsyth found it peaceful—the sisters at the mission fed the soldiers breakfast—he heard firing by the creek in the direction of the hostile camp on White Clay Creek. He decided to see if the soldiers there were in a tangle with the Indians and needed his help. On this reconnaissance, he marched his men into a cul-de-sac surrounded by bluffs, then neglected to secure the heights. A small handful of Brulé warriors on the hills pinned down his command and threatened to inflict heavy casualties before the Ninth Cavalry, rushing to his aid from Pine Ridge, managed to protect their retreat. One soldier was killed and six wounded, one fatally. In the aftermath of the Drexel Mission fight, on January 1, warriors briefly attacked a regimental train and killed an agency worker.[113]

Miles arrived at Pine Ridge on December 31 and took control. He fortified the agency against attack, surrounding it with trenches and earthworks. But he also used his personal relationships with the Sioux leaders at White Clay Creek to try to end the standoff. On the first day of the new year, he wrote to Red Cloud, Little Wound, Two Strike, Big Road, No Water, Kicking Bear, Short Bull, and others, promising that he was their friend and encouraging them to come in. "A great many troops are on all sides," he wrote, "but not a shot will be fired or a hand raised against any [Indians] if they do as I direct them."[114]

Miles also wrote a separate letter to Red Cloud, expressing his sorrow that the chief had been carried away with the other Indians and assuring him that it had been Indian police, not soldiers, who had shot at his house on the twenty-ninth. Miles explained to Red Cloud that, since they had seen each other in late October, he had gone to Washington twice to help the Indians. "I know all the wrongs that have been done to the Indians and the wrongs the Indians have done. If they do whatever I tell them it will be best for all the Indians."[115]

Over the next few days, Miles's communications convinced Red Cloud to go back to Pine Ridge. The old chief knew "Bear Coat" from the past, and trusted that he spoke the truth. Red Cloud also knew the officer's claim to have "a great many troops" was true. The army had mobilized almost half its infantry and cavalry for the Sioux campaign. Thirty-five hundred soldiers were stationed around Pine Ridge agency, and Miles could call in another two thousand. The old chief probably regretted dashing from the agency and throwing in his lot with the "hostiles" after maintaining his good standing at the agency for so long. "I want you to send away these soldiers that are around me," he told Miles. "I will live together again."[116]

Red Cloud was not alone in longing for the safety and relative plenty of the agency. Little Wound also wanted to return, as did a number of Oglalas, especially when Miles replaced Royer with an officer they trusted. What with cold weather, little food, and their own receding fear, they were ready to try the agency again, where Miles was distributing food and clothing freely. But Kicking Bear, Short Bull, and Two Strike refused to let them go. The Messiah wanted the Indians to stay together, they counseled. If Indians were to die, it was best to die all together. They fought angrily against defections back to Pine Ridge—threatening to kill even Red Cloud if he left—and pointed to what had happened to Big Foot's people when they trusted the army.

But a number of factors pushed wavering Sioux into deciding to surrender. On January 4, Miles removed Forsyth from command and launched an investigation into the Wounded Knee affair, reinforcing the Sioux's belief that Miles was on their side. Then, on January 7, Plenty Horses, a young Brulé warrior who had been trained at Carlisle and was anxious to erase the stigma of his non-Indian education, shot Lieutenant Edward W. Casey in the back as he approached the camp to confer personally with the Sioux leaders. Almost certainly worried about reprisals, Oglalas already interested in going back to Pine Ridge began to slip away from the White Clay camp. One hundred fifty of them, including Red Cloud and his family, were back at Pine Ridge by January 9.[117]

With the Oglalas melting away from the group on White Clay Creek, Miles began to move the army cordon around the frightened Indians. He nudged them closer to Pine Ridge at the same time that he upped the number of friendly emissaries he dispatched to the camp. He sent gifts, offered leniency for those who surrendered, and promised that the Sioux leaders could meet with the Secretary of the Interior and the president to explain their grievances. Young-Man-Afraid-of-His-Horse had just arrived back from Wyoming, where he had been hunting, and Miles sent him to counsel the others to return. Miles's coaxing of the frightened Indians was even more painstaking than Brooke's of the Stronghold warriors in the previous weeks.[118]

Miles's efforts threw the Indians into confusion. Scouts reported that the Brulés in camp were quarrelling about whether or not to go back to the agency. Every night the camp was in an uproar, an uproar that often included gunfire. Every morning, a group of tepees would move closer to the agency, and those remaining, suddenly wondering if staying behind was a mistake, would catch up with them. The soldiers moved along with them, making up the distance that the Sioux had covered during the day. At night, the fighting would start again. Quietly, though, family after family slipped away from camp and back to the agency.[119]

By the fourteenth, the Indian camp was only a few miles from Pine Ridge agency. Its leaders would surrender the next day. Miles promised general leniency, although he maintained that he would have to arrest Short Bull, Kicking Bear, and twenty of the other leaders. Still defiant, Kicking Bear and the others were nonetheless out of options. On January 15, the Sioux began riding into the agency, men on horseback, families in wagons, ponies dragging tepee poles and the families' belongings. One officer reported: "It was a spectacle worth beholding. They moved in two columns up White Clay Creek, one on each side, about 5500 people in all, with 7000 horses, 500 wagons, and about 250 travois, and in such good order that there was not at any point a detention on any account."[120]

Over the next several days, unwilling to risk a repeat of what had happened at Wounded Knee, Miles would negotiate repeatedly with leading Indians for the surrender of their weapons. Despite the men's desire to keep their guns, the Indian resistance was broken. The first man to hand his gun to the soldiers was Kicking Bear.[121]

CHAPTER 8

The Aftermath

THE SURRENDER of the Sioux ended the shooting, but the struggle over what had happened at Wounded Knee had just begun. Republicans, Democrats, Interior Department officials, Colonel Forsyth and his men, General Miles, and even surviving Sioux all tried to gain control over the way the nation saw the massacre.

As soon as General Miles arrived at Pine Ridge, he heard reporters, scouts, and Indians who had been at Wounded Knee talking about the troops falling to their own guns and about the killing that followed the initial skirmish. Miles was furious at Forsyth for both the Wounded Knee disaster and his potentially deadly miscalculation the next day at Drexel Mission. He resented the ineptitude that had led Forsyth to turn a delicate and well-planned military maneuver designed to prevent bloodshed into a catastrophe. For all Miles's conviction that the days of the ranging Sioux were over, he respected his adversaries and abhorred the fact that the warriors, along with their women and children, had been murdered. Finally, he recognized that his arguments in favor of increased military presence in the West to manage the Indians had just been badly scarred by what amounted to a massacre. This cut to the quick. He was determined to limit the political damage and make Forsyth pay for his idiocy.[1]

With early reports from Wounded Knee still fresh, General Schofield had sent a telegram to Miles congratulating the "brave 7th Cavalry for their splendid conduct." Miles had responded that such enthusiasm was perhaps inadvisable. Undoubtedly, Forsyth's actions would have to be gravely evaluated, he warned. In light of that information, Commander of the Army Schofield told Miles on January 2 not to relay his congratulations to Forsyth. He also sent a separate telegram informing Miles that President Harrison regretted that blood had been shed in the search for a solution to the Sioux problem, and suggested that "an inquiry be made as to killing of women and children on Wounded Knee Creek."[2]

General Miles jumped on Schofield's suggestion. Politicians from the Interior Department were already blaming the entire military for the disaster, and Miles was eager to establish that the fault was Forsyth's alone. When news of the massacre got to Pine Ridge agency, Royer had written instantly to his superiors pointing out that his Pine Ridge Indians had not been involved and that he was blameless for the turn of events. His missive circulated among the officials at the Interior Department, and within days Noble was telling the newspapers that he "sincerely regretted that the recent action of the military had resulted in bloodshed, and he congratulated himself that his Department was in no sense responsible for it."[3]

Civilian reformers were gaining the upper hand again, turning up in newspapers in support of the Secretary of the Interior. "Secretary Noble has the right ideas if he is given a chance to work them out," according to a South Dakota railroad commissioner interviewed by the *Washington Post*.[4] The *New York Tribune*, which had taken Miles's part only weeks before, declared: "Those who think that the Indians have been driven out should listen to the testimony of those who have lived in the neighborhood of these savages."[5]

The debacle indeed destroyed Miles's chance to win military control of the agencies. The cabinet argued the issue on January 6. The next day, Schofield ordered officers to all the South Dakota agencies, but only the one at Pine Ridge would be in their control. At the other agencies, the military men would work together with civilian agents and be responsible only for military matters.[6]

Miles aggressively countered the charges laid at the door of the military and went after Forsyth as the main culprit. On January 4, he began to take steps to put the blame for the massacre on Forsyth. He removed the general from command, then convened a court of inquiry to decide whether or not Forsyth had placed his troops in dangerous positions. The inquiring officers were also charged with determining whether any noncombatants were needlessly injured or killed.[7]

The inquiry into Forsyth's actions put President Harrison's people in Washington in a difficult position. Many—perhaps most—Americans saw Forsyth as a hero, and the Seventh Cavalry's attack on "hostile" Indians as reasonable payback for Custer's destruction at the hands of the Sioux fewer than fifteen years before. They were quite happy to see Indians killed. Indeed, on January 11, an ex-convict shot up a family related to progressive Young-Man-Afraid-of-His-Horse while they traveled under an Indian agent's protection. After murdering the man and wounding his wife, the killer boasted, "I have shot one of those damned Government pets, and if any more of them want to be fixed, let them come this way."[8]

Administration men were caught flat-footed by Miles's public accusation that something had gone badly wrong at Wounded Knee. When he had suggested an "inquiry," Schofield had meant Miles should ask around quietly, not that he should make any problems public by appointing an official court of inquiry. Harrison's men were quite content to leave the massacre of Sioux in South Dakota well enough alone. They quickly put the responsibility for proving his accusations squarely on Miles. "It was not the intention of the President to appoint a Committee of Inquiry," Schofield telegraphed to Miles on January 6. "You were expected first yourself to inquire into the facts and in the event of its being disclosed that there had been unsoldierly conduct to relieve the officer." Secretary of War Proctor also fumbled for an exit strategy from the investigation. "General Miles did it," he told reporters. "It is a very much mixed-up matter and I may explain it later." Even William Tecumseh Sherman was unnerved. He wrote to his niece, Miles's wife: "If Forsyth was relieved because some squaw was killed, somebody has made a mistake, for squaws have been killed in every Indian war." Sherman told her that Miles should "say little and write less, but create success."[9]

Miles's attack on Forsyth also put the officers of the Seventh in a difficult position, but they quickly came to the support of their popular superior officer. Even before the court of inquiry began to take testimony, army officers strenuously defended Forsyth, telling newspaper reporters that it was impossible to tell the difference between the men and women when they were all wearing blankets. And even if they did kill women and children, well, as the *New York Tribune* put it: "A Sioux squaw is as bad an enemy as a man. . . . The little boys, too, can shoot quite as well as their fathers."[10]

As the court of inquiry began to gather information, Forsyth's men circled their wagons around their commander. Officers rounded up affidavits from participants denying that the soldiers had precipitated the fight, and denouncing the suggestion that the soldiers had fired into each other. They dispatched translator Philip Wells, a strong supporter of Forsyth, to go among the wounded Indians and take statements of what had happened. Wells himself gave a statement, blaming the Minneconjou religious leader who sang the Ghost Dance song during the disarming for starting the trouble. The three accounts he gathered similarly blamed the medicine man. All three also maintained that the soldiers were friendly and that there was no sign of trouble until the Ghost Dancer stirred up the younger men.[11]

These documents were suspect. In one of them, for example, Elks Saw Him allegedly claimed that the Indians weren't at all nervous about the Hotchkiss cannons and soldiers when they had first encountered them at Porcupine Creek. "On a little rise they placed two cannon covering us, having their other guns in readiness for firing. We came right on towards them and finally reached them, our people saying, 'They are only fooling us.'" This statement was simply preposterous. The Minneconjous had crossed South Dakota in three days with a desperately ill leader out of terror of the military. There was no way that, confronted with state-of-the-art modern weaponry, they would have concluded the soldiers were joking.[12]

Forsyth's officers also tried to cover up what had happened at Wounded Knee. Meded Swigert, a hotelkeeper who had gone to see the surrender out of curiosity and gotten more than he bargained for, remembered: "This affair on the W. K. was hushed up; there was anxiety to keep a part of the truth from the public; this was evident from the uneasiness manifested by some in authority; officers had at least one conference with the civilians asking what they knew and warning them not to say too much. This was probably to shield Forsythe." Swigert was right; the officers did intend to protect their commander.[13]

The cover-up continued once the investigation actually began. Officers tried to reject Miles's attack on Forsyth's military management, denying that he had made a blunder by placing his troops across from each other. In their testimony, they stated that Forsyth had not arranged his men badly—despite the fact that men on opposite sides of the council circle fired into each other's lines. His supporters explained this mistake by arguing that Forsyth could not have known he needed to arrange them differently because no one could ever have imagined there would be a battle that morning. Others simply claimed that the Indians had killed all the soldiers, that none had fallen to friendly fire.

Forsyth's supporters went so far as to insist that there had been no massacre at all. They ignored the fact that the women and the men at council had been held separate by the soldiers before the firing started. They claimed that the unfortunate deaths of so many women and children was because the noncombatants were so mixed up with the warriors.[14]

The conclusions of the investigation were fixed from the start. As soon as the testimony had been gathered and even before the report was written, a member of the court of inquiry telegraphed to the papers: "Colonel Forsyth will be cleared."[15]

The court of inquiry reported to General Miles on January 13. It bowed to Miles—and the facts—enough to acknowledge that Forsyth had placed his troops badly, but concluded that no one could have foreseen the outbreak of fighting.

Miles was furious at what was virtually an exoneration of Forsyth. Three days after he received its report, Miles asked the committee to reconvene. He asked it to consider, specifically, that he had repeatedly warned his subordinates to be careful to keep the Indians and the soldiers separate at all times. Required to answer new questions on this point, Brooke initially claimed not to remember whether or not he had passed those orders to Forsyth. Ultimately he conceded that he had. While the committee then was forced to rap Forsyth for his disregard of Miles's explicit warning, it went on to conclude that Forsyth could not possibly have expected "that the Indians would deliberately plan their own destruction." They sent their revised report to Miles on January 18.[16]

Almost two weeks later, on January 31, Miles passed the findings of the court of inquiry to General Schofield, but added his own harsh verdict on the whole mess. His aide-de-camp noted that Miles was indignant at Forsyth's mismanagement and disgusted by the butchery at Wounded Knee. The aide had to plead with Miles to tone down the language he used in his comments. Even so, Miles's conclusion was damning. He reported that Colonel Forsyth had been repeatedly warned that Big Foot's people were desperate and deceitful, and had been repeatedly ordered to guard constantly against surprise. Forsyth had ignored these warnings. He had arranged his troops so that none could fire without endangering other soldiers. "It is, in fact, difficult to conceive how a worse disposition of troops could have been made," Miles snarled, and it was impossible not to believe that friendly fire was more deadly than the Indians to the soldiers.[17]

General Schofield, a consummate politician, spun things differently. Sending the report on to the Secretary of War, he added a cover letter that began by dismissing the charges against Forsyth and suggesting he should be reinstated as commander of the Seventh. The evidence in the report, Schofield wrote, showed that the officers and most of the enlisted men had taken great care to avoid killing Indian women and children unnecessarily. Further, the evidence proved that the Seventh Cavalry had exercised "excellent forbearance" in "very trying circumstances." In a slap at Miles, Schofield added: "In my judgment, the conduct of the regiment was well worthy of commendation bestowed upon it by me in my first telegram after the engagement."[18]

The Secretary of War slanted his interpretation of the report even more against Miles. On February 12, Proctor released the official report on the investigation into the events at Wounded Knee. The official conclusion completely exonerated Colonel Forsyth. The testimony Miles's own staff had gathered, he wrote, showed that Sitting Bull's followers had joined Big Foot's band in late December. Together, these two groups were full of the most fanatical and desperate Sioux. They had surrendered to Whitside only because they had to, not because they were truly willing to give in to the army. While they did not actually plan to commit treachery, the younger warriors, at least, had not really submitted to the government in their hearts. Once he was in charge of them, Forsyth had his work cut out for him. It was imperative that no member of the band escape while being disarmed, for if they ran away, they would have launched a raid upon the settlers. Forsyth distributed the troops the way he did simply to prevent anyone from escaping. And there had been no harm done by the fact that they were essentially arranged in a square. There was no evidence that a single soldier had been killed or wounded by friendly fire, according to the Secretary of War.[19]

Proctor even exonerated the soldiers in the deaths of the surrendering Sioux. The massacre was the Indians' fault. They were upset at being disarmed and then were inspired to fight by the Ghost Dancer. After listening to him, according to Proctor's version of the story, they wheeled around and opened fire. Incredibly, Proctor blamed the first wave of fire that mowed down the Indians on the warriors themselves: "Nothing illustrates the madness of their outbreak more forcibly than the fact that their first fire was so directed that every shot that did not hit a soldier must have gone through their own village. There is little doubt that the first killing of women and children was by this first fire of the Indians themselves," he wrote.

The soldiers, Proctor insisted, had conducted themselves with great restraint. They tried hard not to fire on women and children. Officers had explicitly cautioned the soldiers as a group not to shoot "squaws" or children, then pointed out fleeing women to individual soldiers, to keep the women safe. The troops had fired exclusively on the fighting warriors until the Indians had broken through the surrounding cordon of soldiers, at which point they became mingled with their families. Once the men, women, and children were mixed together, the women and children were exposed to the soldiers' guns and were unavoidably killed or wounded. That the Indian men had thus endangered their families was "universally regretted by the officers and men of the 7th Cavalry," Proctor insisted, but he took pains to point out that the Indians were entirely responsible for the sad turn of events. To illustrate just how restrained the soldiers had been, Proctor claimed that the Indians fired at least fifty shots at them before they returned fire. As for the bodies found three miles from the battlefield, such a distance indicated that those deaths must have had nothing to do with the battle itself, and Forsyth was, therefore, not responsible.[20]

Proctor's final pronouncement on the affair showed how completely politics had trumped Miles's determination to recognize what had happened at Wounded Knee Creek as a massacre under the mismanagement of an incompetent officer. Proctor concluded that "the conduct of both officers and men through the whole affair demonstrates an exceedingly satisfactory state of discipline in the 7th Cavalry. Their behavior was characterized by skill, coolness, discretion and forbearance, and reflects the highest possible credit upon the regiment." Proctor endorsed the idea that Forsyth should be reinstated.

President Harrison agreed. In mid-February, Forsyth resumed command of the Seventh Cavalry.[21]

General Miles had lost his campaign to pin the responsibility for the massacre on Forsyth. Government officials were far more interested in letting the entire military take the blame—if blame there was; many people were quite happy with the outcome of the affair. Miles left Pine Ridge for Chicago on January 26. He took with him about two dozen Ghost Dance leaders who would be imprisoned at Fort Sheridan in Illinois. He had left orders for soldiers to escort the various Sioux bands encamped at Pine Ridge back to their home reservations.

While eastern administrators refused to see the events in South Dakota for what they were, those closer to the events understood the tragic nature of the massacre. On Tuesday, February 3, seventy-one survivors of Big Foot's band, along with nine soldiers from the Sixth Cavalry guarding them, camped in the woods near the Oar Lock ranch on the way back to the Cheyenne River Reservation. The Oar Lock's owner recorded in his diary that even the most devout Indian-hater would have to pity this shattered band as they straggled behind the soldiers. He tried to capture the moment in poetry:

The Captives Journey
Subdued, crest fallen and sad,
Followed in the soldiers wake.
The remnant of a once proud band
That battled for loyaltie's sake.

All raged and wounded and helpless,
They journeyed as captives do;
How sad they looked! How weary they moved!
And sadder still, ah, how few.[22]

But sorrow for what had happened to Big Foot's people at Wounded Knee did not last long. Before the month was out, life had resumed its normal course. In late February, the Oar Lock owner recorded the arrival of Indians to bake their bread in his stove—which he permitted—and the animated discussion he had with one of the men about the killing of a deer earlier that day.[23]

The reality of the military intervention in South Dakota was buried; it was already becoming a mythological tale of brave soldiers and treacherous Indians. On January 21, as the Pine Ridge agency braced itself against a howling wind, Miles reviewed 3,500 troops that had participated in the South Dakota affair before they dispersed back to their regular assignments. Unsure that this demonstration was indeed intended to be peaceful, Sioux warriors on their ponies stood guard on the hills around the agency, silhouetted against the sky. Miles was bundled in a greatcoat against the wind, astride a black horse, as the infantrymen tramped shivering before him. The men did not cheer as they marched, but occasionally an officer would salute his general with a saber. Miles would lift his black hat in response. Then the musicians of the Seventh Cavalry drew near Miles. As they approached, they struck up "Garryowen," the catchy Irish quick-time jig that Custer had used as charging music. A reporter recorded that the horses "began to dance to the irresistible melody, Whitside waved to Miles, and General Miles, overcome with emotion, took off his hat and hung it on the pommel of his saddle, letting the storm toss his gray hair as far as it pleased."[24]

The reporter saw in this cold parade not the tramp of raw soldiers who had been forced into a situation in which they butchered a helpless people. Rather, he saw the review as representative of the majesty and pathos of the western army as it held civilization against savages. "The column was almost pathetically grand," the reporter concluded, "with its bullet-pierced gun carriages, its tattered guidons, and its long lines of troopers and foot soldiers facing a storm that was almost unbearable. It was the grandest demonstration by the army ever seen in the West; and when the soldiers had gone to their tents, the sullen and suspicious Brulés were still standing like statues on the crests of the hills."[25]

According to the reporter, the military engagements in South Dakota had pitted these noble soldiers against deceitful savages. The conquest of the Sioux, including the murder of Sitting Bull and the destruction of Big Foot's band, had prevented an uprising that would have killed hundreds of settlers. The Ghost Dance was simply the cover for a plot to hatch in the spring, when the Sioux would begin a war. Killing the two leaders and most of the Minneconjou band was the only way to keep them from launching their bloodthirsty plans. The awful slaughter at Wounded Knee shocked the Sioux into negotiating for peace, he wrote. The killing of the Indians was, in this light, fortuitous.[26]

The image of the Wounded Knee affair as the fight of brave soldiers against savages became part of the era's popular entertainment. Twenty-three of the twenty-seven Ghost Dancers Miles had arrested and taken to prison at Fort Sheridan in Illinois became new performers in Buffalo Bill's Wild West Show. The Commissioner of Indian Affairs had commuted their sentences. On March 30, Buffalo Bill took the men, including Kicking Bear and Short Bull, out of jail to join the Wild West Show for a year-long tour of Europe. Commissioner T. J. Morgan, who before the Wounded Knee affair had fervently objected to the demoralizing influences of Wild West shows on the Indians he was trying to "civilize," now endorsed Cody's plan wholeheartedly. There were some Indians, he had decided, who could never be brought into modern society. Far from being hurt by having their "savagery" put on display, there was no other place for them in the modern world outside of shows that highlighted that their day was over. In May 1891, Cody advertised that he had in his show the prisoners of war from Wounded Knee. He advertised them in a London newspaper as "fifty of the worst Indians engaged in the Wounded Knee fight." As usual, Cody's production represented the theme of civilization triumphing over savagery. The Indians from Wounded Knee played the role of villains.[27]

Morgan had come to see the traditionalist Sioux involved at Wounded Knee as irredeemable criminals whom he no longer wanted to try to bring into American civilization. When some of the Indians with Buffalo Bill asked to come home after a year in Europe, Miles and Noble had to talk Morgan into allowing it. To make sure they understood what was in store for them if they caused any more trouble, he made them tour the state penitentiary in Joliet, Illinois, before he would let them go back to their families.[28]

Morgan did not, however, have the last word. In 1892, following the show's last performance in Glasgow, Kicking Bear lingered on the stage after the show was over. Speaking in Lakota, he told the uncomprehending crowd his own version of his life story. Sadly, that speech, like almost all Indian versions of history, was lost as soon as he spoke the words.[29]

Back East, the Wounded Knee massacre forced the administration to adopt measures to remedy their long neglect of Indian affairs. In the immediate wake of the disaster, horrified reformers and opponents of the president pressed the administration to address Indian issues. On January 18, Harrison signed a bill that honored Crook's promises of 1889. It paid Red Cloud's people for the ponies that had been taken from them in 1876, appropriated money for schools, and, critically, restored the slashed rations.[30]

But the Harrison administration was more interested in damage control than in positive change. Miles had followed through on his promise to arrange a meeting between the Sioux leaders and government officials in Washington, so that the leaders could explain their grievances in person. The Sioux chose their own representatives to this meeting. While they sent progressives like American Horse, Young-Man-Afraid-of-His-Horse, and Hump, they also sent Ghost Dancer leaders Big Road, Two Strike, and Little Wound to confer with the Secretary of the Interior and the president. On February 1 they arrived in Washington, where they toured the city and bought suits.[31]

It was an inauspicious time for a meeting. Harrison's officials had little interest in Indian affairs at the best of times, and a number of recent events were distracting them more than usual. First of all, the administration was still trying to repair the damage caused by the election. Officials were preoccupied with trying to find jobs for Republican politicians who had been turned out by Alliance voters. This involved flurries of letters and long political calculations that absorbed an inordinate amount of time. The election results also meant that the Republicans had to negotiate a new relationship with Alliance members, who backed silver coinage. That relationship had always been rocky, and it wasn't helped by the fact that Harrison and his men were dead set against the Alliance men on the coinage issue.[32]

Adjusting monetary issues to attract Alliance supporters got even harder when the Secretary of the Treasury, William Windom, dropped dead at a dinner given by the Board of Trade and Transportation of New York City at the end of January. Windom had finished a long peroration attacking silver money and its supporters—his last words were: "He that loveth silver shall not be satisfied with silver"—and sat down. Minutes later he fell off his chair, and he died immediately afterward in an anteroom. Administration officials had trusted Windom's judgment and were anxious and tight-lipped over the crisis of finding a new Treasury Secretary. They had no interest in chatting with defeated warriors.[33]

The meetings were a disaster. The Indians had come to deliberate; the administration had agreed to the meeting only to save face. President Harrison would do no more than shake their hands, so they had to deal with the Interior Secretary. On February 7, the delegates met with Noble, who began the meeting by telling them flat out that he did not have time to listen to long speeches. For the secretary, the gathering was not a business meeting so much as a chance to show off his charges. He had invited Secretary of War Proctor, of course, but also Proctor's wife and daughter. Also present were Noble's wife, Senator Dawes's daughter, and a number of other young women.[34]

American Horse began the conversation. He acknowledged the ladies with a compliment, but refused to let their presence derail what he considered a business meeting. He complained that the government was mismanaging the agencies by filling agency jobs with the white friends and relatives of the agents. Whites took all the jobs and then called Indians lazy. The Sioux wanted a chance to rise, he said. Let them fill the jobs on the agencies, working for their people. He also asked for the Carlisle School to be moved to the West, so children would not be separated from their parents in an unhealthy climate.[35]

For his part, Young-Man-Afraid-of-His-Horse was not quite so ready to look forward. He had questions about the past. Why hadn't Congress made the changes to the 1889 treaty General Crook had promised? Why were rations cut? Why hadn't winter annuities come? Why was the whole Sioux nation called to account when some people danced a religious dance? Why shouldn't white men be blamed for what happened?[36]

When it was his turn to speak, Noble told the Indians that the government was trying to do what was right for them. Astonishingly, he told them to have confidence in General Crook's promises. The Indians, he said, must do their best to have their children educated. They must never dream they could get anything from the government by force. He promised to consider the delegation's complaints, but the Sioux could see that nothing would be done. "We had some promises, but they were like all other promises of the Great Father," Young-Man-Afraid-of-His-Horse said sadly. "We are not fooled and we go home with heavy hearts. . . . We shall tell our people that we have got more promises. Then they will laugh at us and call us old men."[37]

On February 11, the last day of their talks in Washington, Sioux delegates told the Commissioner of Indian Affairs, spectators, and reporters their version of what had happened at Wounded Knee. Not surprisingly, their recollections did not have much in common with the official report. Turning Hawk established that the Sioux ran from their agencies initially because they were afraid of the soldiers. He explained that at Wounded Knee, the women had had no weapons, and he thought it "very improbable" that women could have been shot because their clothing looked like that of the men. American Horse concurred. The men and women were separated, after all, and each group was surrounded by soldiers. The women were under a white flag at the lodges, he said; one was shot down as she reached for the flagpole. Another woman killed there "was shot down with her infant. The child, not knowing that its mother was dead, was still nursing, and that was especially a very sad sight." Women and babies were killed, women heavy with child were killed. When most had already died, the wounded were instructed to come out of hiding and they would be saved. But as soon as several "little boys who were not wounded came out of their places of refuge . . . a number of soldiers surrounded them and butchered them there."[38]

American Horse spoke for many of the progressives when he confessed himself to have been blindsided. He had been staunchly loyal to the government, only to see his people murdered at the hands of American soldiers. "I have come to Washington with a very great blame against the Government on my heart," he said.

Reverend Cook, the minister from Pine Ridge, took on the official report directly, calling out the statement in the report that the Seventh Cavalry had been restrained. Cook claimed to have heard a damning story from one of General Miles's scouts, who had been with the soldiers after the fight. One of the officers had told the scout, "with much gluttonous thought in his voice, 'Now we have avenged Custer's death.'" The Sioux had been allowed to tell their side of the story, but it didn't get much traction. It appeared in a few newspaper stories, some reporters used it to condemn government Indian policy, and then it disappeared. The Indian leaders went home, disappointed.[39]

Miles tried to force the administration to honor the delegation's requests, but had no luck. It was "most unfortunate that these men have been ignored, discouraged and disaffected," he wrote to Schofield in March, and even the loyal Sioux would turn from the government if their needs weren't addressed. But Miles was now persona non grata in the administration. He had bucked President Harrison's men over Wounded Knee and, in the immediate aftermath of the Forsyth inquiry, William Tecumseh Sherman had died. Miles had lost his most influential supporter, and his star fell. When the army reorganized in July 1891, the administration stripped Miles of much of his command.[40]

Instead of following Miles's suggestions, Secretary of the Interior Noble based the administration's future approach to the Sioux on his own ideas. In April, he told the Commissioner of Indian Affairs that the agents must impress upon the Indians "that they must obey the law now and keep order and that the government has done everything demanded of it." Noble had only the best interests of the Indians in mind, he claimed, and wanted to treat them magnanimously as they were pushed into civilization as quickly as possible. But they must know that if they caused any more trouble, "it will be an occasion for great severity to them and of punishment . . . sufficient to compel obedience." If they could not be content with all the government did for them, it would hold them "by the strong hand of force, be the consequences what they may." Far from lamenting the massacre, Noble seemed to see it as a useful illustration for the Indians of what would happen if they didn't keep quiet.[41]

The response to Wounded Knee got caught up in the same partisan politicking that had created the crisis in the first place. While Democrats and reformers wanted to see effective changes in American Indian policy, the Harrison administration did only enough to save face. Then, to burnish the president's credentials with voters, it honored the soldiers involved in the massacre.

Easterners defending the Sioux saw the larger story behind Wounded Knee and demanded sweeping changes in America's devastating Indian policy. The *New York Times* noted that the Indian families who had been called to Pine Ridge had returned home to find their belongings plundered by settlers. These progressive Indians had worked to build comfortable log cabins and had stocked their farms with hogs and cows. In their absence, settlers had stolen everything they could use: sewing machines, spring mattresses, chinaware, cook stoves, and lamps, anything that could be taken away. Few Indians expected either to obtain their rights or to receive anything promised them. Their treatment was "simply criminal." They were "robbed when at peace, starved and angered into war, and then hunted down by the Government."[42]

Indian reformers insisted that the root of the 1890 to 1891 trouble had been the spoils system. Their pressure was especially effective after the newspaper coverage of the events in South Dakota, when opponents of the administration had hammered home that Republican appointees like Royer were unfit for their jobs.[43]

The Wounded Knee massacre so horrified voters across the Union that they forced President Harrison to clean up the Indian system—a little. The Indian Rights Association started a petition campaign to place about seven hundred Indian offices under the Civil Service Law. In the spring of 1891, Harrison yielded to these pleas, making it a requirement that applicants for the position of Indian agent must demonstrate proof of their fitness for the job. The fact that Daniel Royer traveled to Washington in February 1891 to get his position at Pine Ridge back, and that Senators Moody and Pettigrew supported him (although President Harrison ultimately did not), probably added urgency as well as indignation to the proposals of the Indian Rights Association.[44]

But although he had to yield some ground to popular outrage, President Harrison remained determined to defend the administration's version of what had happened in South Dakota. His chance came quickly. Harrison had won the presidency in large part by courting the nation's veterans, and he continued to appeal to them in the wake of the massacre. In March, before the new Democratic Congress convened, Secretary of War Proctor began awarding Medals of Honor to soldiers for their valor in engagements from the Civil War onward. He did not neglect the troops from the Wounded Knee affair and the skirmishes that came afterward. On March 6, he awarded the first five of the twenty Medals of Honor that would go to soldiers who had fought in South Dakota.[45]

Most of the Wounded Knee medals rewarded "bravery in action," or "distinguished gallantry," as they so often did in those days when Medals of Honor were awarded largely for the asking. Some of the citations, though, were more specific: "While the Indians were concealed in a ravine, assisted men on the skirmish line, directing their fire, etc., and using every effort to dislodge the enemy," "voluntarily led a party into a ravine to dislodge Sioux Indians concealed therein." "While engaged with Indians concealed in a ravine, he assisted the men on the skirmish line, directed their fire, encouraged them by example, and used every effort to dislodge the enemy." "Conspicuous bravery in action against Indians concealed in a ravine." "Killed a hostile Indian at close quarters."[46]

The military tactics used at Wounded Knee not only won Medals of Honor for the soldiers, they also became the face of the modern American army. Lieutenant Harry L. Hawthorne, who had directed the artillery until he had been shot in the groin, took his Medal of Honor with him to MIT, where in 1891 he became a professor of military tactics.[47]

All the political maneuvering that had produced such disastrous consequences was for naught. The efforts of administration men to court South Dakota voters and later, legislators, did not help the party. South Dakota did not end up sending Republican senator Gideon Moody back to Washington. The state legislature met in January 1891. Initially, it was evenly divided between Republicans and their Democratic and Alliance opponents. But there were a number of contested seats, which eventually went to Alliance claimants. The Republicans fell into the minority, and the legislature adamantly opposed Moody, who was an administration man through and through. The Republicans dropped Moody and tried unsuccessfully to find a compromise candidate. After four weeks and forty ballots, Alliance members and Democrats elected an Independent, James H. Kyle of Aberdeen, as senator. Kyle was a minister known for his attacks on business and corporate wealth. Once in Washington, he sat with the Democrats and worked with the Alliance members.[48]

None of the administration's other efforts to stay in power availed either. Harrison lost the 1892 election to Grover Cleveland, who promised lower tariffs and civil service reform. Harrison fell into an oblivion from which he has never recovered, but which is a kinder historical fate than he deserved.

The Shermans' era was over. The brothers had spent their lives defending the principle that every hardworking man should be able to rise in America; Cump had risked his life for this principle on battlefields, John had changed the nation's economic system to advance it. But Republicans had come to use the rhetoric of individualism to defend the very sort of economic oligarchy the party had organized in the 1850s to oppose. By the 1890s, the Republicans were the party of big business, hated by those trying to rise in American society. Cump died on Valentine's Day, 1891, six days after his seventy-first birthday. John stayed in the Senate, but was scorned by the populist politicians of the 1890s, one of whom went so far as to attack him by name in a lurid novel that detailed the corruption of Gilded Age politicians by "plutocrats." President McKinley honored Sherman with the position of Secretary of State in 1897, but after a year he retired to private life. He died in 1900.[49]

Despite his good intentions, Cleveland didn't get much time to clean up after his predecessor's administration. In May 1893, the stalling economy finally crashed. The stock market began to drop in February, and in June the bottom fell out. The McKinley Tariff, despite the endless protestations of *Frank Leslie's*, proved no panacea. It could not fix the problem that the growth of the 1880s had rested on an unstable railroad boom. When that bubble burst, the disparities in wealth created by Republican economic policies kept the economy from recovering.

The depression that lasted from 1893 to 1897 swept across society. It began in the factories and the fields. By 1894, some 2 million were out of work and an army of unemployed laborers from across the country was marching to Washington to ask for a jobs program. They were turned away by one hundred mounted police—and their leader arrested for trespassing on the White House lawn—but the wealthy leaders who scorned them would find themselves in trouble soon enough. W. J. Arkell, the source of the money that had allowed Russell Harrison to take over *Frank Leslie's* in 1889, was one of those who watched his riches evaporate. In 1894, a bank he directed closed its doors; the next year another of his businesses failed. By 1897, Arkell was trying to lay claim to the newly discovered Klondike gold fields because an expedition his company had funded years before had found a new route to the region. But his efforts to shore up his finances failed, and in 1898, W. J. Arkell's publishing company failed. Arkell took his ex-senator father and at least one colleague down with him. In 1904, he was cadging meals in San Francisco, trying unsuccessfully to recoup his fortune in gold mines.[50]

By the time Arkell was hiding out in California, a public disgusted by the excesses of big business had ushered in the Progressive Era to promote a level economic playing field for workers and employers. They worked to reverse some of the most venal developments of the Gilded Age, developments brought to a new low under President Harrison. Progressives limited working hours and child labor, and tried to improve working conditions. They cleaned up city streets and promoted education. They regulated drugs and inspected meat for disease. To slow the influence of big business in government, they arranged for the direct election of senators. They tried to establish, once and for all, that the government should not do the bidding of businessmen, but should promote the good of everyone.

While the Progressives tried to undo the damage left by men like President Harrison and his administration, they were not completely successful. The late nineteenth-century Republican approach to American government left a lasting legacy. The Harrison Republicans were consummate party politicians, willing to ignore reality, manipulate government machinery to stay in power, and destroy those in the way of their plans. Harrison's men convinced themselves that the protection of big business through the tariff was crucial to the survival of the nation. They refused to recognize the artificial bubble of western growth or the growing gap between rich and poor in America, problems their own policies exacerbated. They saw protests as an attack on the American system rather than as an attempt to save it. They could not acknowledge the faltering economy; they explained away the many signs of a looming depression and convinced themselves that the new tariff, the culmination of their program, would magically make the economy boom. They could not recognize the legitimacy of workers' worries about declining wages in the face of extraordinary wealth, or their widespread concerns about the cozy relationship of business and government. Anyone opposing the Republicans' extreme pro-business policy opposed America, Republicans believed, and must be silenced.

Harrison's men used political machinery and overwrought rhetoric about voter fraud to try to undercut the Democrats' electoral strength. To bolster their dwindling popularity as the divide between rich and poor became a gulf, administration Republicans of 1890 stuffed public positions with unqualified supporters and sought to tilt the polls in their favor by supporting Republican voters and restricting Democrats, under the noble-sounding cry for "ballot reform." Their plans for a heavy-handed Federal Elections Bill did not work. Instead, their rhetoric about the corruption of the ballot provoked a larger movement to purge voters from the rolls.

The argument that America's voting system had been corrupted by unsavory opponents became a driving feature of national politics after 1890, although in a more comprehensive way than the Harrison administration had advocated. On the heels of the 1890 campaign, members of each party worked to purge their opponents from voter rolls. Republicans and Democrats both called for suffrage restrictions, although Southern Democrats, of course, wanted to keep African Americans from the polls, and northern Republicans wanted to exclude immigrants. After 1890, states quickly disenfranchised large numbers of voters. In 1890, Mississippi ratified a new state constitution imposing a poll tax and a literacy requirement. Other states followed suit. By 1903, each Southern state had enacted educational, literacy, or property requirements for suffrage, keeping poor blacks and whites from the polls. Similar laws in the North purged the rosters of those who seemed likely to subvert the government.[51]

The administration's apocalyptic rhetoric about the corruption of the vote and the stealing of elections grew in intensity until, six years after Harrison left office, it became the argument behind one of America's few examples of a political coup. In 1898, the "reputable, taxpaying, substantial men" of Wilmington, North Carolina, took out their guns and overthrew the town's legally elected government of African American Republicans and Populists. Vigilantes terrorized black citizens, killing ten, and forced political opponents to resign their elected offices. There was never any question that a majority of the voters had elected the Wilmington government, but Democrats furious that their opponents had won simply declared that the voters were illegitimate and their votes shouldn't have counted. They refused to recognize a legal election, and baldly declared a new government run by their own people to be the legitimate one. Such a rejection of fundamental American law would have horrified the congressmen who had pressed for the Federal Elections Bill, but it was an extreme version of their own rhetoric that justified it.[52]

The administration's push to bring six western states into the Union to add Republican votes in Congress was a disaster for western ecology. As eastern opponents pointed out, the western Territories admitted in 1889 and 1890 had such low populations that statehood was hardly warranted. Republicans defended their admission of the new states by insisting that settlers would flood in once irrigation made the dry western land productive. The drive for productivity helped tie the government to policies of land "reclamation." In 1902, the Newlands Reclamation Act committed the federal government to fund irrigation projects across the West. The law led to the damming of virtually every western river, dramatically changing the ecology of western America.

These irrigation projects ultimately stunted the population growth of the new states rather than encouraging it. Massive irrigation favored agribusiness over small farmers, creating a new, big business–oriented western economy. This meant that settlers did not, in fact, pour into the new states, and Idaho, Wyoming, Montana, North Dakota, and South Dakota never grew as Harrison's men projected.

South Dakota's early years were a constant struggle to attract settlers and bring money into the state. The effort to lure tourists had an unintentionally ironic by-product. In 1923, one of South Dakota's early settlers and the founder of the state historical society, a man named Doane Robinson, conceived a bold plan. He wanted to have a gigantic monument of a western hero carved into the Black Hills to attract tourists and boost the South Dakota economy. A South Dakota senator and former governor took up the cause with enthusiasm and it moved forward.

Robinson invited sculptor Gutzon Borglum, who had gained a reputation for his work carving a monument at Stone Mountain, Georgia, to design a monument for South Dakota. The son of Danish immigrants, Borglum rejected the idea of a western hero and instead wanted the monument to represent American ideals, his son later recalled. He chose to carve four presidents in the stone of Mount Rushmore in the Black Hills: George Washington, who had founded the nation; Thomas Jefferson, who had launched the country's westward expansion; Abraham Lincoln, who had saved the Union from destruction; and Theodore Roosevelt, who had protected working men and helped fit democracy to industrial development.

Borglum's monument inadvertently evoked the hollowness of the Harrison administration's promises. Harrison's men had assured the public that the West would prosper, and it had taken Sioux land by force to make that dream come true. But the Mount Rushmore statue was conceived to attract tourists to a state that had failed to thrive under the late nineteenth-century Republican plan. It would stand in the heart of the Black Hills that the Sioux had fought so hard to hold. There, deep in the land that the Sioux held sacred, Americans carved their own past. The final irony was that the sculpture was intended, Borglum's son wrote, to illustrate the simple concept on which the nation was founded: "Man has a right to be free and to be happy."[53]

In one way, though, the administration's western plan did accomplish what it was supposed to. Senators from Idaho, Wyoming, Montana, North Dakota, and South Dakota enjoyed more national power relative to their state's population than the senators from states like New York, even into the twenty-first century.

Late nineteenth-century Republicans' emphasis on specific kinds of economic development ultimately crippled Sioux success in the American economy. The Harrison administration liked the patronage opportunities afforded by Indian agencies, but the Sioux themselves were never of much interest to Harrison's men except as an obstacle to clear out of the way of economic growth. While administration Republicans had worked with Indian reformers, their goal had always been to take Indian lands out of the traditional economy of the Sioux and use them for the railroads, farming, and mining that underlay the economy of industrial America. They talked of inviting Indians into the American mainstream, but they were using the language of reform as a cover for relentless economic development.

It looked briefly as though the Sioux might make a successful transition into the American economy. After the crisis of 1890, the army officers in charge of Pine Ridge encouraged the Sioux to range cattle. They did so with great success. The Pass Creek district of Pine Ridge branded as many as two thousand calves a year, and the Indians showed every sign that they would become successful cattle ranchers. This made sense, for the skills of the hunt translated well to those of cattle herding. Sioux men were expert horsemen and were enthusiastic about the management of their herds.[54]

But this sensible solution to Indian poverty fell victim to the American drive to seize Indian lands for development, a drive encouraged and aided by Republican policies. Local residents wanted the Sioux range and also their livelihood. In 1900, the government began to collect a tax of one dollar for every head of cattle exceeding one hundred in herds owned by Indians. Any full-blood Indian who owned more than one hundred cattle sold off or butchered the extras. The range went to big cattlemen, whose herds of thousands became the heart of the western cattle industry.[55]

Congress's light-fingered approach to Indian lands became part of the fundamental law of the nation in the early twentieth century. In 1904, the Supreme Court decided the case of *Lone Wolf v. Hitchcock*, in which the Kiowas, Comanches, and Apaches sued the Secretary of the Interior, the Commissioner of Indian Affairs, and the Commissioner of the General Land Office. In the case, the Indians charged that Congress had violated the Treaty of Medicine Lodge by selling Indian lands without the approval of three-quarters of the tribe. Unanimously—and unsurprisingly, considering the larger principle at stake—the nine justices confirmed Congress's unfettered power to do whatever it wanted with respect to a treaty with a foreign power. The law governing contracts only protected citizens, it ruled. Noncitizens, in this case Indians, had no recourse when Congress chose to abrogate a contract with them.

The decision was short and enunciated very clear principles, but the court went further than it had to. The plaintiffs had argued that there were too few signatures on the agreement to cede lands and that the existing signatures had been obtained fraudulently. The Court decided that it was up to Congress to determine whether or not the signatures were legal. Then, it went on to quote from an 1877 decision declaring that Congress would always manage Indian affairs in good faith. Only fourteen years after the crisis of 1890, the Court concluded: "It is to be presumed that . . . the United States would be governed by such considerations as would control a Christian people in their treatment of an ignorant and dependent race." With this decision, the Court condoned the taking of the Great Sioux Reservation, and all that had come after it.[56]

The Supreme Court justices expressed their faith in American good will, but Red Cloud articulated what that benevolence had really meant for his people. When an anthropologist came to Pine Ridge at the turn of the century to interview him, he told the man about the free "buffalo days" of the past. Then he took the man outside and bade him to look around. Red Cloud himself could no longer see the valley, but he recalled it vividly. Through an interpreter, he told the anthropologist to look at the barren waste around him. The land was poor and worthless. "Think of it!" he said. "I, who used to own rich soil in a well-watered country so extensive that I could not ride through it in a week on my fastest pony, am put down here!" The government had promised to feed and support the Indians, he said, but now they had to beg for food. If they complained too much, officers put them in jail. The young people were going bad, the old were dying. "Young man," he told the anthropologist, "I wish there was some one to help my poor people when I am gone."[57]

But there was not. Red Cloud died in 1909, in his mid-eighties. He had hoped that Jack Red Cloud would take his place, but the younger Red Cloud had neither his father's personality nor his tribal support. Jack Red Cloud died in 1918, outliving his father by less than a decade.[58]

The Harrison administration has wrongly been buried in obscurity, for its effects were far-reaching. Its aggressive use of rhetoric, disseminated by its own media, had frightening repercussions for voting rights. Its rosy promises for the West—and the subsequent need to make those promises come true—spelled disaster for the western landscape. Its focus on economic development doomed the Sioux to poverty, and its manipulation of the electoral map changed the dynamics of politics. The actions of Harrison and those around him regarding legislation and policy were complicated and hard to follow, but they are worth understanding.

No one had paid much attention to the Sioux delegates when they came to Washington in February 1891, but less than a decade later, the Wounded Knee affair was going to get the deep investigation it so badly needed. From 1903 until his death in 1926, Nebraska judge Eli S. Ricker traveled around South Dakota to interview individuals associated with the events at Wounded Knee. He tried to figure out what had really happened there. Scribbling on yellow lined pads like the ones schoolchildren used, and making judicious notes about his witnesses' reputations for veracity, Ricker pulled together a compelling case. Ultimately he concluded that on December 29, 1890, undisciplined and disordered troops had murdered surrendering Indians at Wounded Knee.

That Ricker became the man who collected such damning evidence was odd in itself. He was one of those who had signed the resolutions sent to Secretary of War Proctor in November 1890 by the citizens of Chadron, Nebraska, castigating the Sioux and demanding a permanent solution to Indian outbreaks.

But as he grew older, Ricker's opinions changed. No one knows why, but it's likely that his career as a Populist judge and his role as editor of the *Chadron Times* taught him to study all sides of a question. In any case, he revised his initial hatred of the Sioux. By 1903, his perspective had changed enough that he titled an article about a Wyoming citizens' attack on a Pine Ridge hunting party "The Paleface Outbreak in Wyoming."[59]

That same year, Ricker decided to collect the stories of the people with firsthand knowledge of the Wounded Knee affair. He asked questions of witnesses and wrote down their answers, letting them ramble as they wished. Ricker recorded the stories of scouts, teamsters, traders, sightseers, and grave diggers who had been at Wounded Knee. He also recorded the stories of the Indians. He worked until his death. While he never articulated exactly why he began the project, he made it clear he saw it as his life's great work.[60]

The non-Indian participants in the events at Wounded Knee recited essentially the same story that had been put forward during the investigations of the court of inquiry. The medicine man who had danced before the council and tossed dust became the scapegoat for the disaster. In interview after interview, participants who did not speak Lakota and had not observed the disarming blamed him for prompting the younger men to fire on the soldiers. The medicine man's tossing of dirt had been a signal for the men to fire, they claimed. One of Captain Wallace's couriers told Ricker: "The Medicine man threw dirt in the air and yelled and the braves threw off their blankets and began firing. The soldiers threw themselves on the ground." When asked if an officer had ordered the soldiers to fire on the Indians, the courier said no. Instead, a teamster remembered that that Indians had fired first, deliberately, with women firing from the tents. They had had a plan, the teamster insisted, to pretend to be friendly, "and at a concerted moment to begin a massacre of the white soldiers and people when they did not suspect danger."[61]

Some witnesses explicitly defended the soldiers. Father Francis M. J. Craft, S. J., who had wanted to see the surrender and was stabbed in the right lung during the battle, insisted: "Any reports as to soldiers or officers being in any way to blame for the battle of Wounded Knee Creek, or that they hunted down & killed Indian women & children are entirely false. The women & children were killed—most of them at the beginning of the battle—by the fire of the Indians themselves, when they fired, without provocation, upon the troops, beyond whom the women & children were standing. All the women & children who were saved, were saved by soldiers, at the risk, & in many cases, at the cost of their own lives."[62]

The Indian participants, not surprisingly, told a very different story. Sitting with Ricker for six different sessions in 1907, Dewey Beard talked for almost twelve hours about what had happened to him and the other members of Big Foot's band at Wounded Knee Creek on December 29. He told the story of the flight from Cheyenne River, about meeting with the soldiers by Porcupine Creek, about the council on the morning of December 29 and the gunshot and the fight. It is from these interviews that we know about the fighting in the ravine and the deaths there. In 1907, Beard was still devastated and angry at the relentless murder of women and children.

Ricker had interviewed Beard's brother, Joseph Horn Cloud, in 1906, and his story corroborated Beard's. Horn Cloud also provided Ricker with a detailed list of those killed and wounded in what the Indians knew as Big Foot's Massacre.[63]

Mixed-blood scouts, interviewed separately, confirmed the events as described by the Horn Cloud brothers. George Bartlett, captain of the Indian police, told his version of the battle to Ricker in 1903. This was Ricker's first interview, and in it Bartlett blamed the soldiers for what amounted to a massacre. He had seen the events from horseback, and had ridden to Pine Ridge agency to tell General Brooke what had happened. But he had not spoken about it before, apparently because of the cover-up. "About the investigation which followed?" he responded to his questioner: "Naturally my feelings were with the Seventh, and this is the first time I have ever told the story of what I saw. Many soldiers were afterwards heard to remark that the accounts with the Sioux for the Custer massacre were partly squared."[64]

For years, newspaperman Charley Allen had refused to discuss what he saw on December 29, but he talked to Ricker. He also blamed the soldiers. There had been "a cordon of soldiers thrown around the council, and it was impossible for these soldiers to shoot without killing one another," he insisted. Then Allen began a tirade of rhetorical questions: "Why should the soldiers have fired when no shots had been poured into them? Was there no authority and no discipline among officers and soldiers? Could they not wait until the recalcitrant Indian or Indians who forcibly refused to deliver their guns were overcome and restrained? It is said Indians in the council arose when the first shot occurred. Was it not natural that they should do so without intention to fight?" Allen concluded with his own condemnation of the affair: "The action of the troops was overhasty, premature, and more like a mob than trained soldiery."[65]

After years of sifting through the many stories about what had happened at Wounded Knee, Ricker came to agree with Allen. The Indians at Wounded Knee "were attacked, wantonly, cruelly, brutally, and what little fighting they did was in self defense. The affair at W.K. was a drunken slaughter—of white soldiers and innocent Indians—for which white men were responsible—solely responsible. A little reason and patience & forbearance would have avoided the murderous clash." Ricker's interviews give us a priceless window into the affair. He established the truth—or as close as we can come to it—in his painstaking review of the information he gathered from every participant he could find. Ricker devoted his life to the project because, as he wrote, "history must be true, otherwise it is not history." After his death in 1926, his family donated his tablets to the Nebraska State Historical Society. Until prominent historian Richard E. Jensen painstakingly edited Ricker's notes and published them in 2005, they were not widely known. For almost eighty years, Ricker's damning evidence against the soldiers was buried in a library vault.[66]

In place of history grew mythology. For the American people, believing in the heroism of the soldiers at Wounded Knee became an article of faith. The triumph of the army over those who would "attack" Americans illustrated that the American republic stood for good against evil.

When some writers condemned American policy toward the Indians, the backlash they inspired established that the Indians were the aggressors and the Americans the aggrieved parties in their interactions. In his famous book *The Winning of the West*, Theodore Roosevelt castigated reformers who condemned the government's treatment of Indians. The Indians did not own land, he insisted, and had Americans tried to avoid conflicts with them, the Indians would have gone to war. If it were to be blamed, America's "Indian policy [should] be blamed because of the weakness it displayed, because of its shortsightedness and its occasional leaning to the policy of the sentimental humanitarians . . . but . . . [o]ur government almost always tries to act fairly by the tribes; the governmental agents . . . are far more apt to be unjust to the whites than to the reds." Roosevelt blamed the Indians' bloodthirstiness for conflicts on the Plains and lauded the government for its restraint. He had nothing but contempt for the "purely sentimental historians" who talked about injustices to the Indians and wrote "foul slanders about their own countrymen."[67]

Faith in the soldiers and disdain for the savages was not limited to white Americans. The black buffalo soldiers stood firm for the government against the Sioux in 1890, even as their own lives were increasingly circumscribed by new voting laws. During the South Dakota campaign, black soldier W. H. Prather put his patriotism into a song that was distributed to the soldiers:

The Red Skins left their Agency, the Soldiers left their Post,
All on the strength of an Indian tale about Messiah's ghost
Got up by savage chieftains to lead their tribes astray;
But Uncle Sam wouldn't have it so, for he ain't built that way. . . .
A fight took place, 'twas hand to hand, unwarned by trumpet call,
While the Sioux were dropping man by man—the 7th killed them all,
And to that regiment he said "Ye noble Braves, well done,
Although you lost some gallant man a glorious fight you've won."[68]

By the turn of the century, Wounded Knee had become a symbol of the strength of the American government and its democratic ideals. In 1927, American poet Stephen Vincent Benét wrote of his love for American places, noting the strength in their very names. He suggested that when he died:

I shall not rest quiet in Montparnasse.
I shall not lie easy at Winchelsea.
You may bury my body in Sussex grass,
You bury my tongue at Champmedy.
I shall not be there. I shall rise and pass.
Bury my heart at Wounded Knee.

Not only Benét's, but also the heart of the nation lies at Wounded Knee. It lies there in strength, as Benét acknowledged, for Wounded

Knee shows the great power of the government. It lies there in sorrow, for Native Americans and for those who deplore their treatment at the hands of the federal government. It also lies there in condemnation of extreme American party politics and all who engage in them: the politicians who rely on fear to win support, accusing their opponents of wanting to destroy America, and the voters who accept such tactics. As Charles Eastman wrote in barely veiled disgust as he reviewed the events of the "Ghost Dance War": "There was no 'Indian outbreak' in 1890–90, and . . . such trouble as we had may justly be charged to the dishonest politicians, who through unfit appointees first robbed the Indians, then bullied them, and finally in a panic called for troops to suppress them."[69]

Dr. Eastman spent his life negotiating the terrain between the Sioux and post–Civil War Americans. He and Elaine Goodale married in New York City in June 1891. They had six children, but their marriage was a troubled one. Goodale patronized her husband and resented being stuck at home rearing children while he traveled on speaking tours. He, in turn, resented her condescension and her unflagging insistence that Indians must adopt all aspects of white life. It didn't help, either, that Goodale was both adamantly opposed to birth control and afraid of childbirth. The couple produced six children that Eastman found it almost impossible to support as white prejudice continually undercut the ability of an Indian, even an educated one, to make a living. Finally, the relationship fell apart altogether when Eastman fathered a daughter with another woman. Goodale and Eastman parted company around 1920 and never saw each other again, although Eastman lived for another eighteen years.[70]

As he aged, Eastman gradually lost his faith in the American system. He was forced out of his work at Pine Ridge when he tried to defend the rights of the Sioux. Then he was forced out of private practice when clients realized he was an Indian. Finally, beginning in 1894, Eastman began to tour for the YMCA movement, traveling to missions among the Indians in the West and in Canada to win converts to Christianity and the way of life that went with the religion. This experience would force him to rethink the principles he had learned in late nineteenth-century America, the principles that had inspired his work at Pine Ridge. He asked himself why the simple lives of his people seemed so full of the spirit of worship while church-going Christians seemed to be so selfish and mean-spirited.[71]

Indians' perceptions of Americans began to seem startlingly accurate to Eastman. After one of Eastman's talks on Christianity, "one old battle-scarred warrior . . . got up and said . . . : 'Why, we have followed this law you speak of for untold ages! We owned nothing, because everything is free from Him. Food was free, land free as sunshine and rain. Who has changed all this? The white man; and yet he says he is a believer in God! He does not seem to inherit any of the traits of his Father, nor does he follow the example set by his brother Christ.'" The Indians interpreted Christianity through American economics, and they rejected what they saw. Another old man explained: "I have come to the conclusion that this Jesus was an Indian. He was opposed to material acquirement and to great possessions. He was inclined to peace. He was as unpractical as any Indian and set no price upon his labor of love. These are not the principles upon which the white man has founded his civilization. It is strange that he could not rise to these simple principles which were commonly observed among our people."[72]

After urging Indians to accept Christianity and educate their children, Eastman found himself rebuked by an old chief. The man declared himself glad that Eastman was satisfied by the white man's civilization, but he said he and his tribe wanted none of it. "The white man had showed neither respect for nature nor reverence toward God, but, he thought, tried to buy God with the by-products of nature. He tried to buy his way into heaven, but he did not even know where heaven is. . . . 'As for us,' he concluded, 'we shall still follow the old trail.'"

Once his eyes were opened to this way of looking at American civilization in his era, Eastman found material evidence that the Indians were right. He had dropped his wallet, with train tickets and "a considerable sum of money" in it, early one day, and at the end of his evening lecture the Indian who had found it handed it back to him. "Better let these Indians alone!" Eastman said to the missionary with whom he traveled. "If I had lost my money in the streets of your Christian city, I should probably have never seen it again." Perhaps it was true what the Indians were telling him. Perhaps to honor his principles he would have to reject the American economy that, in the Gilded Age, went hand-in-hand with religion.[73]

That suspicion was confirmed when Eastman saw urban poverty for the first time. Traveling to New York City, Chicago, and Boston to publicize the YMCA's work with the Indians, Eastman got to see urban slums firsthand. Settlement workers took him to visit the cities' dives, and what he saw shocked him. He had seen the poor parts of Boston when a student there, but "not in a way to realize the horror and wretchedness of it." The economic inequality left him aghast. As a child he had learned that some men would take from others and that some would be poor, but in that culture, he recalled, the poor retained their self-respect and dignity. Those who had food divided it with those who did not, and when a loved wife or child died, they gave away everything they owned. Eastman was shocked by the contrasts he saw in the cities. "We could not conceive of the extremes of luxury and misery existing thus side by side, for it was common observation with us that the coarse weeds, if permitted to grow, will choke out the more delicate flowers. These things troubled me very much."[74]

As both a refugee Sioux forced off his land and a well-educated doctor, Eastman had seen both sides of America's post–Civil War economy. He had thought long about what he had witnessed in South Dakota in 1890, and had come to believe that the blame for the murder of the Sioux at Wounded Knee could not be placed on the soldiers alone. The fault was that of American society itself. Eastman concluded that the men who had destroyed the Sioux economy talked a lot about Christianity, but their actions had nothing to do with that generous religion. "I have not yet seen the meek inherit the earth, or the peacemakers receive high honor," he noted. "Why do we find so much evil and wickedness practiced by the nations composed of professedly 'Christian' individuals?" For all their noble talk, such men were no different than the tyrants of the past, eager to take everything for themselves. "The pages of history are full of licensed murder and the plundering of weaker and less developed peoples, and obviously the world to-day has not outgrown this system," Eastman mused.[75]

In the end, the Sioux doctor condemned the America he knew. He had given up his traditional way of life for a promise of a better world in which individuals strove for the good of all. Instead he had found prejudice and butchery in the name of economic progress. Bitterly, he pronounced his judgment on the society that had promised so much and delivered so little: "Behind the material and intellectual splendor of our civilization, primitive savagery and cruelty and lust hold sway, undiminished, and as it seems, unheeded. When I reduce civilization to its lowest terms, it becomes a system of life based upon trade. The dollar is the measure of value, and *might* still spells *right*; otherwise, why war?"[76]

ACKNOWLEDGMENTS

This book was not written in an office, and it absorbed great energy from the wonderful people who were going on with their lives around me as I worked everywhere from the kitchen counter to golf courses. My family lived with the project most as I typed away in one spot or another, and they were instrumental in getting me through it. Rob made it easier by his matter-of-fact questions and good taste in music; Eva by her determination to make sure Mom took some breaks and got some sleep (and lots of chocolate). Marshall suffered as I widged songwriters to learn about rhythm and sound until he came to refer to one of them as "He-Who-Must-Not-Be-Named" and to scream whenever one of his CDs came on. I thank him for his sense of humor and his love of history that helped me keep my own.

Michael R. Pontrelli's enthusiasm for this story was a blessing. It's wonderful when someone else gets as excited about century-old South Dakota politics as you do, and is willing to stay awake at night judging synonyms. I thank him for that encouragement, as well as for helping me to recover from an accident, and, as always, for taking care of the household when I'm so absorbed in writing I forget everything else.

I could not have produced this book or survived the last few years without Nancy Evans and Sarah Matel. While Indian women are virtually invisible in this book, I thought always of how decisions they did not make affected their lives and, more positively, of how networks of kinship and friendship surrounded them. Invariably, those thoughts brought images of Sarah and Nancy, friends since babyhood, who watched children, cooked meals, talked, and listened, to help me through this project, and who were always up for some distracting adventure.

Much of this book was written at Wawenock Golf Club in Walpole, Maine, and I thank Stephanie Russell and Geri McElroy, who made me feel welcome despite the fact that I carried a laptop rather than a golf bag. Thanks for my time at Wawenock are especially due to Sharlene Feltis, who not only let me try out ideas on her, but also reserved for me my own writing table in her restaurant so I could work in comfort. The Woburn Rock Gym in Woburn, Massachusetts, has also been kind as I commandeered the couch every week; thanks to all of you, especially Chris O'Connell, Irina Shuruyeva, and Aleksey Shuruyev.

I have been most fortunate in having a number of advisers to help me make sense of how my material fits into a larger world. Dr. Raymond Bradley always answered my neophyte questions about clouds and climate cheerfully, even when they came in the middle of the night. Rich Cairn shared with me his memories of South Dakota and impressed upon me the magic of the clouds. Guy Crosby, once again, was generous with his knowledge of the cattle industry, answering questions about beeves and winter weight loss. Dr. Peter Goth of Springtide Farm in Bristol, Maine, talked me through both the importance of offal to the human diet and instances of disease in populations that eat offal. Daniel J. Travanti corrected my grammar and ideas about "truth"; Denise Warren shared with me her knowledge of words and how to shape images with them. Dr. Walter T. Weylman gave Red Cloud's photograph an eye exam; Mary Jean Weylman cheered this project—and me—on.

My friends at various universities have also been helpful. This book benefited from an early reading by Michael S. Green and a later one by Joel Wolfe. Ari Kelman at University of California, Davis, saved me from some stupid mistakes. My colleagues at the University of Massachusetts, Amherst, gave me the space to write. I am especially indebted to Barry Levy, who understood that I was driven to finish this project and made sure I could.

While I own the problems in this book, the rest of it really belongs to Lisa Adams and to Lara Heimert. Lisa dissuaded me from writing the book I was contemplating and urged me to write this one instead. When I got frustrated with organization, she listened and made suggestions, and she read material when I was unhappy with it. She then handed me off to Lara, who undertook to teach me to write—*really* write—making me learn more in the last year than ever before. Their inspiration and hard work were at least as important to this book as mine. Agents and editors often fall into the background when a book is finally done, so it seems fitting for a book with quiet heroes to be dedicated to them, with my deepest thanks.

NOTES

Introduction

1. William Fitch Kelley, *Pine Ridge 1890: An Eye Witness Account of the Events Surrounding the Fighting at Wounded Knee*, ed. and compiled by Alexander Kelley & Pierre Bovis (San Francisco: Pierre Bovis, 1971), p. 102.

2. Charles W. Allen, *From Fort Laramie to Wounded Knee*, ed. Richard E. Jensen (1939; rpt. Lincoln: University of Nebraska Press, 1997), p. 153, and p. 256, note 14. *Winning the West: The Army in the Indian Wars, 1865–1890* (Office of the Chief of Military History, U.S. Army), at http://www.history.army.mil/BOOKS/amh/AMH-14.htm.

3. Elizabeth B. Custer, *"Boots and Saddles" or Life in Dakota with General Custer* (New York: Harper & Brothers, 1885), pp. 42, 47, on Google Books.

4. Kelley, *Pine Ridge*, p. 102.

5. *Ibid.*, pp. 102–103.

6. Dewey Beard, in Richard E. Jensen, ed., *The Indian Interviews of Eli S. Ricker, 1903–1919* (Lincoln: University of Nebraska Press, 2005), p. 215.

7. Horn Cloud, in *Ricker Indian Interviews*, pp. 196–197. Beard, in *Ricker Indian Interviews*, p. 215. Kelley, *Pine Ridge*, p. 182.

8. *Technology Quarterly*, 5 (Boston: 1892): 290–291, on Google Books. Robert M. Utley, *The Last Days of the Sioux Nation* (New Haven: Yale University Press, 1963), p. 195. Horn Cloud, *Ricker Indian Interviews*, p. 196. Beard, *Ricker Indian Interviews*, p. 215. Kelley, *Pine Ridge*, pp. 182–183.

9. Horn Cloud, *Ricker Indian Interviews*, p. 196. Kelley, *Pine Ridge*, pp. 185–186.

10. Horn Cloud, *Ricker Indian Interviews*, p. 196. Beard, *Ricker Indian Interviews*, p. 215.

11. Kelley, *Pine Ridge*, p. 183. Beard, *Ricker Indian Interviews*, pp. 216–217.

12. Kelley, *Pine Ridge*, pp. 183–186.

13. Horn Cloud, *Ricker Indian Interviews*, p. 197. Beard, *Ricker Indian Interviews*, pp. 216–217.

14. Kelley, *Pine Ridge*, pp. 183–186. Horn Cloud, *Ricker Indian Interviews*, p. 197.

15. Kelley, *Pine Ridge*, p. 184.

16. Horn Cloud, *Ricker Indian Interviews*, pp. 197–198.

17. Kelley, *Pine Ridge*, pp. 185–186.

18. Jerry Green, ed., *After Wounded Knee: Correspondence of Major and Surgeon John Vance Lauderdale while Serving with the Army Occupying the Pine Ridge Indian Reservation, 1890–1891* (East Lansing: Michigan State University Press, 1996), p. 30.

19. Green, *After Wounded Knee*, p. 30.

20. Kelley, *Pine Ridge*, p. 178.

21. Kelley, *Pine Ridge*, p. 184.

22. Allen, *From Fort Laramie to Wounded Knee*, p. 191.

23. Utley, *Last Days*, p. 204.

24. "Buck Buck, A.K.A. Johnny Ride a Pony" at http://www.gameskidsplay.net/games/strength_games/buck_buck.htm, accessed January 9, 2008. Allen, *From Fort Laramie to Wounded Knee*, p. 194.

25. William Garnett, *Ricker Indian Interviews*, p. 95.

26. Horn Cloud, *Ricker Indian Interviews*, p. 200. Meded Swigert, in Richard E. Jensen, ed., *The Settler and Soldier Interviews of Eli S. Ricker, 1903–1919* (Lincoln: University of Nebraska Press, 2005), p. 19. Philip F. Wells, *Ricker Indian Interviews*, p. 157. Beard, *Ricker Indian Interviews*, p. 219.

27. Wells, *Ricker Indian Interviews*, p. 157. Beard, *Ricker Indian Interviews*, p. 219.

28. Allen, *From Fort Laramie to Wounded Knee*, p. 206.

29. Kelley, *Pine Ridge*, pp. 188–189.

30. I thank Dr. Raymond Bradley, Director of the Climate Research Center, UMass Amherst, for confirming that the blizzard in South Dakota was probably linked to the sleet and snow in the East a few days later. (Raymond Bradley to the author, March 8, 2007.) *New York Times*, January 2, 1891, p. 5.

31. Mary Elizabeth Lease, quoted in John D. Hicks, *The Populist Revolt* (Lincoln: University of Nebraska Press, 1961, p. 160.

32. William T. Sherman to U. S. Grant, W. R. Stanton, and O. H. Browning, Ft. Lyon, Colorado Territory, quoted in Howard Roberts Lamar, *Dakota Territory, 1861–1889* (New Haven: Yale University Press, 1956), p. 25.

Chapter 1

1. *New York Times*, January 1, 1890, p. 1.

2. *New York Times*, December 30, 1890, p. 5.

3. William Tecumseh Sherman, *Memoirs of William Tecumseh Sherman*, volume 1 (New York: D. Appleton and Company, 1889), p. 11. John Sherman, *Recollections of Forty Years in the House, Senate and Cabinet*, volume 1 (Chicago: The Werner Company, 1895), pp. 12–23, 28–32.

4. Sherman, *Recollections*, 1: 78, 81–83, 89, 91–105.

5. Sherman, *Recollections*, 1: 89.

6. Sherman, *Recollections*, 1: 84. W. T. Sherman, *Memoirs*, 1: 41–48, 110.

7. W. T. Sherman, *Memoirs*, 1: 86.

8. W. T. Sherman, *Memoirs*, 1: 110.

9. Sherman, *Recollections*, 1: 94.
10. W. T. Sherman, *Memoirs*, 1: 114–131.
11. Heather Cox Richardson, *The Greatest Nation of the Earth: Republican Economic Policies During the Civil War* (Cambridge, Massachusetts: Harvard University Press, 1997), pp. 15–27.
12. Sherman, *Recollections*, 1: 112–113.
13. Sherman, *Recollections*, 1: 101–105.
14. Sherman, *Recollections*, 1: 201.
15. John Sherman to William Tecumseh Sherman, November 26, 1860, in Sherman, *Recollections*, 1: 235.
16. W. T. Sherman, *Memoirs*, 1: 176.
17. W. T. Sherman, *Memoirs*, 1: 196.
18. Sherman, *Recollections*, 1: 265.
19. Sherman, *Recollections*, 1: 251, 258, 261.
20. Sherman, *Recollections*, 1: 304.
21. Richardson, *Greatest Nation*, pp. 160–169.
22. Sherman, *Recollections*, 1: 185.
23. Richardson, *Greatest Nation*, pp. 101–138.
24. Mark R. Wilson, *The Business of Civil War: Military Mobilization and the State, 1861–1865* (Baltimore: The Johns Hopkins University Press, 2006), pp. 74, 116–117.
25. Wyoming was not organized as a territory until 1868, and Dakota Territory split into South Dakota and North Dakota in 1889.
26. Pekka Hamalainen, "The Rise and Fall of Plains Indian Horse Cultures," *Journal of American History* (December 2003) at http://www.historycooperative.org/journals/jah/90.3/hamalainen.html.
27. Walter Prescott Webb, *The Great Plains* (1931; rpt. Lincoln: University of Nebraska Press, 1981), pp. 60–68. Stanley Vestal, *Sitting Bull: Champion of the Sioux* (1932; rpt., Norman: University of Oklahoma Press, 1898), pp. 59–60.
28. Number 40 million from http://www.nps.gov/archive/wica/bison.htm, accessed January 9, 2008. Webb, *Great Plains*, p. 44.
29. "Uses for Buffalo Parts," Akta Lakota Museum and Cultural Center website, www.aktalakota.org, November 30, 2007. Tom E. Mails, *The Mystic Warriors of the Plains* (Garden City, New York: Doubleday, 1972), p. 190, cited on www.siouxme.com/buff-ind.html, November 30, 2007.
30. James Mooney, *The Ghost-Dance Religion and Wounded Knee* (1896; rpt. New York: Dover Publications, Inc., 1973), p. 1058.
31. Philip Weeks, *Farewell, My Nation: The American Indian and the United States in the Nineteenth Century* (Arlington Heights, Illinois: Harlan Davidson, 2000), pp. 104–111.
32. Charles A. Eastman, *Indian Boyhood* (1902; rpt. Williamstown, Massachusetts: Corner House Publishers, 1975), pp. 11–19. Raymond Wilson, "The Writings of Ohiyesa—Charles Alexander Eastman, M.D., Santee Sioux," *South Dakota History*, 6 (Winter 1975): 55–73. Charles A. Eastman, *From the Deep Woods to Civilization* (1916; rpt. Lincoln: University of Nebraska Press, 1977), pp. 1–6.

33. Herbert S. Schell, *History of South Dakota* (Lincoln: University of Nebraska Press, 1961), pp. 69–72. Frances Chamberlain Holley, *Once Their Home or Our Legacy from the Dahkotahs* (Chicago: Donohue & Henneberry, 1890), pp. 74–79.

34. Mooney, *Ghost-Dance Religion*, pp. 1058–1059. Vestal, *Sitting Bull*, pp. 145, 154–156.

35. Vestal, *Sitting Bull*, pp. 22–25, 50–61.

36. Vestal, *Sitting Bull*, p. 59.

37. Weeks, *Farewell, My Nation*, pp. 112–118, 126, 128.

38. *Ibid.*

39. Vestal, *Sitting Bull*, p. 69.

40. Holley, *Once Their Home*, pp. 378–379.

41. Schell, *History of South Dakota*, pp. 84–86. *New York Times*, June 2, 1870, p. 4.

42. On scope of initial assignment, see *New York Times*, December 3, 1865, p. 3. For Sherman's activities, see W. T. Sherman, *Report*, November 5, 1866, in Report of the Secretary of War, 39th Congress, 2nd sess., H. Exec. Doc. 1 pt. 3, pp. 18–23.

43. Report on Indian Affairs by the Acting Commissioner, 1867, (Washington: Government Printing Office, 1868), pp. 2–3.

44. George E. Hyde, *A Sioux Chronicle* (1965; rpt. Norman: University of Oklahoma Press, 1993), pp. 60–65. Spotted Tail's political murder fifteen years later was hidden for years under a claim that he had stolen the murderer's wife. James C. Olson, *Red Cloud and the Sioux Problem* (Lincoln: University of Nebraska Press, 1965), pp. 30–31.

45. Olson, *Red Cloud*, pp. 27–35.

46. Olson, *Red Cloud*, pp. 27–39.

47. Sherman, *Report*, p. 19.

48. Sherman, *Recollections*, 1: 389–392. W. T. Sherman to John Sherman, October 20, 1866, in Rachel Sherman Thorndike, ed., *The Sherman Letters* (New York: Charles Scribner's Sons, 1894), p. 277. John Sherman to W. T. Sherman, October 26, 1866, in Thorndike, *Sherman Letters*, p. 278.

49. Sherman, *Report*, p. 21.

50. Olson, *Red Cloud*, pp. 41–43.

51. Olson, *Red Cloud*, pp. 43–45.

52. Olson, *Red Cloud*, pp. 50–51.

53. Sherman to Cooke, December 28, 1866, quoted in Olson, *Red Cloud*, p. 52. Sherman to Augur, February 19, 1867, quoted in Olson, *Red Cloud*, p. 53. W. T. Sherman to John Sherman, December 30, 1866, in Thorndike, *Sherman Letters*, p. 287.

54. Olson, *Red Cloud*, pp. 41–53. Vestal, *Sitting Bull*, p. 80. James H. Cook, *Fifty Years on the Old Frontier as Cowboy, Hunter, Guide, Scout, and Ranchman* (New Haven: Yale University Press, 1923), pp. 228–230. Donald B. Connelly, *John M. Schofield and the Politics of Generalship* (Chapel Hill: University of North Carolina Press, 2006), pp. 214–218, 301–306.

55. Connelly, *Schofield*, pp. 214–218, 301–306.

56. Olson, *Red Cloud*, p. 59. Philip Weeks, *Farewell, My Nation*, pp. 124–126, 128.

57. Olson, *Red Cloud*, p. 59.

58. Olson, *Red Cloud*, pp. 60–66.

59. W. T. Sherman to John Sherman, September 28, 1867, in Thorndike, *Sherman Letters*, p. 296.

60. Olson, *Red Cloud*, pp. 66–68.

61. Charles J. Kappler, ed., *Indian Affairs: Laws and Treaties* (Washington, D. C.: Government Printing Office, 1904), 2: 977–989. Frederic Logan Paxson, *The Last American Frontier* (New York: The Macmillan Company, 1922), p. 292.

62. Olson, *Red Cloud*, pp. 68–69.

63. Olson, *Red Cloud*, pp. 70–73.

64. Olson, *Red Cloud*, pp. 73–76.

65. Olson, *Red Cloud*, pp. 76–81.

66. Olson, *Red Cloud*, pp. 81–82.

67. James McLaughlin, *My Friend the Indian* (Boston: Houghton, Mifflin Company, 1910), pp. 265–267, on Google Books. John B. Sanborn, late commissioner to the Indians, in *New York Times*, April 18, 1870, p. 1.

68. W. T. Sherman to John Sherman, June 17, 1868, and September 23, 1868, in Thorndike, *Sherman Letters*, pp. 320–321.

69. Treaty of Fort Laramie, available at: http://www.ourdocuments.gov/doc.php?flash=old&doc=42.

70. Virginia Weisel Johnson, *The Unregimented General: A Biography of Nelson A. Miles* (Boston: Houghton Mifflin Company, 1962), pp. 32–34. Robert Wooster, *Nelson A. Miles and the Twilight of the Frontier Army* (Lincoln: University of Nebraska Press, 1993), p. 51. W. T. Sherman to U. S. Grant, May 8, 1868, in House Ex. Doc 239, 40th Congress, 2nd sess.

71. Wooster, *Miles*, p. 51.

72. Olson, *Red Cloud*, pp. 83–92.

73. Olson, *Red Cloud*, pp. 83–92. Hyde, *Sioux Chronicle*, pp. 4–5.

74. *New York Times*, June 8, 1870, p. 4. Dewitt Clinton Poole, *Among the Sioux of Dakota: Eighteen Months Experience as a Sioux Agent* (New York: D. Van Nostrand, Publisher, 1881), pp. 133–193, on Google Books. Olson, *Red Cloud*, pp. 92–113. *New York Times*, June 2, 1870, p. 4, and June 5, 1870, p. 1.

75. *New York Times*, June 8, 1870, p. 4. *New York Times*, June 8, 1870, p. 1.

76. *New York Times*, June 10, 1870, p. 1.

77. Olson, *Red Cloud*, pp. 107–108. *New York Times*, June 11, 1870, p. 1.

78. Herbert S. Schell, *History of South Dakota* (Lincoln: University of Nebraska Press, 1961), pp. 125–126. Richard White, *It's Your Misfortune and None of My Own: A New History of the American West* (Norman: University of Oklahoma Press, 1991), p. 218.

79. Robert M. Utley, *The Indian Frontier of the American West, 1846–1890* (Albuquerque: University of New Mexico Press, 1984), pp. 150–153, 178.

80. William Garnett, in Richard E. Jensen, ed., *The Indian Interviews of Eli S. Ricker, 1903–1919* (Lincoln: University of Nebraska Press, 2005), pp. 117–118. Olson, *Red Cloud*, pp. 131. Vestal, *Sitting Bull*, p. 128.

81. Robert M. Utley, *The Lance and the Shield: The Life and Times of Sitting Bull* (New York: Henry Holt and Company, 1993), p. 87.

82. McLaughlin, *My Friend the Indian*, pp. 61–64, on Google Books. Vestal, *Sitting Bull*, p. 95.

83. Vestal, *Sitting Bull*, pp. 125–131.

84. Vestal, *Sitting Bull*, p. 131. Wooster, *Miles*, pp. 59–60. Holley, *Once Their Home*, pp. 176–177. Nelson A. Miles, *Serving the Republic* (New York: Harper and Brothers Publishers, 1911), pp. 107–111, on Google Books.

85. Wilson, "Ohiyesa," pp. 56–58. Eastman, *Deep Woods to Civilization*, pp. 6–30.

Chapter 2

1. *New York Times*, November 1, 1865, p. 4; November 22, 1865, p. 1. W. T. Sherman to J. Sherman, September 21, 1865, in Rachel Sherman Thorndike, ed., *The Sherman Letters* (New York: Charles Scribner's Sons, 1894), p. 256.

2. William H. Rowe, *The Maritime History of Maine* (New York: W. W. Norton & Company, 1948), pp. 207–249.

3. Henry Collins Brown, *In the Golden Nineties* (Hastings-on Hudson: Valentine's Manual, Inc., 1928) pp. 48–54, on Making of America, University of Michigan.

4. Heather Cox Richardson, *West from Appomattox: The Reconstruction of America after the Civil War* (New Haven: Yale University Press, 2007), pp. 188–192.

5. Richard B. Morris, ed., *Encyclopedia of American History* (New York: Harper & Brothers, 1953), p. 481.

6. While historians have recognized the higher rainfall in this period from anecdotal evidence, Cary J. Mock has recently compiled climatic evidence for this phenomenon. See Cary J. Mock, "Rainfall in the Garden of the United States Great Plains, 1870–1889," *Climatic Change*, 44 (2000): 173–195, at http://webra.cas.sc.edu/hvri/pubs/2000_RainfallInTheGardenOfTheUSGreatPlains.pdf, accessed October 30, 2009.

7. Kenneth M. Hammer, "Come to God's Country: Promotional Efforts in Dakota Territory, 1861–1889," *South Dakota History*, 10 (Fall 1980): 291–309.

8. On Baum, see Nancy Tystad Koupal, ed., L. Frank Baum, *Our Landlady* (Lincoln: University of Nebraska Press, 1996). Poem on p. 69.

9. Sara L. Bernson and Robert J. Eggers, "Black People in South Dakota History," *South Dakota History*, 7 (Summer 1977): 241–270. Willard B. Gatewood, Jr., "Kate D. Chapman Reports on 'The Yankton Colored People,' 1889," *South Dakota History*, 7 (Winter 1976): 28–35.

10. Todd Guenther, "Lucretia Marchbanks: A Black Woman in the Black Hills," *South Dakota History*, 31 (Spring 2001): 1–25.

11. Herbert S. Schell, *History of South Dakota* (Lincoln: University of Nebraska Press, 1961), pp. 126–128.

12. *Ibid.*, p. 129.

13. *Ibid.*, pp. 140–141.

14. *Ibid.*, pp. 130–133. James McLaughlin, *My Friend the Indian* (Boston: Houghton, Mifflin Company, 1910), pp. 268–269, on Google Books. Doane Robinson, *A History of the Dakota or Sioux Indians* (South Dakota: 1904), pp. 416–420, on Google Books.

15. Robinson, *Dakota or Sioux*, pp. 416–420.

16. *Ibid.*, p. 421.

17. Stanley Vestal, *Sitting Bull: Champion of the Sioux* (1932; rpt., Norman: University of Oklahoma Press, 1898), p. 133. Lame Deer, "How the Sioux Came to Be," in Richard Erdoes and Alfonso Ortiz, eds., *American Indian Myths and Legends* (New York: Pantheon Books, 1984), pp. 93–95.

18. Schell, *South Dakota*, pp. 130–133. McLaughlin, *My Friend the Indian*, pp. 268–269.

19. Sitting Bull quoted in Robert M. Utley, *The Indian Frontier of the American West, 1846–1890* (Albuquerque: University of New Mexico Press, 1984), p. 180.

20. *New York Times*, June 3, 1870, p. 1.

21. Jerome A. Greene, ed., *Battles and Skirmishes of the Great Sioux War, 1876–1877: The Military View* (Norman: University of Oklahoma Press, 1993), p. xvii.

22. Robinson, *Dakota or Sioux*, pp. 423–424. McLaughlin, *My Friend the Indian*, pp. 268–269. Vestal, *Sitting Bull*, p. 139–141. Robert M. Utley, *The Lance and the Shield: The Life and Times of Sitting Bull* (New York: Henry Holt and Company, 1993), pp. 127–128.

23. Vestal, *Sitting Bull*, p. 141.

24. *Ibid.*, pp. 140–147.

25. *Ibid.*, pp. 148–151.

26. *Ibid.*, p. 152.

27. Greene, *Battles*, pp. xvii–xviii.

28. Utley, *Lance and Shield*, p. 140. Vestal, *Sitting Bull*, p. 152.

29. Vestal, *Sitting Bull*, pp. 152–153. Utley, *Lance and Shield*, pp. 140–141.

30. John Gregory Bourke, *On the Border with Crook* (New York: Charles Scribner's Sons, 1896), pp. 312–315, on Google Books. Utley, *Lance and Shield*, p. 141.

31. Bourke, *On the Border with Crook*, pp. 315–316. Utley, *Lance and Shield*, p. 141.

32. Vestal, *Sitting Bull*, pp. 152–160. Greene, *Battles*, p. xviii.

33. Utley, *Lance and Shield*, p. 142.

34. Vestal, *Sitting Bull*, pp. 152–160. Utley, *Lance and Shield*, p. 143–144. Orin G. Libby, ed., *The Arikara Narrative of Custer's Campaign and the Battle of the Little Bighorn* (1920; rpt. Norman: University of Oklahoma Press, 1998), p. 31.

35. Utley, *Lance and Shield*, pp. 145–146.

36. Utley, *Lance and Shield*, pp. 146–147. Libby, *Arikara Narrative*, p. 30.

37. Utley, *Lance and Shield*, pp. 149–150.

38. Utley, *Lance and Shield*, pp. 150–151. Vestal, *Sitting Bull*, pp. 160–162.

39. Garnett, *Ricker Indian Interviews*, p. 118. Utley, *Lance and Shield*, p. 153.

40. William Jackson, "The Battle of the Little Big Horn, June 25–26, 1876," in Greene, *Battles*, pp. 41–62. Utley, *Lance and Shield*, pp. 151, 157–159.

41. Gall in Frances Chamberlain Holley, *Once Their Home or Our Legacy from the Dahkotahs* (Chicago: Donohue & Henneberry, 1890), p. 276.

42. Vestal, *Sitting Bull*, p. 167.

43. Utley, *Lance and Shield*, p. 159. Libby, *Arikara Narrative*, p. 32. Vestal, *Sitting Bull*, p. 176.

44. Vestal, *Sitting Bull*, pp. 176–177. Utley, *Lance and Shield*, pp. 160–161. Greene, *Battles*, pp. xvii–xix.

45. Holley, *Once Their Home*, p. 229.

46. *Ibid.*, pp. 260–261.

47. Sitting Bull, in Utley, *Lance and Shield*, p. 161.

48. Robert Wooster, *Nelson A. Miles and the Twilight of the Frontier Army* (Lincoln: University of Nebraska Press, 1993), pp. 76–79.

49. *Ibid.*, pp. 80–83.

50. *Ibid.*, pp. 83–85.

51. *Ibid.*, pp. 85–93.

52. Wooster, *Miles*, pp. 93–95. Garnett, in Richard E. Jensen, ed., *The Indian Interviews of Eli S. Ricker, 1903–1919* (Lincoln: University of Nebraska Press, 2005), pp. 70–71.

53. George E. Hyde, *A Sioux Chronicle* (1965; rpt. Norman: University of Oklahoma Press, 1993), p. 23. Wooster, *Miles*, p. 94. On Sitting Bull and his time in Canada, see Beth LaDow, *The Medicine Line: Life and Death on a North American Borderland* (New York: Routledge, 2001), pp. 48–66.

54. Wooster, *Miles*, p. 90.

55. Hyde, *Sioux Chronicle*, pp. 3–4.

56. *Ibid.*, p. 23.

57. For Newell's impressions of Spotted Tail, and a record of the chief's stories, see Cicero Newell, *Indian Stories* (Boston: Silver, Burdett and Company, 1912), on Google Books. Hyde, *Sioux Chronicle*, pp. 36–51.

58. Hyde, *Sioux Chronicle*, pp. 36–51.

59. *Ibid.*, pp. 51–53.

60. *Ibid.*, pp. 53–58.

61. *Ibid.*, pp. 31–36.

62. Garnett, *Ricker Indian Interviews*, p. 113. On Sun Dance, see George Sword, in James R. Walker, *Lakota Belief and Ritual* (Lincoln: University of Nebraska Press, 1980), pp. 175–191.

63. Mark R. Ellis, "Reservation *Akicitas*: The Pine Ridge Indian Police, 1879–1885," *South Dakota History*, 29 (Fall 1999): 185–210.

64. Ellis, "Reservation *Akicitas*," pp. 185–210.

65. George Sword, "Foundations," in Walker, *Lakota Belief and Ritual*, p. 74.

66. Sitting Bull in Vestal, *Sitting Bull*, p. 232.

67. *Ibid.*, p. 233.

68. McLaughlin, *My Friend the Indian*, p. 206.

69. Robinson, *History of South Dakota*, pp. 306–308. James F. Hamburg, "Railroads and the Settlement of South Dakota During the Great Dakota Boom, 1878–1887," *South Dakota History*, 5 (Spring 1975): 165–178.

70. William Tecumseh Sherman to Ellen E. Sherman, September 16, 1883, in M. A. DeWolfe Howe, *Home Letters of General Sherman* (New York: Charles Scribner's Sons, 1909), p. 391, on Google Books.

71. On Italians and knives, see *New York Times*, February 24, 1887; May 18, 1887; August 11, 1887.

72. Holley, *Once Their Home*, p. 375. Walter Prescott Webb, *The Great Plains* (1931; rpt. Lincoln: University of Nebraska Press, 1981), pp. 3–26.

73. McLaughlin, *My Friend the Indian*, pp. 12–13. Joanna L. Stratton, *Pioneer Women: Voices from the Kansas Frontier* (New York: Simon and Schuster, 1981), pp. 46–76. Webb, *Great Plains*, pp. 23–24.

74. White, *"It's Your Misfortune,"* p. 263.

75. John Sherman in *Frank Leslie's Illustrated Newspaper* (hereafter *FLIN*), August 3, 1889, p. 431. Sam S. Kepfield, "'They Were in Far Too Great Want': Federal Drought Relief to the Great Plains, 1887–1895," *South Dakota History*, 28 (Winter 1998): 244–270.

76. A. J. Grover, in *New York Times*, May 31, 1878, p. 3.

77. Evelyn H. Walker, et al., *Leaders of the Nineteenth Century* (Chicago, Illinois: A. B. Kuhlman Company, 1900), p. 199, on Google Books.

78. W. A. Croffut, *The Vanderbilts and the Story of Their Fortune* (Chicago: Belford, Clarke & Company, 1886), pp. 190–197, on Google Books. *Boston Globe*, March 26, 1883, p. 1.

79. *FLIN*, March 8, 1890, p. 104; June 14, 1890, p. 401.

80. *FLIN*, March 8, 1890, p. 104.

81. *New York Times* and *Chicago Tribune* quoted in *Harper's Weekly*, February 9, 1884, p. 86.

82. W. M. Rapsher, "Dangerous 'Trusts'," *North American Review*, 146 (May 1888): 509–515, on Making of America, Cornell.

83. *Harper's Weekly*, September 27, 1884, p. 628; September 15, 1888, p. 687.

84. George B. Curtiss, Esq., *Protection and Prosperity: An Account of Tariff Legislation and its Effect in Europe and America* (New York: Pan-American Publishing Company, 1896), p. 630, on Google Books.

85. *Harper's Weekly*, June 30, 1888, p. 470. Wooster, *Miles*, p. 197. John Sherman, *Recollections of Forty Years in the House, Senate and Cabinet*, volume 2 (Chicago: The Werner Company, 1895), pp. 1022–1034. Harry J. Sievers, S. J., *Benjamin Harrison: Hoosier Statesman* (New York: University Publishers Incorporated, 1959), pp. 345–347.

86. Sievers, *Hoosier Statesman*, pp. 426–427.

87. Grover Cleveland, Message to Congress, December 3, 1888, available at John T. Woolley and Gerhard Peters, The American Presidency Project [online], Santa Barbara, California, available at http://www.presidency.ucsb.edu/ws/?pid=29529.

88. Richardson, *West from Appomattox*, p. 233.

89. *New York Times*, January 1889. *FLIN*, "Against the Trust," January 19, 1889, p. 378. See also *FLIN*, May 4, 1889, p. 199. *Harper's Weekly*, July 12, 1890, p. 535.

90. *FLIN*, January 11, 1890, p. 407.

91. *FLIN*, March 16, 1889, p. 87.

92. Amos R. Wells, "The Christian Endeavor Movement II: A New Religious Force," *New England Magazine* (June 1892): 518–528, MOA, Cornell. *FLIN*,

March 23, 1889, p. 103; April 20, 1889, pp. 175, 176; August 10, 1889, p. 2; August 24, 1889, p. 30; September 28, 1889, p. 123; March 1, 1890, p. 83.

93. *FLIN*, May 18, 1889, p. 254. *FLIN*, April 6, 1889, p. 134.

94. For Arkell on election of 1890, see *FLIN*, March 8, 1890, p. 98. *New York Times*, April 27, 1889, p. 4. *New York Times*, February 24, 1889, p. 16; March 16, 1889, p. 2. *FLIN*, May 18, 1889, p. 254; November 16, 1889, p. 270.

95. *FLIN*, May 11, 1889, p. 223.

96. *FLIN*, May 11, 1889, pp. 224–233, supplement.

97. *FLIN*, May 18, 1889, p. 263; August 17, 1889, p. 31; August 24, 1889, p. 40, forward.

98. Edward C. Kirkland, ed., Andrew Carnegie, *The Gospel of Wealth* (1889; rpt. Cambridge: Harvard University Press, 1962).

99. *FLIN*, March 8, 1890, p. 99.

100. *FLIN*, December 14, 1889, p. 330; December 21, 1889, p. 354; January 4, 1889, p. 387.

Chapter 3

1. Stanley Vestal, *Sitting Bull: Champion of the Sioux* (1932; rpt., Norman: University of Oklahoma Press, 1898), p. 18.

2. James C. Olson, *Red Cloud and the Sioux Problem* (Lincoln: University of Nebraska Press, 1965), pp. 286–288.

3. Olson, *Red Cloud*, pp. 289–294.

4. Olson, *Red Cloud*, pp. 286–294. James McLaughlin, *My Friend the Indian* (Boston: Houghton, Mifflin Company, 1910), pp. 265–267, on Google Books, pp. 271–273.

5. McLaughlin, *My Friend the Indian*, pp. 271–273.

6. Testimony of Sitting Bull, 48th Congress, 1st sess., S. Rpt. 283, pp. 79–81.

7. Jerome A. Greene, "The Sioux Land Commission of 1889: Prelude to Wounded Knee," *South Dakota History*, 1 (Winter 1970): 41–72.

8. Elaine Goodale Eastman, *Sister to the Sioux: The Memoirs of Elaine Goodale Eastman, 1885–91*, ed. Kay Graber (University of Nebraska Press, 1978), pp. 18–30.

9. Eastman, *Sister to the Sioux*, pp. 32–33.

10. Eastman, *Sister to the Sioux*, pp. 88–92.

11. Greene, "Sioux Land Commission," pp. 43–44.

12. Greene, "Sioux Land Commission," p. 45. Olson, *Red Cloud*, pp. 309–312.

13. *New York Times*, February 13, 1888, p. 1; February 24, 1888, p. 3.

14. *New York Times*, February 15, 1889, p. 5; February 17, 1889, p. 4; February 25, 1889, p. 1. Frances Chamberlain Holley, *Once Their Home or Our Legacy from the Dahkotahs* (Chicago: Donohue & Henneberry, 1890), p. 393. Greene, "Sioux Land Commission," p. 45.

15. *FLIN*, January 5, 1889, p. 346; March 2, 1889, p. 39; March 16, 1889, p. 91, from New York *World*.

16. *FLIN*, March 16, 1889, p. 91.

17. Greene, "Sioux Land Commission," pp. 45–46.

18. Greene, "Sioux Land Commission," pp. 47–48. William Garnett, in Richard E. Jensen, ed., *The Indian Interviews of Eli S. Ricker, 1903–1919* (Lincoln: University of Nebraska Press, 2005), p. 93.

19. John Frederick Finerty, *War-path and Bivouac, or Conquest of the Sioux* (Chicago: 1890), pp. 419–424, on Google Books.

20. Greene, "Sioux Land Commission," pp. 48–49.

21. George E. Hyde, *A Sioux Chronicle* (1956; rpt. Norman: University of Oklahoma Press, 1993), pp. 202–212. Olson, *Red Cloud*, p. 224.

22. Hyde, *Sioux Chronicle*, pp. 212–218.

23. Hyde, *Sioux Chronicle*, pp. 219–220.

24. Hyde, *Sioux Chronicle*, pp. 220–225.

25. Hyde, *Sioux Chronicle*, pp. 225–228. McLaughlin, *My Friend the Indian*, pp. 283–288. Vestal, *Sitting Bull*, pp. 261–262. Jeffrey Ostler, *The Plains Sioux and U.S. Colonialism from Lewis and Clark to Wounded Knee* (Cambridge University Press, 2004), p. 234.

26. William Garnett, *Ricker Indian Interviews*, p. 93.

27. *New York Times*, November 16, 1889, p. 3.

28. Olson, *Red Cloud*, pp. 225–229. Holley, *Once Their Home*, p. 393.

29. Garnett, *Ricker Indian Interviews*, p. 96. Cornelius A. Craven, in Richard E. Jensen, ed., *The Settler and Soldiers Interviews of Eli S. Ricker, 1903–1919* (Lincoln: University of Nebraska Press, 2005), p. 48. *New York Times*, August 7, 1889, p. 1.

30. *New York Times*, August 7, 1889, p. 1.

31. Col. L. F. Spencer, Report, in Report of Commissioner of Indian Affairs, 1889, pp. 158–161.

32. *New York Times*, August 7, 1889, p. 1.

33. *FLIN*, August 24, 1889, p. 38.

34. *FLIN*, July 6, 1889, p. 366; August 24, 1889, p. 38.

35. *FLIN*, June 1, 1889, p. 287. Montana was fairly well balanced, and Republicans and Democrats both fought to get more of their votes counted. See Hubert Howe Bancroft and Frances Fuller Victor, *History of Washington, Idaho, and Montana, 1845–1899* (San Francisco: The History Company, Publishers, 1890), pp. 781–806, on Google Books. *FLIN*, October 19, 1889, p. 191.

36. *FLIN*, November 2, 1889, pp. 223, 230. *FLIN*, December 14, 1889, p. 331.

37. Holley, *Once Their Home*, pp. 400, 405.

38. Benjamin Harrison, Message to Congress, December 3, 1889, at John T. Woolley and Gerhard Peters, The American Presidency Project [online], Santa Barbara, California: University of California (hosted), Gerhard Peters (database). Available at http://www.presidency.ucsb.edu/ws/?pid=29530.

39. *FLIN*, November 16, 1889, p. 259.

40. Hyde, *Sioux Chronicle*, p. 230. Robert M. Utley, *Last Days of the Sioux Nation* (New Haven: Yale University Press, 1963), p. 54.

41. Holley, *Once Their Home*, p. 185. Eastman, *Sister to the Sioux*, pp. 59–60.

42. Hyde, *Sioux Chronicle*, p. 230.

43. Hyde, *Sioux Chronicle*, p. 230. Utley, *Last Days*, p. 54. I thank Guy Crosby for his confirmation of how much weight an animal could lose over a winter.

44. Hyde, *Sioux Chronicle*, p. 230.

45. Herbert Welsh, "The Murrain of Spoils in the Indian Service," in *Proceedings at the Annual Meeting of the National Civil-Service Reform League* (New York: Published for the National Civil-Service Reform League, 1898), p. 85, on Google Books.

46. T. J. Morgan, Instructions to Indian Agents in Regard to Inculcation of Patriotism in Indian Schools, December 10, 1889, in *Report of the Commissioner of Indian Affairs* (Washington: GPO, 1890), p. lxvii, on Google Books.

47. *Washington Post*, August 28, 1890, p. 6. Hyde, *Sioux Chronicle*, pp. 230–231. Utley, *Last Days*, pp. 54–55.

48. Report of H. D. Gallagher, in Report of the Secretary of the Interior, 1890, pp. 48–49. Utley, *Last Days*, p. 55. Hyde, *Sioux Chronicle*, p. 231. T. J. Morgan, "Instructions to Agents in Regard to Manner of Issuing Beef," July 21, 1890, in *Report of Indian Commissioner*, 1890, p. clxivi, on Google Books. I am indebted to Dr. Peter Goth of Springtide Farm, in Bremen, Maine, for explaining the nutritional importance of offal and its role in human eating patterns.

49. Utley, *Last Days*, p. 55. Hyde, *Sioux Chronicle*, p. 231.

50. Vestal, *Sitting Bull*, p. 268. Hyde, *Sioux Chronicle*, pp. 234–235. Hugh D. Gallagher, Report, in 59th Annual *Report of the Commissioner of Indian Affairs*, 1890 (Washington: GPO, 1890), pp. 48–49.

51. Utley, *Last Days*, pp. 55–56.

52. Utley, *Last Days*, p. 56.

53. Utley, *Last Days*, p. 56.

54. Hyde, *Sioux Chronicle*, p. 235.

55. *FLIN*, April 5, 1890, p. 207. *Harper's Weekly*, January 11, 1890, p. 19.

56. Hyde, *Sioux Chronicle*, p. 236. Utley, *Last Days*, p. 57.

57. *FLIN*, January 25, 1890, p. 440. *Idaho Daily Statesman* (Boise Idaho), January 22, 1890.

58. *New York Times*, February 12, 1890, p. 1.

59. *New York Times*, February 12, 1890, p. 4. *FLIN*, February 22, 1890, p. 59.

60. *FLIN*, March 8, 1890, p. 112.

61. John G. Bourke, *On the Border with Crook* (New York: Charles Scribner's Sons, 1892), pp. 486–487, on Google Books.

62. James Mooney, *The Ghost-Dance Religion and Wounded Knee* (1896; rpt. New York: Dover Publications, Inc., 1973), pp. 820–821.

63. Mooney, *Ghost-Dance*, p. 820. Hyde, *Sioux Chronicle*, p. 240.

64. Hyde, *Sioux Chronicle*, pp. 240, 242. Jensen, *Ricker Indian Interviews*, p. 387, note 17.

65. Mooney, *Ghost-Dance*, pp. 819–820. Utley, *Last Days*, pp. 60–62. Porcupine, in Mooney, *Ghost-Dance*, pp. 793–796. For railroad routes, see the excellent maps in George Franklin Cram, *Cram's Township and Railroad Maps* (Chicago, 1896), LC Railroad maps, 201 and 314, at American Memory Website, g4270 rr002010, http://hdl.loc.gov/loc.gmd/g4270.rr002010 and g4261p rr003140, http://hdl.loc.gov/loc.gmd/g4261p.rr003140.

66. Mooney, *Ghost-Dance*, pp. 775, 807.

67. Porcupine, in Mooney, *Ghost-Dance*, pp. 793–794.

68. "Vegetation of Nevada," at http://www.maycenter.com/arboretum/NvVeg.htm, accessed November 16, 2007.

69. Mooney, *Ghost-Dance*, p. 765. Porcupine, in Mooney, *Ghost-Dance*, p. 794.

70. Laura Ingalls Wilder, *Little Town on the Prairie* (1941; rpt. New York: HarperCollins, 2004), pp. 203, 205, 271. Dunn, Helen, Indians of Nevada, Published by the Nevada Department of Education, 1973), at Nevada State Library and Archives. Mooney, *Ghost-Dance*, p. 770. Sixtieth Annual Report of the Commissioner of Indian Affairs, 1891, pp. 2, 78–79.

71. I thank Michael S. Green for helping me to describe Pyramid Lake. Porcupine, in Mooney, *Ghost-Dance*, pp. 794–795.

72. http://en.wikipedia.org/wiki/Paiute.

73. Mooney, *Ghost-Dance*, pp. 765–767, 771.

74. For an analysis of the Ghost Dance see Ostler, *Plains Sioux*, pp. 243–288. Mooney, *Ghost-Dance*, pp. 771–772.

75. Mooney, *Ghost-Dance*, p. 772.

76. C. C. Warner to James Mooney, October 12, 1891, in Mooney, *Ghost-Dance*, p. 767. Porcupine, in Mooney, *Ghost-Dance*, p. 795.

77. Porcupine, in Mooney, *Ghost-Dance*, p. 795.

78. Ostler, *Plains Sioux*, pp. 264–265.

79. Ostler, *Plains Sioux*, pp. 265–266.

80. Porcupine, in Mooney, *Ghost-Dance*, p. 795. For an analysis of the Ghost Dance see Ostler, *Plains Sioux*, pp. 243–288. Mooney, *Ghost-Dance*, p. 772.

81. Mooney, *Ghost-Dance*, pp. 772, 784, 797.

82. Ostler, *Plains Sioux*, pp. 251–256 points out that the many languages and cultures involved in descriptions make it hard to decipher precisely what people said. Mooney, *Ghost-Dance*, p. 772.

83. Mooney, *Ghost-Dance*, p. 775.

84. Mooney, *Ghost-Dance*, pp. 797–798, 821–822.

85. Hyde, *Sioux Chronicle*, pp. 243, 247.

86. J. George Wright replaced Col. L. F. Spencer at Rosebud on September 14, 1889. See *Report of Commissioner of Indian Affairs*, 1890, p. 57. Hyde, *Sioux Chronicle*, pp. 243, 247.

87. Hyde, *Sioux Chronicle*, pp. 242–243. Utley, *Last Days*, p. 75.

88. Utley, *Last Days*, p. 75.

89. Charles W. Allen, *From Fort Laramie to Wounded Knee*, ed. Richard E. Jensen (1939; rpt. Lincoln: University of Nebraska Press, 1997), pp. 149, 158.

90. Mooney, *Ghost-Dance*, pp. 843–844.

91. *Ibid.*

92. Vestal, *Sitting Bull*, p. 269.

93. Nancy Tystad Koupal, ed., *Our Landlady*, by L. Frank Baum (Lincoln: University of Nebraska Press, 1996), pp. 49, 77.

94. Koupal, quoting L. Frank Baum in *Our Landlady*, p. 49.

95. Utley, *Last Days*, p. 77.

96. Eastman, "Ghost Dance War," p. 29, quoted in Utley, *Last Days*, p. 77.

97. Allen, *From Fort Laramie to Wounded Knee*, p. 164.
98. *FLIN*, December 7, 1889, p. 315.
99. Utley, *Last Days*, pp. 79–80.

Chapter 4

1. *FLIN*, December 21, 1889, p. 363.
2. *FLIN*, December 14, 1889, pp. 330–331, 333; February 2, 1890, p. 3.
3. *Harper's Weekly*, February 15, 1890, p. 118.
4. *FLIN*, September 7, 1889, p. 71. Donald R. Kennon and Rebecca M. Rogers, *The Committee on Ways and Means a Bicentennial History 1789–1989,* H. Doc. 100–244, available at http://www.gpoaccess.gov/serialset/cdocuments/100-244/pdf/1865-1890.pdf, p. 185. *FLIN*, February 15, 1890, p. 26.
5. *Harper's Weekly*, January 4, 1890, p. 16. *FLIN*, February 1, 1890, p. 455.
6. B. Harrison to James G. Blaine, August, 29, 1890, series 2, reel 73, Benjamin Harrison Mss (hereafter BH Mss). On granger laws, see *FLIN*, June 7, 1890, p. 371. *FLIN*, May 24, 1890, p. 341. On antirailroad sentiment causing the bad market, see *FLIN*, July 12, 1890, p. 501. *FLIN*, February 1, 1890, p. 455. *FLIN*, February 22, 1890, p. 55.
7. *FLIN*, October 19, 1889, p. 191. *FLIN*, February 1, 1890, p. 455.
8. *Boston Globe*, January 1, 1890, pp. 1, 4. See also *New York Times*, March 11, 1889, p. 4; November 21, 1889, p. 2.
9. *Harper's Weekly*, January 18, 1890, p. 42.
10. *FLIN*, October 12, 1889, p. 167. *FLIN*, June 8, 1889, p. 303. *FLIN*, July 6, 1889, p. 371. *FLIN*, October 5, 1889, p. 143.
11. Senator Plumb, quoted in George B. Curtiss, Esq., *Protection and Prosperity: An Account of Tariff Legislation and its Effect in Europe and America* (New York: Pan-American Publishing Company, 1896), p. 627, on Google Books. *FLIN*, January 25, 1890, p. 439.
12. *FLIN*, February 8, 1890, p. 1; May 10, 1890, p. 294; May 3, 1890, p. 279; April 26, 1890, p. 259.
13. *FLIN*, March 22, 1890, p. 163. *FLIN*, March 29, 1890, p. 171. Harry J. Sievers, *Benjamin Harrison: Hoosier President* (Indianapolis: Bobbs-Merrill Company, Inc., 1968), pp. 52–53.
14. *FLIN*, April 5, 1890, col. B.
15. On heat in 1890, see *Harper's Weekly*, July 19, 1890, p. 558. *FLIN*, May 24, 1890, p. 331.
16. For charges of ballot box stuffing, see *FLIN*, January 25, 1890, p. 439.
17. Alfred S. Johnson, ed., *The Quarterly Register of Current History* (Detroit, Michigan: The Evening News Association, 1892), 1: 282, on Google Books. For the details of ballot reform, see Eldon Cobb Evans, *A History of the Australian Ballot System in the United States* (Chicago: The University of Chicago Press, 1917), on Google Books.
18. *Harper's Weekly*, January 25, 1890, p. 62.
19. *FLIN*, November 23, 1889, p. 275.
20. George Frisbie Hoar, *Autobiography of Seventy Years*, volume 2 (New York: Charles Scribner's Sons, 1905), p. 150.

21. *FLIN*, September 21, 1889, p. 103; November 9, 1889, p. 239; January 11, 1890, p. 407; January 18, 1890, p. 422. See also Albion W. Tourgee, "Our Semi-Citizens," *FLIN*, September 28, 1889, p. 122.

22. *FLIN*, February 2, 1890, pp. 2–3. Also *FLIN*, March 1, 1890, pp. 78–79.

23. *FLIN*, November 9, 1889, p. 252. *Harper's Weekly*, January 11, 1890, p. 18.

24. *FLIN*, February 2, 1890, pp. 2–3. Also *FLIN*, March 1, 1890, pp. 78–79. Also *FLIN*, April 12, 1890, p. 211. See also *Harper's Weekly*, January 11, 1890, p. 18.

25. *FLIN*, November 23, 1889, p. 275.

26. For terms of Lodge's bill, see *New York Times*, March 16, 1890, p. 12, and March 17, 1890, p. 4. *FLIN*, February 8, 1890, p. 2. See also *FLIN*, March 29, 1890, p. 171.

27. *FLIN*, March 29, 1890, p. 170. *New York Times*, April 10, 1890, p. 4. *FLIN*, March 29, 1890, p. 171.

28. *FLIN*, April 26, 1890, p. 255.

29. On Hoar's bill, see *New York Times*, April 25, 1890, p. 5.

30. On caucus and new bill, see *New York Times*, June 17, 1890, p. 1.

31. *New York Times*, April 29, 1890, p. 4; June 19, 1890, p. 4.

32. *FLIN*, June 28, 1890, p. 435. Henry Cabot Lodge, "Honest Elections," *FLIN*, March 3, 1890, p. 274.

33. Wyoming population figures in *New York Times*, November 7, 1900.

34. http://www.idahohistory.net/dateline.html, accessed October 27, 2009. *FLIN*, March 22, 1890, p. 147. Merle Wells, "Idaho's Season of Political Distress: An Unusual Path to Statehood," *Montana: The Magazine of Western History*, 37 (Autumn 1987): 58–67.

35. *Harper's Weekly*, January 11, 1890, p. 31. *FLIN*, May 3, 1890, p. 275.

36. *Boston Globe*, June 28, 1890, p. 10.

37. *FLIN*, April 12, 1890, p. 211; July 12, 1890, p. 487.

38. *Boston Globe*, June 28, 1890, p. 10; July 2, 1890, p. 6; July 3, 1890, p. 4. *New York Times*, June 28, 1890, p. 1.

39. *Harper's Weekly*, July 19, 1890, p. 551.

40. *FLIN*, November 16, 1889, p. 258.

41. *FLIN*, November 16, 1889, p. 258; November 23, 1889, p. 274.

42. For part of the history of the 1890 census, see: http://www.archives.gov/publications/prologue/1996/spring/1890-census-1.html. *New York Times*, April 30, 1890, p. 1. *FLIN*, July 12, 1890, p. 487; September 27, 1890, p. 113.

43. *FLIN*, May 31, 1890, p. 355. *FLIN* cover illustration of April 26, 1890, was William Tecumseh Sherman. See also April 26, 1890, pp. 257, 259 on U. S. Grant.

44. Richard B. Morris, ed., *Encyclopedia of American History* (New York: Harper & Brothers, 1953), p. 261. *FLIN*, May 17, 1890, p. 311.

45. *New York Times*, July 7, 1890, p. 4. *FLIN*, May 17, 1890, p. 311.

46. *FLIN*, July 19, 1890, p. 507.

47. *FLIN*, March 1, 1890, p. 79.

48. *FLIN*, June 21, 1890, p. 423; June 28, 1890, p. 440; September 6, 1890, p. 83. Joe J. Jordan, "History of Cape May Point—The Early Years," at www.cmpnj

.com/history.html, Cape May Point home page. *New York Times*, July 24, 1890, p. 3; August 17, 1890; October 20, 1890, p. 3.

49. Joke in Robert V. Hine and John Mack Faragher, *The American West: A New Interpretive History* (New Haven: Yale University Press, 2000), p. 340.

50. Richard White, "*It's Your Misfortune and None of My Own:" A New History of the American West* (Norman: University of Oklahoma Press, 1991), pp. 224–225. Sam S. Kepfield, "'They Were in Far Too Great Want': Federal Drought Relief to the Great Plains, 1887–1895," *South Dakota History*, 28 (Winter 1998): 244–270.

51. John D. Hicks, *The Populist Revolt* (1931; rpt. Lincoln: University of Nebraska Press, 1961), pp. 103–104.

52. Larry Remele, "'God Helps Those Who Help Themselves': The Farmers Alliance and Dakota Statehood," *Montana: The Magazine of Western History*, 37 (Autumn 1987): 22–33.

53. *FLIN*, February 22, 1890, p. 51; March 1, 1890, p. 79; May 31, 1890, pp. 350–351; June 28, 1890, p. 439; July 5, 1890, pp. 462–463.

54. Herbert S. Schell, *History of South Dakota* (Lincoln: University of Nebraska Press, 1961), p. 227.

55. *FLIN*, May 17, 1890, p. 315; July 26, 1890, p. 531; August 2, 1890, p. 551; August 16, 1890, p. 31; August 23, 1890, p. 43; September 13, 1890, p. 103.

56. *FLIN*, July 12, 1890, p. 487. Benjamin Butterworth in *FLIN*, August 9, 1890, pp. 566–567. *New York Times*, April 30, 1890, p. 1.

57. *New York Times*, March 3, 1890, p. 4. Sherman in *New York Times*, June 23, 1890, p. 4.

58. John Sherman, *Recollections of Forty Years in the House, Senate and Cabinet*, volume 2 (Chicago: The Werner Company, 1895), p. 1073. *New York Times*, April 1, 1890, p. 4; April 8, 1890, p. 4. *FLIN*, May 1890, p. 315.

59. *New York Times*, June 5, 1890, p. 5. Sherman, *Recollections*, 2: 1062–1069.

60. Sherman, *Recollections*, 2: 1062–1069.

61. *FLIN*, June 28, 1890, p. 435; October 4, 1890, p. 149.

62. *FLIN*, August 16, 1890, p. 23.

63. *FLIN*, August 23, 1890, p. 43.

64. *FLIN*, June 28, 1890, p. 435. See also *FLIN*, July 5, 1890, p. 467.

65. *FLIN*, September 13, 1890, p. 99. Headline of article is: "THE FARMERS' FAULT."

66. *FLIN*, June 14, 1890, p. 395; July 5, 1890, pp. 462–463.

67. *FLIN*, November 1, 1890, pp. 232–233.

68. *FLIN*, June 7, 1890, p. 369; July 5, 1890, p. 467, reprint from *Christian Advocate*.

69. *FLIN*, September 27, 1890, p. 135.

70. Resolution of the Council and House of Representatives of Oklahoma Territory, enclosed in letter from E. L. Gay to BH, September 6, 1890, series 2, BH Mss. C. Mckeever to Commanding General, Department of the Missouri, September 6, 1890, telegram, enclosed in letter of Redfield Proctor to E. W. Halford, series 2, BH Mss.

71. John M. C. Marble to Harrison, July 29, 1890, series 2, BH Mss. James A. Foster to Hon. H. T. Mitchner, forwarded to Harrison, August 31, 1890, series 2, BH Mss.

72. *FLIN*, November 15, 1890, p. 261. J. S. Runnells to E. W. Halford, October 3, 1890, series 2, BH Mss. Benjamin Harrison to Sallie H. Devin, October 2, 1890, series 1, BH Mss. T. N. Haskell to Harrison, September 30, 1890, series 2, BH Mss. See also Philip M. Crapo to BH, October 8, 1890, series 2, BH Mss. And A. O. [?] Dawes to E. W. Halford, October 8, 1890, series 2, BH Mss.

73. Kepfield, "Federal Drought Relief," pp. 244–270. *FLIN*, October 25, 1890, p. 201. *Boston Globe*, October 12, 1890, p. 1.

74. *FLIN*, April 19, 1890, pp. 230–231.

75. New York *Sun*, quoted in *FLIN*, July 26, 1890, p. 527. *FLIN*, April 5, 1890, p. 191.

76. *New York Times*, April 15, 1890, p. 4. *FLIN*, March 22, 1890, p. 151; April 5, 1890, p. 191.

77. *New York Times*, April 1, 1890, p. 1.

78. *New York Times*, April 1, 1890, pp. 1, 4.

79. *New York Times*, April 17, 1890, p. 5; April 25, 1890, p. 4.

80. *New York Times*, April 28, 1890, p. 1; May 3, 1890, p. 4; May 8, 1890, p. 1. St. Paul, Minnesota, *Pioneer Press*, quoted in *New York Times*, April 30, 1890, p. 4. *FLIN*, April 19, 1890, p. 239.

81. *New York Times*, May 8, 1890, p. 1. *FLIN*, May 24, 1890, p. 339.

82. *New York Times*, May 16, 1890, p. 5; May 22, 1890, p. 1.

83. *FLIN*, June 7, 1890, pp. 370–371. For a collection of quotations from other newspapers, see *New York Times*, May 12, 1890, p. 4.

84. *New York Times*, May 27, 1890, p. 1.

85. *New York Times*, July 15, 1890, p. 3. *Harper's Weekly*, August 2, 1890, p. 590.

86. *FLIN*, July 26, 1890, p. 527. *New York Times*, July 16, 1890, p. 4; July 17, 1890, p. 1. *Harper's Weekly*, August 16, 1890, p. 630.

87. *Harper's Weekly*, August 16, 1890, p. 630.

88. *New York Times*, August 16, 1890, p. 4.

89. *New York Times*, July 3, 1890, p. 1. *FLIN*, July 19, 1890, p. 511. *Harper's Weekly*, July 12, 1890, p. 535. *Harper's Weekly*, July 26, 1890, p. 574.

90. *Harper's Weekly*, July 12, 1890, p. 535.

91. *Harper's Weekly*, July 12, 1890, p. 534; August 30, 1890, p. 674.

92. *Harper's Weekly*, October 18, 1890, p. 803; November 8, 1890, p. 863.

93. *Harper's Weekly*, September 20, 1890, p. 730. See also *Harper's Weekly*, October 11, 1890, p. 786.

94. *New York Times*, August 23, 1890, p. 4.

95. *FLIN*, August 16, 1890, p. 23. On New York ballot law, see *New York Times*, October 15, 1891, p. 4.

96. *FLIN*, August 16, 1890, p. 27; September 20, 1890, p. 115.

97. *Harper's Weekly*, September 6, 1890, p. 694; October 4, 1890, p. 766.

98. *FLIN*, August 30, 1890, p. 63; September 27, 1890, p. 113. *Harper's Weekly*, August 30, 1890, pp. 674–675.

99. *New York Times*, October 28, 1890, p. 4.

100. *Boston Globe*, October 1, 1890, p. 4; *New York Times*, October 2, 1890, p. 1; September 30, 1890, p. 1. *FLIN*, October 11, 1890, p. 165; October 18, 1890, p. 185.

101. *Boston Globe*, October 2, 1890, p. 1. *New York Times*, October 1, 1890, p. 4.

102. *Harper's Weekly*, October 25, 1890, p. 822.

103. *FLIN*, October 25, 1890, p. 201.

104. Edward H. Ammidown, president of the American Protective Tariff League, November 12, 1890, to Benjamin Harrison, series 1, BH Mss.

105. *FLIN*, October 11, 1890, p. 179.

106. *FLIN*, October 18, 1890, p. 185.

107. *FLIN*, October 18, 1890, p. 195; October 25, 1890, pp. 201, 215; November 1, 1890, p. 235.

108. *FLIN*, October 4, 1890, p. 148; November 1, 1890, p. 221.

Chapter 5

1. Howard Roberts Lamar, *Dakota Territory, 1861–1889: A Study of Frontier Politics* (New Haven: Yale University Press, 1956), pp. 18–19.

2. On appointments to help election, see F. H. Doran to L. T. Michener, October 7, 1890, series 2, BH Mss, enclosed in L. T. Michener to E. W. Halford, October 10, 1890, series 1, BH Mss; and N. Portz to Harrison, October 8, 1890, series 2, BH Mss.

3. Doane Robinson, *A History of the Dakota or Sioux Indians* (South Dakota, 1904), p. 301. Welsh, "Murrain of Spoils," pp. 86–87. Jerry Green, ed., *After Wounded Knee: Correspondence of Major and Surgeon John Vance Lauderdale while Serving with the Army Occupying the Pine Ridge Indian Reservation, 1890–1891* (East Lansing: Michigan State University Press, 1996), p. 24.

4. *Daily Inter Ocean*, October 19, 1890, p. 30, from Rapid City *Republican*. Green, *After Wounded Knee*, p. 24.

5. Elaine Goodale Eastman, *Sister to the Sioux: The Memoirs of Elaine Goodale Eastman, 1885–91*, ed. by Kay Graber (Lincoln: University of Nebraska Press, 1978), p. 137.

6. James Mooney, *The Ghost-Dance Religion and Wounded Knee* (1896; rpt. New York: Dover Publications, Inc., 1973), pp. 820–821.

7. George E. Hyde, *A Sioux Chronicle* (1956; rpt. Norman: University of Oklahoma Press, 1993), pp. 243, 247, 250–251. James C. Olson, *Red Cloud and the Sioux Problem* (Lincoln: University of Nebraska Press, 1965), pp. 209, 250, 252, 260, 308.

8. Hyde, *Sioux Chronicle*, pp. 251–252. Mrs. Z. A. Parker, quoted in Mooney, *Ghost-Dance*, pp. 916–917. For a discussion of violence in the Ghost Dance, see Jeffrey Ostler, *The Plains Sioux and U.S. Colonialism from Lewis and Clark to Wounded Knee* (Cambridge University Press, 2004), pp. 255–263.

9. *Report of the Commissioner of Indian Affairs*, 1891, p. 124. P. F. Wells to James McLaughlin, October 19, 1890, in Stanley Vestal, *New Sources of Indian History* (Norman: University of Oklahoma Press, 1934), pp. 5–6.

10. P. F. Wells to James McLaughlin, October 19, 1890, in Vestal, *New Sources*, pp. 5–6.

11. Mooney, *Ghost-Dance*, p. 847. Hyde, *Sioux Chronicle*, p. 266n.

12. Hyde, *Sioux Chronicle*, p. 258. Mooney, *Ghost-Dance*, p. 848.

13. Perain P. Palmer to T. J. Morgan, October 29, 1890, in *Records of the Adjutant General's Office*, "Reports and Correspondence Relating to the Army Investigation of the Battle at Wounded Knee and to the Sioux Campaign of 1890–1891," microfilm M-983, NARA (hereafter RAGO).

14. Mooney, *Ghost-Dance*, p. 847.

15. James McLaughlin to T. J. Morgan, October 17, 1890, in *Annual Report of the Commissioner of Indian Affairs, for the Year 1891*, pp. 328–330.

16. Mooney, *Ghost-Dance*, p. 849.

17. Eastman, *Sister to the Sioux*, pp. 137–138. James McLaughlin to T. J. Morgan, October 17, 1890, in *Report of the Commissioner of Indian Affairs*, pp. 328–330.

18. *Daily Inter Ocean*, October 19, 1890, p. 30, from Rapid City *Republican*.

19. *Ibid.*

20. See T. J. Morgan to R. V. Belt, November 18, 1890, series 2, BH Mss. Robert M. Utley, *Last Days of the Sioux Nation* (New Haven: Yale University Press, 1963), pp. 103–105.

21. *New York Times*, October 15, 1890, p. 2; October 22, 1890, p. 2. Robert Wooster, *Nelson A. Miles and the Twilight of the Frontier Army* (Lincoln: University of Nebraska Press, 1993), pp. 176–177.

22. Jeffrey Ostler, "Conquest and the State: Why the United States Employed Massive Military Force to Suppress the Lakota Ghost Dance," *Pacific Historical Review*, 65 (May 1996): 233. Royer to Belt, October 30, 1890, RAGO.

23. Wooster, *Miles*, p. 177. Hyde, *Sioux Chronicle*, p. 254. Royer to Belt, October 30, 1890, RAGO. Royer to Morgan, November 8, 1890, RAGO, recounts the meeting again.

24. Ostler, "Conquest and the State," p. 233. Royer to Belt, October 30, 1890, RAGO.

25. Royer to Morgan, November 8, 1890, RAGO.

26. Royer to Belt, October 30, 1890, RAGO.

27. William T. Hagan, *The Indian Rights Association: The Herbert Welsh Years, 1882–1904* (Tucson: The University of Arizona Press, 1985), pp. 113–114. *Washington Post*, August 28, 1890, p. 6. On Wright's call to Washington, see William S. E. Coleman, *Voices of Wounded Knee* (Lincoln: University of Nebraska Press, 2000), p. 55.

28. Reynolds was from Hagerstown, Indiana. His politics show up in Charles Kettleborough, *Constitution Making in Indiana*, volume 2, 1815–1916 (Indianapolis: Indiana Historical Commission, 1916), p. 277, on Google Books. E. B. Reynolds to Belt, November 2, 1890, RAGO.

29. E. B. Reynolds to Belt, November 2, 1890, RAGO.

30. *Ibid.*

31. *Ibid.* Mooney, *Ghost-Dance*, pp. 849, 788–789.

32. Mooney, *Ghost-Dance*, pp. 849, 788–789, 916.

33. *FLIN*, October 25, 1890, p. 205.

34. Harrison to Secretary of War, October 31, 1890, series 1, BH Mss. Sam. Breck, Asst. Adjutant General to Commanding General, Division Missouri, October 31, 1890, RAGO.

35. Ostler, "Conquest and the State," pp. 217–248. R. Williams, Assistant Adjutant General to Miles, November 16, RAGO. Utley, *Last Days*, p. 110.

36. Utley, *Last Days*, p. 110.

37. *FLIN*, August, 9, 1890, p. 567; August 16, 1890, p. 27; August 30, 1890, p. 71; October 4, 1890, p. 148. George W. Steele, Governor of Oklahoma, to Benjamin Harrison, November 6, 1890, in series 1, BH Mss. On the strategy of emphasizing to Westerners what the administration could offer them, see also *FLIN*, October 18, 1890, p. 185. R. B. Harrison to E. W. Halford, October 14, 1890, series 1, BH Mss.

38. *FLIN*, September 27, 1890, p. 137.

39. *FLIN*, November 15, 1890, p. 262.

40. *Harper's Weekly*, October 18, 1890, p. 802; November 1, 1890, p. 842; November 15, 1890, p. 886. Elliott F. Shepard to E. W. Halford, November, 10, 1890, series 1, BH Mss.

41. *FLIN*, November 22, 1890, p. 278. Mr. Tibbott's diary, recounting walk and conversation with Harrison, November 8, in series 1, BH Mss. Benjamin Harrison to Hon. R. S. Taylor, November 29, 1890, series 1, BH Mss.

42. *FLIN*, November 8, 1890, pp. 240, 255; November 15, 1890, pp. 260–261, 273.

43. Frederick Douglass blamed the defeat largely on the lack of the election bill (*FLIN*, November 29, 1890, p. 302). *FLIN*, November 22, 1890, p. 279.

44. *FLIN*, November 22, 1890, p. 279.

45. *FLIN*, November 22, 1890, p. 278. *Harper's Weekly*, November 29, 1890, pp. 934–935.

46. *Harper's Weekly*, November 29, 1890, pp. 934–935.

47. *Harper's Weekly*, November 29, 1890, pp. 934–935. *FLIN*, November 29, 1890, p. 307.

48. *FLIN*, November 22, 1890, pp. 278–279. Benjamin Harrison to "Howard," November 17, 1890, series 1, BH Mss.

49. *FLIN*, November 15, 1890, p. 261. C. W. Ernst to George Frisbie Hoar, December 4, 1890, in George Frisbie Hoar Mss, Massachusetts Historical Society.

50. *FLIN*, November 15, 1890, p. 260; December 6, 1890, pp. 330–331.

51. *New York Times*, November 7, 1890, p. 1.

52. *New York Times*, November 7, 1890, p. 1; November 29, 1890, p. 4.

53. Herbert S. Schell, *History of South Dakota* (Lincoln: University of Nebraska Press, 1961), p. 228.

54. Robinson, *History of South Dakota*, pp. 296–297. See also R. F. Pettigrew, *Imperial Washington: The Story of American Public Life from 1870 to 1920* (Chicago: Charles H. Kerr & Company Co-Operative, 1922), pp. 150–162. *New York Times*, November 5, 1890, p. 5; November 6, 1890, p. 5; November 9, 1890, p. 1.

55. *New York Times*, November 13, 1890, p. 5; November 30, 1890, p. 3.

56. Perain P. Palmer to T. J. Morgan, November 4, 1890, and Perain P. Palmer to Belt, November 5, 1890, RAGO.

57. Visit was on November 7. Perain P. Palmer to T. J. Morgan, November 10, 1890, RAGO.

58. Royer to Belt, October 30, 1890, RAGO.

59. Royer to Belt, October 30, 1890; Royer to Noble, in Belt to Noble, November 12, 1890; Royer to Morgan, November 8, 1890; Noble to Harrison, November 7, 1890, all in RAGO.

60. Richard E. Jensen, ed., *The Indian Interviews of Eli S. Ricker, 1903–1919* (Lincoln: University of Nebraska Press, 2005), p. 52. Royer to Morgan, November 8, 1890, RAGO.

61. Royer to Commissioner of Indian Affairs, November 11, 1890; Belt to Royer, November 12, 1890; Royer to Belt, November 12, 1890; Belt to Royer, November 12, 1890, all in RAGO.

62. Raymond Wilson, "The Writings of Ohiyesa—Charles Alexander Eastman, M.D., Santee Sioux," *South Dakota History*, 6 (Winter 1975): 58.

63. Charles A. Eastman, *From the Deep Woods to Civilization: Chapters in the Autobiography of an Indian* (1916; rpt. Lincoln: University of Nebraska Press, 1977), pp. 76–87.

64. *Ibid.*

65. *Ibid.*, pp. 84–85.

66. *Ibid.*, pp. 84–91.

67. Donald B. Connelly, *John M. Schofield and the Politics of Generalship* (Chapel Hill: University of North Carolina Press, 2006), pp. 214–218, 301–306.

68. "102 Sioux Indians"—led by Hollow Horn Bear—to Great Father, November 6, 1890, RAGO.

69. C. A. Earnest to Bvt. Lt. Col. M. V. Sheridan, November 12, 1890, confidential, series 1, BH Mss.

70. *Ibid.*

71. *Ibid.*

72. Royer to Belt, November 13, 1890, RAGO.

73. Hyde, *Sioux Chronicle*, pp. 263–264; Eastman, *Deep Woods to Civilization*, pp. 93–95. Royer to Belt, November 13, 1890, RAGO.

74. Eastman, *Deep Woods to Civilization*, pp. 94–95.

75. *Ibid.*, pp. 95–96.

76. *Ibid.*, pp. 95–98.

77. Royer to Belt, November 13, 1890, RAGO.

78. Noble to Harrison, November 7, 1890, RAGO.

79. Belt to Noble, November 8, 1890, RAGO.

80. Palmer to Morgan, November 10, 1890; Belt to Noble, November 14, 1890; Noble to Proctor, November 15, 1890, RAGO.

81. Belt to Noble, November 12, 1890; Belt to Noble, November 13, 1890, RAGO.

82. Two communications from George Chandler, Acting Commissioner of Indian Affairs to Benjamin Harrison, November 13, 1890, RAGO.

83. Ostler, "Conquest and the State," pp. 217–248. J. M. Schofield to Miles, November 13, 1890, RAGO.

84. Connelly, *Schofield*, pp. 214–218, 301–306.

85. J. M. Schofield to Miles, November 13, 1890, RAGO. Harrison to Secretary of War, November 13, 1890, series 1, BH Mss.

86. Harrison to Secretary of the Interior, November 13, 1890, series 1, BH Mss. Mooney, *Ghost-Dance*, p. 850.

87. Miles to Schofield, November 14, 1890, series 2, BH Mss.

88. *Ibid.*

89. R. Williams, Assistant Adjutant General to Miles, November 16, 1890, containing telegram from Ruger, RAGO.

90. *Ibid.*

91. Royer to Commissioner of Indian Affairs, November 15, 1890, in J. M. Schofield to Major General Miles, series 1, BH Mss. Schofield to Miles, November 17, 1890, RAGO.

92. Telegrams of Royer in John R. Brooke to Assistant Adjutant General, November 16, 1890, RAGO.

93. *Ibid.*

94. Telegrams, letter, and endorsements in John R. Brooke to Assistant Adjutant General, November 16, 1890, RAGO.

95. Telegrams, letter, and endorsements in John R. Brooke to Assistant Adjutant General, November 16, 1890, RAGO. J. M. Schofield to Major General Miles, series 1, BH Mss.

96. R. Williams to Commanding General Department Platte, and two telegrams to Commanding General Department Dakota, all November 17, 1890, RAGO.

97. See, for example, Commercial Club of Albuquerque to Benjamin Harrison, December 10, 1890, RAGO.

Chapter 6

1. Donald B. Connelly, *John M. Schofield and the Politics of Generalship* (Chapel Hill: University of North Carolina Press, 2006), pp. 214–218, 301–306.

2. Robert Wooster, *Nelson A. Miles and the Twilight of the Frontier Army* (Lincoln: University of Nebraska Press, 1993), p. 90.

3. *New York Times*, February 1, 1891, p. 17. Report on Population of the United States at the Eleventh Census: 1890 (Washington, D.C.: GPO, 1895), part 1, p. xxxiv, at http://www2.census.gov/prod2/decennial/documents/1890a_v1-01.pdf.

4. *FLIN*, March 1, 1890, p. 78.

5. Richard Morris, ed., *Encyclopedia of American History* (New York: Harper & Brothers, 1953), p. 283. *FLIN*, April 13, 1889, p. 158.

6. *Harper's Weekly*, February 8, 1890, pp. 98–99. *FLIN*, April 13, 1889, p. 150; May 24, 1890, p. 335.

7. Grover Cleveland, Message to Congress, December 3, 1888, at John T. Woolley and Gerhard Peters, The American Presidency Project [online], Santa Barbara, California, available at http://www.presidency.ucsb.edu/ws/?pid=29529. *FLIN*, November 9, 1889, p. 239.

8. *FLIN*, December 14, 1889, p. 330; December 21, 1889, p. 347.

9. Charles A. Eastman, *From the Deep Woods to Civilization: Chapters in the Autobiography of an Indian* (1916; rpt. Lincoln: University of Nebraska Press, 1977), pp. 101–102.

10. Robert M. Utley, *Last Days of the Sioux Nation* (New Haven: Yale University Press, 1963), pp. 113–114. On caliber of shells, see Document 641 in RAGO.

11. Eastman, *Deep Woods to Civilization*, p. 101.

12. Jensen, in Charles W. Allen, *From Fort Laramie to Wounded Knee*, ed. Richard E. Jensen (1939; rpt. Lincoln: University of Nebraska Press, 1997), pp. 254–255, note 9. Elaine Goodale Eastman, *Sister to the Sioux: The Memoirs of Elaine Goodale Eastman, 1885–91*, ed. Kay Graber (Lincoln: University of Nebraska Press, 1978), p. 156. Eastman, *Deep Woods to Civilization*, p. 103. George E. Hyde, *A Sioux Chronicle* (1956; rpt. Norman: University of Oklahoma Press, 1993), p. 265. Eastman, *Deep Woods to Civilization*, p. 103.

13. Hyde, *Sioux Chronicle*, pp. 265, 272. I thank Dr. Walther T. Weylman for suggesting the cause of Red Cloud's poor vision.

14. *Ibid.*, p. 268.

15. Eastman, *Sister to the Sioux*, p. 151.

16. Allen, *From Fort Laramie to Wounded Knee*, pp. 167–174.

17. Hyde, *Sioux Chronicle*, pp. 265–266.

18. Richard Jensen, et al., *Eyewitness at Wounded Knee* (Lincoln: University of Nebraska Press, 1991), p. 29. Miles to Adjutant General, November 26, 1890, Chicago, RAGO. *Report* (1891), p. 128, and Turning Hawk, "Account," February 11, 1891, in *Report* (1891), p. 179. Hyde, *Sioux Chronicle*, p. 269. Miles to Adjutant General, November 27, 1890, RAGO. Utley, *Last Days*, p. 118.

19. Jeffrey Ostler, "Conquest and the State: Why the United States Employed Massive Military Force to Suppress the Lakota Ghost Dance," *Pacific Historical Review*, 65 (May 1996): 220–225.

20. A. C. Mellette to Miles, November 26, 1890; Miles to Adjutant General, November 26, 1890, containing A. C. Mellette to Miles, November 26, 1890, RAGO.

21. A. A. McFadon to Proctor, November 26, 1890, RAGO. Citizens' meeting is on November 25. Miles to Adjutant General, December 11, 1890, 3rd endorsement of A. A. McFadon letter, RAGO.

22. Williams to Brooke, by Miles, November 18, 1890, RAGO.

23. Nelson A. Miles to Adjutant General, November 24, 1890, series 1, BH Mss.

24. John W. Noble to E. W. Halford, November 25, 1890, series 1, BH Mss.

25. Noble to Proctor, November 25, 1890, RAGO. R. V. Belt to the Secretary of the Interior [John W. Noble], November 25, 1890, series 1, BH Mss.

26. R. V. Belt to the Secretary of the Interior [John W. Noble], November 25, 1890, series 1, BH Mss.

27. Noble to Proctor, November 25, 1890, RAGO. R. V. Belt to the Secretary of the Interior [John W. Noble], November 25, 1890, series 1, BH Mss.

28. Belt to Noble, November 21, 1890; Belt to Noble, November 22, 1890; Belt to Noble, November 22, 1890, with A. P. Dixon's telegram; Noble to Proctor, November 22, 1890, RAGO.

29. Schofield to Miles, November 24, 1890, RAGO.

30. *Ibid.*

31. Utley, *Last Days*, pp. 118–119. Miles to Adjutant General, November 27, 1890, RAGO. Jensen, et al., *Eyewitness at Wounded Knee*, p. 31.

32. Allen, *From Fort Laramie to Wounded Knee*, pp. 153, 168, and note 14, p. 256.

33. *New York Times*, October 28, 1899, p. 7. Charles L. Kenner, *Buffalo Soldiers: Officers of the Ninth Cavalry, 1867–1898* (Norman: University of Oklahoma Press, 1999), pp. 117–137. Utley, *Last Days*, p. 118.

34. Utley, *Last Days*, p. 202.

35. William Fitch Kelley, *Pine Ridge 1890: An Eye Witness Account of the Events Surrounding the Fighting at Wounded Knee*, ed. and compiled by Alexander Kelley and Pierre Bovis (San Francisco: Pierre Bovis, 1971), pp. 52–53.

36. Kelley, *Pine Ridge*, p. 56. *Washington Post*, November 30, 1890, p. 1. V. T. McGillycuddy on the Ghost Dance, in Stanley Vestal, *New Sources of Indian History* (Norman: University of Oklahoma Press, 1934), pp. 81–90.

37. Kelley, *Pine Ridge*, p. 53.

38. Eastman, *Sister to the Sioux*, p. 152.

39. Utley, *Last Days*, pp. 118–119, 121. James H. Cook, *Fifty Years on the Old Frontier as Cowboy, Hunter, Guide, Scout, and Ranchman* (New Haven: Yale University Press, 1923), pp. 201–202, 240–242. Allen, *From Fort Laramie to Wounded Knee*, p. 174. Jensen, et al., *Eyewitness at Wounded Knee*, p. 31.

40. Allen, *From Fort Laramie to Wounded Knee*, p. 173. Also V. T. McGillycuddy on the Ghost Dance, in Vestal, *New Sources*, pp. 81–90.

41. Jensen, in Allen, *From Fort Laramie to Wounded Knee*, p. 259, note 4. L. G. Moses, "Wild West Shows, Reformers, and the Image of the American Indian, 1887–1914," *South Dakota History*, 14 (Fall 1984): 193–221.

42. Allen, *From Fort Laramie to Wounded Knee*, p. 169.

43. Miles to Adjutant General, November 26, 1890; Miles to Adjutant General, November 27, 1890, RAGO.

44. Allen, *From Fort Laramie to Wounded Knee*, pp. 151, 171.

45. Allen, *From Fort Laramie to Wounded Knee*, p. 176. Eastman, *Sister to the Sioux*, p. 153. Kelley, *Pine Ridge*, pp. 43, 47, 94.

46. See images in Jensen, et al., *Eyewitness at Wounded Knee*, p. 46. Allen, *From Fort Laramie to Wounded Knee*, pp. 167, 171, 178–181.

47. Allen, *From Fort Laramie to Wounded Knee*, p. 178. George R. Kolbenschlag, *A Whirlwind Passes: News Correspondents and the Sioux Indian Disturbances of 1890–1891* (Vermillion, South Dakota: University of South Dakota Press, 1990), p. 19. *Chicago Herald*, November 20, 1890, p. 1.

48. W. A. Birdsall, in Richard E. Jensen, ed., *The Settler and Soldiers Interviews of Eli S. Ricker, 1903–1919* (Lincoln: University of Nebraska Press, 2005), p. 46.

49. Utley, *Last Days*, pp. 121–122.

50. *Ibid.*

51. Eastman, *Sister to the Sioux*, pp. 142, 148.

52. Thomas R. Buecker, ed., "'The even tenor of our way is pursued undisturbed': Henry P. Smith's Diary during the Ghost Dance Movement, 1890–1891," *South Dakota History*, 34 (Fall 2004): 197–236.

53. 102 Sioux Indians to Great Father, November 6, 1890, RAGO. Noble to Harrison, November 29, 1890, series 1, BH Mss. *Boston Globe*, November 20, 1890, p. 1. *Boston Globe*, November 29, 1890, p. 7.

54. *Boston Globe*, November 27, 1890, p. 6. *Harper's Weekly*, November 22, 1890, p. 902.

55. *Boston Globe*, November 27, 1890, p. 6; November 29, 1890, p. 7.

56. *FLIN*, November 22, 1890, p. 280.

57. Stanley Vestal, *Sitting Bull: Champion of the Sioux* (1932; rpt., Norman: University of Oklahoma Press, 1898), p. 272. James McLaughlin, *My Friend the Indian* (Boston: Houghton, Mifflin Company, 1910), pp. 265–267, on Google Books. Vestal, *Sitting Bull*, p. 270 says 200, with 50 warriors, but 300 run to Big Foot. Calculation of one-quarter comes from formula used repeatedly in army reports.

58. *Washington Evening Star*, November 21, 1890, quoted in Wooster, *Miles*, pp. 181–182.

59. See C. McKeever, Acting Adjutant General to Commanding General, Division Missouri, November 1, 1890, RAGO. Wooster, *Miles*, pp. 191–192.

60. R. V. Belt to the Secretary of the Interior [John W. Noble], November 27, 1890, series 1, BH Mss.

61. *Ibid.*

62. Noble to Harrison, November 29, 1890, series 1, BH Mss.

63. Belt to Noble, November 28, 1890, series 1, BH Mss.

64. *Ibid.*

65. Noble to Harrison, November 29, 1890, series 1, BH Mss.

66. James P. Boyd, *Recent Indian Wars* (Philadelphia: Publishers Union, 1892), pp. 236–239, on Google Books. Hyde, *Sioux Chronicle*, pp. 273–275. Utley, *Last Days*, pp. 137–140.

67. Boyd, *Indian Wars*, pp. 206–210. Hyde, *Sioux Chronicle*, pp. 276–277.

68. Boyd, *Indian Wars*, p. 240. *Atlanta Constitution*, December 13, 1890, p. 1. Kelley, *Pine Ridge*, pp. 121–122.

69. Wooster, *Miles*, pp. 180–181.

70. Utley, *Last Days*, pp. 123–124. Wooster, *Miles*, p. 181.

71. McLaughlin to Commissioner of Indian Affairs, November 28, 1890, series 1, BH Mss. McLaughlin to T. J. Morgan, November 29, 1890, series 1, BH Mss.

72. Redfield Proctor to Major General Miles, November 28, 1890, series 1, BH Mss.

73. Utley, *Last Days*, pp. 125–126.

74. Miles to Adjutant General, November 28, 1890, RAGO.

75. Miles to Adjutant General, November 28, 1890, RAGO. Hawley, in William S. E. Coleman, *Voices of Wounded Knee* (Lincoln: University of Nebraska Press, 2000), p. 137.

76. R. Williams to Proctor, November 29, 1890, RAGO. *Washington Post*, November 26, 1890, p. 1; November 30, 1890, p. 1. *New York Times*, December 2, 1890, p. 2.

77. *Harper's Weekly*, November 29, 1890, pp. 922–923; December 6, 1890, pp. 946–947.

78. *Harper's Weekly*, December 13, 1890, p. 967. *New York Tribune*, December 1, 1890, p. 7; December 14, 1890, p. 6.

79. Proctor to Miles, December 1, 1890, RAGO. *Washington Post*, December 5, 1890, p. 1.

80. Noble to Harrison, November 29, 1890, series 1, BH Mss. Noble to Commissioner of Indian Affairs, December 1, 1890, RAGO.

81. Belt to Noble, December 2, 1890, enclosing letter of November 28, 1890, from A. T. Lea, series 1, BH Mss.

82. *Ibid.*

83. *Harper's Weekly*, December 6, 1890, p. 942.

84. *New York Times*, December 4, 1890, p. 5. W. R. Bush of Lake City, Florida, November 12, 1890, to M. S. Quay (obviously forwarded to Hoar), George Frisbee Hoar Mss, carton 47, Massachusetts Historical Society. *Washington Post*, December 1, 1890, p. 1. *Congressional Record*, 51st Congress, 2nd sess., pp. 45, 128–129.

85. *Congressional Record*, 51st Congress, 2nd sess., p. 45. *New York Times*, December 4. *Washington Post*, December 4, 1890, p. 2.

86. *Congressional Record*, 51st Congress, 2nd sess., p. 47.

87. *Congressional Record*, 51st Congress, 2nd sess., p. 47. *New York Times*, November 11, 1890, p. 1. *Congressional Record*, 51st Congress, 2nd sess., pp. 45–48.

88. William S. E. Coleman, *Voices of Wounded Knee* (Lincoln: University of Nebraska Press, 2000), pp. 130–139. *New York Times*, December 4, 1890. *Washington Post*, December 4, 1890, p. 2. See, for example, *New York World*, December 3, 1890, in Coleman, *Voices*, p. 146.

89. *Congressional Record*, 51st Congress, 2nd sess., pp. 45, 68–71.

90. Garnett, in Richard E. Jensen, ed., *The Indian Interviews of Eli S. Ricker, 1903–1919* (Lincoln: University of Nebraska Press, 2005), p. 98. *Washington Post*, December 9, 1890, p. 1. Congressional Record, 51st Congress, 2nd sess., p. 68.

91. *Congressional Record*, 51st Congress, 2nd sess., p. 197.

92. *Congressional Record*, 51st Congress, 2nd sess., pp. 198, 200.

93. William T. Hagan, *The Indian Rights Association: The Herbert Welsh Years, 1882–1904* (Tucson: The University of Arizona Press, 1985), pp. 100–101, 117–118. W. H. Hare to Herbert Welsh, December 12, 1890, series 1, BH Mss. T. J. Morgan to E. W. Halford, December 16, 1890, series 1, BH Mss.

94. Eastman, *Sister to the Sioux*, pp. 152–153, 156–160.

95. Eastman, *Sister to the Sioux*, pp. 169–170, 172.

96. Miles to Adjutant general, December 10, 1890, RAGO. Utley, *Last Days*, p. 173.

97. Sumner Report, February 3, 1891, in *Annual Report of the Secretary of War* (1891), 1: 223–224, in Utley, *Last Days*, p. 174. Miles to Adjutant General, December 10, 1890, RAGO.

98. Letter from Georgia to Sitting Bull, December 8, 1890, in Vestal, *New Sources*, pp. 76–77. *FLIN*, December 13, 1890, p. 351.

99. See Belt to McLaughlin, December 5, 1890, series 1, BH Mss, ordering him not to arrest anyone without orders from the army.

100. Signed by H. C. Corbin, Assistant Adjutant General, in the absence of the Division Commander signs for Miles, a letter to the Adjutant General. Message of

December 16 sent on December 24 from Noble to Harrison, series 1, BH Mss. James Mooney, *The Ghost-Dance Religion and Wounded Knee* (1896; rpt. New York: Dover Publications, Inc., 1973), p. 855.

101. Mooney, *Ghost-Dance*, p. 855.

102. Noble to Harrison, December 24, 1890, series 1, BH Mss. John M. Carignan to McLaughlin, from Grand River, December 14, 1890, series 1, BH Mss.

103. John M. Carignan to McLaughlin, from Grand River, December 14, 1890, series 1, BH Mss.

104. The following account comes from "The Arrest and Killing of Sitting Bull, Told by John Loneman, one of the Indian Police ordered to arrest the Chief. Translated and Recorded by his relative, Robert P. Higheagle," in Vestal, *New Sources*, pp. 45–55.

105. On Sitting Bull's legendary hospitality, see "'Note on Crowfoot' by Robert P. Higheagle," in Vestal, *New Sources*, pp. 55–56.

106. "'Note on Crowfoot' by Robert P. Higheagle," in Vestal, *New Sources*, pp. 55–56.

107. "The Arrest and Killing of Sitting Bull, Told by John Loneman," in Vestal, *New Sources*, pp. 45–55. An official account of the fight is in McLaughlin to T. J. Morgan, December 16, 1890, series 1, BH Mss.

108. McLaughlin to T. J. Morgan, December 16, 1890, series 1, BH Mss.

109. "The Arrest and Killing of Sitting Bull, Told by John Loneman," in Vestal, *New Sources*, pp. 45–55.

Chapter 7

1. Robert M. Utley, *Last Days of the Sioux Nation* (New Haven: Yale University Press, 1963), p. 174. Joseph Horn Cloud, in Richard E. Jensen, ed., *The Indian Interviews of Eli S. Ricker, 1903–1919* (Lincoln: University of Nebraska Press, 2005), p. 195.

2. Joseph Horn Cloud, *Ricker Indian Interviews*, pp. 192–193.

3. Sumner, in *Report of the Secretary of War, 1891*, pp. 223–224.

4. Barber to Sumner, December 16, 1890, *Report,* p. 229.

5. Sumner to Miles, December 18, 1890, *Report*, p. 229. Sumner to Ruger, Miles, and Carr, all December 19, 1890, Sumner, *Report*, pp. 229–231.

6. Joseph Horn Cloud, *Ricker Indian Interviews*, pp. 192–193. Dewey Beard, *Ricker Indian Interviews*, pp. 209–211. Utley, *Last Days*, p. 177.

7. Joseph Horn Cloud, *Ricker Indian Interviews*, pp. 192–193. Dewey Beard, *Ricker Indian Interviews*, pp. 209–211. Utley, *Last Days*, p. 177.

8. Joseph Horn Cloud, *Ricker Indian Interviews*, pp. 192–193. Dewey Beard, *Ricker Indian Interviews*, pp. 209–211. Utley, *Last Days*, p. 177. Numbers of refugees in Miles to Merriam, December 24, 1890, *Report*, p. 209.

9. *Report*, pp. 207–209. Utley, *Last Days*, pp. 176–179.

10. Sumner, *Report*, p. 224. Jeffrey Ostler, *The Plains Sioux and U.S. Colonialism from Lewis and Clark to Wounded Knee* (Cambridge University Press, 2004), pp. 326–327.

11. Sumner, *Report*, p. 224. Ostler, *Plains Sioux*, pp. 326–327.

12. Ostler, *Plains Sioux*, pp. 326–327.

13. Beard, *Ricker Indian Interviews*, pp. 211–212. Horn Cloud, *Ricker Indian Interviews*, pp. 193–194. Sumner, *Report*, pp. 224–225; Sumner to Miles, December 22, 1890, *Report,* p. 233.

14. Beard, *Ricker Indian Interviews*, pp. 211–212. Horn Cloud, *Ricker Indian Interviews*, pp. 193–194.

15. Sumner, *Report*, pp. 224–225.

16. Sumner, *Report*, pp. 225.

17. Sumner, *Report*, p. 112. Sumner to Miles, December 22, 1890, *Report*, p. 233.

18. Miles to Sumner, December 22, 1890, *Report*, p. 233.

19. Jensen, in Charles W. Allen, *From Fort Laramie to Wounded Knee*, ed. Richard E. Jensen (1939; rpt. Lincoln: University of Nebraska Press, 1997), p. 262, note 2. Horn Cloud, *Ricker Indian Interviews*, pp. 194–195. Beard, *Ricker Indian Interviews*, pp. 212–213. Sumner, *Report*, p. 226. Dunn, *Report*, pp. 235–236.

20. Jensen, in Allen, *From Fort Laramie to Wounded Knee*, p. 262, note 2. Horn Cloud, *Ricker Indian Interviews*, pp. 194–195. Beard, *Ricker Indian Interviews*, pp. 212–213. Dunn, *Report*, pp. 235–236.

21. Jensen, in Allen, *From Fort Laramie*, p. 262, note 2. Horn Cloud, *Ricker Indian Interviews*, pp. 194–195. Beard, *Ricker Indian Interviews*, pp. 212–213. Dunn, *Report*, pp. 235–236. Felix Benoit, *Report*, p. 237.

22. Horn Cloud, *Ricker Indian Interviews*, p. 195. Beard, *Ricker Indian Interviews*, p. 213. Utley, *Last Days,* pp. 183–184. Horn Cloud, *Ricker Indian Interviews*, p. 195. Benoit, *Report*, pp. 237–238.

23. Benoit, *Report*, pp. 237–238.

24. Sumner to E. A. Carr, December 23, 1890, *Report*, p. 234.

25. James White, in Richard E. Jensen, ed., *The Settler and Soldiers Interviews of Eli S. Ricker, 1903–1919* (Lincoln: University of Nebraska Press, 2005), pp. 50–51.

26. Ostler, *Plains Sioux*, pp. 331–332.

27. *Washington Post*, December 12, 1890, p. 1. *Congressional Record*, 51st Congress, 2nd sess., pp. 797–798. William S. E. Coleman, *Voices of Wounded Knee* (Lincoln: University of Nebraska Press, 2000), p. 233.

28. Robert Wooster, *Nelson A. Miles and the Twilight of the Frontier Army* (Lincoln: University of Nebraska Press, 1993), p. 185. Miles to Adjutant General, December 11, 1890; Miles to Adjutant General, December 12, 1890, RAGO.

29. Miles to Dawes, December 19, 1890, in Miles, *Report*, p. 149.

30. Miles to Schofield, December 19, 1890, RAGO. Also *Report*, p. 149.

31. Miles to Adjutant General, December 11, 1890, endorsed by John Schofield, December 13, 1890, in RAGO.

32. Harrison notes, December 1890, series 1, BH Mss.

33. *FLIN*, December 20, 1890, p. 367.

34. *FLIN*, January 3, 1891, p. 407. *Washington Post*, December 16, 1890, p. 1; December 17, 1890, p. 4.

35. Horn Cloud, *Ricker Indian Interviews*, pp. 195–196. Ostler, *Plains Sioux*, p. 330. Utley, *Last Days*, pp. 189–191.

36. Horn Cloud, *Ricker Indian Interviews*, p. 195. Dewey Beard, *Ricker Indian Interviews*, pp. 214–215. Ostler, *Plains Sioux*, p. 330. Utley, *Last Days*, pp. 189–191.

37. Utley, *Last Days*, p. 192.

38. Utley, *Last Days*, p. 193.

39. Utley, *Last Days*, p. 193.

40. Horn Cloud, *Ricker Indian Interviews*, p. 196.

41. Beard, *Ricker Indian Interviews*, p. 216.

42. Nelson Miles and John Brooke correspondence, December 28, 1890, in Brooke Testimony, RAGO.

43. *Ibid.*

44. *Ibid.*

45. McFarland, *Ricker Settler Interviews*, p. 2. William Fitch Kelley, *Pine Ridge 1890: An Eye Witness Account of the Events Surrounding the Fighting at Wounded Knee*, ed. and compiled by Alexander Kelley and Pierre Bovis (San Francisco: Pierre Bovis, 1971), p. 185. Utley, *Last Days*, p. 198. For annotated aerial maps, see William B. Thomasson, "Images of Wounded Knee (they speak for themselves)," November 8, 2007, to February 24, 2008, http://hoist.hrtc.net/~wbt/wounded knee.htm.

46. Utley, *Last Days*, p. 198.

47. McFarland, *Ricker Settler Interviews*, p. 16.

48. Utley, *Last Days*, p. 202. William Peano, *Ricker Indian Interviews*, pp. 233–234.

49. McFarland, *Ricker Settler Interviews*, p. 2. Dewey Beard, *Ricker Indian Interviews*, p. 217.

50. Kocer, *Ricker Settler Interviews*, p. 40. Allen, *From Fort Laramie to Wounded Knee*, p. 191. Utley, *Last Days*, pp. 201–202.

51. Utley, *Last Days*, p. 204.

52. Utley, *Last Days*, pp. 204–205. Beard, *Ricker Indian Interviews*, p. 218.

53. Allen, *Fort Laramie to Wounded Knee*, p. 193.

54. Allen, *Ricker Settler Interviews*, p. 14. Meded Swigert, *Ricker Settler Interviews*, p. 17.

55. Allen, *Ricker Settler Interviews*, pp. 13–14. George Sword, Account, in *Annual Report of the Commissioner of Indian Affairs* (1891), p. 180.

56. Allen, *From Fort Laramie to Wounded Knee*, pp. 194–195. Horn Cloud, *Ricker Indian Interviews*, p. 199.

57. Wells, *Ricker Indian Interviews*, pp. 121–122, 155.

58. Utley, *Last Days*, p. 208. Horn Cloud, *Ricker Indian Interviews*, p. 199.

59. Ostler, *Plains Sioux*, p. 340. Allen, *From Fort Laramie to Wounded Knee*, p. 195.

60. J. W. Butler, *Ricker Settler Interviews*, p. 23.

61. Allen, *From Fort Laramie to Wounded Knee*, p. 195. Utley, *Last Days*, pp. 209–210. Allen, *Ricker Settler Interviews*, p. 13. Horn Cloud, *Ricker Indian Interviews*, p. 199.

62. Joseph Horn Cloud, *Ricker Indian Interviews*, p. 199.

63. Horn Cloud, *Ricker Indian Interviews*, p. 200.

64. Horn Cloud, *Ricker Indian Interviews*, p. 199. Beard, *Ricker Indian Interviews*, p. 219.

65. *Ibid.*

66. Horn Cloud, *Ricker Indian Interviews*, p. 201. Wells, *Ricker Indian Interviews*, p. 128.

67. Garnett, *Ricker Indian Interviews*, p. 95.

68. Utley, *Last Days*, p. 211.

69. Horn Cloud, *Ricker Indian Interviews*, p. 200. Beard, *Ricker Indian Interviews*, p. 219.

70. Meded Swigert, *Ricker Settler Interviews*, p. 19. Wells, *Ricker Indian Interviews*, p. 157. Beard, *Ricker Indian Interviews*, p. 219.

71. Wells, *Ricker Indian Interviews*, pp. 156–157. George Bartlett, *Ricker Settler Interviews*, p. 38. Rough Feather, quoted in James H. McGregor, *The Wounded Knee Massacre From the Viewpoint of the Sioux* (1940; rpt. Rapid City, South Dakota: Fenske Printing, Inc., 1987), pp. 99–101. Bertha Kills Close to Lodge, in McGregor, *Wounded Knee Massacre*, pp. 106–107. Afraid of the Enemy, in McGregor, *Wounded Knee Massacre*, pp. 118–119. Frank Sits Poor, in McGregor, *Wounded Knee Massacre*, pp. 120–121.

72. Meded Swigert, *Ricker Settler Interviews*, p. 18. John W. Butler, *Ricker Settler Interviews*, p. 23. George Bartlett, *Ricker Settler Interviews*, p. 36. Allen, *From Fort Laramie to Wounded Knee*, pp. 197–198. Kelley, *Pine Ridge*, p. 2.

73. Garnett, *Ricker Indian Interviews*, p. 95. Wells, *Ricker Indian Interviews*, pp. 129, 157.

74. Beard, *Ricker Indian Interviews*, p. 220.

75. Ostler, *Plains Sioux*, p. 343. Utley, *Last Days*, p. 216. Invaluable for understanding this are the annotated aerial photographs of William B. Thomasson, at http://hoist.hrtc.net/~wbt/woundedknee.htm.

76. George Bartlett, *Ricker Settler Interviews*, p. 34. George A. Stannard, *Ricker Settler Interviews*, p. 39.

77. George A. Stannard, *Ricker Settler Interviews*, p. 39. Allen, *Ricker Settler Interviews*, pp. 14–15. James H. Cook, *Fifty Years on the Old Frontier as Cowboy, Hunter, Guide, Scout, and Ranchman* (New Haven: Yale University Press, 1923), pp. 197–198.

78. Beard, *Ricker Indian Interviews*, pp. 220–224.

79. *Ibid.*

80. Bartlett, *Ricker Settler Interviews*, p. 33. Stannard, *Ricker Settler Interviews*, p. 39. Stannard identifies the people in the wagon as "nine bucks" traveling "leisurely." There are a number of ways this makes no sense. In any case, Bartlett and Ricker both identified the people in the wagon as women.

81. Beard, *Ricker Indian Interviews*, p. 224.

82. McFarland, *Ricker Settler Interviews*, pp. 5–6.

83. Horn Cloud, *Ricker Indian Interviews*, pp. 202–203. Beard, *Ricker Indian Interviews*, pp. 225–226.

84. Allen, *From Fort Laramie to Wounded Knee*, pp. 198–203.

85. Allen, *From Fort Laramie to Wounded Knee*, pp. 203–204, and p. 265, note 3.

86. Allen, *From Fort Laramie to Wounded Knee*, p. 204. Wells, *Ricker Indian Interviews*, p. 130. Paddy Star, *Ricker Indian Interviews*, p. 238.

87. Wells, *Ricker Indian Interviews*, p. 130. Paddy Star, *Ricker Indian Interviews*, p. 238. Allen, *From Fort Laramie to Wounded Knee*, p. 205. Allen, *Ricker Settler Interviews*, p. 14.

88. Kocer, *Ricker Settler Interviews*, p. 42. Allen, *Ricker Settler Interviews*, p. 14. Allen, *From Fort Laramie to Wounded Knee*, p. 206.

89. Allen, *Ricker Settler Interviews*, p. 14. Allen, *From Fort Laramie to Wounded Knee*, p. 206.

90. Bartlett, *Ricker Settler Interviews*, p. 33. McFarland, *Ricker Settler Interviews*, pp. 6, 10.

91. Allen, *From Fort Laramie to Wounded Knee*, p. 208.

92. Allen, *From Fort Laramie to Wounded Knee*, p. 207.

93. Allen, *From Fort Laramie to Wounded Knee*, p. 207.

94. Kelley, *Pine Ridge*, p. 189.

95. Schofield to Miles, December 30, 1890, RAGO. Wooster, *Miles*, p. 186.

96. Miles to Schofield, January 1, 1891, RAGO. Utley, *Last Days*, p. 228.

97. Elaine Goodale Eastman, *Sister to the Sioux: The Memoirs of Elaine Goodale Eastman, 1885–91*, ed. Kay Graber (University of Nebraska Press, 1978), pp. 18–30.

98. Utley, *Last Days*, p. 235. Eastman, *Sister to the Sioux*, pp. 160–162.

99. George E. Hyde, *A Sioux Chronicle* (1956; rpt. Norman: University of Oklahoma Press, 1993), p. 307. Charles A. Eastman, *From the Deep Woods to Civilization: Chapters in the Autobiography of an Indian* (1916; rpt. Lincoln: University of Nebraska Press, 1977), pp. 111–114. Eastman, *Sister to the Sioux*, p. 166.

100. Bartlett, *Ricker Settler Interviews*, p. 35. Horn Cloud, *Ricker Indian Interviews*, p. 202.

101. Bartlett, *Ricker Settler Interviews*, pp. 33–36. Kocer, *Ricker Settler Interviews*, pp. 41, 43.

102. Eastman, *Deep Woods to Civilization*, pp. 111–114. Eastman, *Sister to the Sioux*, p. 166.

103. Birdsall, *Ricker Settler Interviews*, p. 46. The men were Birdsall and Lt. Cloman or Kloman.

104. James Mooney, *The Ghost-Dance Religion and Wounded Knee* (1896; rpt. New York: Dover Publications, Inc., 1973), image and caption between pp. 788–789. Birdsall, *Ricker Settler Interviews*, p. 46.

105. Eastman, *Sister to the Sioux*, p. 166.

106. Number from Jensen note 72, *Ricker Settler Interviews*, p. 389, and W. A. Birdsall, *Ricker Settler Interviews*, p. 45. Detail from William Peano, *Ricker Indian Interviews*, pp. 235–237. There are various counts of those killed at Wounded Knee. The total number who died there or of their wounds either at the agency or in the places they crawled for shelter was probably between 225 and 250.

107. Eastman, *Deep Woods to Civilization*, pp. 107–110.

108. James C. Olson, *Red Cloud and the Sioux Problem* (Lincoln: University of Nebraska Press, 1965), pp. 329–331. William Peano, *Ricker Indian Interviews*, pp. 234–235.

109. Wells, *Ricker Indian Interviews*, pp. 162–163. Horn Cloud, *Ricker Indian Interviews*, p. 203.

110. Horn Cloud, *Ricker Indian Interviews*, pp. 202–203. Beard, *Ricker Indian Interviews*, pp. 225–226.

111. Eastman, *Deep Woods to Civilization*, pp. 107–110.

112. Garnett, *Ricker Indian Interviews*, p. 100. Wells, *Ricker Indian Interviews*, p. 154.

113. Utley, *Last Days*, pp. 236–241, 253–254.

114. Utley, *Last Days*, p. 251. Miles to Red Cloud, et al., January 1, 1891, quoted in Utley, *Last Days*, p. 255.

115. Miles to Red Cloud, January 1, 1891, quoted in Olson, *Red Cloud*, p. 331.

116. Utley, *Last Days*, p. 251. Olson, *Red Cloud*, p. 331.

117. Olson, *Red Cloud*, pp. 332–333. Hyde, *Sioux Chronicle*, pp. 308–311. Utley, pp. 256–258.

118. Olson, *Red Cloud*, pp. 332–333.

119. Hyde, *Sioux Chronicle*, pp. 309–310.

120. Olson, *Red Cloud*, p. 333. Hyde, *Sioux Chronicle*, pp. 313–314. Capt. W. E. Dougherty, "The Recent Messiah Craze," *Journal of the Military Service Institution of the United States*, 12 (1891): 577, quoted in Utley, *Last Days*, p. 260.

121. Miles, quoted in James P. Boyd, *Recent Indian Wars* (1891; rpt. Digital Scanning, Inc, 2000), p. 276, on Google Books. Hyde, *Sioux Chronicle*, p. 314. *Washington Post*, January 16, 1891, p. 1. *New York Tribune*, January 18, 1891, p. 13.

Chapter 8

1. Louis Mousseau, in Richard E. Jensen, ed., *The Indian Interviews of Eli S. Ricker, 1903–1919* (Lincoln: University of Nebraska Press, 2005), p. 229.

2. Robert M. Utley, *Last Days of the Sioux Nation* (New Haven: Yale University Press, 1963), pp. 244–245.

3. Royer to Morgan, December 29, 1890, enclosed in Morgan to Noble, December 30, 1890, in RAGO. *Washington Post*, January 6, 1891, p. 2.

4. *Washington Post*, January 6, 1891, p. 2.

5. *New York Tribune*, January 3, 1891, p. 7.

6. *Atlanta Constitution*, January 7, 1891, p. 1. *Washington Post*, January 8, 1891, p. 2.

7. Jensen, note 198 in *Ricker Indian Interviews*, p. 414.

8. Utley, *Last Days*, pp. 261–267.

9. *New York Tribune*, January 6, 1891, p. 1. W. T. Sherman to Mary, January 7, 1891, quoted in Robert Wooster, *Nelson A. Miles and the Twilight of the Frontier Army* (Lincoln: University of Nebraska Press, 1993), p. 188.

10. *New York Tribune*, January 6, 1891, p. 1.

11. See James W. Forsyth to Adjutant General, March 5, 1891, *Ricker Indian Interviews*, p. 138.

12. Philip F. Wells, *Ricker Indian Interviews*, pp. 126–130. Statement of Elks Saw Him, *Ricker Indian Interviews*, pp. 131–132. Statement of Frog of Big Foot's Band, *Ricker Indian Interviews*, pp. 132–135. Statement of Help Them, son of Heart Man, living on Wounded Knee, *Ricker Indian Interviews*, pp. 135–136.

13. Meded Swigert, in Richard E. Jensen, ed., *The Settler and Soldiers Interviews of Eli S. Ricker, 1903–1919* (Lincoln: University of Nebraska Press, 2005), p. 20.

14. See, for example, testimony of S. M. Whitside, A. Capron, L. S. McCormick, and H. J. Nowlan in RAGO.

15. *New York Tribune*, January 11, 1891, p. 1.
16. Wooster, *Miles*, pp. 189–190.
17. Eli L. Huggins, quoted in Wooster, *Miles*, p. 190. *Boston Globe*, February 13, 1891, p. 10.
18. *Boston Globe*, February 13, 1891, p. 10.
19. *Ibid.*
20. *Ibid.*
21. *Boston Globe*, February 13, 1891, p. 10. *New York Times*, February 13, 1891, p. 6.
22. Thomas R. Buecker, ed., "'The even tenor of our way is pursued undisturbed': Henry P. Smith's Diary during the Ghost Dance Movement, 1890–1891," *South Dakota History*, 34 (Fall 2004): 224. [all sic, indents in original]
23. *Smith's Diary*, p. 227.
24. Charles Seymour, "The Sioux Rebellion: The Final Review," *Harper's Weekly*, February 7, 1891, p. 106.
25. *Ibid.*
26. *Ibid.*
27. Richard Jensen, et al., *Eyewitness at Wounded Knee* (Lincoln: University of Nebraska Press, 1991), p. 171. *Harper's Weekly*, May 9, 1891, p. 339; September 3, 1892, p. 847.
28. L. G. Moses, "Wild West Shows, Reformers, and the Image of the American Indian, 1887–1914," *South Dakota History*, 14 (Fall 1984): 193–221.
29. Joy S. Kasson, *Buffalo Bill's Wild West: Celebrity, Memory, and Popular History* (New York: Hill and Wang, 2000), p. 191.
30. *New York Times*, February 1, 1891, p. 17.
31. Jensen, et al., *Eyewitness at Wounded Knee*, p. 172.
32. *New York Times*, February 1, 1891, p. 4; February 2, 1891, p. 1.
33. *Harper's Weekly*, February 7, 1891, p. 107.
34. *New York Times*, February 8, 1891, p. 8. *Washington Post*, February 8, 1891, p. 2. *Washington Post*, February 13, 1891, p. 5.
35. *New York Times*, February 8, 1891, p. 8.
36. *Harper's Weekly*, February 21, 1890, p. 131.
37. *New York Times*, February 8, 1891, p. 8. Man-Afraid-of-His-Horses, in *Washington Post*, February 20, 1891, p. 7.
38. *New York Times*, February 12, 1891, p. 6. *Washington Post*, February 12, 1891, p. 5.
39. *New York Times*, February 12, 1891, p. 6.
40. Miles to Schofield, March 13, 1891, in Utley, *Last Days*, p. 277. Wooster, *Miles*, pp. 192–194.
41. Noble to Commissioner of Indian Affairs, April 2, 1891, quoted in James C. Olson, *Red Cloud and the Sioux Problem* (Lincoln: University of Nebraska Press, 1965), pp. 335–336.
42. *New York Times*, February 1, 1891, p. 17.
43. Herbert Welsh, "The Murrain of Spoils in the Indian Service," in *Proceedings at the Annual Meeting of the National Civil-Service Reform League* (New York: Published for the National Civil-Service Reform League, 1898), p. 86, on Google Books.

44. Welsh, "Murrain of Spoils," pp. 87–88. *Chicago Tribune*, March 15, 1890, p. 35.

45. *Los Angeles Times*, March 7, 1891, p. 5.

46. For citations, see "Medal of Honor Recipients, Indian Wars Period," at http://www.history.army.mil/html/moh/indianwars.html.

47. *Technology Quarterly* (1892), p. 291, on Google Books.

48. Herbert S. Schell, *History of South Dakota* (Lincoln: University of Nebraska Press, 1961), pp. 228–229.

49. Milford W. Howard, *If Christ Came to Congress* (1894; rpt. New York: Living Books, 1964).

50. On Arkell's business troubles, see *New York Times*, July 23, 1894, p. 2; February 5, 1895, p. 14; July 15, 1897, p. 10; July 25, 1897, p. 2; August 23, 1897, p. 5; June 8, 1898, p. 12; October 5, 1898, p. 4; August 12, 1900, p. 11. George Graham Rice, *My Adventures with Your Money* (Boston: Richard G. Badger, 1913), pp. 46–53, 75–76, on Google Books.

51. See, for example, *New York Times*, January 21, 1890, p. 4. *Harper's Weekly*, February 1, 1890, p. 79. *FLIN*, October 11, 1890, p. 164. J. Morgan Kousser, *The Shaping of Southern Politics: Suffrage Restriction and the Establishment of a One-Party South, 1880–1910* (New Haven: Yale University Press, 1974), pp. 32, 49, 57.

52. Henry Litchfield West, "The Race War in North Carolina," *Forum*, 26 (1898–1899): 578–591. Glenda Elizabeth Gilmore, *Gender and Jim Crow* (Chapel Hill: University of North Carolina Press, 1996), p. 111.

53. Lincoln Borglum and Gweneth Reed Dendooven, *Mount Rushmore: Heritage of America* (Las Vegas: KC Publications, 1980), pp. 1–19.

54. Charles W. Allen, *From Fort Laramie to Wounded Knee*, ed. Richard E. Jensen (1939; rpt. Lincoln: University of Nebraska Press, 1997), p. 154; on officers and agents at Pine Ridge after Wounded Knee, see Jensen, in Allen, *From Fort Laramie to Wounded Knee*, pp. 256–257, note 13.

55. Allen, *From Fort Laramie to Wounded Knee*, pp. 154–155. Jensen, in Allen, *From Fort Laramie to Wounded Knee*, p. 256, note 16.

56. I thank Michael R. Pontrelli, for walking me through the *Lone Wolf v. Hitchcock* decision.

57. Warren King Moorehead, *The American Indian in the United States* (Andover, Massachusetts: The Andover Press, 1914), p. 186, on Google Books.

58. Olson, *Red Cloud*, pp. 335–340.

59. Richard E. Jensen, Introduction, *Ricker Indian Interviews*, pp. xi–xxvii.

60. Donald F. Danker, "The Wounded Knee Interviews of Eli S. Ricker," *Nebraska History*, 62 (Summer 1981): 151–243.

61. Guy Vaughn, *Ricker Settler Interviews*, p. 21. McFarland, *Ricker Settler Interviews*, pp. 4, 10.

62. James H. Cook, *Fifty Years on the Old Frontier as Cowboy, Hunter, Guide, Scout, and Ranchman* (New Haven: Yale University Press, 1923), pp. 235–236. Francis M. J. Craft, *Ricker Settler Interviews*, p. 22.

63. Horn Cloud, *Ricker Indian Interviews*, p. 191.

64. Bartlett, *Ricker Settler Interviews*, p. 38.

65. Allen, *Ricker Settler Interviews*, p. 16.

66. Ricker, *Ricker Indian Interviews*, p. 425, note 5.

67. Theodore Roosevelt, *The Winning of the West*, volume 1 (New York: 1910), pp. 247–253, on Google Books.

68. James Mooney, *The Ghost-Dance Religion and Wounded Knee* (1896; rpt. New York: Dover Publications, Inc., 1973), p. 883.

69. Charles A. Eastman, *From the Deep Woods to Civilization: Chapters in the Autobiography of an Indian* (1916; rpt. Lincoln: University of Nebraska Press, 1977), p. 117.

70. *Washington Post*, June 19, 1891, p. 4. Elaine Goodale Eastman, *Sister to the Sioux: The Memoirs of Elaine Goodale Eastman, 1885–91*, ed. Kay Graber (University of Nebraska Press, 1978), pp. 172–175. Theodore D. Sargent, *The Life of Elaine Goodale Eastman* (Lincoln: University of Nebraska Press, 2005), pp. 106–120.

71. Eastman, *Deep Woods to Civilization*, p. 141.

72. *Ibid.*, pp. 142–143.

73. *Ibid.*, pp. 148–149.

74. *Ibid.*, pp. 147–148.

75. *Ibid.*, pp. 193–194.

76. *Ibid.*, pp. 193–194.

SUGGESTIONS FOR FURTHER READING

The best place to begin learning more about Wounded Knee is the wonderful book of photographs by Richard Jensen, R. Eli Paul, and John E. Carter, *Eyewitness at Wounded Knee* (1991). Richard Jensen has also edited and annotated a number of illuminating documents that deal with the Wounded Knee affair: *The Indian Interviews of Eli S. Ricker, 1903–1919* (2005); *The Settler and Soldiers Interviews of Eli S. Ricker, 1903–1919* (2005); and Charles W. Allen, *From Fort Laramie to Wounded Knee* (1939; rpt. 1997).

The classic study of Wounded Knee remains James Mooney, *The Ghost-Dance Religion and Wounded Knee* (1896; rpt. 1973); it is available online. Also classic is George E. Hyde, *A Sioux Chronicle* (1956; rpt. 1993), which takes an engaging look at the Sioux experience from the 1870s onward. Harder to find, but worth the search, is Jerome A. Greene, "The Sioux Land Commission of 1889: Prelude to Wounded Knee," *South Dakota History*, 1 (Winter 1970). For a book that places Wounded Knee in the larger context of colonialism, see Jeffrey Ostler, *The Plains Sioux and U.S. Colonialism from Lewis and Clark to Wounded Knee* (2004). In 1963, Robert M. Utley wrote an account of Wounded Knee in *Last Days of the Sioux Nation* (1963); this is a good place to find a study of military maneuvers.

A good overview of Indian history in the nineteenth century is Philip Weeks, *Farewell, My Nation: The American Indian and the United States in the Nineteenth Century* (2000). For a look at the Sioux War specifically, Jerome A. Greene, ed., *Battles and Skirmishes of the Great Sioux War, 1876–1877: The Military View* (1993) is especially interesting.

There are excellent biographies of many of the individuals involved in the Wounded Knee affair. Good places to start are: James C. Olson, *Red Cloud and the Sioux Problem* (1965); Stanley Vestal, *Sitting Bull: Champion of the Sioux* (1932; rpt. 1989); Robert M. Utley, *The Lance and the Shield: The Life and Times of Sitting Bull* (1993); Robert Wooster, *Nelson A. Miles and the Twilight of the Frontier Army* (1993); and Donald B. Connelly, *John M. Schofield and the Politics of Generalship* (2006).

Memoirs and collections of letters from the time of the events at Wounded Knee help a reader to understand how individuals interpreted what was going on around them. Notable are Charles A. Eastman, *From the Deep Woods to Civilization: Chapters in the Autobiography of an Indian* (1916; rpt. 1977); Elaine Goodale Eastman, *Sister to the Sioux: The Memoirs of Elaine Goodale Eastman, 1885–91*, ed. Kay Graber (1978); William Fitch Kelley, *Pine Ridge 1890: An Eye Witness Account of the Events Surrounding the Fighting at Wounded Knee*, ed. and compiled by Alexander Kelley and Pierre Bovis (1971). Stanley Vestal, *New Sources of Indian History* (1934), has Loneman's account of Sitting Bull's death and various other documents from the time. Jerry Green, ed., *After Wounded Knee: Correspondence of Major and Surgeon John Vance Lauderdale while Serving with the Army Occupying the Pine Ridge Indian Reservation, 1890–1891* (1996), looks at events from the perspective of a doctor on the scene—a fascinating angle I couldn't include here.

Walter Prescott Webb, *The Great Plains* (1931; rpt. 1981), is still a good place to start for the history of the Great Plains region; Howard Roberts Lamar, *Dakota Territory, 1861–1889* (1956), covers the early history of what became South Dakota, and Nancy Tystad Koupal, ed., L. Frank Baum, *Our Landlady* (1996) is a gem of a book that explores the early state history with both detail and humor.